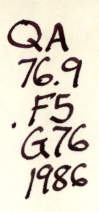

File Systems

Design and Implementation

File Systems
Design and Implementation

Daniel Grosshans

Prentice-Hall, Inc., Englewood Cliffs, New Jersey 07632

Library of Congress Cataloging-in-Publication Data

GROSSHANS, DANIEL.
   File systems.

   Bibliography: p.
   Includes index.
   1. File organization (Computer science)   I. Title.
QA76.9.F5G76 1986   005.74   85-24483
ISBN 0-13-314568-9

Editorial/production supervision and interior design: Dee Amir Josephson.
Cover design: 20/20 Services, Inc.
Manufacturing buyer: Gordon Osbourne

Printed in the United States of America
10 9 8 7 6 5 4 3 2 1

ISBN 0-13-314568-9

Prentice-Hall International (UK) Limited, *London*
Prentice-Hall of Australia Pty. Limited, *Sydney*
Prentice-Hall of Canada Inc., *Toronto*
Prentice-Hall Hispanoamericana, S.A., *Mexico*
Prentice-Hall of India Private Limited, *New Delhi*
Prentice-Hall of Japan, Inc., *Tokyo*
Prentice-Hall of Southeast Asia Pte. Ltd., *Singapore*
Editora Prentice-Hall do Brasil, Ltda., *Rio de Janeiro*
Whitehall Books Limited, *Wellington, New Zealand*

Figures 3–5 through 3–11, Tables 3–3 through 3–6, Figure D–0 and all label definitions in Appendix D are reproduced with permission from
American National Standard Magnetic Tape Labels and File Structure for Information Interchange, ANSI X3.27–1978, copyright 1978 by the
American National Standards Institute. Copies of this standard may be purchased from the American National Standards Institute of 1430 Broad-
way, New York, N.Y. 10018.

UNIX is a registered trademark of Bell Laboratories.

IBM is a registered trademark of the International Business Machines Corporation.

To my wife, Maria, and
my children, Kristin, Lisa and Amie

Contents

Preface   *xiii*

1   File Processing Overview   1

1.1   Overview   1
1.2   Why Study I/O?   3
1.3   I/O From a User's Perspective   5
1.4   I/O From a System Perspective   6
1.5   Terminology   7
1.6   Key Issues in File Design   15
1.7   Key File Deisgn Ratios   19
1.8   Summary   20

PART I   DEVICE CHARACTERISTICS   23

2   Device I/O   25

2.1   Overview   25
2.2   Hardware Configurations   26
2.3   Device I/O   30
2.4   I/O Programming   35
2.5   Implementation Requirements   36
2.6   Summary   37

3   Magnetic Tape Devices   41

3.1   Overview   41
3.2   Tape Hardware Characteristics

3.3   File Structure
3.4   Tape I/O
3.5   I/O Exception Handling
3.6   Compatibility Issues
3.7   Cost/Benefit Trade-offs   69
3.8   Performance Characteristics   70
3.9   Implementation Requirements   72
3.10 Summary   73

4   **Random Access Devices**   **77**
4.1   Overview   77
4.2   Disk Hardware Characteristics   78
4.3   Disk File Structure   83
4.4   Disk I/O   95
4.5   I/O Exception Handling   97
4.6   Compatibility Issues   101
4.7   Cost/Benefit Trade-offs   102
4.8   Performance Characteristics   103
4.9   Implementation Considerations   107
4.10 Summary 110

PART II   FILE SYSTEMS   113

5   **Basic File Systems**   **115**
5.1   Overview   115
5.2   What Is a Basic File System?   116
5.3   Basic File System Interface: File Operations   117
5.4   Basic File System: File Operations   120
5.5   Basic File System Interface: Block Operations   130
5.6   Data Flow   134
5.7   Performance Considerations   135
5.8   Implementation Requirements   136
5.9   Summary   140

6   **Basic I/O Supervisor**   **143**
6.1   Overview   143
6.2   Basic File Support Functions   144
6.3   Device Drivers   149
6.4   I/O Request Queueing   149
6.5   I/O Initiation   151
6.6   I/O Termination Process   151
6.7   Interrupt Handling   154
6.8   Performance Considerations   158
6.9   Implementation Requirements   159
6.10 Summary   163

7   Logical I/O Concepts   166

    7.1   Overview   166
    7.2   File Attributes   168
    7.3   Data Flow To/From User   169
    7.4   I/O Buffering Techniques   173
    7.5   File Reorganization   180
    7.6   Performance Considerations   181
    7.7   Design Trade-offs   182
    7.8   I/O Status Handling   183
    7.9   Implementation Requirements   184
    7.10 Summary   185

8   Access Method I/O   187

    8.1   Overview   187
    8.2   File Design Considerations   189
    8.3   File Operations   190
    8.4   Record Operations   199
    8.5   Performance Considerations   213
    8.6   Design Trade-offs   215
    8.7   Implementations Requirements   216
    8.8   Summary   221

PART III   ACCESS METHODS   225

9   Sequential Files   27

    9.1   Overview   227
    9.2   File Design Considerations   228
    9.3   File Operations   230
    9.4   Record Operations   232
    9.5   Performance Considerations   237
    9.6   Design Trade-offs   238
    9.7   Implementation Requirements   240
    9.8   Summary   243

10   Relative Files   246

    10.1 Overview   246
    10.2 File Design Considerations   247
    10.3 File Operations   252
    10.4 Record Operations   253
    10.5 Performance Considerations   259
    10.6 Design Trade-offs   261
    10.7 Implementation Requirements   264
    10.8 Summary   267

11   *Direct Files*   *270*

    11.1 Overview 270
    11.2 File Design Considerations 271
    11.3 File Operations 281
    11.4 Record Operations 283
    11.5 Performance Considerations 290
    11.6 Design Trade-offs 291
    11.7 Implementation Requirements 294
    11.8 Summary 299

12   *Indexed Sequential Files*   *302*

    12.1 Overview 302
    12.2 File Design Considerations 304
    12.3 File Operations 313
    12.4 Record Operations 316
    12.5 Performance Considerations 324
    12.6 Design Trade-offs 328
    12.7 Implementation Requirements 330
    12.8 Summary 334

13   *Indexed Files*   *336*

    13.1 Overview 336
    13.2 File Design Considerations 338
    13.3 File Operations 343
    13.4 Record Operations 345
    13.5 Performance Considerations 353
    13.6 Design Trade-offs 357
    13.7 Implementation Requirements 359
    13.8 Summary 364

14   *VSAM Files*   *367*

    14.1 Overview 367
    14.2 File Design Considerations 369
    14.3 File Operations 378
    14.4 Record Operations 379
    14.5 Performance Considerations 384
    14.6 Design Traade-offs 388
    14.7 Implementation Requirements 390
    14.8 Summary 391

15   *Multikey Indexed Files*   *394*

    15.1 Overview 394
    15.2 File Design Considerations 395
    15.3 File Operations 403

15.4   Record Operations   404
15.5   Performance Considerations   410
15.6   Design Trade-offs   411
15.7   Implementations Requirements   413
15.8   Summary   416

PART IV   MISCELLANEOUS TOPICS   419

16   File System Issues   421

16.1   Overview   421
16.2   File Sharing   422
16.3   Distributed Data Processing   423
16.4   High Availability   424
16.5   Data Security   425
16.6   Impact of Personal Computers   426
16.7   Programming Language Incompatibilities   427
16.8   Internationalization   428
16.9   Summary   429

Appendix A   Internal Data Structures   430

Appendix B   Common File Structures   440

Appendix C   Disk File Structures   444

Appendix D   Tape File Structures   451

Glossary   458

Bibliography   471

Index   473

Preface

The objective in writing this book was to discuss I/O from two perspectives. First, from the vantage point of a user writing a program that performs READs and WRITEs, how does the user's progam tie into the rest of the file system to perform these tasks? Second, how does the file system accomplish its work of managing all the I/O that goes on within a system?

The book covers not only the traditional access methods, such as sequential files and ISAM files, but also the internal processing that is required to support these access methods. Tied in with the latter point are the data and file structures that must be built to successfully process all user and system I/O. These structures are discussed in enough detail to provide the reader with an insight into how a file system could be implemented. Thus, in addition to the access methods, the I/O supervisory functions are discussed, as are device drivers and resource allocation routines. Finally, there is a discussion of how devices, specifically disks and tapes, work and what the file system must do to transfer data to and from the devices.

The methodology used was to discuss each component of the entire file system from the actual devices, such as tapes and disks, through the file system itself, and finally all the way up to the user interface to the access methods. Real-world design, implementation, and performance issues are discussed in order that the reader may understand the trade-offs that are made in any system design. In fact, the emphasis is on real issues and problems, not on the theory of how things might be done.

Since I/O is one of the major constraints to overall system performance, it is important to spend time improving performance and system throughput. There are programming assignments at the end of each chapter which will not only walk the reader through a file system implementation, but also serve to highlight the design and performance issues within the file system.

The structure of this book corresponds to the ACM Curriculum '78 core course *CS.5 Introduction to File Processing*. It is assumed that a data structures course has, or will be taken, and therefore data structures theory is not explicitly discussed, although it ripples through all the structures used as examples. The goal here is to cover the broad area of I/O and file systems. Since this covers such a wide area, only the major highlights are dealt with in detail. This was done in order that this book could be used in a one-semester course in file processing. The highest priority is given to getting the reader to *understand* I/O design and performance issues. A secondary priority is to give the reader firsthand implementation experience by providing programming assignments which result in the step-by-step construction of a mini file system that works.

1

File Processing Overview

CHAPTER OBJECTIVES

When you complete this chapter, you will be able to:

- Understand the user's perspective on file processing and why file processing is critical to overall system performance
- Discuss the impact of file processing on the performance of both user and system programs
- Understand the standard file terminology
- Understand and be able to discusss the key issues in file design
- Identify the key I/O performance criteria

1.1 OVERVIEW

When most programs are written, they usually include statements such as READ or WRITE. Although languages vary on the specific syntax, the concept is the same. Specifically, the user is trying to READ data from, or WRITE data to, some kind of medium for permanent storage. What *really* happens next? How does the "system" know what to do? How does the user's program know when the READ or WRITE request has been completed so that the program can resume processing?

These, and other questions, are all related to input/output (I/O) which deals with data transfers in to, or out of, the main memory of the computer. The term

1

"I/O" is analogous to the terminology of READ/WRITE. As can be seen in Figure 1-0, *The I/O interface between the user's program and the peripheral devices is known as the file system.* I/O will be analyzed in detail, both from the user's point of view and from the file system's perspective, with the following overall goals:

- Understand how each of the hardware and software I/O components work together
- Understand the *internal* data structures required to process I/O requests
- Understand the design of the disk and tape file structures
- Understand how the data and control information flows through the entire system

We will discuss in detail what it takes to design and implement a file system. In addition, we will always keep in mind the issue of maintaining a competitive level of overall performance, or system responsiveness.

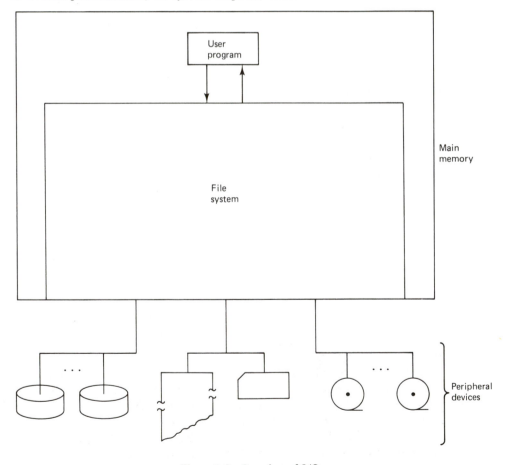

Figure 1-0   Overview of I/O.

What is most important here is to understand the *concepts and ideas* presented. This is because the industry in general, and file systems, I/O, and devices in particular, are changing so rapidly.

Finally, we must consider the growing impact of the personal computer on all activities in this industry. For example, a user may decide to run applications, such as payroll or inventory, on a large IBM mainframe computer. This machine could cost several millions of dollars and have gigabytes of on-line storage capacity. At the other extreme, a user may decide to run a payroll application on a personal computer costing several thousand dollars and perhaps having several megabytes of on-line storage. For which user do we design file systems? Can we design a system that can be beneficial to both large and small computer users? For these reasons, it is best if we can understand the whys and hows of file systems. Then we can try and apply those ideas to the current task.

1.2 WHY STUDY I/O?

The fundamental reason for the importance of studying I/O is that *I/O is slow* in comparison to the internal speeds of computers (see Figure 1–1). In fact, relative to the speed of an I/O device, the speed of a central processing unit (CPU) is increasing more rapidly. The primary reason for this is that I/O devices are mechanical and are thus significantly slower than the electronic speeds of semiconductors and microprocessors.

Second, a user may think that a single READ or a WRITE statement in a program causes only one I/O operation to occur. In reality, *zero to many* actual I/O operations could occur. This is analogous to the situation in which one line of code written in a high-level language such as COBOL can result in zero to many actual machine instructions.

There are several other reasons why I/O is important to study:

- There is much I/O occurring in a system on behalf of each user, over and above the I/O that the user specifically requested (e.g., compiling programs, editing memos, listing directories, etc.).
- The capacity of the media (e.g., tapes and disks) is increasing at about 30% per year. This means that more and more I/O can be performed on the same devices, thus causing another bottleneck at the device level.
- I/O capacity is severely limited. For example, the average time that a disk takes to mechanically reposition itself to another place on the disk is about 20 milliseconds (ms). Also, assume that we are working on a 1-mips (million instructions per second) machine. In the time it would take to process *one* I/O request, the CPU could have executed over 20,000 instructions. This is greatly exacerbated if the CPU runs at 100 mips. Then, in the span of a single I/O instruction, over *2 million* CPU instructions could have been executed!

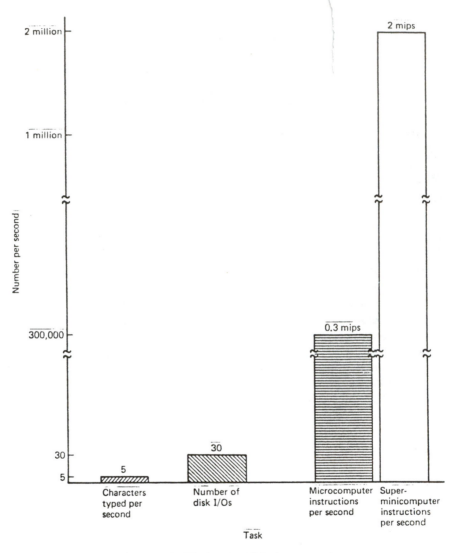

Figure 1-1 Work accomplished per second.

One reason that multiuser operating systems came into being was to try to use these CPU cycles that would otherwise go unused while a program is waiting for an I/O operation to complete. The way this is done is to allow other programs to execute while the I/O is going on.

If we perform the calculation above in a different manner, we can see another major reason that I/O is so critical. If the average I/O time is 20 ms, we can calculate that there can be at most 50 I/O operations completed per second. Due to a variety of factors, such as having multiple jobs running in the system at any give time, the maximum I/O load is rarely achieved. Usually, it is considered good if a system reaches

75% to 80% of I/O capacity at any given time. Note that this percentage includes *all* the I/O going on in the system against that specific device (e.g., paging, program loading, compiling, and other utilities). How can we possibly have 50 or more students working on the same machine? How can there be 5000 airline travel agents making reservations without running into each other?

What we have just discusssed is one of the critical constraints on the performance of any system. Specifically, the amount of I/O that can be performed in any given interval of time is severely limited. Thus *the file system must treat I/O as a precious commodity that is utilized only when it is absolutely necessary.* We shall examine this topic, and determine where the constraints really are and what can be done to solve the I/O performance and throughput problems.

There is one other observation that can be made. For reasons of greater productivity, the software development industry is moving toward the use of higher-level languages, such as COBOL, FORTRAN, or Pascal. However, high-level languages tend to hide completely from the user the amount of I/O that is really being performed. The benefit of this is that users do not need to understand in a great amount of detail how the system works in order to get their jobs done. However, it also means that users have become unaware of how to take advantage of the system and thus improve its overall performance and throughput levels.

Finally, each high-level language provides the user with a different set of I/O capabilities. Thus the functionality that a user requires will tend to dictate in which language the user will choose to write the application. Either this will happen, or the user will try to make the application work within the constraints of the language primarily utilized at the user's installation.

1.3 I/O FROM A USER'S PERSPECTIVE

What does a user expect, or require, when an I/O request is made? What does a user think will happen, and what actually will happen?

When a user runs a program, or works interactively at a computer terminal, the objective is to complete the task at hand as soon as possible. Often, *the limiting factor in the responsiveness of the executing program is the underlying I/O performance of the system.* To understand why this is the case, we need only investigate the kinds of work the user performs.

Typically, the user wants to be able to perform the following kinds of activities without having to be concerned with all the technical details:

- To write data into a file today and be guaranteed that the data will be readable tomorrow
- To create files from one higher-level language, such as COBOL, that will be readable when accessed from any other language (e.g., FORTAN, Pascal)
- To be able to access the records in the file either sequentially or randomly, as required by the job being processed

- To have a reasonable combination of functionality, performance (i.e., response time), and stability, meaning that the system is reliable and will not adversely affect the integrity of the data
- To have the flexibility of choosing when to define file characteristics and when to let the system choose the parameters itself
- To *not* have to know all the technical details of the machine to get the job done
- To have the system make optimal use of the available resources so that the user is not forced into purchasing more hardware than is required to do the job
- To have the assurance that the data will not be inadvertently "lost"

Fundamentally, the user wants to be able to complete the work that needs to be done and not have the "computer" get in the way. Unfortunately, for most users, I/O is the "black box" shown in Figure 1-0. This is because the usual contact with I/O is either indirect, through a higher-level language, or invisible, meaning I/O that is performed on behalf of the user. For example, there is the paging that goes on in a virtual memory machine, the I/O performed by the operating system to load the user's program, and the I/O to compile the user's program. It is the intent of this book to break down this mysterious "I/O black box." We will do this by examining how the various system components work together to get the I/O completed successfully, at the right time, and in the most efficient manner.

1.4 I/O FROM A SYSTEM PERSPECTIVE

The objective of any file system is to meet the data management needs and requirements of its users. If any file system does not meet these needs, users will go elsewhere in search of software that allows them to do their job properly. Thus the file system is providing an I/O service to its user base. The basic goals and objectives of a file system are as follows:

- To meet the data management needs and requirements of the user
- To guarantee to the highest possible degree that only *valid data* are ever actually written into a file
- To maximize overall system performance and throughput by minimizing the number of *actual* I/O operations that need to be performed
- To provide I/O support for multiple users, not just a single user
- To provide I/O support for a variety of different device types
- To minimize, or eliminate, the potential for lost or destroyed data (i.e., *never lose data*)
- To optimize the control and utilization of the devices installed in the computer configuration
- To provide a standardized set of I/O interface routines that either the user can call directly, or the various system modules, acting on the behalf of the user (e.g., compilers, linkers, system utilities, etc., can call

In summary, the file system must provide an efficient and effective I/O service that provides the functionality and performance required by the user and by the pressure of competition. However, no statements made regarding file processing can be "guaranteed" to be correct in every application. The best that can be done is to make us all aware of how a file system works. Then each of us can decide what is the best technique to use in a given situation. Also, it can be demonstrated that if the user has some knowledge of how I/O is performed, the performance of the user's task can be dramatically improved *without changing one line of code in the user's application.*

Not all the features and functions that are discussed in this book are accessible from higher-level languages. However, these features are available on most systems in either the monitor, file system, utility programs, job control language, or interactive system commands. As the various components of a file system are discussed, we will also explain where the required information comes from.

1.5 TERMINOLOGY

To understand what I/O and file systems are all about, it is necessary to have common definitions on which to base the discussions. One problem in the computer industry is that there is no commonly accepted and used standard set of definitions. Most software development companies use similar words, but words that have different meanings. In this book we attempt to use the most common definitions for the terminology, but you still need to be aware that different vendors and writers may use different terms or definitions.

1.5.1 Fields

A field is an elementary data item such as a name, employee number, city, and so on (see Figure 1-2). It is characterized by its size, or length, and its data type (e.g., ASCII string, packed decimal, integer, etc.). Fields can even vary in length. In this book fields are assumed to be of fixed length, since in most standard applications, as well as in most higher-level languages, variable-length fields are not supported.

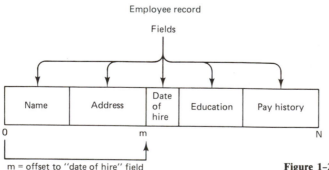

m = offset to "date of hire" field

Figure 1-2   User data record structure.

1.5.2 Records

A record is a collection of related fields that can be treated as a unit by some processing program. For example, you could have a person's payroll record, a student record, or a health record. All the data in the record are related to, or associated with, the same person or entry. A record can contain many fields of information, as shown in Figure 1–2. For example, within a person's employment record, one could have individual fields containing home address, telephone number, past work history, pay, and even school and degree held. How can a specific field within a record be located? *The field offset is the number of bytes from the beginning of the record to the start of the field in question.* Thus, if we know where the record begins, we can add the field offset to obtain the location of the desired field.

Records also have certain characteristics, such as:

- Records must somehow be created.
- Records should have a maximum defined size, although in some circumstances, not all data need be present. The reason for this is that the file system must have guidelines as to what record sizes should be considered valid and which records should be rejected. Remember, the file system must guarantee that only valid records are placed into a file.
- Records within a particular file have the same fields, field offsets from the start of the record, and field data types. This fact not only makes it easier to program, but also improves performance since the record does not have to be scanned to locate the field to be used.
- Records have a particular format. *There is one and only one record format for any specific file,* although different files can have different record formats. *If all the records within a file are of identical size, we have fixed-length records (FLRs),* as shown in Figure 1–3a.

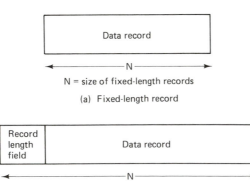

N = size of fixed-length records

(a) Fixed-length record

N = length of entire record, including attached length field

(b) Variable-length record

Figure 1–3 Record formats.

Alternatively, *if the size of each record in a file can change, we have variable-length records* (VLRs), as shown in Figure 1–3b. VLR records can vary in size only up to some predefined maximum length. For VLR records, there must be some way in which the length of the record can be known so that the data can be written or read correctly. This is done by *appending a length field to the front of each record* in the file. Thus VLR records only take up as much room as they really require.

In contrast with VLR records, FLR records *always* take up the maximum space, whether or not all of the fields have data in them. Finally, fixed-length records do *not* need a length field, because all records are the same size.

1.5.3 Files

A file is a collection of related records. For example, in a payroll file, each employee has one data record, and all the fields in that record relate to that employee. Similarly, all of the records in the file are related since they all contain payroll data. I/O is concerned with the reading and writing of data records between a user's program and the peripheral device. All related records are stored in a structure called a *file* (see Figure 1–4). This is analogous to a file cabinet. Here, someone puts data (i.e., file folders) into the cabinet (i.e., file) in an organized way so that the information can later be retrieved (i.e., read), updated, and put back into the file (i.e., write).

A file in a computer system is a structure designed to contain data (e.g., file folders). The data are organized in such a way that they can be easily retrieved, updated or deleted, and put back into the file with all changes made. Just as we can set up many different filing systems, there are many ways in which we can organize the data in computer-based files so that they can be used by applications and other programs, as well as interactively from a terminal.

There are several characteristics of files that are important to understanding them. Files can be *created* or *deleted* by the user. For example, you might create a personnel file, an inventory file, or a work file that you will use for a short period and then delete because that file is no longer needed.

Files have unique *filenames*. When a particular file is wanted, it is only necessary to give its name and the file system will locate it. However, filenames must be unique, or the file system will not know which is the correct version of the file wanted by the user. *The entire unique filename is known as the file's pathname.* The pathname consists of the following information:

pathname = device + user + directory + filename

The *device* parameter is required since there could be many different devices connected to the system at any one time. Therefore, on which device does the file reside? Typically, the device need not always be specified since the default can be the device on which the major directory, or account, resides.

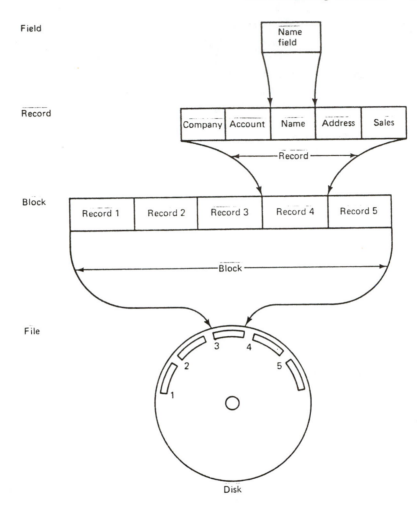

Figure 1-4 Fields, records, and files.

The *user and directory* parameters are needed to adequately define the location of the file on the device. For example, there could be several files named "ABC." However, each one belongs to a different user and/or resides in different directories. The combination of device, user, and directory specifies the unique directory in which the file called *filename* exists (see Figure 1-5).

Just as we can have an inventory file, or a personnel file, the *filename* defines not only which file the user wants out of all the files that may exist, but also implies a *location* and *size*. Of all the file cabinets we may have, when someone wants the "parts file," we know exactly where to look for it. In a similar manner, the file system maintains within a directory entry the file name, its location on the medium, and the size of the file itself (i.e., the number of blocks written into the file).

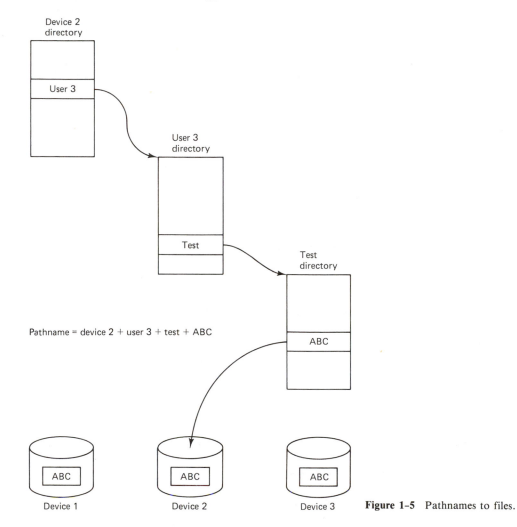

Figure 1-5 Pathnames to files.

Files can also be *shared* or *nonshared* between multiple users. Some files may contain sensitive data, and any access to the data should be restricted (e.g., a personnel system's files). Other files, such as those files used in an airline reservation system, need to be shared by all the travel agents and airline ticket offices around the world. Sharing can mean that only certain users will be allowed to READ or WRITE data to the actual file, or that no user has access to the data until the owner allows access.

The last file characteristic that will be discussed is that of performance. *Performance is the user's perception of the system's responsiveness.* Also, it is seen as how long the software can work until it breaks. Depending on how you organize the data within a file, you can retrieve data, or insert new data, slowly or quickly. Sometimes we may want to look at all records in the file so as to organize the records in such a manner that it is a fast process to sequentially access the next record. On the other hand, the records in a doctor's office need to be rapidly accessed by patient's last name in a completely *random* manner. We will learn that once it is known how the data in the file will be used, we can then design a means of organizing those records to get the performance and access capabilities that are required by the user of those data.

1.5.4 Blocks

A block is the unit of data that actually gets transferred (i.e., READ or WRITTEN) to, or from, the user's file that is located on a particular device. A block is the smallest amount of data that can be transferred with a single I/O operation. A block may contain one, or more, records. In fact, a block may contain only a partial record, so that to access the entire record, more than one block will need to be read.

This raises a question as to whether a block can vary in length. If this were the case, we could force all records to fit within a block simply by increasing the size of that block. As was the case for records, blocks can be either fixed or variable in length. If the block is variable in length, a *block length field* must be appendded to the front of each block. Also, to be able to read and write entire blocks into main memory, we will require that blocks be allowed to vary only up to a predefined *maximum block size*. The file system will then be able to allocate enough space in main memory for I/O at least at large as the maximum block size. For fixed-length blocks, the maximum block size is equivalent to the specified fixed length.

Figure 1-6 shows two different conditions that can occur when putting records into a block. In some file structures, records are not required to be smaller than the maximum size of a block, and in fact could be of almost unlimited length. When records are allowed to cross block boundaries, we say that the "system" allows *spanned* records (see Figure 1-6b and d).

In this situation, all blocks then become of maximum size. Any records that do not completely fit within the block are divided between two or more blocks. Thus, with spanned records, there is no wasted space within a particular block. However, as we shall see later, the price for not wasting space in the file is paid with slower access times. This is because a *single I/O* operation (e.g., read or write a block) may not be enough to transfer the entire record. Thus at least one more I/O operation will be required.

Alternatively, where records are prohibited from crossing, or spanning, block boundaries, we say that the "system" supports *unspanned* records only (see Figure 1-6a and c). In this case, the maximum record size must fit completely within a block. In addition, the file system will pack as many records in each block as can possibly fit. If the last record in the block can fit only partially, it must be completely moved into the next block. In this situation, file space is potentially wasted, since not every byte of the block may be used (see Figure 1-6a).

The goal of a file system is to be able to READ and WRITE records quickly. One way to accomplish this is always to guarantee that when a block is READ, it contains one or more *complete* records (i.e., do not allow spanned records). Thus

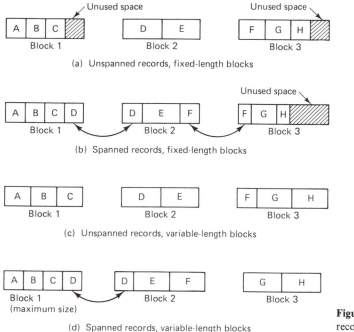

(a) Unspanned records, fixed-length blocks

(b) Spanned records, fixed-length blocks

(c) Unspanned records, variable-length blocks

(d) Spanned records, variable-length blocks

Figure 1-6 Spanned and unspanned records.

multiple I/O requests will not required to READ or WRITE any record in the file, and time will be saved.

On the other hand, it can be argued that by allowing records to span blocks, you can package the records together more densely and without wasted space (see Figure 1–6b and d). Unspanned record structures always run the risk that space will be wasted because there could be room in the block, but not enough room to hold the next record. Thus space is being wasted. Here again, we are trading off optimal use of media space against reducing the number of I/O operations required to READ or WRITE any record in the file. In other words, we are trading media space for improved performance and user response time.

Another characteristic that is important in relation to file system performance is the concept of a *blocking factor*. For example, if a file had fixed-length records, and if the block size were known, we could calculate how many records could fit into any block in the file. *The number of records that can fit into a block is called the blocking factor* (see Figure 1–7). If we had variable-length records, or even spanned records, we could not predict with 100% accuracy what the blocking factor for that file would be. However, we should be able to determine how many records *on the average* will fit into any given block in the file, and therefore calculate the blocking factor for the file.

The importance of a blocking factor, or more precisely, the placing of more than a single record into a block, may not be fully understood at this point. However, to illustrate, let us assume that we had two files. One of them wrote only one record

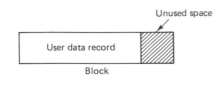

(a) One record per block (blocking factor = 1)

Figure 1-7   Blocking factors.

(b) Multiple (N) records per block (blocking factor = N)

into each block (i.e., a blocking factor of 1). The other file had a blocking factor of 10 (i.e., there were 10 records per block). If each file contained 1 million records, the second file would require 900,000 *fewer* I/O operations to read all the records! It is not uncommon on microcomputers to have disks with an average access time of 90 milliseconds. If this were the case, the first file would take about *24 hours longer* to read all the records in the file.

A significant point to remember is that a reasonable blocking factor greater than 1 will always improve overall performance and system throughput, by cutting down on the amount of I/O that the system must perform. However, we need to be sensitive to the impact of block size on main memory. Memory allocated to data blocks is unavailable for program use. Thus we need to make a trade-off between improved performance gained by using larger block sizes and the amount of main memory available for program use.

1.5.5 File Attributes

How can we determine the size of the records in a file containing only fixed-length records, since the records do not have a length field? Or, to put it another way, how can the file system know what the size and format of the records are in the file that was created last week? *There are certain characteristics that define precisely what a file is and how the records in that file must be processed. These characteristics are known as the file's attributes.* Specifically, some file attributes that we have all ready discussed are the following:

- Filename
- Maximum record size
- Record format (i.e., VLR or FLR records)
- Maximum block size
- Block format (i.e., fixed- or variable-length format)
- File size
- File location

Since a file's attributes are critical, they are permanently recorded within the file. Some of the common attributes, such as filename, may be stored within the directory entry. Then the *file specific* attributes (e.g., key size) can be stored within the file itself.

1.6 KEY ISSUES IN FILE DESIGN

As we examine various techniques for organizing user data records within a file structure, we must always keep in focus our overall goals and objectives. It makes no sense at all to design a file structure, and to write all the supporting code, if the resulting file is not what the user needs. When this situation occurs, as it does far too frequently, the user will simply not use the product—no matter how sophisticated and elegant the design. To maximize the probability of designing a file structure that meets the user's needs, we need to keep in mind the following overall guidelines, which are listed *in order of decreasing priority:*

1. Meet the needs and requirements of the *user*
2. Minimize the number of *actual* I/O operations performed
3. Trade-off of functionality versus performance versus resources
4. Never lose data
5. Use the 80/20 rule when deciding costs versus benefits of some feature

In making the trade-offs noted above, we must understand that unlike some other disciplines, there are no right answers to such decision guidelines. The only ''cookbook'' approach that can be used is to keep focused on these issues.

1.6.1 Needs and Requirements of the User

This point is so obvious that perhaps it should not even be mentioned. For example, let us assume that we went out to purchase a brand new automobile. For most of us, the cost of such a purchase is quite significant relative to most of the other kinds of purchases we make. Therefore, we carefully set out to find a car that meets our requirements. We may not be formal about this process and actually write down a list of requirements, but we have at least the major ones tucked away in the recesses of our mind. By a comparison process, we drop dealer after dealer from our list of possibilities. We may do this because of styling considerations, reputation of dealer, availability of the car, or other factors. Nevertheless, what we have done is to not even consider a broad range of products for one reason or other.

In the same manner, a computer user will shop for software or hardware and will decide *not* to purchase a product for any number of reasons. High on that list, however, is the perception that the product does not meet the needs and requirements of the particular user. Also high on the list are those products which have, correctly or incorrectly, a poor reputation for performance, quality, functionality, or responsiveness to customer requests. In summary, if the user's requirements are not met, nothing else matters, since the product developed will not be purchased.

1.6.2 Number of Actual I/O Operations

This is a critical issue, since the number of *actual* I/O operations needed will directly affect the overall performance as seen by the user. An actual I/O operation means one in which we have to go to the device itself to transfer the data. We will discuss this more later, but many I/O requests are processed between buffers in main memory and never get out to the device itself. For now, it is sufficient to know that devices are mechanical in operation. Thus it takes a comparatively long time to access a device compared to the time it takes to execute a single CPU instruction.

In addition, consider that one line of code written in a higher-level language, such as FORTRAN, COBOL, and Pascal, will actually generate one to many actual CPU instructions. In a similar vein, a simple READ or WRITE from the user can result in zero to many actual I/O operations. Thus designers of file systems need to be aware that the actual number of I/O requests should be kept at a minimum to provide the user with the "best" level of performance.

1.6.3 Functionality versus Performance versus Resources

Whenever we design and implement any project, we always end up consciously, or even unconsciously, making design and implementation trade-offs. Maybe we are running behind schedule, so we need to drop some functionality, not achieve all our performance goals, and so on. In any case, we must be acutely aware of what can and cannot be traded off.

First (see Figure 1–8, step 1), we must provide the user with at least the amount of functionality that the user requires, and possibly more if we are to be fully competitive against the other file systems on the market. Functionality can mean many things to different people. Here, functionality will mean not only the features provided to the user via some programming language, but also the quality of the error messages that are generated and how "user friendly" we can make our system. We should never trade off so much functionality that our product becomes noncompetitive. Thus we must walk the fine line between developing a competitive file system, while not making it overly complex so that it is never completed.

Performance is generally second in line behind functionality in importance to the user (see Figure 1–8, step 2). Performance will not become an issue until the user is satisfied with the amount of functionality that has been provided. Once this level of functionality has been attained, the user will then demand that the system "go faster"!

In a file system, this generally means that we must cut down the amount of time that it takes before we can give the user a response to an I/O request. This time interval is directly related to how well we can minimize the actual number of I/O operations that are performed. There are buffering and blocking techniques, as well as several other techniques, that can be used to reduce dramatically the amount of

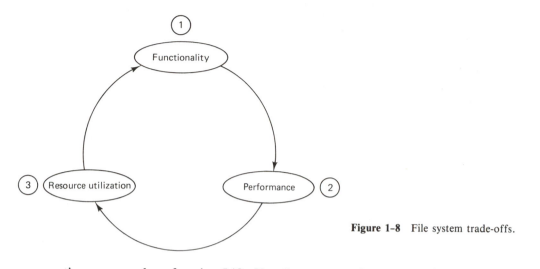

Figure 1-8 File system trade-offs.

time we spend performing I/O. Usually, we must be concerned with how fast we can READ a record for the user, or conversely WRITE a record for the user. If we can do this well, the user will tend to be more satisfied.

Finally, if our file system meets the functionality and performance expectations of the user, we must be concerned about how much of the user's resources are required to use our file system properly (see Figure 1-8, step 3). Resources that must be analyzed are as follows (see Figure 1-9):

- The amount of *main memory* (a) needed for each user
- The *code size* (b) of the file system and operating system, which can affect how much main memory is left for the user's programs
- How well we use the *media space* (c) on the peripheral devices (e.g., disk space)

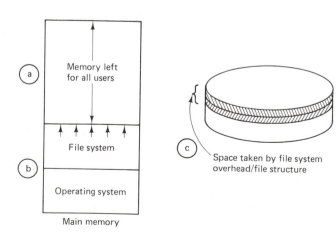

Figure 1-9 File system resources.

Resources cost money. In particular, mechanical devices such as disks and tapes cost relatively large amounts of money, and the file space available tends to be limited. Available media resources form a hard constraint on what we can, and cannot, assume exists at a user's installation. Therefore, the file system must use the space and resources as best it can.

In summary, the user's highest priority is functionality, followed in order by performance and then resources. The inherent difficulty in this task is that we must achieve the functionality and performance levels required by the user *within the constraints of the resources provided*.

1.6.4 Loss of Data

The reason that users want to WRITE their data onto various media, such as disks and tape, is so that they can access the data whenever they need them. They also know that by saving the data in a "computer" they will be able to access any piece of data significantly faster than if the same data were kept in traditional filing cabinets. However, if they ever discovered that a file system, no matter how sophisticated, occasionally and mysteriously lost data, they would drop it like a hot potato.

Consider for a moment what would happen if a file system lost only one piece of data in a file of a million records. The system is 99.999% accurate! No user would complain if we could guarantee this level of accuracy, would they? What would happen if that lonely piece of lost data was *your* payroll check?

1.6.5 The 80/20 Rule for Deciding Costs versus Benefits

It is always a difficult problem to try to decide what to do next when making a trade-off, either one such as that described in the preceding paragraph, or any other. A nineteenth-century Italian economist named Pareto developed a principle that is just as applicable today as it was then. What he hypothesized can be referred to as *the 80/20 rule*. What this states is that *for a wide range of activities, 80% of the results are generated by 20% of the tasks*. For example, 80% of a company's revenues are generated by 20% of the salespeople. Eighty percent of the code written in a software organization is written by 20% of the programmers. Or to be more specific to file systems, 20% of the functionality will be used 80% of the time. Twenty percent of the code written has 80% of the performance problems, and so on. Although the percentages may vary somewhat, they tend to be consistent over a broad range of activities.

What is important here is not how precise the rule is, but what it is really trying to say. From the perspective of file system design, it is important to do an analysis to find and identify that critical 20% of the functionality which most users want; to locate that 20% of the code that has most of the performance problems; and to test the reliability of our file system to find the 20% of the modules that will contain the vast majority of the bugs.

These questions and issues can be answered by performance analysis tools, histograms, test suites, and a careful analysis of customer needs over both the short and the long term. That result of spending the effort to get this information will be that the file system developed will be efficient, stable, and competitive. The bottom line is that designing any software product in general, but more specifically a file system, encompasses much more than the code itself.

1.7 KEY FILE DESIGN RATIOS

As we proceed through our analysis of various file organizations, it will frequently be necessary for us to make a series of trade-offs to accomplish our tasks. Although there are no ''right answers'' that are guaranteed to be correct in all situations, we do have for analysis purposes two key formulas that help us to determine what kinds of trade-off decisions to make. These two ratios, however, only provide some insights into how records are expected to be processed within a file [3,4]. Thus they are really only inputs into our file design decisions.

1.7.1 File Activity Ratio

The file activity ratio, also known as the hit ratio, provides us with a measure of how many records in a given file are typically accessed in any job. Specifically, the file activity ratio is defined as follows:

$$\text{file activity ratio} = \frac{\text{number of records accessed}}{\text{number of records in file}}$$

If, in any given job, the ratio approaches a value of 1, it indicates that almost every record in the file is READ by the job. Thus sequential performance, or the ability to READ all records in a file, becomes critical to overall performance.

On the other hand, when few of the records are accessed in any given job, the ratio approaches zero. When the activity ratio is small, it means that most of the records in the file are *not* READ, only very specific ones. Thus *random* access to data records becomes a critical attribute toward high performance.

Finally, if the ratio is somewhere in the middle, we must look for other measures of performance and functionality with which we can make our design decisions. What is important, however, is that we understand how a file will be used.

1.7.2 File Volatility Ratio

The file volatility ratio is a measure of how fast the original version of a file is changing. If the file is changing rapidly, we should aim to make our change routines (i.e., WRITE and DELETE) as fast as possible. On the other hand, if the file is not changing rapidly, READ performance can be emphasized.

Specifically, the file volatility ratio can be defined as follows:

$$\text{file volatility ratio} = \frac{\text{no of additions} + \text{number of deletions}}{\text{number of records in original file}}$$

If the file has many records that have been added or deleted since the original file was built, this ratio will be high (i.e., approaches 1). This indicates that the *change functions*, WRITE and DELETE, must be designed and implemented for high performance.

On the other hand, a low volatility ratio (i.e., one approaching zero) means that overall the file is not changing very rapidly. Thus the *nonchange functions,* such as READ, should have a high performance. Finally, a ratio somewhere in the middle should force users to look for other measures to make the correct design and implementation decisions.

1.8 SUMMARY

The purpose of this chapter has been to introduce the topic of I/O. We examined I/O not only from the vantage point of the file system, but also from the perspective of the user. It is critical to understand both of these viewpoints to design a file system that meets the needs of both parties.

Finally, we discussed some of the important definitions that will be used throughout this book. These definitions, as well as some file system analysis ratios, will become the basis for our future discussions on the design of file systems.

KEY WORDS

Block	Maximum record size (MRS)
Blocking factor	Nonshared files
80/20 Rule	Pathname
Field	Performance
Field offset	Record
File	Record formats (RFM)
File activity ratio	Shared files
File attributes	Spanned records
File system	Unspanned records
File volatility ratio	Variable-length records (VLR)
Fixed-length records (FLR)	
Input/output (I/O)	

SUPPLEMENTAL REFERENCES

1. Claybrook, Billy G., *File Management Techniques*. New York: John Wiley & Sons, Inc., 1983, Chap. 1. This book provides a general introduction to file systems.

2. Freeman, Donald E., and Olney R. Perry, *I/O DESIGN: Data Management in Operating Systems*. Rochelle Park, N.J.: Hayden Book Company, Inc., 1977, Chap. 1. This text gives an excellent introduction to file systems. In addition, the authors provide a good perspective as to how file systems fit in the overall scheme of things within the operating environment of a computer system.

3. Hanson, Owen, *Design of Computer Data Files*. Rockville, Md.: Computer Science Press, Inc., 1982, Chap. 1. Hanson's introduction to file systems includes not only definitions, but also an overview of some of the major access method components within a file system.

4. Martin, James, *Computer Data-Base Organization,* 2nd ed. Englewood Cliffs, N.J.: Prentice-Hall, Inc., 1975, Chaps. 17, 18. The major feature of these chapters is Martin's ability to discuss many of the trade-offs that need to be considered when designing file systems.

EXERCISES

1. Why are *file attributes* critical to the correct processing of a file?

2. What is the major constraint on overall system performance and throughput? Explain.

3. File systems must make trade-offs between functionality, performance, and resources. Assume that you were designing a file system for a microcomputer. How would these trade-offs affect the methodology and decision making in your design?

4. Assume that an average disk I/O operation takes 20 milliseconds. If a system has three disks, what is the maximum number of disk I/O operations that can be processed in 1 second?

5. Why do most users consider functionality more important that performance?

6. If the file activity ratio is low and the file volatility ratio is high, what kinds of record operations should we try to optimize?

7. How does the *blocking factor* file attribute affect performance? Explain.

8. What is the difference between a field and a record? Explain.

9. Why is the *name* of a file not good enough to locate a particular file? How does the file's *pathname* solve these problems?

10. What are the advantages and disadvantages of having *spanned* records in a file? Explain.

PROGRAMMING EXERCISE

1. Examine the I/O statements in COBOL and one other language. Then define what functions and data structures would be required in a file system to support these languages.

Part 1

Device Characteristics

Next, we examine how the hardware portion of the computer system performs I/O operations. Why discuss hardware in a book concerned about file system software? Because how the I/O software works is dependent on how well we can take advantage of the hardware to achieve the highest combination of functionality and performance. This section of the book answers the following key questions:

- How do disk and tape devices work?
- How can software get the hardware devices to do the work needed to be done?
- How can we start an I/O operation, and how will we know when the operation has completed?
- How can we tell if our request was successful or whether there was a problem during the I/O processing?
- If the I/O request failed, are there any actions that can be taken to recover successfully, or must we give up trying?

In Chapter 2 we discuss how a computer system is interconnected with all the various devices. Also, we discuss in general terms how I/O requests can be made by software programs residing in main memory.

In Chapter 3 we cover tape devices in some detail. We learn what can, and what cannot, be done with tape drives. In addition, we discuss the trade-offs in using tapes versus other kinds of devices. Also, we begin to address performance issues. These will become extremely important, since an understanding of I/O performance is critical to understanding how file systems should be designed and why certain trade-offs are made.

    Chapter 4 concludes Part I with a discussion of disk devices. Disks are the primary on-line storage medium in use today. Their performance characteristics are critical to the operational efficiency of most applications as well as systems programs. With one exception, all the access methods discussed in Part III are "disk-only" file systems. We need to understand the importance of disks and how they work mechanically.

2

Device I/O

When you complete this chapter, you will be able to;

- Understand the various hardware components that make up an I/O configuration
- Understand how the I/O operations work and how the file system makes requests to perform I/O operations
- Describe how the file system knows when an I/O request has completed, so that the user can be notified
- Describe how data flow between the user's program, the file system, and the actual hardware devices
- Understand the concept of exception-handling and error recovery techniques
- Understand some of the criteria for performance consideration and improvement

2.1 OVERVIEW

Much of what is discussed in this book relates not only to file systems and data management, but also indirectly to the hardware itself. We are concerned with overall file system performance, which is intimately tied into the hardware and how it works.

Performance of tapes and disks is largely dependent on the mechanics of the device. We discuss how the file system software interacts with the devices. This is an important part of the entire file system design. An understanding of how the devices communicate with the software will enable us to understand and make better trade-offs in our file system designs. *Device I/O is performed by the device drivers in the file systems. The device drivers are the lowest-level software routines that communicate directly with the peripheral devices (see Figure 2–0).*

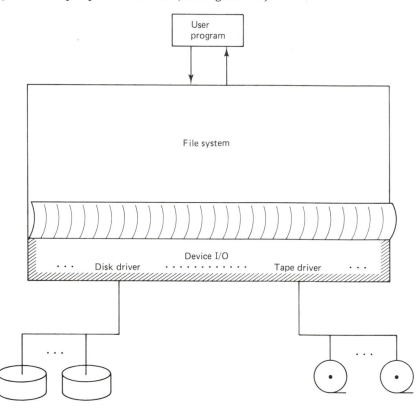

Figure 2–0   File system: hardware component.

2.2 HARDWARE CONFIGURATIONS

For many programmers who code in higher-level languages, the "machine" and the associated peripheral devices are almost completely invisible. In fact, the trend within the industry recently has been to make the computer easier and easier to use. One way to do this is to totally remove from the user the technical details of the hardware. The use of high-level languages such as Pascal or FORTRAN, access methods, and operating systems serve to insulate the user completely from the technical details of the hardware. For most applications this may be acceptable, since for the user, the underlying software will take advantage of the machine characteristics. However, the file system is a major piece of the underlying software and it has no choice but to know and understand the hardware, including the CPU and all devices.

Figure 2–1 shows the major components within a computer system. Although every system has similar components, not all vendors use the same terminology. Thus we will describe the components in more general terms.

2.2.1 Channels

Programs run in main memory of the computer. The program can access data outside the main memory of the machine by sending commands to the *channel* (see Figure

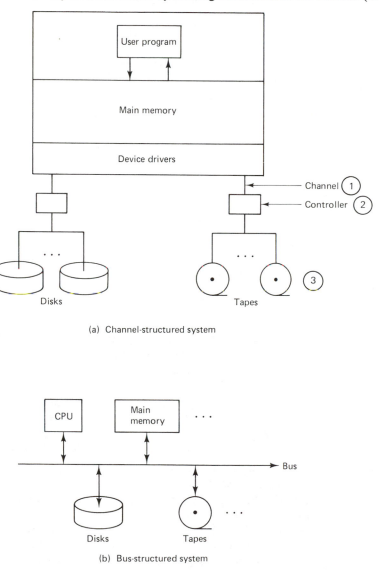

(a) Channel-structured system

(b) Bus-structured system

Figure 2–1   Computer system configuration.

2-1, a-1). The channel is the connection between the programs in main memory and the devices. A term sometimes used instead of channel is *bus*. Although technically different in implementation, the functions of a bus and channel are similar (see Figure 2-1b). *Functionally, the channel, or bus, is the vehicle for transmitting data between the CPU and the devices.*

A channel can be connected to multiple *controllers* which are of the same type. *A controller is a hardware component that understands the specific details of the devices connected to it, as well as the interface to the channel itself (see Figure 2-1, a-2).* For example, there could be a series of disk controllers connected to the same channel. In addition, there can be mutliple *devices* connected to each of the individual controllers. Thus one channel has the capacity to support many devices.

There is another benefit to having channels—that of providing a standard interface to perform I/O. All channels can be built to respond to the same set of internal instructions. In days and systems past, there was one interface to perform I/O to card readers, another interface to access tapes, and a third software interface to access disks. This was an intolerable situation. Channels eliminate this problem by defining a common software interface to all devices.

There are several kinds of channels, as described below.

Selector channel.   *A selector channel supports high-speed data transfer between main memory and a single device,* at any one time. To achieve high throughput, *only one device can be executing a request at any one time.* All other devices connected to the channel will remain idle until the device currently operating has completed. This frees the channel to perform useful work on other devices.

The obvious benefit of a selector channel is its high data capacity throughout. On the other hand, its major limitation is that it can support only a single I/O request at a time.

Byte multiplexer channel.   This type of channel can support up to 256 I/O requests being processed simultaneously. *The byte multiplexer channel operates as if it were really 256 individual channels, each of which could be connected to an I/O request.*

These channels are typically used for slower-speed devices, such as card readers, printers, and tapes. *Effectively, the channel is a small computer that can switch from one subchannel to another fast enough to keep all I/O requests working simultaneously.* Realistically, we can think of a multiplexer channel as a multiprogramming operating system with up to 256 jobs (i.e., devices) to be executed. Whenever any of the I/O requests needs service, the channel responds and then moves onto the other jobs in process. The multiplexer channel interleaves bytes of data from multiple devices during data transfer operations.

The major benefit of a byte multiplexer channel is to be able to overlap the mechanical movements of the various devices while supporting data transfer between the device and the memory of the computer. The drawbacks are that this type of channel costs more than a selector channel, and the actual number of simultaneous data transfers is limited.

   Block multiplexer channel.   *The block multiplexer channel can support up to 256 high-speed devices,* such as disks. It is similar to the byte multiplexer channel, except that it can support faster devices. This is because *it interleaves data in blocks, not bytes* as was the case with the byte multiplexer channel.

   In addition, the block multiplexer channel has more built-in intelligence. For example, it can start moving the access arm on one disk while waiting for another disk to rotate to the correct block, and simultaneously be transferring data to or from a third device. Again, this is important because it enables us to overlap the mechanical operations of moving the access arm on a disk or waiting for the disk to be rotated to the position wanted. Remember that mechanical operations take time, and anything that can be done to overlap these operations, and thus minimize the total delay to the system, is more than welcome.

2.2.2 Controllers

Channels provide a standard software interface to perform I/O. However, there is the severe problem that a *channel does not understand device specific processing.* In addition, the problem is compounded because so many different devices can be connected into any system that it would be difficult at best for the channel to understand even a small subset of the devices. Thus there needs to be another hardware box that lies between the actual devices and the channel. This "box" must perform two functions:

  • Understand and interface to the standard channel interface definition
  • Understand and interface to the devices themselves

   This interface box is called a *controller.* Thus *the controller acts as a translator by taking channel inputs and translating them into commands the device will understand, and vice versa.* All devices require a controller to run correctly, although several devices of the same device type, or class, can be connected to the same controller. Thus a controller has the intelligence to drive one type of device (e.g., Winchester disks, $5\frac{1}{4}$-inch floppy disks), but no more than one.

2.2.3 Devices

Finally, we arrive out at the device itself (see Figure 2–1, a–3). *A device can support only one I/O request at any time.* On the other hand, a device controller can be operating several devices simultaneously, and the channel could also be running several controllers at the same time. The bottom line, however, is that the device is the critical item in the environment outside the memory of the computer. It has the means of storing and later retrieving data for programs excuting in main memory.

An important point to remember is that the channel and controller components are nonmechanical and thus can execute at high speeds. Devices, on the other hand, are mechanical and tend to operate orders of magnitude slower than their nonmechanical counterparts. It is this dramatic time differential that is cause for major concern. The slowness of the I/O has a direct impact not only on the time it takes to complete the user's job, but also on the overall throughput of the system itself.

There are many kinds of devices, such as:

- Card readers and card punches
- Printers
- Tapes
- Hard disks
- Floppy disks
- Terminals
- Optical character readers
- Color plotters

We will be concerned only with tapes and disks, since these devices represent where the vast majority of all data files are stored. The other devices, although interesting, are left to the reader to investigate.

2.3 DEVICE I/O

How do software programs interface with the channel to get I/O requests completed? It cannot be via the high-level-language "commands," since each lanaguage tends to use different syntax and semantics to define its own I/O calls. Therefore, the simplest approach would be to define a standard interface to a series of software modules which are collectively known as a *file system*. Then we can let the file system be concerned with device specifics.

Given that there is a way in which software can request I/O to be performed, *what information is needed to perform I/O operations?* (See Figure 2–2.)

I/O commands.   First, we must be able to instruct the device to do something for us. We can do this by means of a series of *I/O commands (refer to Figure 2–2a)*. Commands are similar to op-codes in an assembler language program, or verbs within a high-level-language program (e.g., MOVE, ADD, IF, COMPARE, etc.). More specifically, there are two classes of I/O commands, *device control* and *data transfer* commands. The latter commands actually instruct the device to READ or WRITE a block of data. Device control commands relate to the mechanical movement of the device, such as rewinding a tape.

Address of the data record buffer.   Second, we need to specify the address of an area in main memory, known as a record buffer, into or from which the data will be transferred (see Figure 2–2b). For example, if we wanted to write a block to

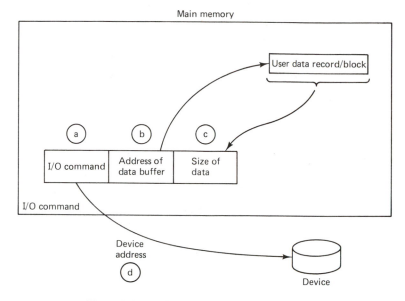

Figure 2–2   Device I/O command requirements.

disk, we would need to issue the WRITE__BLOCK command and point to the location in main memory where the data record to be written was located.

Amount of data to be transferred.   In reading or writing a block of data, how can the device know how much data it should read or write? It does not, unless we also tell it how much data to transfer (see Figure 2–2c). Thus, to perform I/O, we need to tell the device exactly how much data to transfer (i.e., how large the data record really is).

Device.   Finally, the I/O operation must be performed on one of the devices connected to the computer system. Each device has a unique address, or name (see Figure 2–2d). This is similar to houses having unique addresses, or people having unique telephone numbers. Thus before an I/O operation can be performed, the specific device address must be known.

There are as many ways of passing the device all this information as there are devices, or more. We can issue one command at a time. When it completes, we can send the device the next command. Alternatively, we can package up all the commands into a *channel program. A channel program is a program to be executed by a channel, just as the CPU executes a software program.* Specifically, there is:

- A known beginning and ending (Figure 2–3 a and d)
- A series of instructions that must be executed in a particular sequence (Figure 2–3b)
- An ability to branch from one point in the program to another (Figure 2–3c)

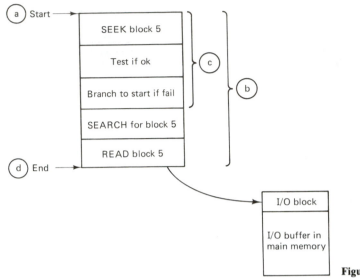

Figure 2-3   Channel program.

What happens to a program when an I/O operation is being executed on its behalf? *Most programs will stop executing from the time the I/O request is made until the I/O request has been completed. This is known as synchronous I/O.* This means that the program is synchronized to the completion of the I/O operation. Almost all the major high-level languages (e.g., COBOL, FORTRAN, BASIC) support only synchronous I/O. On the other hand, *if a program requests an I/O operation and can continue to do its own work until it requires the data record, we have asynchronous I/O.* Here, the programming language would have to have the syntax that would allow the programmer to test, or wait, to see if the I/O request had completed. It is asynchronous because the program and the I/O operation are executing simultaneously. The file system must use asynchronous I/O to successfully support multiple users running on many separate devices.

2.3.1 Device Control Commands

To correctly READ or WRITE the block of data we need, it is necessary to mechanically reposition the device to the location of the desired block on the medium (i.e., tape or disk). This is strictly a mechanical operation and therefore will take substantially longer to execute than will CPU instructions. These mechanical operations are performed via *device control commands* (see Figure 2–4a).

```
SEEK                    READ_BLOCK
REWIND                  WRITE_BLOCK
BACKSPACE
FORWARD_SPACE
    .
    .
    .
```

(a) Device control commands   (b) Data transfer commands   **Figure 2-4**   Device I/O commands.

We can, with magnetic tape drives, for example, rewind to the beginning of the tape, or forward-space to the end of the tape. We can also move forward or backward *n* blocks to reposition to a specific block of data.

On a disk we can move the read/write access arm in, or out (i.e., SEEK), to the proper location. We must then wait for the correct block to rotate underneath the read/write heads (i.e., SEARCH). Then, and only then, can we actually read or write that specific data block.

There are two key points to remember here. First, there are specific commands available to reposition a device to the correct block of data. Second, all mechanical movements take a long time, and we should therefore try to minimize their usage to improve overall performance. *Mechanical I/O is one of the major bottlenecks to overall system performance.*

2.3.2 Data Transfer Commands

Once we have mechanically repositioned the medium to the correct block of data, it is necessary to command the device to either read, or write, that block on the device. These operations are collectively known as *data transfer commands* (see Figure 2–4b). There are only two data transfer commands:

- WRITE-BLOCK: *transfer the data record from main memory to the device itself*
- READ-BLOCK: *transfer the data record from the device into main memory*

For example, we can WRITE to the printer, READ from the card reader, or WRITE a block of data to disk or tape. All data get transferred from, or into, a block of allocated main memory known as an *I/O buffer*. This buffer must be large enough to hold the largest block of data that will ever be written or read from the file. The block I/O buffer is not directly visible to the user. Thus the file system must move the desired data between the user's *record buffer* allocated within the user's address space and the system's I/O buffer.

More precisely, let us examine Figure 2–5. In a user's program there is usually some kind of declaration of a record area. Thus, when the program wishes to write a record onto a disk, it copies the data to be written into this record area, also called a user record buffer. The program then executes a "WRITE" type of statement (step 1). The file system then takes control (step 2) and proceeds to copy the data record from the user's record buffer into the appropriate location in the I/O buffer in main memory (step 3). Note that other records could already reside within that block, so the file system makes certain that the record is copied into the correct position within the block. Then, when the block is full, the file system finally writes the block in the I/O buffer in main memory onto the appropriate sector on the disk (step 4).

Alternatively, assume that the user wants to READ a specific record from the file. The file system determines which block of the file the record is in and then proceeds to read that file block from the disk into an I/O buffer in main memory (step 5). Then the file system extracts the desired record from the I/O buffer (step 6) and copies it into the user's record buffer (step 7). Again, there could be more than one record in the file block just read into memory, so it is up to the file system to *know*

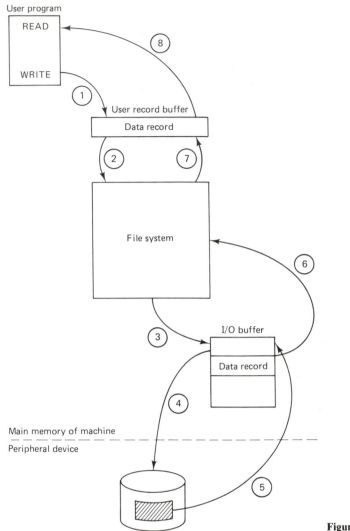

Figure 2-5 I/O data movement.

which of the records is the correct one to access. Finally, control is returned to the user (step 8) and the user program resumes execution.

It is critical to understand the foregoing sequence. The only way in which data records on a device can be manipulated by a program is by reading the block containing the records into an I/O buffer in main memory. Only after the file system has copied the record into the user's buffer can the user's program access the data. To put it another way, *programs cannot directly access and manipulate data on the device itself. The data must first be read into the main memory of the machine. Then, and only then, can the data be accessed.*

The size and number of I/O buffers is critical to overall I/O performance and throughput, and will be discussed throughout this book. For comparison purposes, the time it actually takes to *transfer* the data to or from the device is negligible compared to that of mechanically moving the device itself.

For example, if data can be transferred at 1 million bytes per second, which is not unreasonable, an average 200-byte data record can be read in just 200 microseconds. In the time it would take to perform an average I/O operation on disk (e.g., 50 milliseconds), almost 50,000 characters of data could have been transfered, which is approximately the number of characters in this chapter!

2.4 I/O PROGRAMMING

We have discussed some of the commands that software can issue to tell the devices what to do next. However, several major questions must still be asked, such as:

- How can we put these I/O commands together into a program?
- How can we actually start, or initiate, the I/O program?
- How can we know when the I/O program has completed?
- How can we tell if our request completed correctly or whether errors were encountered?
- If errors were detected, can anything be done to recover from the error?

These questions are covered in detail in Chapters 5 and 6. However, it is useful now to show some examples of I/O programs.

2.4.1 I/O Program Examples

To write an I/O program, it is first necessary to determine what operations, either mechanical repositioning or data transfer commands, will be required to complete the I/O request. Once we have determined the commands needed, we can then put all the needed commands into the proper sequence. This sequence is known as an *I/O channel program*.

Notice how similar this activity is to "normal" computer programming. First we design and develop a solution to a problem. Then we implement the program by writing the instructions in the correct sequence. I/O instructions have op-codes (i.e., commands), main-storage addresses, and are fetched from main memory before their execution. Channel programs terminate after the last command. They also have looping capability. In fact, there can be more than one channel program in execution at the same time. Thus the channel programs are effectively multiprogrammed.

Tape I/O.   For example, if we want to read the first block of data on a tape device, we need to do the following:

1. REWIND Tape.   This command repositions to the beginning of the tape. This is done to ensure that we are correctly positioned at the actual beginning of the tape (i.e, at the first record). If we were *not* trying to access the first record on the tape, this command must not be used.

2. READ_BLOCK ptr, count.   This will cause *count* bytes of the first block of data to be read from the tape and transferred into the I/O block buffer in main memory pointed to by *ptr*. The file system then extracts the desired data record from the I/O block buffer and copies the data record into the user's record buffer.

Disk I/O.   Conversely, the sequence of I/O commands required to write a block of data to a disk is as described below.

1. SEEK cylinder, track.   The SEEK command repositions the read/write access arm to the cylinder and track on which the block of data is to be written. *Since the disk arm could be located anywhere on the disk, this command is always required to reposition to the correct cylinder.*

2. SEARCH track, block number.   The SEARCH command allows us to wait while the disk rotates beneath the read/write heads to the correct position on the track. The SEARCH command examines each block as it passes underneath the read/write heads to see if the proper location on the track (i.e., block number) has been reached. When it is correctly positioned, the next command is executed.

3. WRITE_BLOCK ptr, count.   This command transfers *count* number of bytes of data from the I/O block buffer in the main memory location addressed by *ptr* to the disk itself.

I/O programs can get substantially more complicated depending on what is being done and now intelligent the disks and their controllers are. However, the concepts are the same as in FORTRAN and COBOL programming, even though programs may vary in difficulty. *The major benefit of a channel program is that the device can execute many instructions without interrupting the CPU for something to do next.* Thus the file system is interrupted only when the entire channel program has completed.

Not all machines, especially in the mini- and microcomputer area, have channel program capabilities. For one reason, it is a more expensive way of performing I/O. In their place, the same series of device commands are executed, except that now they are requested one at a time. When one I/O command completes, the file system then issues the next I/O command. Therefore, the file system must get involved with every command issued to the device. Thus more of the available CPU cycles must be spent processing I/O than was the case for channel programs.

2.5 IMPLEMENTATION REQUIREMENTS

In each of the following chapters, we describe some of the data and file structures required to implement a real file system. Although only the major data elements of these structures are discussed, enough detail is provided to see how a file system really goes about its work and does its tasks.

Within almost every structure discussed will be a set of data know as the header information. This information includes the following types of information.

Version ID.   It will be assumed that these structure definitions will change over time as new functionality and features are added to the system. In order for the file system to know what features are, and are not, available on a particular system, each control block is self-identified by a version number.

Link field.   All main-memory data structures of the same type will be connected together in a linked list. This allows the file system to be able to determine at all times what is, and is not, currently being processed. It has the secondary effect of allowing the file system to perform an orderly shutdown of a user's job should that job come to an abnormal halt.

Status.   Some, although not all structures have a status field at a standard location in the structure's header in order to be able to pass status information to different modules of the system.

Finally, in each chapter we discuss only the new fields that had to be created based on the functionality discussed in that section. This will allow us to define only as much of the structure as is relevant up to that point in the book. The full structure definitions are incorporated in the appendices.

The file system can keep track of the state of all the devices in the system configuration by maintaining a control block, or table of critical information, known as the *device control table (DCT)*. This control block resides within main memory. Within the device control table (see Table 2–1, p. 38), the file system maintains the following kinds of information:

- Current device status, such as available or unavailable
- A pointer to the I/O request queue for that device
- Device-specific parameters
- Error-processing information
- The name of the volume currently mounted on that device

What is important to understand is that there does exist a table that contains all the relevant information about the device and the jobs running on it. *There is one DCT for every device in the system.*

2.6 SUMMARY

In this chapter we have covered a wide range of topics relating to the hardware aspects of I/O. These are important to know and understand, since how well a file system

TABLE 2-1   DEVICE CONTROL TABLE

Header information	
Version ID	Identifies which format this DCT conforms with; also allows for future expansion
Link to next DCT	All DCTs reside in a linked list
Address of IORQ	IORQ associated with this specific device
General device information	
Device status	Status information sent back from the device itself
	I/O successful
	I/O successful after error recovery
	Device not ready
	Illegal command
	Write-protected media
	Unrecoverable error
	Invalid HW address
	Device busy
	I/O in progress
	Invalid block/sector number
HW address of device	How to access the device
Volume name	Name of the volume currently mounted on this device
Device type	$5\frac{1}{4}$ -inch floppy disk
	$3\frac{1}{2}$ -inch floppy disk
	300-MB disk
	600-MB disk
	Cartridge tape
	Streamer tape
	Standard tape
	etc.
Exception-processing information	
Device-specific information	

knows and takes advantage of the hardware will dictate how good that file system really is.

The second thing that should be becoming more and more clear is how much time I/O really requires relative to CPU speeds. This is one of the most misunderstood areas of systems design. Thus products are produced that perform less than expected because the I/O impact was not properly considered.

Finally, it is important to understand the hardware, and how I/O is performed, because it is the file system that is the interface between the user, other ssytem routines, and the external peripheral devices. Thus we have no choice in designing and implementing file systems but to know in great detail how the hardware and devices perform I/O.

KEY WORDS

Asynchronous I/O	Device control commands
Block Multiplexer channel	Device control table (DCT)
Bus	I/O buffers
Channel programs	I/O commands
Channels	Record buffer
Controller	Selector channel
Data transfer commands	Synchronous I/O

SUPPLEMENTAL REFERENCES

1. Brown, D. T., R. L. Eibsen, and C. A. Thorn, "Channel and Direct Access Device Architecture." *IBM Systems Journal,* Vol. 11, No. 3, 1975, pp. 186–199. This article discusses some of the I/O problems of medium- and large-scale computers. It goes on to discuss the design and architecture of IBM channels, and how IBM tried to solve various I/O problems.

2. Freeman, Donald E., and Olney R. Perry, *I/O DESIGN: Data Management in Operating Systems.* Rochelle Park, N.J.: Hayden Book Company, Inc., 1977, Chaps. 2, 3. These chapters provide a rather detailed discussion of the hardware aspects of file systems and I/O. In addition, there is an entire chapter that deals with I/O programming, which includes many examples.

3. Prasad, N. S., *Architecture and Implementation of Large Scale IBM Computer Systems.* Wellesley, Mass.: QED Information Sciences, Inc., 1981, p. 327. For those who want to learn and understand the nitty-gritty details of the software-to-hardware I/O interface, this is the book. It covers channels, interrrupts, channel programming, and much more. Although the book is targeted at IBM systems, it is very applicable to other systems as well.

4. Toby, J. Teorey, and James P. Fry, *Design of Database Structures.* Englewood Cliffs, N.J.: Prentice-Hall, Inc., 1982, Chap. 9. For those who want to investigate the performance aspect of I/O, this chapter contains many different formulas and perspectives.

5. Wiederhold, Gio, *Database Design.* New York: McGraw-Hill Book Company, 1977, Chap. 2. This book is rather a complete investigation of device I/O. There are some disk-oriented formulas and performance curves.

EXERCISES

1. Why does the file system *require* asynchornous I/O in order to operate efficiently and effectively? Explain.

2. Assume that you were assembling a computer system that had two disks, a tape, and a printer connected to the CPU. What types of channels would you select for each of these device types? Explain why.

3. Why is it possible to connect a *block* multiplexer channel to high-speed disk devices but not to a byte multiplexer?

4. Why are device control commands needed? Is it possible to do without them?

5. Do any of the high-level languages allow the user to continue processing after an I/O request has been made? If there are none, describe what features would be needed in that language for it to support asynchronous I/O.

6. Why are both block buffers and user record buffers needed? Is it possible to eliminate either, or both, of them?

7. What is the function of the device control table, and how many are there in any given system?

8. What is the major benefit that channel programs have over "traditional" I/O, meaning that the file system has to issue every individual I/O command after the previous command completed?

9. Why is it necessary to rewind a tape before reading it? What would happen if you did *not* rewind the tape before reading it?

10. Where is an I/O buffer located? How many are there in a system, and how large are they?

PROGRAMMING EXERCISE

1. Design and implement a module that allocates space for device control tables and then initializes them. Note carefully how and from where you get your initialization information.

3

Magnetic Tape Devices

CHAPTER OBJECTIVES

When you complete this chapter, you will be able to:

- Describe how I/O is performed on tape drives
- Understand the file structure that is written onto a tape by the file system and why it is required
- Discuss how error recovery is performed and what the risks are in utilizing these techniques
- Understand the performance implications, both positive and negative, of using tapes
- Begin to understand the concept of compatibility

3.1 OVERVIEW

One of the most useful and common devices that can be connected to a computer is the *magnetic tape* device. Although disks, which are discussed in Chapter 4, are used for on-line storage, tapes are an inexpensive medium for saving or transporting files. Tapes have high data capacities, do not take up much space, and are quite reliable. In addition, tapes are simpler and easier to understand than disks, yet have similar file structure requirements to disks. Thus by first discussing tapes, we can begin to learn the details of what a file structure is and why it is required. Figure

3–0 shows that the tape-handling modules in the file system are part of the lowest-level software interface to the devices themselves. More specifically, device-driver software modules as a group form *the* interface between the software in the CPU and the external world of peripheral devices.

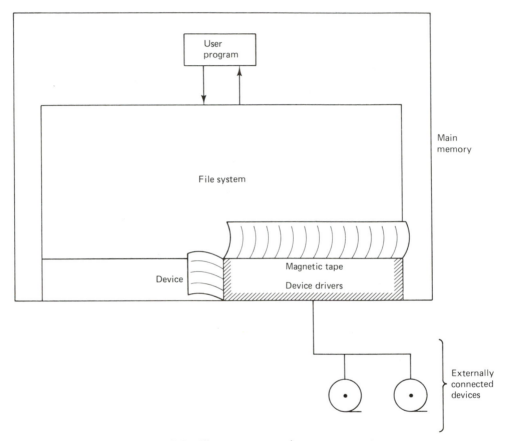

Figure 3–0   File system: magnetic tape component.

3.2 TAPE HARDWARE CHARACTERISTICS

A tape is a tape is a tape. It does not matter whether it is large or small, the ideas and requirements are the same. Take, for example, a cassette tape on which your favorite song has been recorded. If we examine it in detail, we can list some of its characteristics:

- All cassettes are the same size. If we tried to play one in our eight-track stereo tape deck, we would fail. Also note that the tape in a cassette is much narrower than the tape in an eight-track tape deck. Thus the *physical size* of the medium is important.

- Cassettes can be purchased that can record or play back for various lengths of time (e.g., 10 minutes to 90 minutes).

- All cassettes must have the music technically recorded, (i.e., written onto tape) identically. It is only in this manner that cassette recorders can be used to play cassettes originally recorded on other machines. If we had used records as our example, we can observe the problem of buying standard records versus digitized records. Each requires its own unique machines to record and play back the music.

- Tapes have a beginning and an end.

- We have the capability of either recording (i.e., writing) on the tapes or playing the tapes back (i.e., reading the tapes). In addition, we can forward-space or rewind the tapes. Thus we have *device control commands* (e.g., FORWARD-SPACE, BACKSPACE, and REWIND) as well as *data transfer commands* (e.g., READ and WRITE).

- There is a mechanism on cassettes, specifically a plastic tab in each corner at the rear of the cassette case, such that if these tabs are removed, the user *cannot* record on the cassette. This is a protection mechanism to prevent accidental destruction of a song or other recording that may have been made on the medium.

The list above illustrates some of the characteristics of tapes that we frequently take for granted. In the realm of tape processing, we also have these features and protection mechanisms. The fact that in one case we are recording music, or voice, and in another case we are recording data for use on a computer does not change the necessity for having these features. Let us now examine tapes in a more detailed manner.

3.2.1 Recording Surface

As can be seen in Figure 3–1, data are written onto *tracks* on the surface of the tape itself. *Tracks are a series of parallel lines on the surface of the tape on which a single*

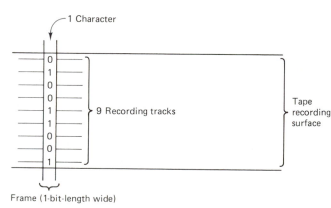

Frame (1-bit-length wide)

Figure 3–1   Tape recording format.

bit of information can be recorded. Depending on the device in question, the information is typically recorded on either seven or nine tracks, although 18-track tape drives are also available. In addition, 32-track tape drives are now being developed. The most common approach in use today is to record data onto nine tracks. Since one bit is recorded onto each of the parallel tracks, nine tracks have enough room to record an 8-bit byte plus a control, or *parity,* bit. The parity bit is used by the tape device to detect single-bit error conditions, such as the dropping of a bit in a character. All the bits that make up a byte of information are recorded within a *frame* on the tape which is just a single bit wide.

3.2.2 Tape Density

Besides recording the data on a specific number of tracks, the amount of data that can be recorded per inch of tape can also vary. *The number of bits that can be recorded per inch is known as the density of the tape.* Currently, the more popular tape densities range from 800 bpi (bits per inch) to 6250 bpi. In the future, given the current trends within the industry, tapes could be developed that support 38,000 bits (or bytes) per inch [2, 3] (see Figure 3–2). Since the bits representing a particular character are recorded on parallel tracks within a frame, the density really represents the number of *bytes* per inch. With the newer 18- and 32-track tapes, there are two and four characters, respectively, written within each frame.

3.2.3 Protection

To protect a tape from inadvertently being destroyed by someone writing other data onto it, there has to be a way, similar to the use of plastic tabs in the back of cassettes, to protect the data. This is accomplished with a small plastic ring, called a *write-ring,* which can be inserted or removed from the back of the tape itself (refer to Figure 3–3). Although it varies from vendor to vendor, the most common practice is that *when the write-ring is present, then and only then can data be written onto the tape itself.* The tape drive *hardware* detects that the write-ring is present and allows write operations to occur. Conversely, when the write-ring is removed, the tape *hardware* prohibits all writing of data onto the tape.

3.2.4 Beginning and End of Tape Detection

The tape device itself has to be able to detect where the first block of data is on the tape. This is needed so that the device can always position to the first block and *know* that it is the correct block. On a cassette, if you forget to rewind the tape, you will begin playing or recording in the middle of the tape. Thus the first thing you need to do is to rewind the tape to a known place on the medium, namely the beginning. In a similar manner, we can always try to position the tape medium to the beginning of the first data block. *The method used to locate the beginning of the tape is to look for a small aluminum reflector strip placed on the tape when it was manufac-*

Linear density (bpi per track)	Year	Product	Tape width (in.)	Tracks	TPI	Areal density (bpsi)
100	1953	IBM 726	1/2	7	14	1,400
200	1955	IBM 727	1/2	7	14	2,800
556	1959	IBM 729 III	1/2	7	14	7,784
800	1962	IBM 729 V	1/2	7	14	11,200
800	1963	IBM 2401-1	1/2	9	18	14,400
1,600	1965	IBM 2401-4	1/2	9	18	28,800
6,250	1973	IBM 3420-4	1/2	9	18	112,500
1,600	1973	3M DCD-3	1/4	4	16	25,600
6,400	1977	DEI Funnel	1/4	4	16	102,400
8,000	1981	Archive Sidewinder	1/4	4	16	128,000
10,000	1981	3M HCD-75	1/4	16	64	640,000

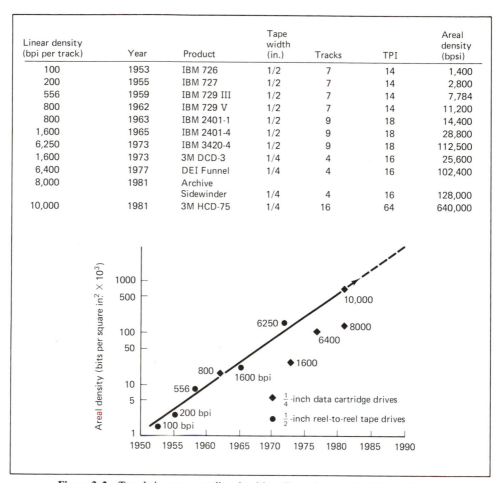

Figure 3–2   Trends in tape recording densities. (From Stanley H. Miller & Robert Freese, "Recording densities push the limit." *Mini-Micro Systems,* October, 1983, pp 287–292.

tured (see Figure 3–4). By repositioning to this marker, the device knows that it is at the true beginning of the data.

If it is important to know the location of the beginning of the data on the tape, it is equally important to know where the end of the tape is located. We do not want to record data to the physical end of the tape itself, because then the tape would unravel off the end of the reel. Thus *if a reflector strip could be used to identify the start of the tape, a similar reflector strip can signal the end of the tape* (see Figure 3–4).

We could ask ourselves how a tape drive can tell the difference between the beginning and the end of a tape if they are both identified by reflector strips. The way this is done is to place the reflector strips on opposite edges of the medium itself.

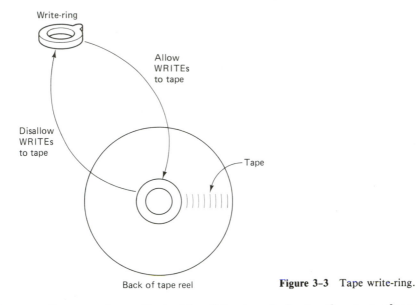

Figure 3–3 Tape write-ring.

Thus *a reflector strip on the inside of the tape indicates the start-of-tape, while a reflector strip on the outside edge of the tape indicates the end-of-tape.*

The physical length of the tape medium can also vary considerably. Just as we can purchase cassette tapes that can record for just 30 minutes, we can also buy tapes that can record for 90 minutes or more. Similarly, standard $\frac{1}{2}$-inch-width tape can come on reels with 600 to 2400 feet of tape. Thus the amount of data that can actual-

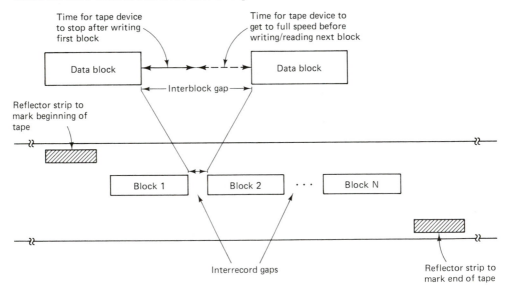

Figure 3–4 Physical structure of the tape.

ly be recorded on the tape itself is dependent on both the length of the tape and its recording density. Unlike disks, tape media can be variable in length.

3.3 FILE STRUCTURE

What is a file structure, and why is it important? We can begin to answer this question by investigating how data are actually recorded onto a tape. For now, consider *file structure* to be the overhead in the file. In other words, *the file structure is the additional information that is recorded on the medium, over and above the data that were written by the user.* The file structure is used by the file system to correctly record and retrieve the data on the media.

First, information will get written onto the tape in units of data called blocks. A block can be of different sizes, but it will always be a block of data that gets transferred onto the tape. Referring to Figure 3–4, we can see that all the blocks on the tape are separated by spaces called *interrecord gaps* (IRGs). They are also known as *interblock gaps (IBGs),* since they do, indeed, separate blocks on the medium.

The size of the IRG is determined by the mechanics of the tape drive itself. Fundamentally, the tape drive must be running at full speed before it can correctly read or write data on the medium. Since we are dealing with a mechanical device, it takes a relatively lengthy period of time to reach full speed. Therefore, the IRG must be large enough for the tape drive to slow down and come to a halt after reading, or writing, a block of data, *and* then to restart and get up to full speed before encountering the next block of data. Therefore, *the first half of the gap is to allow the tape to slow down and stop, while the other half of the gap is the amount of space required for the drive to get up to full speed.*

Since tapes are made by many different manufacturers, and the start/stop times and distances can vary widely, we could potentially have a significant problem in reading back tapes that were created on another manufacturer's tape drive. One benefit of tapes is that not only are they relatively inexpensive, but they are easy to carry from one machine to another, independent of the brand of tape drive. Therefore, to solve this potentially serious problem, there are conventions that all manufactuers follow so that all IRGs are of the same size, regardless of where, or how, they were created. The standard IRG size is approximately $\frac{1}{2}$ inch.

A block consists of one or more records. The set of all the related records is called a file. If we put related records into blocks and then write the blocks onto tape, how can we distinguish to which file the blocks belong? Somehow, we must be able to partition the blocks in one file separately from the blocks in another file.

There is a special bit pattern that is written onto a tape that can be recognized by the tape hardware as being a special kind of identifier. This bit pattern is called a *tape mark.* To partition all the blocks of a file into one logical entity separate from all the other blocks on the tape, we will need to write this tape mark just before the first block in the file and just after the last block in the file. Thus *all the blocks of data in a file are located between two tape marks* (see Figure 3–5). If there were other files on the tape medium, those files would also be surrounded by a matching pair of tape marks. Now we have almost accomplished what we set out to do, namely to come up with a method of determining which blocks belonged to a specific file.

We have one other problem, however. If there is more than one file on the tape, how can we be sure which file is the one we really want? We can locate the correct file if each file can be identified by a unique name. We could then search the tape until we found the name of the file we wanted. The standard way this is accomplished is by writing *labels* on the tape to identify each file.

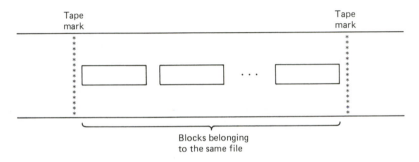

Figure 3–5   Overview of tape file structure.

3.3.1 Labels

File labels are blocks of data that the file system can use to uniquely identify, and correctly process, each file on the medium. File labels may seem like a trivial thing to create. However, we must understand some of the serious ramifications involved if we choose to create the labels ourselves. First, other users who might need your tapes must be able to read and understand the file labels. Thus the size, location and field-by-field content of the file labels must be known and understood in advance by everyone. This self-regulation has been accomplished by having a *tape standard* [1] written and agreed on by all parties. In the area of tape labels, the standard defines the size, location, and content of these labels.

Where should the file label be placed so that everyone, and every piece of software that needs to use the information within it, can find and read it? *The easiest and most straightforward rule is to make the file label block(s) the first block(s) in a file.* Then, any software that needs to access the file label need only read the first block of the file.

There is another problem that must be solved. Even if we can locate the file label, how can the software programs know how much data there is or how big the first block is? This problem is solved by defining within the tape label standard the length of all labels. Specifically, *all labels are 80 characters long.* Any software that needs to read, or write, a label can use the standard length of 80 bytes. If everyone follows these conventions, labels can be created by anyone and can be read by any other person or program.

What information do we need to know about a tape? First, we must guarantee that the file being processed is the correct one. Before labels were standardized and put onto tape files, tapes were *unlabeled*. The only way to tell if the file was the correct one was either by the handwritten label on the outside of the tape reel or by seeing if the program worked successfully. Otherwise, there was no way of really knowing if the correct tape volume was being accessed.

Second, we need to be able to guarantee that the *correct tape volume* is being accessed. This further guarantees that the correct *version* of the file is being used.

To meet both of these objectives, we will define several different kinds of tape labels. One set of labels will be associated with each file, and another set will be associated with each tape volume. Labels can provide this distinction if the following conventions hold:

- All labels are of fixed length and exactly 80 bytes long.
- Each label uniquely identifies itself so that it can be recognized by the file system.
- The field definitions in the labels conform with an agreed standard.

By convention, there is a tape label standard [1] which all vendors support. Thus it is possible for one system to be able to correctly read and write tapes generated by another system.

Volume labels.   How can we tell that the correct version of the file is mounted? More specifically, if we saved versions of the file every night for security and backup reasons, how can we make sure that we have not mounted last week's or last year's version of the file? If a file can have a name, so can a volume. Specifically, every volume has associated with it a volume label. *The volume label is the first label on the tape and uniquely identifies this tape volume.* In this label is all the critical information related to the tape volume (see Figure 3-6). The following data are recorded in the volume label:

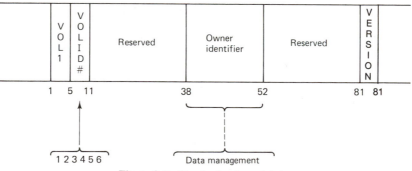

Figure 3-6   Standard volume labels.

- *Label identifier "VOL":* Used to uniquely identify this block as the one and only VOLume label block on this tape.
- *Label number:* Always set to 1.
- *Volume identifier:* Assigned by the user as a number which specifically identifies this volume from among the set of all tape volumes at a particular computer installation. This is usually the same *identifier* that is written on the outside of the tape to uniquely identify this particular volume. For example, tape "123456" is different from tape "123457."
- *Owner identifier:* Field that can be used to record who owns this volume. This is typically the name of the person or organization that created this particular tape volume.
- *Label standard version:* Field that indicates to which version of the tape standard this tape conforms. Over time, standards have a way of being modified to add new features. It is important for the file system to know which standard was used to create this tape. Thus this field tells the file system what features are, and are not, supported.

With this set of information, we can be sure that the correct volume containing our file has been mounted on the tape drive. As part of the process of using a tape, the software in the file system validates that the correct volume has been mounted. The information used to validate the label is provided either by the user's program or via information passed in the job control language or command language used on the system.

File labels.   Immediately following the volume label block on the tape is the first *file* label block. There can, and will be, more than one label block associated with a file. *These labels are known as the file's header labels.* It is not important to realize which block contains a certain piece of data, since this can always be looked up in a reference book. However, it is important to understand that the key information specifying what the file looks like can be found within the set of blocks consisting of the file's labels. The following file-related information is a subset of the data that can be found within the file label set (see Figure 3–7):

- *Label identifier "HDR":* Serves to specifically delineate this label from any other label or data block in the file.
- *File identifier:* Unique name of the file both on this volume and within the set of all the files at this computer installation. Thus, given a volume name and a file name on that volume, we have uniquely specified the file that we need to access.
- *Creation and expiration dates:* These dates can be used to ensure that the desired version of the file has been mounted. In addition, the expiration date allows us to purge files that are older than a prespecified interval. In this manner, we can reuse the tapes themselves rather than keep all data forever!

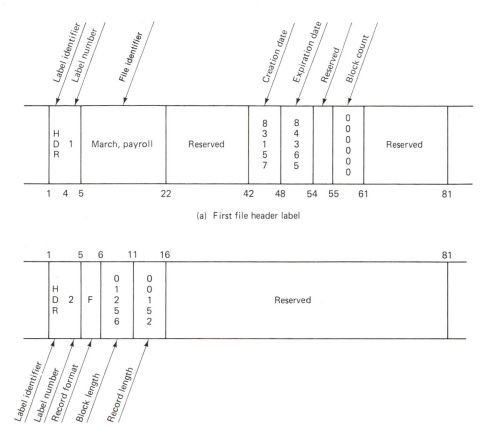

(a) First file header label

(b) Second file header label

Figure 3-7   File header labels.

- *Block count:* Indicates the actual number of blocks written into the file when it was created.
- *Record format:* Defines whether the records in the file are fixed or variable in length.
- *Block length:* Defines the size of the largest possible block that can exist within this file. This information is needed so that we can be sure to allocate I/O buffer space internally in main memory that is large enough to hold the largest block in the file.
- *Record length:* Defines the maximum length of any record in the entire file.

There are also file labels that are placed at the end of a file, which are known as *end-of-file labels* or *trailer labels* (see Figure 3-8). These labels have almost all of the same information that the file's header labels contained. However, there is one additional critical piece of information, the block count. *The block count*

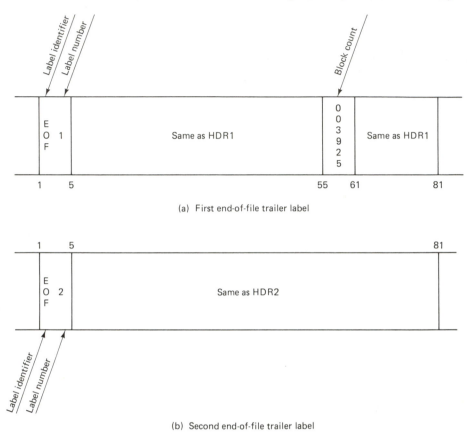

(a) First end-of-file trailer label

(b) Second end-of-file trailer label

Figure 3-8   File trailer labels.

*represents the actual number of data blocks that were written to the file, not counting
any of the label blocks.* In the file header label, this field is set to zero, since it is
not known how many blocks will subsequently get written into the file.

This field is used to double check that after reading all the blocks in a file, the
number of blocks actually read corresponds to the number of blocks in the file as
identified by the block count in the end-of-file label. If the numbers are not identical,
we know that one or more blocks were incorrectly processed.

3.3.2 Single File per Tape

Where are the user data blocks? Certainly, we do not want to examine every block
on the tape to check to see if it was a label. Thus how can we easily and consistently
know which blocks are data and which blocks are labels? By convention, all the user
data blocks are surrounded by a special bit sequence called a tape mark. As can be
seen in Figure 3-9, the user data start after the first tape mark, and the last data

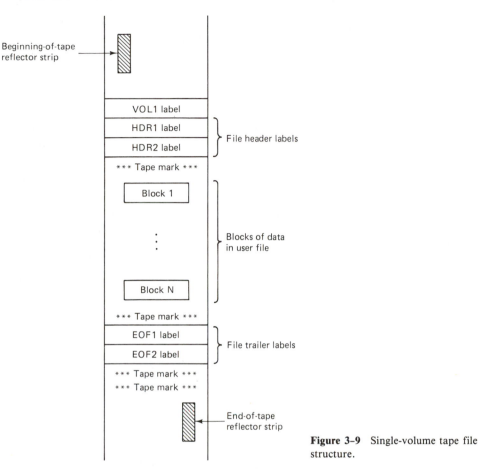

Figure 3-9 Single-volume tape file structure.

block is immediately followed by a tape mark. In this manner, we know precisely which blocks are label blocks and which contain user data.

Finally, it is important to understand why labels are so vital to the overall file system processing and to data integrity. It is true that all the information that is stored in the volume and file labels could have been passed to the file system via a program or command language interface. However, it is critical to remember that what we are dealing with data that are important to the user, be it payroll data, inventory data, or anything else.

Second, these data are being used to run businesses, and without the correct data, or without the files because of a mysterious system crash, those businesses could be hurt substantially. Thus we cannot assume that the person who writes the programs, or enters the job control language, is perfect and that the data provided will always be correct. The only data that can be trusted are those that were written into the file itself when the file was created. Only those data can and should be trusted to specify correctly the characteristics of the file. That is why tape labels are so important. It is not a question of whether we can ever trust anyone to provide the correct information, but rather is it worth the risk of possibly damaging the files if and when an error is made?

3.3.3 Multivolume Files

In the preceding section we discussed the format of one file existing on one tape volume, and how the user's data were surrounded by tape marks and labels. However, what if the file is too large to fit on a single tape volume? In that case we would still have the user's data encapsulated between labels. Instead of having an end-of-file label, we would have an end-of-volume label. The end-of-volume label is identical to the end-of-file label discussed earlier. However, the label identifier is now set to *EOV* instead of *EOF*. *An EOV label indicates to the file system that more of that file exists on another tape reel* (refer to Figure 3–10). In this manner, we can read to the end of the first tape volume and then find out that this was only the end of the first volume of the file. Thus labels are used not only to provide critical file definition information to the file system, but they also provide control information which allows the file system to process the file correctly and completely.

   If a file extends onto multiple tapes, how can we be sure that the tapes are processed in the correct sequence? In the file label, HDR1 or EOF1, there is also a field that indicates which *file section* or piece of the file this specific volume contains. Thus the first volume would identify itself as file section 2, the second volume would be file section 2, and so on. In this manner, the tapes can be processed successfully and in the correct sequence.

3.3.4 Multifile Tapes

Just as one file can overflow onto multiple tape volumes, it is also possible to have more than one file exist on a single volume of tape. How can we tell where one file ends and the next begins? Or for that matter, how can we tell whether or not another file exists on a particular volume? As we stated previously, the user's data exist between the tape marks that indicate the start and end of the file. Along with the tape marks, there are labels that precede the start of the data and follow the end of the data. All these conventions still hold.

   Now, however, we need to separate one file's trailer labels from the next file's beginning labels. The method in which this will be done is to *separate the end of one file from the beginning of the next file by a single tape mark* (see Figure 3–11). We previously used a tape mark to separate user's data from labels. Now we are using a tape mark to indicate the dividing line between files.

   How is this done? Assume that the file system has read the user's data out of one file and has read the end-of-file labels. *If the next read encounters only one tape mark, the file system knows that there is another file on that volume.* On the other hand, *if two consecutive tape marks are encountered, this indicates that there are no more data on this volume.*

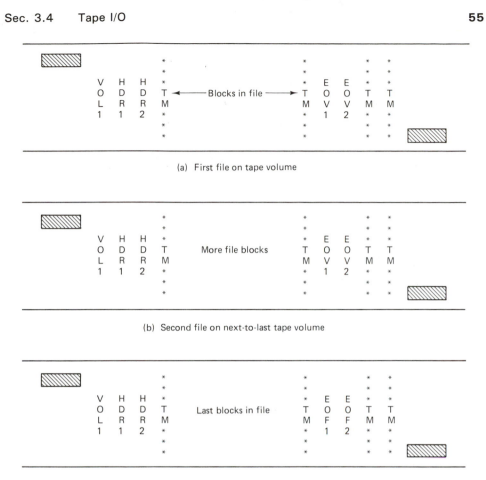

(a) First file on tape volume

(b) Second file on next-to-last tape volume

(c) Last file on last tape volume

Figure 3-10   Multivolume tape files.

In summary, tape labels provide the information necessary to process the file(s) on the tape correctly and completely. In addition, tape marks are used as identifiers to separate label blocks from user data blocks and to separate one file from another on the tape. It is important to understand why labels exist, and also what kind of information they contain.

3.4 TAPE I/O

Up to this point we have discussed only how files look once they get onto the tape medium itself. We have avoided talking about how we transfer the data to and from the tape medium. In this section we discuss how tape drives work and how we can program them to do what we want them to do.

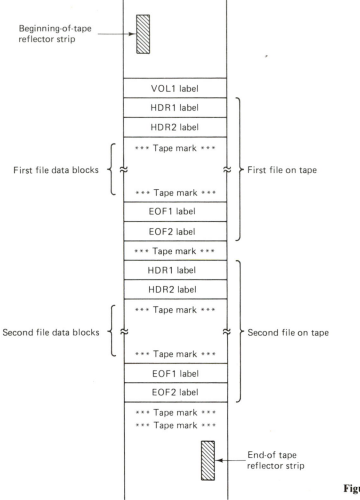

Beginning-of-tape
reflector strip

VOL1 label

HDR1 label

HDR2 label

*** Tape mark ***

First file data blocks

*** Tape mark ***

First file on tape

EOF1 label

EOF2 label

*** Tape mark ***

HDR1 label

HDR2 label

*** Tape mark ***

Second file data blocks

*** Tape mark ***

Second file on tape

EOF1 label

EOF2 label

*** Tape mark ***
*** Tape mark ***

End-of tape
reflector strip

Figure 3-11 Multifile tapes.

When we write programs in Pascal, COBOL, or any other language, what we are really doing is writing the sequence of instructions that we want the CPU to execute. If the sequence is wrong or incomplete, the program does not work. In essence, we are providing the instructions to the computer to perform our work. Similarly, when we want a device to work for us, (e.g., a tape drive), we must provide it a set of instructions, called commands, telling the tape drive what to do next. Again, the set of device commands, as were the CPU instructions, must be in the correct sequence and must be complete. There is one major difference, however; the number of device commands is much less than the number of instructions that can be written in a program. The commands really fall into two distinct categories, *device control commands* and *data transfer commands*.

3.4.1 Device Control Commands

All devices, be they tapes, disks, card readers, printers, or anything else, are mechanical in nature. This is important, because it requires us to have a set of commands that allow us to mechanically reposition the medium on the device so that we can get at the records we need. Being mechanical as opposed to electronic, they are slow in relation to the speed in which a CPU instruction can execute. In fact, therein lies one of the key factors in I/O performance—that the device positioning and control commands take a long time to execute.

If we look at any cassette recorder, we see push buttons for the I/O commands that it is possible to execute on the recorder. For example, there are buttons to *forward-space, backspace,* and *stop,* as well as the data transfer commands of *play* (i.e., READ) and *record* (i.e., WRITE). A tape drive is similar in operation, and has the following device control command repertoire:

- Forward-space to a block ahead of us on the tape.
- Backspace to a previous block.
- Rewind-Tape to the beginning of the tape.
- Erase-Block immediately.
- Write-Tape-Mark immediately.

The commands listed above allow us to position the tape medium to the correct block of data, or else let us perform some very specific processing, such as the Write-Tape-Mark command. None of these commands allows the user to transfer data to or from the tape device.

Forward-space and backspace commands.   *The Forward-space and Backspace commands allow us to skip over blocks of data that already exist on the tape.* On a cassette recorder, we may want to forward-space to the next song. On a computer tape, we may want to skip over a block(s) until we get to the one we really want.

Rewind-tape command.   *The Rewind-Tape command rewinds the tape until the reflector strip at the beginning of the tape is encountered.* As a result, the tape is repositioned to the start of the block immediately *following* the reflector strip. This command allows us to reposition the tape as rapidly as is possible to the beginning of the tape.

Erase-block command.   *The Erase-Block command allows us to physically get rid of a specific block of data on the tape.* Once erased, the block is gone. Thus great care should be exercised before using this command. The goal of this command is to *lose data* (i.e., erase them), and a file system must allow this kind of function to succeed only in well-controlled and well-understood situations.

Write-tape-mark command. *The Write-Tape-Mark command allows the file system to separate the file labels from the file's data blocks.* Thus this command enables the file system to build a file structure on the tape that can be used in accessing the data correctly.

In summary, with the device control commands, the file system has the capability to reposition the tape to any location. In addition, it has the capability of building a workable file structure on the tape itself.

3.4.2 Data Transfer Commands

We have now arrived at the point where we can discuss how user data can really be written onto, and later read from, a tape. There are only two commands that transfer data to or from a device:

- WRITE_BLOCK transfers a block of data *from* the I/O buffer in memory *to* the device and onto the medium.
- READ_BLOCK transfers a block of data *from* the medium on the device *into* the I/O buffer in main memory.

When writing to a tape, the tape drive itself must have an indication as to whether or not the operation is legal. This is done by inserting a plastic ring, known as a *writering*, into the back of the tape medium. This causes a switch to be set inside the tape drive that allows writing to occur. Conversely, if we did not want to write onto a tape, we could remove the write-ring and the tape drive would not write onto the medium, even if so requested.

How large is the block of data being transferred to or from a device? If you recall the discussion of file labels, one of the parameters stored in a file label is the *block size* of the largest possible block in the file. Thus *all blocks read, or written, in a file must be equal to, or smaller than, the value of the block size parameter in the file label.*

By knowing the size of the largest block in a file, we can then allocate space in main memory large enough to hold the largest block in the file being accessed. Thus we can be guaranteed that no matter what block in the file is being accessed, the space in memory that we have allocated will always be large enough to hold the block. This space allocated internally in main memory is called an *I/O buffer*.

To use one of the data transfer commands, we need to specify the following information to the device:

- The specific *command* itself (i.e., READ_BLOCK or WRITE_BLOCK)
- The main memory *address* of the I/O buffer into which the block will be transferred or from which the data will be taken
- The *count* (i.e., number of bytes) of data to be transferred

The count field represents the exact amount of data to be transferred, whether more or less data actually exist. If more data exist in main memory, they are lost forever (i.e., there is a bug in the program). If *more data* exist on the tape medium, the user should be told that the entire block was not READ, and thus data may be missing. This can only occur on READ_BLOCK commands when the file system intentionally tries to read a block by using a count field that is smaller than the size of the largest possible block in the file. On WRITE_BLOCK commands, the count specified represents the precise amount of data that is to be transferred to the tape media, whether or not it represents the maximum amount of data possible.

In summary, if we need to transfer data to or from a device, we must use either the READ_BLOCK or WRITE_BLOCK command. Also note that all data get transferred in increments of a block, never partial blocks, and never more than a block of data. Finally, it is important to observe that blocks of data are always transferred without having any knowledge of the content of the block. In Part III, when we discuss access methods, we will discover that only then is any part of the content of a block known and understood. For now, the blocks are simply transferred to and from a device.

3.4.3 Block Addressing Techniques

How can we read or write a particular record, or more specifically a particular block, on magnetic tape media? Since a tape is made up of many blocks of data, is it possible to randomly access any of these blocks? To answer these questions, we need to understand the structure of the data on a tape volume.

First, consider a tape as being similar to a deck of cards sitting in a box. If we want to find a particular record, we must look at the first card. If this is not the correct card, we must go to the next card. This must be repeated until we have either found the desired card or until there are no more cards to scan. Thus we must sequentially read all the cards. What this means is simply that in order to find the next block in the file, we can only read the next block. Thus, *in sequential access, the location of the next block of data is defined to be the next physical block in the file.*

Next, consider the case of a cassette tape. To get to the third song on the tape, it is necessary to skip over the first two songs. The reason for this is that all of the data (i.e., music) must pass underneath a single read/write head. Thus, to get to any specific song on a tape, we must read, or skip over, all of the tape from where we are now to where we want to be. Therefore, the only way we can achieve random access to blocks on a tape is to sequentially read all the intermediate blocks first. The bottom line is that although it is technically feasible to allow random access to blocks of data on a tape, it actually ends up being sequential access.

In a similar manner, if we are writing to a tape, *we can only write the next physical block on the medium.* We cannot write block 5 unless the first four blocks already exist. Thus we can only sequentially write blocks of data to tape.

In summary, on tapes we have only sequential access to the data records. Specifically, this means that the next sequential block of data on the tape is literally the next physical block that can be accessed.

3.5 I/O EXCEPTION HANDLING

We cannot assume that if we build all the right I/O command sequences, and do all the correct things, the I/O requests will always be successful. Remember that we are dealing with primarily mechanical devices, and anything mechanical can break, malfunction, or lose the precise level of tolerance required to process correctly. Thus not only do problems arise, but they tend to occur frequently enough to concern ourselves about how best to handle these situations. Also, some of the errors, or exception conditions, that arise are an expected part of the processing. For example, the following exception conditions occur all the time and act as signals to the program so that the data can be processed correctly.

3.5.1 Normal Exceptions

The following conditions could be classified as being normal in occurrence (refer to Figure 3–12).

Beginning-of-tape (BOT) detected. This occurs when the tape is rewound, or a Backspace-Block encounters the beginning of the tape. This condition is reached when the tape device detects the reflector strip at the beginning of the tape medium.

Beginning-of-file (BOF) dectected. This condition occurs when either a Backspace command detects a single tape mark, or when the file system encounters a tape mark after processing the file labels at the beginning of the file. It is up to the file system to *know* the circumstances under which the tape marks were encountered.

End-of-file (EOF) detected. This condition occurs whenever a tape mark is detected immediately following the last valid block of user data within a file. Its purpose is to tell the user program that all the data in the file have been processed and that the program should process accordingly. For example, in COBOL the program can specify the AT END clause, and when the EOF condition is encountered, a different block of code is executed.

End-of-tape (EOT) detected. This occurs when a Forward-space-Block command skips over the last block on the tape and hits the double tape mark that is written at the end of every tape.

End-of-volume detected. This condition occurs when we are either reading or writing on the tape. Basically, the device detects the end-of-volume reflector strip. This is an indication to the device that the end of the data on this volume has been

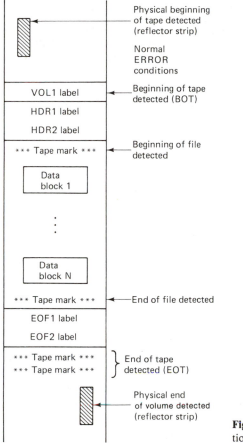

Physical beginning
of tape detected
(reflector strip)

Normal
ERROR
conditions

VOL1 label — Beginning of tape
detected (BOT)

HDR1 label

HDR2 label

*** Tape mark *** — Beginning of file
detected

Data
block 1

Data
block N

*** Tape mark *** — End of file detected

EOF1 label

EOF2 label

*** Tape mark ***
*** Tape mark *** } End of tape
detected (EOT)

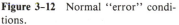

Physical end
of volume detected
(reflector strip)

Figure 3-12 Normal "error" conditions.

reached. However, there are two distinctly different ways of processing this condition, depending on whether the condition was detected during a read or during a write operation.

If end-of-volume is detected during a WRITE command, the write is allowed to complete successfully. This is done because there still should be plenty of tape left at the end of the reel to complete the write operation. When that operation has terminated, the file system then writes out all necessary file labels onto the tape. Finally, the tape is dismounted and the next volume, if any, is mounted in its place. The file system then writes all beginning-of-volume labels, as well as initial file labels. Once all this has occurred, the tape is positioned immediately following all volume and file labels (i.e., at the first data block). Now the user can resume writing to the tape.

If a READ was in progress when the reflector strip was detected, the device allows it to complete. Why? Because, we let the Write operation complete when this same condition was detected. Thus, to retrieve all the data that were written on the tape, we must allow the READ operation to access all data written. Then the file labels are read to determine if the correct number of blocks were read, based on the block count field in the trailer label. The next tape is then mounted and the volume and file labels processed. We are then positioned to continue the reading of the data in the file.

Notice that each of these ''errors'' is normal, and is simply utilized as a signal to the program running that the event has occurred. The program, if written correctly, promptly reacts by executing a different block of instructions. There are, however, other errors that can occur which could be fatal either to the file itself or to the executing program. Thus there are different kinds of errors, some wanted and expected, and others which could cause serious problems. It is the latter set of exception conditions that will be discussed next.

3.5.2 Undesirable Exceptions

There are two subcategories of ''undesirable'' errors, *unrecoverable* (i.e., fatal) *errors* and *recoverable errors*.

Unrecoverable errors. Fatal errors usually occur when a piece of hardware simply breaks down. The tape drive no longer works, or the cable connecting the drive to the computer has problems. In each of these cases, there is status that is returned to the file system which indicates the problem that occurred and that there is nothing that can be done now to recover from the error. In these cases, the file system can only return status to the user, indicating that a fatal hardware problem was encountered and that the device is no longer operational.

Recoverable errors. For those errors that are not fatal, the file system can attempt to recover from the error by performing a procedure called *error recovery*. This is an attempt to retry the request that failed up to N times. The hope here is that by retrying the request, any transient problem might go away and the data can be successfully processed. The operation is retried N times, where N is usually 10. The reason that N is not significantly larger is that the possibility of success after 10 or so retry attempts is not very large. Thus there is a trade-off being explicitly made that says that it does not make sense to retry forever, since the error might indeed be unrecoverable. Thus some number of retries must be chosen. That number must be a reasonable compromise between the expectation of success and the time the retries take that might be better utilized by some other working program.
Whenever a failing operation is retried, care must be taken to avoid *noise blocks. These are blocks on the tape that are less than 12 or so bytes long.* The mechanics of the tape drive are such that any record shorter than a noise block cannot be guaranteed to be a valid record rather than dirt on the medium. Thus any short block is called noise and skipped over. This can cause the tape drive to reposition to the wrong block on the tape.

What, then, is *error recovery* on tape? Let us assume that any of the following errors could occur for which a recovery attempt is reasonable:

- A WRITE_BLOCK operation failed because of a write-protected device or tape.
- A READ_BLOCK operation failed because of problems detected on the tape itself.
- A WRITE_BLOCK operation failed.

In each of the situations above, the device drivers could attempt to retry the operation that failed. To retry the operation, however, the tape must be repositioned to the place on the medium where the failing operation originally began. The method used to reposition the tape is simply to backup to where we began the last request.

How do we back the tape up? We use the *Backspace-Block* command. This will backup over the block that we tried to Read or Write, and then stop in the inter-record gap (IRG) just before the block we last accessed. Once this repositioning has been accomplished, we can retry the last request that failed. *Note:* Some recovery algorithms backspace multiple blocks and then forward-space to the desired block. In both cases, the objective is to move the tape past the Read/Write heads multiple times in the expectation that if there was any dust on the medium itself causing the problem, the tape movement would end up brushing the dirt off the tape. This in turn could allow the retried operation to be successful. Remember that the goal of the BFS is to be successful in handling every user request.

3.5.3 Error Recovery

READ_BLOCK error recovery.   Assume that a READ_BLOCK request (see Figure 3–13, step 1) has failed and the tape is positioned in the gap immediately following the block unsuccessfully read (step 2). A retry sequence for READ_BLOCK-type errors might look something like the following sequence:

- Backspace *m* blocks (step 3).
- Forward-space *m* - 1 blocks (step 4). The tape is now repositioned to the block in which the error was detected.
- Retry the READ_BLOCK operation (repeat step 1).

Retry the foregoing sequence either until the READ_BLOCK operation is successful or until the number of retries attempted equals *N*. *If the retried operation is successful, the file system should return to the user a success status code.* If the retries failed, the user should be notified that the request failed and is unrecoverable.

In either case, statistics concerning the error, and the recovery tried, should be written into a system error log for later analysis. This kind of information can be invaluable to a field engineer who is called to fix a system or perform standard maintenance. Also, these data can give the field service person an insight into which

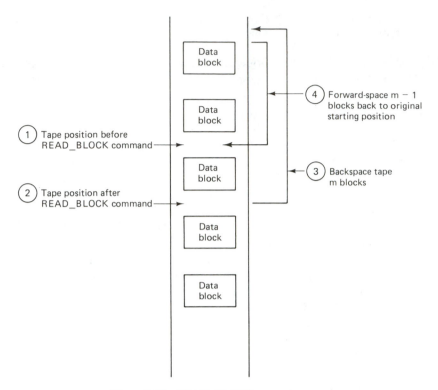

Figure 3–13   READ_BLOCK error recovery.

components of the entire computer system have been failing and where preventive maintenance would be beneficial.

WRITE_BLOCK error recovery.   If a WRITE_BLOCK operation failed (see Figure 3–14, step 1), the retry sequence is similar to, but not exactly the same as, a Read-Block failure. Specifically, if a WRITE_BLOCK request fails, we would then be positioned in the gap following the block just written (step 2). Next, we could retry in a manner similar to the READ_BLOCK failure discussed above, namely reposition and then retry the request. However, if these retries fail, we may have simply encountered a bad strip of tape. If we could skip over that section of the tape, we might be able to retry the operation successfully. Therefore, a more complete retry procedure for WRITE_BLOCK failures on tape is as follows:

- Backspace *m* blocks (step 3).
- Forward-space *m* - 1 blocks (step 4), to reposition back to the failing block.
- Retry the WRITE_BLOCK command (step 1).
- If successful, exit the retry sequence.
- Otherwise, skip over several inches of tape medium (step 5).

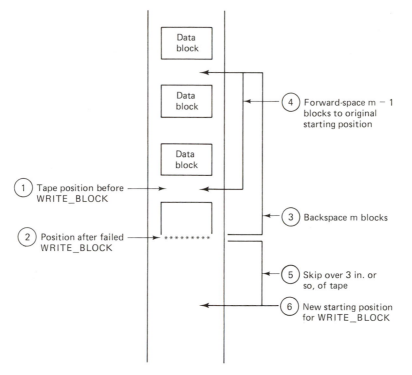

Figure 3-14   WRITE_BLOCK error recovery.

- If successful, retry the **WRITE_BLOCK** sequence (step 6).
- If not successful, repeat the last two instructions (steps 5 and 6) up to *N* times.
- If still not successful, return a fatal error status to the user.
- if successful, return a successful status to the user.

There is no guarantee that if error recovery is performed, the operation will eventually be successful. However, success occurs frequently enough to make it worth the effort.

Miscellaneous error recovery.   Finally, there may be cases in which the error recovery is simply nothing more than sending a message to the system operator. For example, assume that a WRITE_BLOCK failed because the tape was write-protected (i.e., the write-permit ring was missing). Then a message to the operator to remount the tape in the drive with a write-ring would allow the operation to succeed on the next retry. This category of errors is known as *manual intervention* errors.

Write-Protected Tape.   This condition occurs when an attempt is made to *write* a block of data onto the tape. The tape device then detects that the write-ring is not present, and thus the device itself aborts the data transfer. This error can easily be corrected by inserting the write-ring into the back of the tape itself.

Tape Drive Not Ready, or Tape Not Mounted.   These two conditions simply mean that operator intervention is required to correct the situation. In the case of the device not being *ready,* the operator must either turn the tape drive on or push a button which indicates that drive and tape are available. In the second case, the drive is powered on, but the tape medium itself has not yet been properly mounted into the drive. Here again, an operator can easily correct the error condition merely by mounting the proper tape correctly.

There is one final critical point that we should all be aware of when we attempt to perform error recovery on tapes. Specifically, *during a recovery sequence, it is possible to either skip blocks or reread a prior block* and think that the procedure was successful. In these cases, *there is no indication that skipping over blocks or duplicating a prior block ever occurred.*

How can this happen? Assume that a READ_BLOCK of the third block fails (see Figure 3–15a). If we were backspacing (step 2) and there just happened to be dust (i.e., garbage) in the interrecord gap, the tape electronics might not recognize the presence of the gap and might therefore continue to the *next* gap (i.e., block 1 instead of block 2). This can happen because the tape drive only knows to space over a block on the tape and to stop in the next *recognized* interrecord gap. Next, we can Forward-space (step 3) to where we thought we started the initial Read-Block operation. Then we can reread the original block, block 3, of the file. However, because we are not positioned correctly, we will end up actually rereading block 2 (step 4). Thus block 2 has now been read twice, and block 3 has yet to be read at all.

In a similar manner, blocks of a file can be skipped over if the interrecord gaps are incorrectly detected *following* the block being accessed (see Figure 3–15b). It is left to the reader to follow through on the steps in the diagram.

This condition could be detected once the end-of-file label block was read. However, this is long after the user has processsed the invalid sequence of blocks. Thus it would be difficult for the user to recover, short of restoring the file to its last backed-up version and rerunning all the jobs and resubmitting all changes. Although time consuming, this may be the only way out of the problem.

The end-of-file label has within it a field which contains the block count of the number of blocks that were written to the tape when the file was originally created. Thus *if the count is higher than the current block count, it implies that blocks were skipped over. On the other hand, if the original block count is lower than the current block count, we can suspect that blocks were duplicated.* The reason this cannot be more specific than "implies" or "suspects" is that we can tell only that the block counts do not match. We cannot tell what combination of skipped or duplicated blocks resulted in the mismatch. Furthermore, we cannot tell which blocks were duplicated or skipped over.

The worst case possible would be if the block counts *matched* only because the same number of blocks that were skipped over also happened to have been duplicated.

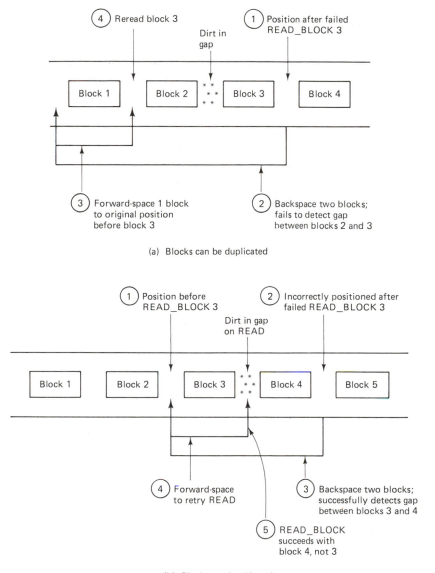

(a) Blocks can be duplicated

(b) Blocks can be skipped

Figure 3-15   Risks in tape error recovery.

Then we would believe that all was okay. There are methods, such as embedding block numbers inside each block, that can help avoid these situations, but there are still many files in existence that do not contain these safeguards, and thus these errors can, and will, arise.

3.6 COMPATIBILITY ISSUES

We have discussed tapes and how they work, but we have generally avoided the topic of tape compatibility. This is an important topic, because it can seriously limit the overall usefulness of tapes. Fundamentally, compatibility boils down to understanding when we can take a tape written on one machine, mount it on another machine, and know that we will be successful in reading the tape. There is nothing quite as discouraging as mounting a tape into a tape drive only to find out that the tape and the system being utilized are incompatible.

What kinds of considerations must we make in determining whether a tape will be compatible? The following list illustrates the topics that must be analyzed:

- The *number of tracks* (i.e., seven, nine, or more) on which data have been recorded onto the tape
- The *density* at which the data were recorded
- The *recording technique* that was used to write the bit patterns onto the tape
- The *tape standard,* if any, that was followed in formatting the tape files.
- The *character set* used (e.g., EBCDIC, ASCII)

3.6.1 Physical Compatibility

The number of tracks, tape density, and recording technique all relate to how the data were physically written by the hardware onto the tape medium. Tape drives typically can recognize one or two densities but will support only nine-track or seven-track recording convention, not both. Thus we must ensure that each of these technical details is selected carefully so that every machine on which we would like to be able to access the tape has tape drives that can read the tapes.

3.6.2 Logical Compatibility

The tape standard chosen, or for that matter not chosen, is critical for the software to be able to interpret the data blocks correctly. There are two standards for tape file structure formats: IBM's and the ANSI standard for tapes [1]. The IBM standard is different from the ANSI standard, so it is important to know which standard has been used.

Finally, it is also important to know the character set being utilized. For example, were the files on the tape written using the ASCII-8, ASCII-7, or EBCDIC character sets? Typically, if we stay within one vendor's machines, we will not encounter a character set problem, since the same character set definition will be used consistently across all the machines. The problem can arise when we try to port tapes from one vendor's machines to another vendor's machine.

In summary, tapes are easy to use to transport data from one machine to another. However, whether or not we will be able to access the data written onto the tape once we get to the new machine is totally dependent on whether the tape is compatible with the characteristics and attributes of the hardware and software on the new machine. If we can do our analysis correctly, before we create our tapes, we can gain all the advantages of tape portability and not have to deal with the problems and difficulties caused by incompatible tapes.

3.7 COST/BENEFIT TRADE-OFFS

Why select tapes instead of some other device or media type? To answer this question, it is necessary to examine some of the costs and benefits of using tapes as our medium for data. There is no right answer to the question above. The reasons for selecting a particular device type depend on the criteria and requirements of the task at hand.

For example, if we need a recording medium for saving files for historical or security reasons, tapes would be a good choice. Why? Tapes have relatively high data capacity, are reliable, and yet are physically small and light in weight. Thus they would take up a minimum amount of storage space, as opposed to the physically much larger disk packs. Also, tapes are relatively inexpensive compared to the costs of disk packs. For example, 2400-foot tapes may cost $10 to $20, and less in volume quantities. Hard disks, on the other hand, could cost as much as $1000 or more for roughly the same data capacity.

The major benefits and the significant costs or drawbacks of using tapes are as follows.

Benefits

- Tapes are inexpensive.
- Tapes have high data capacities.
- Tapes physically occupy a minimum amount of space.
- Tapes are reliable.

Costs

- The data can be accessed by only one user at a time.
- To access any specific block, all blocks preceding it on the tape must be read first.
- Tape compatibility issues could be a problem in multivendor installations.

That data can be accessed only by one user at a time may not be a drawback. However, if an application requires multiple users to be able to access the data simultaneously, we cannot choose tape as our medium. Also, if it is required that blocks within a file be randomly accessible, without accessing all preceding blocks, again we cannot select tape as the medium of choice.

Finally, if we know ahead of time that there are either hardware and software compatibility problems, and if we must be able to transport files between machines, then again we cannot select tape. Or, at a minimum, we must set up procedures to alleviate the problems within the incompatibilities.

To summarize, before we can select a media type for our files, we must understand the needs and requirements of our applications. We must also understand the characteristics and attributes of the hardware/software systems on which we will be running. Then, and only then, can we make a reasonable choice that will not come back to haunt us at some future time.

3.8 PERFORMANCE CHARACTERISTICS

All devices are slow relative to the speed of today's CPUs. Therefore, it is imporant for us to do whatever possible to improve the performance of the devices connected to the system.

Recall for a moment that a tape reads and writes blocks. Thus the tape simply moves from one IRG to the next IRG. When a gap is reached, the tape drive slows down and stops. When we make another I/O request to the tape, the device restarts and must cycle up to full speed before it encounters any data. This starting and stopping takes an enormous amount of time. We must therefore examine how we process our blocks of data on a tape drive to see if there is any conceivable way in which we could improve the overall performance and responsiveness of the device.

One of the major bottlenecks in tape performance lies in the starting and stopping of the drive in each of the gaps. What can be done to minimize this problem? First, the number of blocks, and thus IRGs, in a file is dependent on the number of user records in the file. Thus to have a positive impact on performance, we need to cut down on the number of blocks that must be written into a file, as well as to cut down on the physical size of each individual block on the tape itself. The latter consideration will reduce the amount of tape movement required to physically access all the data blocks.

How can we reduce the physical size of the blocks? To do this, we should attempt to select as high a tape density as is reasonable, given other constraints, such as compatibility. For example, at 800 bpi, assuming 8 bits per byte, a 100-byte block would take up 1 inch of tape. However, at 6250 bpi the same record would take approximately $\frac{1}{8}$ inch. If we had a file of 250,000 blocks, we could readily calculate the amount of tape we could save simply by selecting the most appropriate recording density.

By choosing different tape densities, we can reduce the amount of tape that must be accessed. However, it does not affect the number of blocks or the number of IRGs that exist within a file. We can affect that characteristic by selecting a larger block size, in order that each block in the file might contain more user data records.

For example, if we had a 1-million-record file, if we could hold only a single record per block, the resultant file would require 1 million blocks and 1 million IRGs. On the other hand, if we could put, on the average, 10 records into a single block, the file would require only 100,000 blocks and gaps—an order of magnitude less than

before. What this really means is that the second file would require one-tenth of the
I/O operations to read the entire file than the first file would require (see Table 3–1).

TABLE 3-1 EFFECT OF BLOCKSIZE AND DENSITY ON PERFORMANCE

	Block size (bytes)	Tape density (bpi)	Size of block on tape	Gap size	# feet of gaps	# Blocks/ tape	#Bytes tape
			2.400 foot tape reel				
	400	800	4″	$\frac{1}{2}″$	267′	6,400	2.56 MB
	400	1600	2″	$\frac{1}{2}″$	480′	11,520	4.61 MB
$\frac{1}{2}$ tape is just Gaps	400	6250	$\frac{1}{2}″$	$\frac{1}{2}″$	1200′	28,800	11.52 MB
	2000	800	20″	$\frac{1}{2}″$	58′	1,405	2.81 MB
	2000	1600	10″	$\frac{1}{2}″$	114′	2,743	5.49 MB
	2000	6250	2.5″	$\frac{1}{2}″$	400′	9,600	19.2 MB

3.8.1 How Large Is a File on a Tape?

For example, assume that we wanted to determine how much space a particular file
will take up on a tape. To determine this, we first need to calculate the total number
of blocks that the file will contain, as follows:

$$N = \frac{\text{number of data records in file}}{\text{average blocking factor}}$$

Next, we need to calculate how much space a single block will take on the tape.
This can be determined from the tape density and average block size, as follows:

$$M = \frac{\text{tape density in bytes per inch}}{\text{average block size}}$$

Finally, we can calculate the amount of space a file will take on a tape, as follows:

$$\text{total file space} = N \times (M + \text{IRG size})$$

For calculation purposes we can assume that a gap is roughly $\frac{1}{2}$ inch in length.

3.8.2 How Much Data Can Be Written onto a Tape?

If we want to calculate how much data can be written onto a single tape, we can
do the following. First, calculate the length of the tape *in inches*. If *L* is this length,
we can calculate the maximum number of blocks that will fit on the tape as follows:

$$\text{maximum number of blocks on tape} = B = \frac{\text{length of tape, } L}{M + \text{IRG size}}$$

Now, we almost have the answer in hand. The maximum number of records
that can be written onto a tape can be calculated as follows:

$$\text{maximum number of records on tape} = B \times (\text{average blocking factor})$$

These algorithms can be quite useful when it is necessary to determine how many tapes will be required to back up a file, for example. There are also many variants of these, such as modifications for the case of multiple files per tape.

3.9 IMPLEMENTATION REQUIREMENTS

In Chapter 2 we introduced the concept of the *device control table*. This table contains device-specific data to allow the file system to process I/O requests to a device correctly and efficiently.

In the case of tapes, the file system needs to know certain tape-specific data (see Table 3–2). Thus a tape device control table could contain the following kinds of data:

- Number of retries to perform on READ_BLOCK errors
- Number of retries to perform on WRITE_BLOCK errors
- Various error recovery information fields
- Tape density
- Volume sequence number, when a file spans more than one tape.
- Version of the labels used with the files on this tape.

There can be other data also kept in the device control table, but the list above indicates both the breadth and depth of the data required. It is important to understand that these data are maintained on each tape device that is connected to the system.

In this chapter, several types of labels were described. Tables 3–3 through 3–6, on pp. 74 and 75, show a more detailed definition of these 80-character labels. The definition for these labels comes from the tape standard [1] that most vendors follow. Note that some fields have been left out for clarity. Also, it is more important to understand the kinds of information that get saved with a file than it is to remember every field of a label.

3.10 SUMMARY

In this chapter we have been introduced to the meaning of device-specific processing. One of the intentions of this chapter was also to convey the tremendous level of effort required to correctly process all possible conditions on a tape. Finally, we should now be sensitized to how software, or more specifically a file system, can command devices to work for them.

TABLE 3-2   TAPE DEVICE CONTROL TABLE

Header information

Version ID
Link to next DCT
Address of IORQ

General device information

Device status
HW address of device
Volume name
Device type   Cartridge tape
                                         Streamer tape
                                         Standard tape

Address of device driver

Exception-processing information

Address of system error log   Central file into which all errors are written
Maximum number of retries: tape   Limit on number of retries
  positioning commands
Maximum retries: READs   Limit on number of retries to
Maximum retries: WRITEs   be performed
Number of current retry counter   For current error processing
Recoverable errors   Total number of errors detected and
                                           successfully recovered

Device-specific information: tape

Tape density   800 bpi
                                         1600 bpi
                                         6250 bpi
                                           etc.
Volume sequence number   Multivolume tapes only
Label version standard   Labels can change format
Character set   ANSI 8-bit
                                         ANSI 7-bit
                                         EBCDIC
                                           etc.

KEY WORDS

Compatibility   Noise blocks
Density   Reflector strips
Device control command   Tape mark
Error recovery   Tracks
File header labels   Volume label
File structure   Write-protect
Interrecord gap (IRG)

TABLE 3-3 TAPE VOLUME LABEL

Byte offset	Field	Description
1	Label identifier	"VOL" explicitly identifies this as a VOLume label
4	Label number	"1"
5–10	Volume identifier	Name of this volume, usually the same as the label on the outside of the tape
11–37	Reserved	Reserved for future use
38–51	Owner identifier	Name of the owner of this tape
80	Label-standard version	Number of the standard to which these labels will conform

TABLE 3-4 TAPE HEADER LABELS

Byte offset	Field	Description
	First header label	
1–4	Label identifier	"HDR1" identifies label
5–21	File identifier	*Name* of this file
22–41	Reserved	
42–47	Creation date	Date this file was created
48–53	Expiration date	Date this file can be deleted
54	Reserved	
55–60	Block count	Always set to 0
61–80	Reserved	
	Second header label	
1–4	Label identifierr	"HRD2"
5	Record format	F = fixed length D = variable length S = spanned
6–10	Block length	Maximum number of bytes per block
11–15	Record length	Maximum number of bytes per data record
16–80	Reserved	

TABLE 3-5   TAPE END-OF-VOLUME LABELS

Byte offset	Field	Description
	First end-of-volume label	
1–4	Label identifier	"EOV1" identifies label
5–54	Same as HDR1	
55–60	Block count	Set to *actual* number of blocks written into file
	Second end-of-volume label	
1–4	Label identifier	"EOV2" identifies label
5–80	Same as HDR2	

TABLE 3-6   TAPE END-OF-FILE LABELS

Byte offset	Field	Description
	First end-of-file label	
1–4	Label identifier	"EOF1" identifies label
5–54	Same as HDR1	
55–60	Block count	Set to *actual* number of blocks written into file
61–80	Reserved	
	Second end-of-file label	
1–4	Label identifier	"EOF2"
5–80	Same as HDR2	

SUPPLEMENTAL REFERENCES

1. ANSI, *American National Standard Magnetic Tape Labels and File Structures for Information Interchange.* New York: American National Standards Institute, Inc., 1977, ANSI-X3.27-1978. This is *the* standard for all tape processing. It contains not only all the required label and file formats, but also how certain tape conditions are to be processed.

2. Miller, Stanley H. and Robert Freese, "Recording Densities Push the Limits." *Mini-Micro Systems,* October 1983, pp. 287–292.

3. Welter, Jaques, and Paul E. Schindler, Jr., "Firm May Design IBM Tape." *Information Systems News,* July 9, 1984, p. 2. What is of most use in each of the two books above are the trends discussed concerning increasing recording densities on tape.

EXERCISES

1. When error recovery is performed, the failing device command is retried a certain prede-termined number of times. Should we always use the same retry count for every kind of error, or should we use a different retry count depending on whether we are retrying a failing READ_BLOCK or a WRITE_BLOCK command? Explain why the retry counts should be the same, or different. If the retry counts should be different, state whether a failing READ_BLOCK command should have a higher or lower retry count than a retry of a failing WRITE_BLOCK command.

The following list applies to the remaining questions in this section.

Density	200 Bpi
Number of tracks	9
Record size	800 bytes
Block size	800 bytes
Size of file	1000 records
Interrecord gap	0.5 in.
Length of tape	2400 ft
Speed of tape drive	75 ips
Average start/start time	30 ms

2. (a) How many inches will be taken up for the user only?
    (b) If the record size changes to 200 bytes each, how many times is it faster, or slower?

3. How long will it take to read all the data blocks in this file?

4. If the tape density was changed to 800 Bpi, and the tape speed was increased to 150 ips, then:
    (a) How long would it now take to read the entire file?
    (b) How much data space would the file take up on the tape?
    (c) How much space would be taken up by interrecord gaps?

5. Develop a formula for calculating the total number of tapes required for a single file. Take into consideration record and block sizes, blocking factor, tape density, number of records in the file, IRG size, length of tape, and so on.

6. How can you *really* be sure that you successfully read all the blocks in a file? Explain.

7. Why are aluminum reflector strips required on a tape? What would happen if they did not exist? Could you successfully read and write data on the tape without them?

8. What is the difference between the block count field in the header label and the block count field in the end-of-file label?

9. Before file header labels became standardized, tapes had no labels. What are the major benefits and disadvantages of unlabeled tapes?

10. Is it ever possible for two users to share a tape simultaneously? Explain why or why not.

PROGRAMMING EXERCISE

1. Draw a flowchart of the tape error recovery procedure in sufficient detail that another person could code and test the routine. Differentiate between device control, data transfer, and attention types of errors.

4

Random Access Devices

CHAPTER OBJECTIVES

When you complete this chapter, you will be able to:

- Discuss the file structure that is built onto the disk medium, and why it is required
- Discuss in detail the kinds of I/O operations that can be performed on a disk drive
- Describe the trade-offs among the various kinds, sizes, and formats of disk media
- Describe how disk error recovery is performed and what kinds of exceptions can occur when accessing a block on the disk
- Discuss the performance criteria of disks and how they can affect both the user's and the system's performance

4.1 OVERVIEW

The single major device type that is used today for on-line data storage is the disk drive. It has a large data capacity while allowing random access to any specific block on the disk itself. The lack of random access is one of the major drawbacks of tapes. We will examine disks and the file structure that is built on top of them which enable us to have one or more users and multiple files residing on the same disk. The disk-handling component of the file system is shown in Figure 4–0.

The overall performance and throughput of a system is highly dependent on the performance of the I/O to and from the disk drive. We discuss several ways in

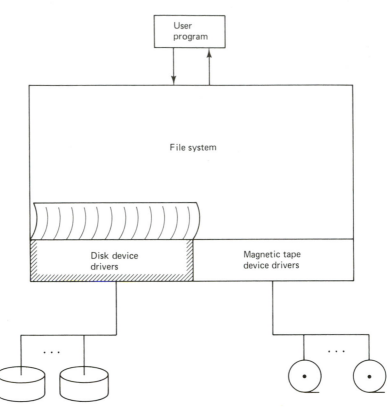

Figure 4-0 File system: disk component.

which disk I/O performance can be significantly improved. Finally, performance is especially important in the area of personal microcomputers. This is because those disks tend to be significantly lower in data capacity and slower in performance.

4.2 DISK HARDWARE CHARACTERISTICS

First, what is a disk? The general overall picture of a disk is shown in Figure 4-1. The disk itself is made up of one or more circular platters, which are similar to a phonograph record. The platters rotate on a fixed central spindle. There is one read/write head per surface. Data are recorded on the surface of the platter as it rotates underneath the read/write head for that platter. When there is a request for a different track, or cylinder, the entire read/write access arm mechanism must be moved to the desired cylinder and track.

If the disks platters are made up of rigid material, they are known as *hard disks*. Alternatively, they can be made of a very thin flexible material and be called *floppy disks*. How they are made is not relevant. Their operational concepts are the same. Hard disks have greater data capacities and higher data transfer rates than floppy disks. On the other hand, floppy disks are inexpensive and highly portable. Therefore,

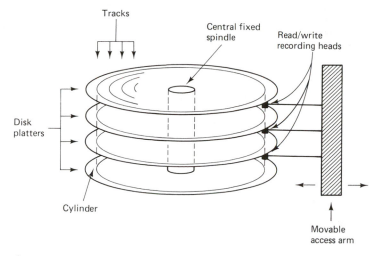

Figure 4-1   Disk hardware.

floppy disks tend to be used more in microcomputers.

Disks themselves are really not that old an invention. They first began to get popular in the mid-1960s. Since that time, the data capacities of a disk have been doubling roughly every two years. The early disks held up to several million bytes of on-line data storage. Today, disks are available that can hold over 1 billion bytes of data! There are even laser disks under development, whose data capacities dwarf those of the disks commonly in use today (see Table 4-1).

TABLE 4-1:   DISK CAPACITIES [3]

IBM model	First shipment	BPI	Density TPI	BPSI (000)	Megabytes per spindle
350	1957	105	20	2	4.4
1311	1963	1,025	50	51	2.7
2311	1965	1,100	100	110	7.3
2314	1966	2,200	100	220	29
3330-1	1971	4,040	192	780	100
3330-11	1974	4,040	370	1,500	200
3340	1973	5,636	300	1,700	70
3350	1976	6,425	478	3,100	317
3370	1979	12,134	635	7,700	571
3375	1981	12,134	800	9,700	820
3380	1981	15,240	800	12,200	1,260
3380DD?	1985E	20,000?	1220?	24,400	2,520

BPI = bits per inch   TPI = tracks per inch   BPSI = bits per square inch

From Don Collier, Paul Frank, and Chris Aho, "Rigid disk heads keep pace with growing storage needs." *Mini-Micro Systems*, December, 1984, pp 127–133.

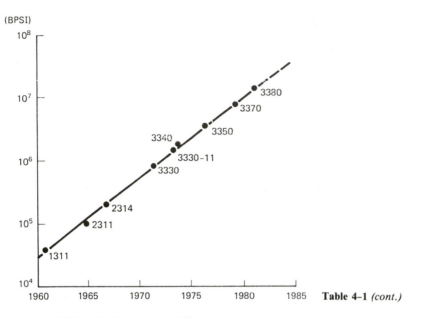

(BPSI)

Table 4-1 *(cont.)*

4.2.1. Cylinders and Tracks

How do the data get written onto a disk? As the disk rotates in the drive, the read/write heads remain stationary over the surface of each platter. *A track is the recording surface that rotates directly underneath a read/write head during a single revolution of the disk platters.* We can record data onto each track until there is no more space. Then the disk drive can switch to another track to allow the operation to complete successfully.

All the tracks that the set of read/write heads pass over in one revolution make up a cylinder. *A cylinder is comprised of all the tracks that can be accessed by the read/write heads without moving the read/write access arm mechanism.*

The moving of the access arm (i.e., all read/write heads are fixed as a unit known as the access arm) takes a relatively long time. However, switching between tracks within a single cylinder is all electronic and is instantaneous. *The movement of the access arm from one cylinder to another cylinder is know as SEEKing.* After the access arm has moved to the cylinder it needs, it must then wait as the platter rotates underneath the read/write heads while waiting for the particular data block to read or write. *The lag time waiting for the disk to rotate is known as rotational display.* Although considerably faster than performing a SEEK to a new cylinder, it is still slow compared with the amount of work that the CPU could have done.

Before a disk can be read or written, it must be initialized. This means that enough information must be written onto the disk to ensure that the data files can be located and managed properly. For example, the following kinds of information are written to disk whenever it is initialized or formatted:

• An empty disk directory or volume table of contents.

- A space allocation table, which is used to manage all the available disk space on the media.
- One or more bootstrap records which allow the operating system to be started up after the machine is turned on.
- Each block or sector is initialized with information to identify each block uniquely. This is used by the hardware to determine if an operation succeeded is accessing the correct block.

Initialization cuts down the amount of space available for the user on the disk itself. The reason for this is that during initialization, many blocks are written onto the medium. However, there is a gap between each block as there was for tapes, which is needed for the hardware to be able to detect the end of each physical block. Typically, the formatted blocks or sectors are fixed in length.

In summary, it is important to remember that the mechanical movements of a disk, SEEKing and SEARCHing, take a long time. Thus it is up to the file system software to try and minimize this delay as much as possible to improve overall system performance.

4.2.2 Device Types

There are a variety of disks available today. The following list shows the breadth of devices currently in use or being developed for future usage.

- *3-inch floppy disks:* There are currently several sizes, ranging from 3 to $3\frac{1}{2}$ inches.
- *3-inch hard disk:* These will have a higher data capacity than the floppy above, but will be more expensive.
- $5\frac{1}{4}$*-inch floppy disks:* These disks are the standard for microcomputers today.
- $5\frac{1}{4}$*-inch hard disks:* These disks are becoming more and more popular on micros. Their capacity can exceed several hundred million bytes of data.
- *8-inch floppy disks:* These have a relatively high data capacity. However, they take up considerably more room than the other sizes.

These disks are targeted primarily at the personal computer and home computer markets. They also tend to be inexpensive, which is one requirement for most microcomputer products. Today, the trend is toward smaller, higher-capacity, more reliable disks.

Multiplatter hard disks, approximately 14 inches in diameter, are in widespread use in minicomputer and mainframe computer installations. These are high-capacity, relatively fast, highly reliable disks. The number of platters on the central spindle effectively dictates the overall capacity of the disk. The number of platters tends to range from a single platter up to 11 platters (i.e., 22 recording surfaces if data are recorded on both sides of each platter). If this disk is rotating at 3600 rpm, the outside track on a 14-inch disk is moving at a linear speed of over 150 *miles per hour*. This last example is given to demonstrate the extremely tight tolerances under which the disks typically operate under.

A disk that has one read/write head per recording surface is called a moving-head disk. All these heads are connected to a central movable access arm. All read/write heads move together. This type of disk is the most popular kind of disk in use today. There are several reasons for this. First, moving-head disks are less expensive than fixed-head disks. Second, they have the advantage of being both removable and transportable. Thus we can carry a disk full of data from one machine to another just as we could with tapes.

Fixed-head disks have one read/write head for every track on every platter. The advantage of this approach is that the read/write arm does not need to move to reposition itself over the data we need. Thus when we need the highest possible level of performance, we can use fixed-head disks since they eliminate head movement. The disadvantage of fixed-head disks is that they tend to be quite expensive. Also, fixed-head disks themselves are usually not removable. Thus it would be impossible to transport a fixed-head disk from one computer to another. Finally, if a fixed-head disk breaks, there is no alternative but to wait for it to be fixed. If it were a movable-head disk, we would only need to move the disk pack to another machine.

4.2.3 Block and Sector Addressing Techniques

On some disks, the size of a block can vary from file to file. However, within the boundary of a particular file, the blocks tend to be the same size. On other disks, all blocks on the entire disk pack are the identical size. *These fixed-length blocks are called sectors*. If there are many tracks and cylinders on a disk pack, how can we address, or find, the particular block of data that we need? As with tape, all data transfer commands copy entire blocks of data between the device and the main memory of the computer, and vice versa. *The actual address of the desired disk block on the medium is called the physical address of the block or physical block number (PBN)*. The PBN of a disk block consists of the following components:

Cylinder number.   This represents the number of the actual cylinder on which the desired block resides.

Track number.   Since there can be more than one track per cylinder, this is the number of the track within the cylinder on which the data block is located.

Record number.   *Record* in this case is the terminology in use, yet in actuality it represents the number of a specific block (i.e., record) on the designated track.

Alternatively, if the device has sectors, only the sector number is needed. Unlike a block, whose address is relative to a particular cylinder and track, sector numbers range from 1 for the first sector on the disk, to *n* for the last sector on the disk.

The file system will then convert this sector number into the correct physical block number on the device.

Since every cylinder has a unique number on a specific disk, the combination of cylinder-track-block number, or sector number, is unique within a disk pack. Therefore, all that needs to be done is to instruct the access arm to move to a specific cylinder and then to electronically select the desired track within that cylinder. Finally, it must wait for the desired block to rotate underneath the read/write head so that we can read or write the block.

Must every program that reads and writes to a disk device understand the technical details of physical block addressing? Consider, for example, what would happen to all those programs if the disk were changed in the middle of the night and a new disk with a different number of cylinders and tracks, or sectors, was installed? Could the old programs still run? They could not if they were dependent on the characteristics of a specific device. Also, why should every program have to write and maintain code to perform the same function?

An argument can be made for having the function of knowing their device specifics isolated to a reusable system routine. All user programs need only pass what is known as a logical block number (LBN) to this routine, which would then convert the LBN into a PBN. *A logical block number is the number of the desired block relative to the first block in the file.* For example, the first block in a file has a LBN of 1, the second block has an LBN of 2, and so on. Therefore, the devices can change continually, yet the programs need not change. This LBN-to-PBN conversion is performed in a basic file system module called a device driver.

4.3 DISK FILE STRUCTURE

We have discussed several attributes of disks by implying that things simply happened. Quite the opposite, we are able to locate files and blocks because of the information structure, or system overhead, which has been intentionally written onto the disk itself. Specific blocks on each disk pack are allocated and reserved for the sole use of the file system (refer to Figure 4–2). Recall that the file structure on tape consisted of a variety of labels and block separators called tape marks. In this section we discuss what kind of structure is built on the disk which will enable users to locate the specific file and block within a file that is needed by them.

Before we proceed, it is important to understand that, unlike tape, there is no standard for the on-disk file structure that is recorded onto every disk. Thus a disk created on one system is unreadable on another system which understands only *its* own unique file structure. This is very painful for most users, since it limits the portability of their data and software. There has been a *proposed* standard [2], but little progress has been made relative to all vendors agreeing on it or any other proposal. Therefore, we discuss the typical components of any disk file structure without being tied down to one of a specific vendor or design.

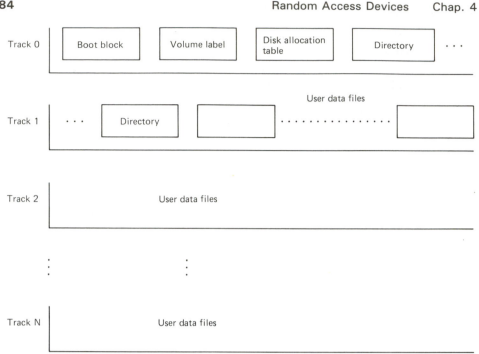

Figure 4-2 On-disk file structure.

4.3.1 Boot Block

This is usually the very first block of cylinder 0 and track 0. *The boot block is really a short program that gets automatically read into main memory when the power is turned on for the machine.* The hardware passes control over to this boot program, which then proceeds to read into memory the rest of the operating system. This is how a bare machine gets "bootstrapped" up and running. For the hardware power-on sequence to read in this program, the boot block must be at a predefined (i.e., known) location on the system disk. This is why the first block on the first track is usually selected for the boot block.

How can the hardware, or boot program, know where the operating system is or how large it is? This is an important issue since the size of the operating system can change from release to release. Note also that we do not want to change the hardware every time there is a new version of the operating system. How can we solve this problem?

First, we will leave the hardware's boot program in ROM unchanged. It will be sufficient if this program simply reads in the first block of the other boot program on the disk. However, it is the boot program on the disk that can be changed at will from release to release of the operating system.

If the hardware's boot program can always locate the other boot program on the disk, then whenever necessary, we can just modify the boot program that is on the disk. Therefore, whenever the operating system changes in size or its location on the disk, only the boot program on the disk needs to be changed. Thus the hardware's ROM boot program can remain stable, even though everything else related to the operating system and the on-disk boot program can be changed completely.

4.3.2 Volume Label

How can we tell if the correct disk pack has been mounted in the device? As was the case for magnetic tape, the volume label is located at a predefined block on the disk. This is usually the block immediately following the boot block(s). *The volume label contains a volume name that serves to uniquely identify the disk pack.* There may be an identification name or number written on the outside of the disk. However, the only identification that can and should be trusted is what is contained within the volume label.

It is the responsibility of the file system to verify that the correct disk volume has been mounted on the device. *The function of verifying that the correct volume is mounted is known as automatic volume recognition.* If the correct disk has been installed, it should continue processing. If not, the file system should return an error message requesting that the correct disk volume be mounted into the device. For the file system to check this, the user must somehow provide the correct volume name to the file system. This is usually done through the systems command, or job control, language. In many small systems, such as microcomputers, this capability is not implemented and it is left to the user to determine whether the correct disk was placed into the disk drive.

4.3.3 Disk Allocation Table

There can be many files on a disk. How can we guarantee that the space used by one file can never be taken and used by another file? *The purpose of the disk allocation table is to control how space gets allocated (i.e., specific blocks, tracks, or cylinders) on the disk itself.* This table knows explicitly what has and has not been allocated to user or system files.

There are many ways in which space can be allocated and controlled on a disk pack. The two methods discussed here are bit maps and extents. Bit maps are most commonly used on small machines such as micros, while extents are used on larger computers and mainframes.

Bit maps.   If the disk is made up of fixed-length blocks, sometimes called sectors, we can control the space on the disk by having a disk space allocation file. This file contains both a bit map and all of the unallocated blocks on the disk. In other words, the disk space allocation file is a real file with blocks allocated to it. However, it is a special kind of file, since whenever another file needs more disk blocks, they are taken from this file.

A bit map contains one bit for every block on the media. If the block is not allocated to any file, the bit is set to 1 (i.e., the block is allocated to the disk space allocation file). When a user program requests more disk space, a search can be made of the bit map looking for a nonzero (i.e., unallocated) block. If found, that specific bit is set to zero (i.e., allocated). Conversely, when a user no longer needs a block, the appropriate bit would be set back to 1. Refer to Figure 4–3, which shows an example bit map.

To complete the picture, each user file also needs to have associated with it a *file allocation bit map*. The format and usage are identical to those of the disk's allocation bit-map file. However, the bits that are in use by the file have their bits set to 1 in the file bit map. In other words, when space is taken out of the disk's allocation bit-map file, a bit is zeroed. In addition, the corresponding bit is turned on in the file's bit-map structure. Conversely, when a file returns a block, the bit is cleared in the file allocation bit map and turned on (i.e., not allocated) in the disk's allocation file. Thus, each block on the disk is allocated either in the disk space allocation file or in a specific file's bit map. All blocks on the disk are always accounted for.

Notice that space is allocated in single-block chunks only. This can result in poor performance since it does take a fair amount of time to read and scan and rescan the bit maps. Therefore, to improve performance, as well as to cut down on the size of the bit maps, we can have a bit-map file in which each bit represents not one, but several contiguous blocks on the disk. *This contiguous chunk of disk space allocation is known as a cluster. A cluster is the minimum amount of disk space that will*

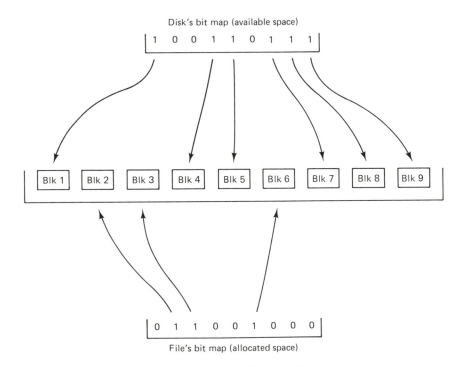

Figure 4–3   Bit-map allocation file.

be allocated per request. Thus every time that space was needed, the user would be given a number of blocks, whether that many were requested or not. This is also known as allocating in clusters, where *the cluster size is the number of blocks controlled by each bit in the bit-map file* (see Figure 4-4). In this manner, users will run out of space less often, and thus performance and throughput on the machine will improve.

Another advantage of allocating in clusters is that each block in a cluster is physically contiguous. This is because each bit in the bit map can only be converted to the starting block of the sector. Then the cluster is made up of the next *n* blocks, or sectors, where *n* is the cluster size. Contiguous blocks means that no SEEKS will be required to access all of the blocks in the cluster. When we allocated only one block per bit in the bit map, each block could be located on different areas of the disk. A SEEK would be required to go from one block to the next. Thus, when sequentially accessing a file, contiguous blocks can cut down the number of SEEK I/O operations dramatically and therefore improve overall performance.

Extents.   Since disks are made up of tracks and cylinders, why not allocate space in chunks of tracks or even cylinders instead of blocks or clusters of blocks?

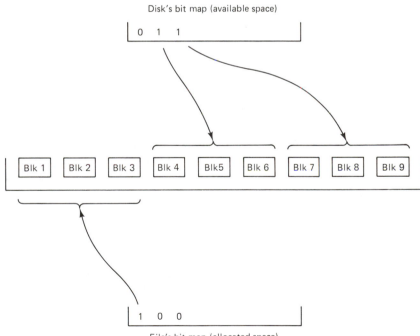

Figure 4-4 Space allocation via clusters.

When space is allocated in units of entire tracks or cylinders, the units are called extents. An extent is equivalent to a cluster, the only difference being the size of the unit of allocation. If space is allocated in this manner, more of the blocks in a file will be contiguous (i.e., physically adjacent to each other). Therefore, the read/write access arm will need to move much less to access the data. Thus performance should be improved.

When space is allocated in this manner, each file in the system has associated with it an extent table which shows the tracks, or cylinders, allocated to the file. Each extent represents a contiguous chunk of allocated space. Refer to the extent allocation table shown in Figure 4–5. Note that no search algorithm is required to scan bits, only an algorithm to search a much smaller extent table. Therefore, since we allocate in larger chunks and require less searching time than the bit-map strategy, the performance should be greatly improved.

	Starting cylinder	Starting track	Ending cylinder	Ending track
First extent	1	1	2	19
Second extent	3	1	3	6
Third extent	10	7	12	14

Figure 4–5 Extent table allocation.

Bit maps versus extents.   Why use bit maps at all? First, bit maps optimize space allocation around individual blocks or clusters. On systems in which disk space is at a premium, usually small systems, the ability to allocate what is needed now, and no more, is a critical requirement. On large computers, which usually have many, many disks available, space is less of a problem than are overall performance and system throughput. Thus on large machines it may be preferable to allocate in considerably larger chunks, such as entire tracks or cylinders. This is true even when we know that some of the space may be unused for a period of time.

It is also important to understand the system usage and the available resources before deciding on the algorithm to be used in a job. Remember the point made in Chapter 1—we will always be trading off functionality, performance, and resources. Understanding the crucial issues related to a task will provide the keys as to how to trade these items off against each other.

Performance.   To understand how space allocation on a disk can affect performance, let us walk through the steps of allocating space. It does not matter which allocation scheme is utilized, since the steps are the same; only the quantity allocated is different.

First, to prevent the same space from being allocated to two files, it will be necessary to continually rewrite the allocation file back to disk after every allocation. Then, should the system crash, at least the space already allocated is correct.

Since it is theoretically possible for two users to request space simultaneously, there must be some way in which to gate the access to the allocation structure. This is known as locking and is discussed later in the book. For now, simply understand that it is possible for the blocks in a file to be locked to prevent anyone else from accessing them. Now let us examine the steps required to allocate, or return, space on a disk.

1. Lock the Disk Allocation Table.   This step is required to prevent another user from looking for space at the same time this request is being processed. This prevents the same space from being allocated to two different files. However, until the allocation process has been completed, all other users who need space must wait until this request has been completely processed.

2. Read the **Disk's** *Allocation Table.*   This step guarantees that the latest version of the space allocation on the disk is being used. In some systems, this information is kept in memory all the time to improve performance. However, we will assume that it is not kept in memory and must be read in each time that space is required.

This process can be very nontrivial if the bit map occupies a number of disk blocks. For example, if we had a 300-megabyte disk with 1000-byte blocks, the entire disk would have 300,000 blocks. If we used one bit per block in our bit map, the bit map itself would occupy over 40 disk blocks. Then, whenever space would be needed, a relatively full disk could require the file system to read up to 40 disk blocks before enough disk space could be found. Forty I/O operations just to give the user the space requested!

3. Search the Disk Allocation Table for Available Space.   Here, we need either to scan a bit map that is one or more blocks long, depending on the size of the disk, or we need to scan an available extent list. Since this is a CPU operation, it should be relatively fast.

4. Allocate Space and Rewrite Updated Blocks Back to Disk.   Once space has been found, mark it as being allocated and then rewrite it back to disk. This updates the allocation file for other users as well as protecting against a system crash or brownout. If we delayed rewriting the allocation blocks for performance reasons, we would be taking a rather large risk. If the system crashed, all files created or extended since the last time the allocation table was rewritten would be lost.

5. Read the **File's** *Allocation Table.*   This step is required to add the allocated space to a specific file. Note again that we have deallocated space out of the disk's allocation table and are now allocating it into a specific file's allocation table.

6. Write the File's Updated Allocation Table to Disk.   Now that we have added the space to the file itself, we need to rewrite it back to disk in case of a system crash. If the system crashed before this rewrite, the space allocation blocks on the disk will not have been updated to reflect this allocation. Thus it would be as if the request had never been made.

7. Unlock the Disk Allocation Table.   This reopens the allocation file for use by other programs.

Steps 2 through 5 can each require one or more I/O operations to completely process the request. Each I/O operation takes considerably longer than CPU instructions take to execute. Also, remember that other users may be waiting for this process to be completed so that they can get the space they need. Thus we can understand how rapidly the performance of the overall system can degrade.

Besides allocating disk space in large cluster sizes, there is another way in which performance could be improved during the space allocation process. Up until now we have assumed that users had to allocate space on an as-needed basis. However, what if we could calculate the amount of space that our file would require once it were fully populated with data? If we could do this, we should be able to *preallocate* the entire file once, when the file is initially created. Then we would never run out of space unless we either calculated wrong or the file simply grew larger than anyone imagined it would.

When space is preallocated, all the requested space is allocated when the file is first created. The disk space allocation routine allocates individual clusters, or extents, until the total amount of requested space has been allocated. This algorithm can result in *noncontiguous* space allocation on the medium. An alternative is to allow the user to request *contiguous* disk space. This means that all of the allocated blocks must be in one physically contiguous space on the medium. This improves performance. However, it is an all-or-nothing allocation. Space may be available on the disk, but not all of it contiguous. Thus an allocation request could fail even though "space was available."

An alternative to noncontiguous and contiguous-or-nothing space allocation is contiguous-if-possible. In this situation, contiguous space is requested and returned if at all possible. If not, instead of failing the request, the file system just tries to get the requested space even if it cannot be contiguous.

When a preallocated file runs out of space, a dynamic allocation scheme is utilized to add more space to the file. Thus preallocation is not an "all-or-nothing" algorithm. Rather, it allows performance to be dramatically improved if, and only if, the system allows us the capability of preallocating file space.

4.3.4 Directories

Once we validate that the correct volume has been mounted, how can we find what files have been written on the disk? There are many schemes that can be used to track the allocation of disk space. Here we discuss two of the more popular algorithms. First, the volume label contains a pointer (i.e., cylinder, track, and block number) of another block, which is the first block of the master directory file. Sometimes this file is referred to as the volume table of contents (VTOC). Alternatively, the directory could be placed at a known location on the disk pack. For example, it could be placed immediately following the disk allocation table. *The master directory con-*

tains within it a list of all the major directories that have been created to date on the disk pack.

Directory structures can either be single-level or multilevel in scope. Figure 4–6 shows a single-level directory structure which is similar to that found today on many microcomputers. *In a single-level directory structure, all the files that exist on the disk are listed in the same directory.* In this structure there is no differentiation of file types (e.g., word processing versus databases, etc.) other than perhaps by using a consistent naming convention. On the other hand, it is easy to implement and takes up a relatively small amount of space on the disk. The latter point is important for microcomputers, since disk space tends to be more limited.

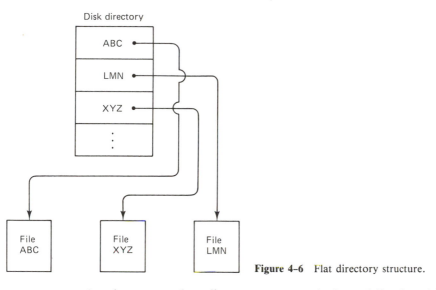

Figure 4-6 Flat directory structure.

Another approach to directory structures is the multilevel, or hierarchical, directory, shown in Figure 4–7. The multilevel directory can have within it not only data files, but also other directories, known as subdirectories. *A subdirectory is simply another directory that exists within another directory.* There can be as many subdirectories as space on the disk permits. Note that each directory requires disk space to hold the list of files in that directory. Thus the more directories that are created, the more disk space that is taken away from user files and turned over to the file system.

One of the benefits of a multilevel file structure is that files can be logically separated via directories. Therefore, all word processing files can be placed within one directory, and all financial files can be placed in another directory. In this manner, the user can partition files into logically related units.

For example, assume that we had a 200-kilobyte (KB) floppy disk. If we used a flat directory structure, a directory listing would fill a screen or two. On the other hand, if we had a 300-megabyte (MB) hard disk, a directory listing would be unbearably long and unwieldly.

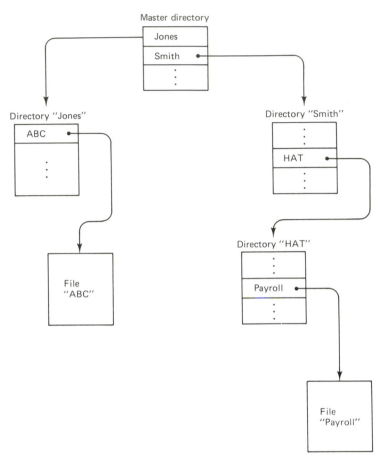

Figure 4-7 Hierarchical file system.

Another reason for moving to a hierarchical file system is to provide a better environment for multiuser systems. If all files were in one directory, all users would have visibility to everyone else's files, and vice versa. However, in a hierarchical structure, the master directory could point to individual user directories (see Figure 4-8). In this manner, the files and subdirectories of one user can be partitioned from all other users. Thus we can achieve a degree of privacy and security.

Each entry in a directory contains the following kinds of information:

File name.   This is the name of the file as chosen by the user. This name must be unique within a specific directory. Thus two files can have the same name as long as they exist in different directories. Note also that there is usually a maximum amount of space set aside in the file directory entry for the filename. The amount of space allocated then dictates the size of filenames that users can declare.

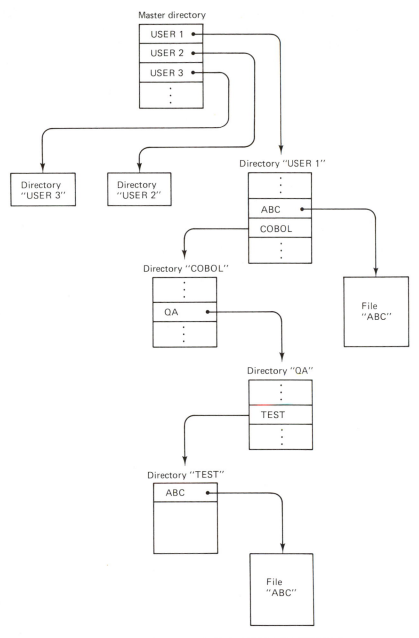

Pathname: /USER 1/COBOL/QA/TEST/ABC

Figure 4–8 Multiuser directory structure.

For example, on many microcomputer systems, the primary filename is limited to eight characters. It is sometimes difficult to come up with meaningful filenames when the user is limited to too few characters. On the other hand, larger systems usually allow 32 or more characters for more descriptive filenames.

Address of the file.   This address is like any disk address: cylinder, track, and block number of the first block in the file. Thus if we find a filename that matches the name that we are searching for, we can locate it on disk from its directory entry.

File security and protection information.   This could be as simple as the user's log-in name and password. Alternatively, there could be an access list showing those users who can access this file as well as those who cannot. This kind of data is required in multiuser environments to protect the integrity and security of the data files. In microcomputer, single-user environments, a file password scheme is needed to allow only those users who know the password to be able to access the data. Thus it is not just a matter of slipping in the floppy disk and all data become instantaneously available.

File attributes.   Entries within a directory can include both files and subdirectories. The purpose of this field is to have a way in which we can identify a directory entry. Specifically, is it another directory name, in which case we need to walk down more of the tree structure? Or, alternatively, is it a filename, in which case we have located the file we were looking for? File attributes comprise an important concept and are discussed in much more detail in subsequent chapters.

For example, some of the possible attributes could be as follows:

- This is a *filename* entry.
- This is a *directory* entry.
- This is a *deleted* file.
- This entry is *unused*.

The file attributes used on the IBM PC are as follows [6]:

- Read-only
- Hidden file: This is used to "hide" the system files so that a user could not inadvertently delete these critical files from the disk.
- *Volume label:* Here the volume label occupies a single-block *file* on the disk.

Thus, to locate a particular file on a disk, we need to walk the index structure as shown in Figure 4-7. First, the master directory must be read. By convention, this is always located at a predefined disk address or is pointed to by the volume label, which is at a predetermined location. In any case, the file system can always locate the master directory. Then the directory is searched for a matching name. If found and the entry is a file, the search is over. On the other hand, if the entry is a directory file, the file system must go to that subdirectory and continue the search. This cycle continues until either the file is located or until all directories have been searched.

For example, Figure 4–8 shows a hierarchical UNIX file structure that includes several directories and files. To locate file "ABC" in the TEST directory, the user must specify the following pathname:

$$A:/USER1/COBOL/QA/TEST/ABC$$

Alternatively, to locate file "ABC" in the USER1 directory, we need only specify the following:

$$A:/USER1/ABC$$

Thus, although the filenames are identical, the pathnames are unique. In a similar manner, we can locate any file on the entire disk. Also, file ABC on disk "A:" in the example above is different from file "ABC" on disk "C:" because the pathname to the file on "C:" is defined as follows:

$$C:/USER1/ABC$$

In summary, if the file system is given a device name and a user name, it will be able to locate any of the user's files. *This combination of volume (i.e., device and volume name), all relevant subdirectory names, and the filename is known as the pathname of a particular file.*

4.4 DISK I/O

To transfer data to and from the disk, we must issue a series of commands to the device. Since there are many tracks and cylinders on a disk, there are a set of *device control, or positioning, commands.* Then, to actually cause the data to be transferred, there are *data transfer commands* that can be issued. What is of critical importance here is that the time it takes to reposition the access arm is enormous compared with the number of CPU instructions that could have been executed in the same amount of time.

The only way in which an I/O operation can be performed is if the device driver knows the actual physical address on the medium. Since most users work in logical record numbers, it falls to the basic file system, or device driver, to convert this logical address into a physical device address.

4.4.1 Device Control Commands

The primary purpose of device control commands is to reposition the disk access arm to the desired cylinder and track so that the correct data block can be read or written. We will discuss the most important commands here, although there are others which some systems and devices also support.

SEEK command.   *The command that enables us to move the access arm on the disk is the SEEK command.* How is this done? First, the user makes a request for a logical block (LBN) in a file. This LBN is then converted by the file system into a physical block number (PBN). Once we have calculated the precise physical block on the media, we can calculate the cylinder and track number on the disk medium. We can do this since we know the number of blocks per track as well as the number of blocks on the entire disk itself. Once we have calculated the cylinder and track address, we can issue the SEEK command to reposition the access arm to the required cylinder.

SEARCH command.   Once we have repositioned the access arm to the correct cylinder and track, we must wait for the disk to rotate the block we want underneath the read/write heads. *The SEARCH command reads the track looking for the desired block as it rotates beneath the read/write head.* The disk and the disk controller have enough intelligence built into them to actually compare what is on the disk against what block has been requested.

4.4.2 Data Transfer Commands

Now that we have repositioned to the correct location on the disk, we can then read or write the desired block. The SEARCH command was instructed to be on the lookout for a particular block of data. When the block in question rotates underneath the read/write heads, *a data transfer command is then issued to actually transfer the data to (i.e., WRITE_BLOCK), or from (i.e., READ_BLOCK) the block just located.* Switching from one command to the next can be done fast enough so that all the work can be done before the block spins beneath the read/write head. Thus there is time to actually switch from the SEARCH command to the Read/Write commands that follow.

WRITE_BLOCK command.   *The purpose of the WRITE_BLOCK command is to transfer data from the I/O buffer in main memory to the disk device itself.* The information required to execute this command successfully consists of the following inputs:

- Actual *command* to request a WRITE_BLOCK command
- The *address* in main memory of the block of data to be written to the disk
- The *count* of bytes of data in the main-memory buffer that are to be written out onto the disk device

The *address* in main memory tells the hardware where to look for the data to be written. This address is usually the pointer to the I/O block buffer in the main memory of the file system. The *count* is the actual number of bytes that will be read or written.

At the completion of the WRITE_BLOCK command, the data have been transferred onto the disk medium. If the system crashed, we would know that the data have been correctly written onto the disk.

A sample I/O channel program to write a block to disk could look like this:

- SEEK Cylinder#, Track#
- SEARCH Block#
- WRITE_BLOCK Block#

On completion of the WRITE command, the device will return an interrupt message to the file system stating whether the request completed successfully. If so, a success status code is returned to the user. If not, the user must be informed of the problem.

READ_BLOCK command.   The READ_BLOCK command is the opposite of the WRITE_BLOCK command. Whereas WRITE_BLOCK transfers data to the device, *the READ BLOCK command transfers a block of data into an I/O buffer in main memory*. The WRITE_BLOCK channel program described earlier can also be used to READ_BLOCKs simply by changing the names of the two commands.

The inputs to the READ_BLOCK command are similar to those for the WRITE_BLOCK command. This is a *command* READ_BLOCK. The *count* represents the maximum number of bytes that will be transferred from the disk into the I/O buffer in main memory. If the block on disk is equal to or larger than the value of the count field, only *count* number of bytes will be transferred into memory. If the disk block being read is smaller than the count value, only the block itself is read, no more.

A sample I/O channel program to read a block from the disk might look like this:

- SEEK Cylinder#, Track#
- SEARCH Block#
- READ_BLOCK Block#

One final word on disk I/O. As can be seen by examining all the disk I/O commands, there are no commands to actually CREATE, OPEN, DELETE, or CLOSE files. These are really file system, or access method, features that impose a structure onto the disk itself. Also, there are no commands to delete or rename files. These, too, are software commands, and thus the hardware (i.e., disk) is not involved in the implementation.

4.5 I/O EXCEPTION HANDLING

Whenever an I/O operation has been initiated, its completion is signaled by an interrupt which also provides status information. This information provides the software with the data to determine whether the I/O request completed successfully. Since the disk is the primary storage medium for on-line data, it is imperative not only to detect error conditions correctly, but also to recover from the errors whenever possible. Two overall goals are *never to lose data,* and *always to try to do whatever is necessary to make the I/O operation completely successful.* Let's investigate the kinds of error conditions that can be detected, and then what software can do to recover from the error.

As with magnetic tape, there can be exception conditions that occur because of mechanical problems, and there can be errors that are detected during data transfer commands. The mechanical problems are typically more difficult to recover from since one or more of the parts on the device may be failing.

For example, Figure 4-9 shows the relationship between the distance the disk head flies over the disk medium and some typical foreign matter that could exist on the device if we were not careful. Given that, and the fact that disks are rotating at up to 3600 rpm, and you can begin to visualize the problem. To drive home this point even further, the disk read/write head flies so close to the surface of the disk medium that it is as if you were flying a Boeing 747 jumbo jet at 600 miles per hour just 2 feet above the ground [1]! Thus error recovery and exception handling is one of the critical tasks of any file system.

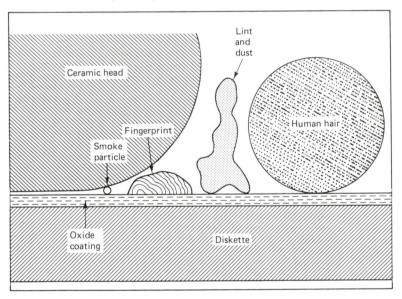

Figure 4-9 Disks and foreign matter. (From ''Clean Machine,'' *Forbes Magazine,* December 5, 1983, p. 242.

4.5.1 Device-Positioning Error Recovery

The device-positioning commands will probably encounter the mechanical difficulties on the device. This is because the positioning commands exercise the mechanical components of the device more than does a data transfer command. The typical kinds of errors that can be encountered are as follows:

SEEK errors.   In this situation, a SEEK command has been executed and the access arm has been repositioned to the cylinder and track needed. The hardware within the device then detects the fact that although the access arm has stopped on a track, it does not correspond with the track *actually* desired. This comparison is done by the device itself reading preinitialized records on the destination track which serve to identify the track itself. When these self-identification data do not equal the desired destination cylinder and track, the hardware knows that a problem has occurred.

What can be done? There are several techniques that can be tried. First, the entire request can be retried several times in the hope that some fluke occurred that will not reoccur. Alternatively, there is usually a *recalibrate I/O command* which allows the file system to move the access arm, not in increments of single tracks, but in fractions of a track. The intent here is to assume that somehow the tracks and the access arm have gotten out of alignment. Thus a small movement of the access arm might reposition correctly over the desired track. This microrepositioning can be performed in both directions from the current position, since we do not know whether we actually passed the track or have not yet reached the track. If these operations fail, there is nothing that can be done, short of remounting the disk in another drive and retrying the entire operation.

SEARCH errors.   After arriving at the *correct* cylinder and track, we must wait while the disk rotates the desired block of data underneath the read/write heads. This is the function of the SEARCH command. This command can fail if it cannot successfully read the blocks on the track to determine which block of data is the correct one.

To perform an error recovery retry, the following sequence of operations should be attempted:

1. Re-SEEK to Cylinder 0, Track 0.   This is done so that the access arm can reposition itself back to the desired track and perhaps center itself in a better position over the desired track.

2. SEEK to the Desired Cylinder and Track.   This is part of the original I/O request that failed.

3. SEARCH the Track for the Desired Block.   This is the operation that failed before, so we are retrying it.

4. If the Sequence Fails, Retry Steps 1, 2, and 3.   This recovery procedure can be retried up to a predetermined number of times. Usually, this sequence is retried 10 times. Then, if an error still exists, the request must be aborted.

If this sequence fails, all the error data should be written into a system error log file so that not only can the error history of a device be tracked, but the information will be available for preventive maintenance purposes.

Device not ready.   This usually means that the device itself was never powered-on. Alternatively, there is a possible error in one of the I/O tables within the file system. Our only choice here is to notify the computer room operator, to verify that the device in question has really been powered-on correctly.

4.5.2 Data Transfer Error Recovery

Data-transfer-related exception conditions are usually split between anticipated errors and unexpected errors. Some errors are indeed expected because they signal an event that is more a logical error than a physical problem with the device or media.

End-of-file.   For example, after the last allocated block in the file has been read, if we try to access the next block, we will cause an *end-of-file* exception condition. This is the only way in which the software can tell when the last piece of data has been read and when there are no more data to be read. This condition occurs over and over again as programs read all the data in a file and then make one too many reads, encountering the end-of-file condition.

Device write protected.   A *write-protect* error can occur in one of two ways on a disk. First, the device itself may have a switch that can be pushed which write-protects (i.e., prohibits all WRITE_BLOCK commands) the disk. This is useful as a safety precaution. Second, the medium can be write protected. For example, assume that we have a floppy disk. These diskettes have a rectangular notch cut out of one side. When that notch is open, all operations are allowed on the device. However, when a piece of tape covers the notch, the hardware is prohibited from writing anything to the disk. Thus the state of the notch, open or covered, dictates whether or not the diskette is to be write protected.

Error recovery in this situation is straightforward. If the device, or medium, was inadvertently write protected, an operator can easily unprotect it. On the other hand, if the device or medium was correctly write protected, the program attempting the write operation must be terminated.

Bad tracks.   There will be times in which, for one reason or another, a track, or portion of a track, is found to be bad. Instead of losing a track from the disk, usually a pool of tracks is set aside for use when other tracks in the primary area of the disk fail. Therefore, when a READ_BLOCK or WRITE_BLOCK tries to access one of these bad tracks, the file system detects from the first block on the track that the track is not to be used. In addition, the first block provides the cylinder and track address of an *alternate track* which can be utilized in its place. Thus instead of failing the I/O commands then and there, the file system retries the I/O request on the alternate track.

As bad tracks are discovered, they are allocated to a *bad track file*. Hence all the known bad tracks are effectively removed from circulation by the process of allocating them to a file that will never be used. In this manner, the user will be totally unaware of the bad tracks.

READ_BLOCK error recovery.   If a READ_BLOCK command fails, error recovery must be attempted, in order to try not to lose any data. The error recovery procedure is identical to the SEARCH error recovery discussed previously. Effectively, the entire failing command sequence is retried up to 10 or so times. If the retries continue to fail, the user must be notified that the record has become unreadable. Thus data have been lost!

WRITE_BLOCK error recovery.   Errors are *not* usually detected during WRITE_BLOCK operations. The reason for this is that there is only one read/write head per track. Tapes have two heads. Thus, as soon as a record has been written onto a tape, it can be read back by the tape drive to ensure that the written block can be correctly read. Disks do not have this capability. The only way to accomplish this is to write the block itself and then wait while the disk makes another complete revolution. When the block just written again rotates under the read/write head, the disk hardware can try and reread that block. The problem with this is that each write would now be forced to consume an additional disk revolution. This would adversely affect the performance and throughput of the system, and thus it is rarely done.

In summary, unless the disk hardware fails in some detectable manner, a WRITE_BLOCK error will not be detected until the block is later accessed via the READ_BLOCK command. Although this may apppear to be "bad," the trade-off being made is one of known disk reliability versus a degradation of performance.

4.6 COMPATIBILITY ISSUES

Compatibility and portability of disk media between machines and vendors is critical. In the realm of microcomputers it is even more important since there are so many different models. The types of compatibility issues that may arise are listed below in two categories, *physical compatibility* and *logical compatibility*.

4.6.1 Physical Compatibility

Physical compatibility relates to how closely the hardware characteristics of the device and medium compare with, or are different from, similar competitive products.

Type of medium.   Is the medium a hard disk, floppy disk, or a nonremovable disk? Once the medium is determined, we need to know the physical size of the disks. For example, we could have all floppy disks and yet have no compatibility. We could have 8-inch, $5\frac{1}{4}$ -inch, and $3\frac{1}{2}$ -inch sizes. Thus if we need to move a disk from one machine to another or from one vendor's machines to another, we first need to ensure that the physical size and types of the disks are the same.

Density and recording technique.   With what density are the data recorded onto the disk? For floppy disks, there is a choice of single, double, and quad density diskettes. Furthermore, the recording density on disks is doubling roughly every two years. For that matter, what technique is used to record the data? If either of these characteristics is incompatible, there will be problems.

Number of sides.   In the world of floppy disks, data can be recorded on one side (i.e., single-sided disks) or can be recorded on both sides of the disk platter (double-sided disks). It is better to record data on both sides of the platter since the data capacity can be doubled inexpensively. However, because of cost in small systems, the price of the additional read/write head for the reverse side may be too high. This is, however, becoming less and less of a problem because hardware prices have been decreasing rapidly.

4.6.2 Logical Compatibility

Logical compatibility relates to how well the on-disk file structures compare with what the current system expects.

File structure used.   Where are the blocks that show where the space allocation of the disk is, and where is the volume label? If we transport a disk that matches all the physical attributes of the target machine, we could still have a problem if the file structure understood by the target machine was different from the file structure that was used in creating and building the disk. While there are standards to be followed in many areas of hardware development, there are precious few to be supported in software, and none relative to the definition of the on-disk file structure.

On every disk there are critical blocks that the file system writes out which are needed for three reasons. First, the directory is needed to keep track of all the files that have to be written onto the medium. Second, there must be an allocation area where we can keep track of all the allocated disk space. This means that the file system must know which blocks are allocated to specific files and which blocks remain unused. Third, there is a *boot block* that is written to allow the system to boot itself into main memory when the power is turned on.

Every file system writes these blocks out to standard locations on the disk itself. The problem is that each system writes these blocks to *different areas on the disk*. Thus it is nearly impossible for one file system to read and recognize the disks from another file system.

4.7 COST/BENEFIT TRADE-OFFS

Why use tapes if disks do so many things well? For example, the benefits and costs of disks compared with magnetic tapes can be listed as follows.

Benefits
- Random access to any block on the disk. With tapes there is no random access.

- Reasonably fast sequential access to blocks within a file. Although perhaps not quite as fast as tape, if allocated contiguously, the performance will be comparable.
- Data capacities are high and reliability is extremely good. In addition, the error recovery capabilities of the newer disks can recover from most single-bit errors.
- LBNs allow files to be accessed by users without knowing the actual disk addresses of the blocks in the file.
- LBNs allow files to be copied from one disk to another much more easily. With PBNs, the file must be copied into the identical blocks on the second disk. Since the target disk may have files written onto it, the needed PBNs may already have been used. Thus no copy can be made.

Costs

- Disks, especially hard disks, tend to be much more expensive than tapes.
- Disks, with the exception of floppies, also tend not to be very portable. They are large, awkward to carry, and are fairly heavy.

The choice depends on how the device will be utilized. If random access or on-line data is a requirement, we really have no choice but to go with disks. On the other hand, to transport data files from one machine to another, or to save data in backup files for security reasons, it is difficult to beat tapes. Thus both here and in other design decisions that we will need to make, there is no single correct answer. The decision depends on the specific application and requirements that the user has defined.

4.8 PERFORMANCE CHARACTERISTICS

Since disks are used for on-line data storage, it is important to understand the performance characteristics of disks in a fair amount of detail. Throughout the remainder of this book, we will be referring to the following principle:

The limiting factor on overall performance is the number of SEEK operations that must be performed.

Current disks can transfer 30 megabytes of data per *second,* and more. They can also hold into the gigabyte range of data (i.e., billions of bytes of data). However, the time it takes for the disk to reposition (i.e., SEEK) to the correct cylinder and track can range up to a very slow third of a second. Thus it is this SEEK time which is the bottleneck to overall performance.

The time it takes to read or write a block on the disk can be represented by the following formula:

$$t_{\text{read/write}} = t_{\text{seek}} + t_{\text{search}} + t_{\text{data transfer}}$$

where t represents time. The largest component in the formula is the time it takes to complete a SEEK operation. One way to improve overall performance is to cut down on the *actual* number of SEEK operations that must be performed. The reason for this is that SEEKs take comparatively long periods of time compared to CPU-type instructions. Also remember that a SEEK operation is needed with every I/O request to ensure that the access arm is repositioned to the correct cylinder and track. For example, if we had a system with only a single disk connected, what is the maximum number of I/O operations that can be performed per second? The formula is as follows:

$$\frac{1 \text{ second}}{\text{average SEEK time}} = \text{maximum number of I/O operations per second}$$

Thus, if an average SEEK operation took approximately 30 ms, the maximum number of SEEKs that could be performed in a second would be about 33. This represents the physical limit of the hardware. On the other hand, since I/O requests consist of more than just SEEK commands, and since it is nearly impossible not to lose processing time between I/O requests, the real number of I/O requests that could be performed at a user installation is considerably less. In addition, the operating system must perform I/O operations to read in programs from the disk to run them as well as to perform other I/O operations on behalf of all the users in the system. Therefore, the actual number of I/O requests that a user can make per second is lower still.

Furthermore, what if on this single disk system there were 20 users running simultaneously? Not an unusual case! With luck, each user might get to make one I/O request per second. If this were a bank, and if it took an average of four or five I/O requests to retrieve and update a customer's account, and if there were 10 teller stations in the bank, it could be 45, 55, or 60 seconds or more just to get an account record. How often are customers unwilling to stand in line waiting for this long?

Indeed, consider for a moment an airline reservation system which might have several thousand travel agents connected to it. How long would customers have to wait in this case? Is there any way in which we could ever guarantee no worse than a 3-second response time?

If an average of five I/O operations were required to completely process a travel agent's request, and if 1000 travel agencies required a 10-second response time, how many disks are needed? Is it even possible? The number of disks is equal to the following:

$$\text{number of disks} = \frac{\text{number of users} \times \text{average number of I/Os per request}}{\text{response time} \times \text{maximum number of I/Os per disk drive}}$$

Thus for 1000 agents and a 10-second response time, we would need 20 disk drives. If, on the other hand, the agencies demanded a 3-second response time, we would need 65 disks, assuming that we could spread the processing equally over all the drives. Thus at $25,000 per disk drive, a 3-second response time requirement would cost in excess of $1.6 million dollars just for disks.

The point here is that when we consider applications, be it customer or system applications, we must be intimately aware that most of the I/O being performed will be done on disk. In addition, there is a physical limitation to the maximum number of operations that can be performed in any given interval. Thus, if there are performance or response-time requirements, we must know how many I/O requests will be made on the average during peak periods so that we can determine whether the requirement is reasonable and can be met.

Other factors affecting performance are the rotational delay waiting for the desired block to be rotated underneath the read/write heads, and the actual data transfer time. The rotational delay can mount up but is still much smaller than the SEEK time. For example, if a disk rotates at 3600 rpm, the average rotational delay is half a rotation or about 8 ms. The data transfer time is insignificant; most machines today can transfer data at rates of 5 to 10 million bytes of data per second, or more.

Therefore, *the key issue is how to minimize the number of actual SEEK operations that must be performed.* The number of SEEKs required can be minimized by the following:

   1. Allocate Space within a File on Contiguous Tracks, and/or Cylinders.   This will allow the file system to read consecutive blocks of data without performing a real SEEK. Indeed, a SEEK operation is still incorporated within the I/O request, but a SEEK to the current cylinder takes zero time, thus having the effect of no SEEK at all.

   2. Use a Fixed-Head Disk Where Feasible.   This type of device completely eliminates SEEK time since there is one read/write head for each track on the device. The only drawback here is that with so many read/write heads the cost of these disk drives is considerably higher than that of moving-head disks.

   3. Spread Users over Multiple Disks (i.e., Don't Place All User Accounts on the Same Disk).   The reason for this is to spread the I/O burden across several devices. If all requests went to the same drive, the access arm would be moving back and forth continuously and that disk would become a bottleneck to overall system performance.

   4. If Possible, Overlap the SEEK I/O Requests across Several Drives.   Since the SEEK operation takes the greatest amount of time, while it is executing, everything else is waiting for it to complete. On the other hand, if there were multiple disks in the system, we could start the SEEK requests on as many drives as possible based on the user requests we had queued in the file system. The newer disk controllers have enough "intelligence" to coordinate the SEEK and SEARCH operations across multiple drives. Therefore, the controllers end up overlapping much of the I/O on the devices attached to them. Thus we can overlap the lengthy time delay and improve overall performance and throughput.

   5. Distinguish I/O-Bound Jobs from CPU-Intensive Jobs.   Many commercial business applications perform a lot of I/O and a relatively small amount of computing. Alternatively, many scientific and engineering applications are compute bound.

The key here is to have a job scheduling algorithm that gives a higher priority to the I/O-bound jobs. The reason for this is that the I/O-bound jobs will not monopolize the CPU. They only need a short burst of CPU time before they perform an I/O operation and thus have to stop and wait. During this waiting period, other jobs, such as the CPU-intensive jobs, can execute. The reverse of this algorithm would give preference to CPU-intensive jobs that would rarely voluntarily give up control of the CPU. Thus fewer jobs would get access to the CPU, and therefore the throughput in the system would decrease dramatically.

6. Perform Intelligent SEEK Queueing.   When an I/O request is submitted, it usually ends up in the queue of I/O requests for that device. This is because there is usually another request ahead of this one that is currently executing on the device. Once that request has terminated, it is up to the basic file system to select the next request to be executed. There are many possible algorithms (see [4]) for this selection, only a few of which will be discussed here.

- *First-in, first-out (FIFO):* In this algorithm, the requests are selected and executed in the order they were submitted. There is no attempt to optimize performance, only to give everyone a "fair" shot at the device. This is the simplest algorithm to implement and is the one that usually exists in microcomputer operating systems.
- *Ordered SEEK queueing:* Here, the selection algorithm scans the queue of requests for the one that results in the *shortest SEEK* from where we are currently positioned on the device. The justification is that shorter SEEKS take less time than longer SEEKS.

    There are two variations of this algorithm. First, we can follow the algorithm in a very strict sense and literally select the next request that results in the shortest SEEK. However, this approach has the potential of stranding requests in the queue which just happen to lie outside the interval that continually gets chosen. Therefore, it is possible to minimize SEEKS on the device and to end up never executing some of the requests. Since this is unacceptable, how can we modify the algorithm to still meet the intent of the algorithm, yet not risk stranding any requests?

    If we make a modification simply to take the next shortest SEEK *in the direction that the disk arm last moved,* we will solve the stranding issue. Here the objective is to move the disk arm all the way into the innermost cylinder and then to turn around and move all the way back to the outermost cylinder. The direction taken for a SEEK is never changed until one of two things occurs. First, we have reached the innermost or outermost cylinders and thus we have no choice but to turn around, or second, there are no other requests in the device queue for cylinders in the direction in which we are currently moving. In this case, we would select the request with the shortest SEEK going in the opposite direction.

7. Install a RAM Disk.   Many microcomputers today use floppy disks. These tend to be low in capacity and slow in operation. However, they are quite inexpensive and reliable. To improve the performance of these devices, it is possible to stimulate the device in main memory. Thus a block of main memory would be allocated to a "disk drive." Also, the device tables would be changed to show that this device really exists. Thus users can read and write to the disk without knowing that the device is really a memory disk. To implement this, there must be a special disk driver that knows the size of the disk, and so on, since the user can define the disk to be any size desired.

What is gained here is that all SEEKS are performed instantaneously *in main memory*. Thus performance improves dramatically. There is, however, another side to this improvement. If the system should crash, or power be lost, before the data were transferred to a real disk, all the data would be lost. The key to using RAM disks is to frequently save or write the files to a real disk.

In summary, to improve performance we must expect to make trade-offs between the response time requirements and the associated cost of selecting a particular approach. How we make these decisions depends on the job to be accomplished. What we have established here are some guidelines and techniques that can be utilized in making these design decisions.

8. Provide Disk Block Caching in the Disk Controller.   This is more expensive than the other methods since it requires the disk and the controller to have more intelligence built into them. Basically, the disk would buffer an entire track, or tracks, in the device itself so that when the next request comes along, it first checks its buffer. If found, no actual disk I/O has occurred and performance improves dramatically [6].

4.9 IMPLEMENTATION CONSIDERATIONS

To keep track of the processing of I/O requests, the disk *device control table (DCT)* must contain at least the information listed below (see Table 4–2). Also, there must be one DAT for each device connected into the system in order that every device can be managed properly.

- Device type
- Number of tracks per cylinder
- Number of cylinders per disk
- Number of blocks or sectors per track
- Number of device-positioning retries to perform
- Number of data transfer retries to perform

TABLE 4-2   DISK DEVICE CONTROL TABLE

Header information	
Version ID	
Link to next DCT	
Address of IORQ	
General device information	
Device status	
HW address of device	
Volume name	
Device type	$5\frac{1}{4}$ -inch floppy disk
	$3\frac{1}{2}$ -inch floppy disk
	300-MB disk
	600-MB disk
Address of device driver	
Exception-processing information	
Addresses of system error log	Central file into which all errors are written
Maximum number of retries: disk positioning commands	Limit on number of retries
Maximum number of retries: READs	
Maximum number of retries: WRITEs	
Number of current retry counter	For current error processing
Number of recoverable errors	Total number of errors detected and successfully recovered
Device-specific information: disk	
Number of tracks per cylinder	
Number of cylinders per disk pack	
Number of sectors per track	

The *disk allocation table (DAT)* contains the following data in order to accurately track which files own all the space on the disk itself (refer to Figure 4–10). There is one DAT on each disk. Sometimes, especially on microcomputers, there is a second DAT which is an identical copy of the primary DAT. This second copy is used only in case the primary DAT gets destroyed or becomes unreadable.

- Minimum cluster or extent size (i.e., track, cylinder, or *n* number of blocks/sectors)
- If a bitmap, one bit for every possible cluster on the disk pack

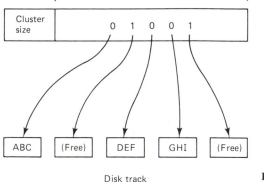

Figure 4-10   Disk allocation table.

- If extents are used, each extent contains the following information:
  —Starting cylinder or track of this extent
  —Number of cylinders or tracks in this extent

The *file allocation table (FAT)* is identical to the device allocation table described above. However, instead of describing all the space as yet unallocated to other files, the FAT describes all the space currently allocated to this specific file. Thus there is one FAT for every file on the disk. In this manner all possible space on the disk is allocated in either the DAT or all of the FATs.

The *directory* file contains the following fields in order to keep track of all the files currently on the disk pack (refer to Table 4–3). There is one directory per disk pack, although a second copy may be kept for security and backup purposes.

- Filename
- Number of the *first block* in the file
- Address of associated disk, or file, allocation table
- Flags, such as:
  —Valid file name entry
  —Valid directory entry
  —Deleted file or directory entry
  —Unused or available directory entry
- Security or protection information for this particular entry

Finally, the label that is written onto each disk to identify its contents is described in Table 4–4. Among other items, the label usually contains the following fields:

- Name of the disk volume
- Owner of the disk pack
- Creation and expiration dates for the data on the entire disk pack
- Security information which specifies who is allowed to access this volume

TABLE 4-3 DISK DIRECTORY ENTRY

Header information

Version ID	Used to identify the definition standard used for this directory structure; also allows for future expansion
Alternate directory	Optional; location where a mirror image of this directory exists, used primarily for backup purposes in case the regular directory gets destroyed

Directory record entry

Flags	Unused, or available, entry Valid file entry Deleted file Directory entry
Filename	Name of this specific file, or directory
Block number	First block in the file
Address of file allocation table	Describes space allocated to this specific file
Security, access information	Full access Read-only access Update access No access
Password	For sensitive files, such as payroll
File size	Number of blocks allocated to this file

TABLE 4-4 DISK VOLUME LABEL

Volume name	Name of the disk pack
Version ID	Definition to which this label conforms; also allows for future expansion
Owner name	Person or organization that owns this disk
Creation date	Date this disk was originally initialized
Expiration date	Date this disk volume can be reinitialized
Security information	Information needed to restrict access, if necessary

4.10 SUMMARY

Disks are the most important device today for on-line storage purposes. In this chapter we have learned what a disk is as well as how a disk operates. What is important is to understand that every disk access takes a relatively long time. Therefore, since most activity in a system is against disks, it is critical that disk I/O be performed only when it is absolutely necessary.

KEY WORDS

Automatic volume recognition (AVR)
Bit map
Cluster
Contiguous allocation
Cylinders
Directory
Disk allocation table (DAT)
Extent
File allocation table (FAT)
Fixed-head disk (FHD)

Floppy disk
Logical block number (LBN)
Physical block number (PBN)
RAM disk
Sector
SEEK Time
Tracks
Volume label
Volume table of contents

SUPPLEMENTAL REFERENCES

1. Ahl, David H., "Floppy Disk Handling and Storage." *Creative Computing,* December 1983, p. 205. This is a short article on how to handle and care for disks for personal computers. The most interesting point is the picture that shows the relationships between disk drive tolerances and "normal" everyday matter, such as fingerprints and smoke dust.

2. Card, Chuck, "A Proposed Floppy-Disk Format Standard." *BYTE,* February 1983, pp. 182–190. This article is the only disk file structure standard that I have seen. It proposes a *media-parameter table* which contains references to the directory, bad-track table, volume label, and so on. Overall, it is a good introduction to both on-disk file structures and the issues involved in the standardization process.

3. Collier, Don, Paul Frank, and Chris Aho, "Rigid Disk Heads Keep Pace with Growing Storage Needs." *Mini-Micro Systems,* December 1984, pp. 127–133. This article contains a variety of interesting charts, diagrams, and pictures related to disk technologies. For those interested in a brief overview of disk technology and trends, this is very good.

4. Deitel, Harvey M., *An Introduction to Operating Systems.* Reading, Mass.: Addison-Wesley Publishing Company, Inc., 1984, Chap. 12. This chapter discusses a variety of disk queueing algorithms, as well as each one's effect on overall performance.

5. "Clean Machine." *Forbes Magazine,* December 5, 1983, p. 242. This article supplements [1] in that it gives another perspective on the care and feeding of disks.

6. Krastins, Uldis, "Cache Memory Quickens Access to Disk Data." *Electronic Design,* May 13, 1982, pp. 77–80. Performance is the name of the game, and disk performance in particular is critical to overall system performance. This article investigates caching as a way of dramatically improving disk performance and throughput.

7. Microsoft, *Disk Operating System.* Boca Raton, Fl: International Business Machines Corporation, 1983, Version 2.0. The appendices here are excellent sources of the details of

the implementation of a small operating system and file system. Specifically, I/O buffers known as *disk transfer areas,* disk directory formats, file allocation table formats, and I/O interrupt handling are discussed in detail.

EXERCISES

1. Discuss the advantages and disadvantages of floppy versus hard disks for microcomputers.

2. Is it better or worse to have a space allocation algorithm that allocates tracks across a surface of the disk rather than down a cylinder? Explain the performance differences.

3. Why is it important to make a distinction between *physical block numbers* and *logical block numbers?*

4. What is the purpose of a *boot block* on a disk, and when/how is it read? Must every disk have a boot block? Explain why or why not.

5. What are the trade-offs to consider when selecting a cluster size to be used by the disk space allocation algorithm?

6. Why must there be a *disk* allocation table as well as *file* allocation tables?

7. If you were the system administrator of a computer, would you recommend that users preallocate their files? Explain.

8. When would you recommend contiguous file allocation? Would you ever recommend that a file not be preallocated? If yes, explain when you would make this recommendation.

9. Why is it necessary to precede a READ_BLOCK or WRITE_BLOCK disk command with a SEEK command? Would you ever want to avoid using the SEEK?

10. What is the function of a bad-track file? Are there any other solutions that would provide the same functionality? Explain.

PROGRAMMING EXERCISES

1. Design and implement a *shortest-seek-first* disk queueing algorithm. Run a simulation to demonstrate how it would function differently from a FIFO queueing algorithm.

2. Design and implement a routine to perform disk error recovery. Define the error conditions that are passed to this module, as well as the algorithm to process each error.

3. Design and implement an *error log file* that will keep track of all errors that occur on the disks. Define all the fields that you would keep in the log file. Make sure that there is enough information saved to be of use to a maintenance person.

Part II

File Systems

Part I discussed individual devices and how they worked. In Part II, we discuss how the I/O software manages these devices and controls what they do and when they do it. The file system can be logically divided into two major pieces, the basic file system and the access methods. The basic file system is the primary interface with the external world of peripheral devices, and thus must process *blocks* of data. The access methods, however, are the interface between the user program and the basic file system and devices. Thus the access methods process the *data records* which the user programs understand, and convert them into the blocks of data which the basic file system understands.

As can be seen for Figure 5-0, *the basic file system (BFS) is that piece of software which interfaces with the environment outside the computer's main memory.* As such, it includes the support for disks, tapes, and all other devices, as well as some other functionality. To understand the BFS, we will examine the following topics:

- How can software control and run the devices?
- How does the software know when an I/O operation has completed?
- How can an interface to a file system be defined?

In Chapter 5 we look outward from the BFS software to the world of the I/O devices to see how they cooperate to get a job done. Then we turn our attention inward to begin an investigation of how user programs interface with the file system.

In Chapter 6 we discuss how the *I/O supervisor* portion of the basic file system controls and monitors I/O activity in the system. This task is usually buried inside

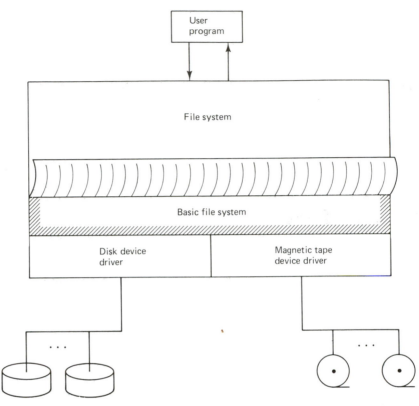

Figure 5-0 File system: basic file system component.

most operating systems. However, to understand I/O processing requirements, it is included here for completeness.

The typical user program does not interface directly with either the I/O supervisor or the basic file I/O routines. Instead, user programs interface with *access methods,* which are discussed in Chapter 7. Access methods allow users to read and write *records* instead of the blocks processed by the I/O supervisor.

Finally, Chapter 8 describes the functionality that the access methods provide user programs. This includes the reading, writing, updating, and deleting of user data records. Also included is the ability to create, extend, and delete files.

5

Basic File Systems

When you complete this chapter, you will be able to:

- Discuss the functions of a basic file system (BFS)
- Describe what information is required to perform I/O operations on behalf of the user
- Understand the concept of "defaults" and how they can be used in a file system
- Describe the basic primitives of a file system
- Begin to understand the concepts of I/O performance and why it is so critical to overall system throughput

5.1 OVERVIEW

To understand how an I/O system works, several questions must be asked, such as:

- How is the file that I need located within the computer system?
- How can I create a new file?
- How can the system find the specific record that I want?
- How is space on a medium allocated so that the space that I own will not be taken by some other user?

115

- How does the system start and stop an I/O request for one of the files in the system?

- How can I determine whether or not my I/O requests have completed successfully?

To answer these and other questions relating to how I/O is performed on a computer system, we must explain exactly how I/O is done. In the process of discussing I/O, we need to take into consideration the kind of CPU that we will be using.

Today, machines can range in size from a small microcomputer to a very large mainframe computer. Micros tend to be limited in both main memory and peripheral device capacity. Mainframe and "supermini" computers can usually support significantly greater storage and memory capacities. Thus, depending on what the actual target machine is, we may need to optimize memory and media space against performance. Or if memory and storage capacity is large, we may want to optimize our I/O routines for performance at the potential cost of using more storage space.

These issues are critical, since the range of machines and their capabilities is so wide. Probably no single file system will work best on all machine configurations. Thus when we design a file system, we need to pay close attention to how it can be made configurable to a wider range of machines and applications. Also, if we add the capability of allowing users to customize individual modules, we will have designed a flexible and extensible file system.

5.2 WHAT IS A BASIC FILE SYSTEM?

A basic file system is the only software that interfaces directly with the peripheral devices attached to the system. The BFS knows how to transfer blocks of data to and from a device. The function of a basic file system is sometimes referred to as *physical I/0.* This is because it deals with the physical reading and writing of blocks of data on the peripheral devices. However, *the BFS does not understand the content and meaning of the data being transferred.*

Sometimes, the BFS is considered to be part of the operating system on the machine. This is primarily because the operating system usually contains the core software that must exist for users to run the system. Since all users utilize I/O to one degree or another, the BFS is packaged as part of the operating system. In the following sections we investigate the BFS software, with just enough discussion of an operating system to tie them both together.

Users and computer systems need a BFS for the following reasons:

- To provide a common interface to perform block I/O. This frees users from having to know and understand the device characteristics of each of the devices connected to the system. Similarly, it allows users to write programs to solve their own needs and not have to be concerned with the intricacies of the hardware they happen to be using.

- To provide a centralized control program to ensure that the devices connected to the system are being allocated and scheduled properly, in other words, to guarantee that all users are able to get their jobs done without interfering with any other program in the system.

- To provide a central resource to ensure data integrity by providing error recovery and exception handling for all users.

5.3 BASIC FILE SYSTEM INTERFACE: FILE OPERATIONS

The BFS interface provides a standardized set of function calls for performing I/O requests. Every program in the system that wants to perform I/O must use this interface. In this section we define what such a BFS interface looks like, as well as discussing what is required to actually implement such an interface.

If we are to define the I/O interface that exists between user programs and the peripheral devices, we must first decide what I/O capabilities are required. Second, we must determine what information we must have in order to complete the I/O processing supplied by the BFS interface. Once we have defined the data required, we must determine how, and from where, the BFS can get this information.

A program can provide only a small portion of all the data the BFS needs. One of the best definitions of I/O requirements in a higher-level-language can be found in COBOL. It has substantially more I/O capability and language syntax than almost any other major language currently in use. Yet the COBOL program itself can provide only a portion of the data that the BFS needs.

Occasionally, a user may not want or be able to supply the BFS with all the data required. What should the BFS do when this happens? First, and most obvious, the BFS could simply abort the request due to insufficient data. This is a rather harsh reaction, although there may be cases where this approach is needed.

Alternatively, the BFS could itself fill in the missing parameters with predefined values. As long as these substitute values are known, this is an acceptable solution. *These substitute values for missing parameters are known as the default values.* Many users, knowingly or not, accept default values as a standard mode of operation and thus assume the following:

- They know the default values.
- The correct processing will occur.
- The performance and space utilization will be acceptable.

The data the BFS needs to perform its work must come from one of the following sources (see Figure 5–1):

- The program itself
- The command language, otherwise known as the JCL (job control language), utilized at the user's site
- A stand-alone utility program that interactively requests the data from the user

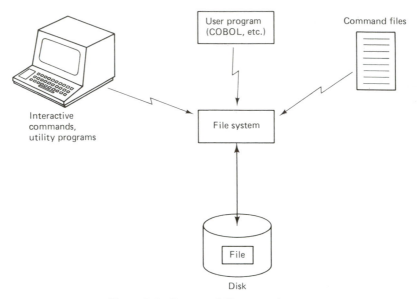

Figure 5-1   Sources of file system inputs.

Of these three sources, the only one that has the capability of providing all the data needed is the stand-alone utility. Such a program can prompt the user for each of the required parameters, check inputs for validity, and then store the information within the file itself.

Finally, we must determine what other kinds of housekeeping the BFS must perform in order to get its work done, yet which is not directly visible to most users. This is work that must be done to guarantee the security, sharability, and integrity of the user's data.

To accomplish all the work implied within the BFS interface definition, the BFS controls the following system resources to guarantee the integrity of the user's data (see Figure 5-2):

- The allocation of all space on the devices.
- The centralization of all I/O through the BFS. This means that the BFS must have one or more queues into which it can put incoming I/O requests. The BFS then becomes responsible for the *initiation* of all the I/O requests on all the devices.
- The control of the devices themselves, which usually requires a rather detailed knowledge of device-specific details.
- The processing of all the I/O *terminations* (i.e., interrupts) to ensure that the correct processing is performed. Also, it must then initiate the next I/O request targeted for that device.

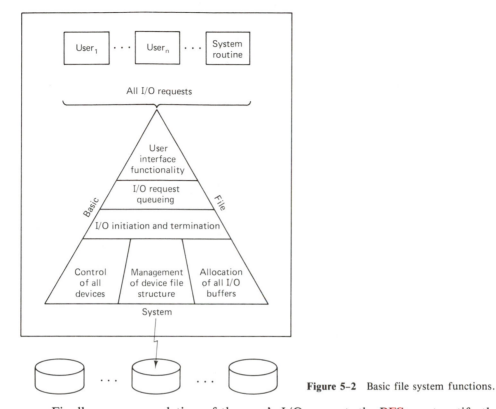

Figure 5-2 Basic file system functions.

Finally, upon completion of the user's I/O request, the BFS must notify the user as to whether the I/O request completed correctly. This is done by returning a status field, which indicates how the I/O request terminated. For example, if everything processed successfully, the BFS could return a status field which indicated success. On the other hand, if an error was encountered, the BFS must notify the user, with some indication as to what went wrong.

One critical aspect of any file system is to be able to process, both efficiently and effectively, each exception condition that may arise. Recall that one of the guidelines discussed in Chapter 1 was that a file system must always ensure the integrity of the user's data. The user's program can then take this status notification and intelligently make a decision as to what should be done next.

We begin to define the BFS interface by asking what kind of I/O work, or activities, most users perform. To get these data, we need to begin with any higher-level-language program to see what kinds of features are typically used. For example, most programs will perform the following kinds of functions:

- CREATE brand new files.
- OPEN, or start using, a file that was CREATEd prior to the running of this program.

- Increase the size of the file (EXTEND), if and when the file has exhausted its current allocated space.
- Stop using (CLOSE) the file after the program has finished using it.
- DELETE, or get rid of, a file that already exists.
- Transfer data from (READ) or to (WRITE) the device designated by the program.

Thus it is possible to divide all BFS functions into two categories:

- *File operations:* CREATE_FILE, OPEN_FILE, EXTEND_FILE, CLOSE_FILE, and DELETE_FILE
- *Block data transfer operations:* READ_BLOCK and WRITE_BLOCK

One of the key functions of a basic file system is to map the functionality described above into commands that the devices themselves can understand. None of the file operations has a corresponding disk or tape I/O command. Thus the basic file system must map the file operations into a sequence of data transfer commands for the devices (see Figure 5–3). On the other hand, the basic file system data transfer commands map directly into the read and write device data transfer commands. We will see a similar division of functionality when we examine logical I/O in detail in Chapters 7 and 8.

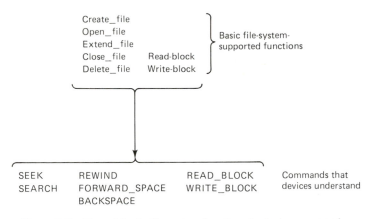

Figure 5–3 Map of basic file system functions to device commands.

5.4 BASIC FILE SYSTEM: FILE OPERATIONS

Before any data can be written, or read, from a file, the file must be created on the device itself. Also, the BFS must be notified of the coming activities so that it can perform its own initialization procedures. *File operations deal with the file structure itself, not the data records within the file.*

5.4.1 CREATE_FILE Request

The purpose of a CREATE FILE function is to allow all users to create new files whenever it is necessary to do so. It also forces all users to go through the same routine in order to get all files created. No files *should* be created outside the BFS. This allows the BFS to ensure that no two files get created with the same name on the same device, and so on. This centralization of control over all files is a critical one that the BFS must have to be able to guarantee that the integrity of the user's data files will always be maintained.

Before any user can process a file, someone must take the time to create the file. This is analogous to a secretary creating a new file that will contain, for example, competitive information. The process of setting up the file (i.e., creating the file) occurs relatively infrequently, and only as the need arises. Once the file has been created, most users will simply want to access the file and the information contained within it.

If a secretary is to create a new file for competitive information, what information must he or she have? First, the secretary must understand the content of the new file so that it can be distinguished from all the other files that exist. The easiest way to accomplish this is simply to give it a *unique filename*. Thus we could have a personnel file, or a competitive information file. To purchase the correct size of cabinet, the secretary must estimate the potential *size* of the file, which is impossible without understanding how the records (i.e., file folders) in the file are to be *organized*. Thus we are beginning to see what information is required to actually create a file.

In an analogous manner, if we wanted to create a new file within a computer system, a similar set of information must be provided. For example, the following data are needed to create a file:

- *Device/user name:* tells the BFS where to place the file when it is created
- *Filename:* identifies the file among all the other files in the computer system
- *File size:* tells the BFS how much room to allocate when it is creating the file
- *File organization:* needed so that the file system, or more specifically the access methods, can know how to insert and later retrieve the blocks within the file
- *Block size:* amount of data that will be read or written in every I/O operation (e.g., a file folder)

The list above should be considered to be the minimum set of data to successfully create a file. An interesting exercise to pursue would be to take any higher-level language (e.g., COBOL, FORTRAN) and examine it to see how it interfaces with the I/O world, and more specifically, how that language *creates* files.

If we assume that the user has provided this information to the BFS, what tasks must the BFS perform in order that the file be successfully created? In other words, what really has to be done to create a file? The tasks listed below are in the sequence in which the actual CREATE_FILE processing would take place.

1. Validate the User's Input Data.   The first step that the BFS must perform is to validate all the input data provided by the caller of the BFS in order that errors can be caught before they can cause problems. Also, from the user's point of view, if the CREATE_FILE request completes successfully, all is well and correct within the new file. If any errors are detected, the calling program would be notified.

2. Check to See if the File Already Exists.   Second, the BFS must check to see if there is any other file with the same name that already exists on the device specified by the user. If there is another file with the same name, we will take the position that the CREATE_FILE request has failed and the BFS will appropriately notify the calling program. The create processing cannot continue without a unique name, since there would be no way in which to specify which of the identically named files to select when a user requested that filename. *Although many options and parameters can be defaulted, filename is not one of them.*

The question can arise as to how the BFS knows what files have already been created and which files have not. The answer is that there is a list, or directory, of all the files currently existing on that specific device. When we want to see what files we own, we type an operating system command that generates a list of all our files. This list comes from the contents of the *directory file.* This file contains, among other things, the names of all the files on that specific device. Thus the basic file system must locate and read into main memory the directory file. Then if the BFS finds a matching file name in this directory, the BFS cannot simply create another file, but must notify the calling user program that a duplicate filename conflict has been detected. If the BFS does not find a matching name, it CREATES the file by placing its name into the file directory on the device.

3. Allocate Space on the Medium for the File.   Third, the BFS must check and see if the device specified by the user has enough space on it for this new file. The BFS can tell if enough space exists by comparing the projected file size, as seen from the vantage point of the user, against the device allocation table on the target device (see Chapter 4).

If there is not enough space on the medium, the BFS has no choice but to abort its processing. Then it must return to the user an error status message stating that there was not sufficient space on the device to successfully create the file using the higher-level language selected by the user. On the other hand, if space is available, the BFS takes from the available space list an amount of space equal to the file size specified by the user. The space taken is marked as allocated so that no other user can make a request for space and then have the same space allocated to another user.

4. Insert a Pointer to the First Block Allocated to the File.   Fourth, the master directory contains a pointer to the first block of the file. By adding this function, anyone who wishes to use this file in the future need only specify the file's name and device, and the BFS will be able to locate it.

5. Allocate and Initialize I/O Buffers and Control Blocks.   Fifth, the BFS must do some internal housekeeping chores so that when the user(s) want to READ or WRITE to that file, the BFS will be ready. The BFS must do two major tasks. First, it must allocate space in memory large enough to READ in the largest block in the file. *The blocks of memory, which are dedicated to the transferring of the data from memory to and from the peripheral devices, are called I/O buffers.* The BFS may allocate one or more of these I/O buffers to successfully process all user requests.

Next, *the BFS must allocate and build a table, also known as a file control block, in which the critical information about the file will be saved.* For example, the BFS must keep track of the file name, the size of the file so that it will not read or write outside the boundaries of the file, the block size so that the BFS can know how much data to transfer in any I/O operation, and so on.

All critical data are saved elsewhere on the disk, usually within the file itself. The reason for this is that in order to process user requests, the BFS needs to know more than the typical user will or can provide. This critical set of data is defined when the file is being CREATEd.

6. Return Success or Fail Status Back to the User.   Sixth, the file has now been created (see Figure 5–4). However, the user does not yet know whether the BFS was successful. Therefore, the next important task for the BFS to perform is to return status information to the user. This information will either inform the user that all went well or that errors were detected which first need to be corrected.

The CREATE_FILE processing has now almost been completed. The only step left to perform is to return control back to the calling program. Note, however, that *at the completion of a CREATE_FILE request the file is left open.* Thus blocks can be READ or WRITTEN immediately.

At any point in the foregoing sequence of events, an error could occur. What kinds of errors can occur, and how should they be processed? Following is a list of some of the possible CREATE_FILE errors.

- Another file with the same name already exists.
- The device has no available space to create another new file.
- The device is, or has become, nonoperational.
- There was a hardware problem which aborted the processing.
- One or more of the input parameters given to the BFS were wrong.

In each case, the only choice that the BFS has is to notify the user of the specific problem. We shall see later that there are other kinds of errors that can arise, in which the BFS can try to fix or get around the problem so that the user's request may succeed.

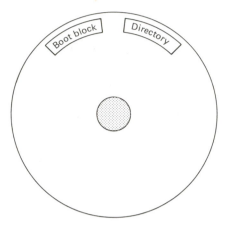

(a) Disk prior to a CREATE_FILE request

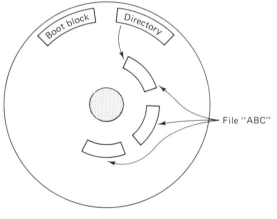

File "ABC"

(b) Disk after CREATE_FILE request

Figure 5-4   CREATE_FILE processing.

5.4.2 OPEN_FILE Request

The purpose of the OPEN_FILE request is to allow users to locate and access files that were created at an earlier time. Note that the difference between an OPEN_FILE request and a CREATE_FILE request is that the file did not exist prior to a CREATE_FILE call, but is assumed to exist prior to an OPEN_FILE request.

The information that the BFS requires in order to open a file is different from the list of information required to create a file. The reason for this is that all of the critical pieces of data which really describe the file were written out into the file structure during the CREATE_FILE processing. Therefore, OPEN_FILE only needs to locate and read this information, known as the file's attributes. Thus the question can be asked: What data are *really* required in order for the BFS to locate a file?

On any given device, the filename is unique within any particular directory. Thus we only need to specify the following data, which is also known as the file's pathname:

- Device name
- User name, or account identification
- Filename

From these data, the BFS can locate and scan the appropriate directories and locate the file wanted by the user program. Next, let us examine the processing that goes on as part of the OPEN_FILE task. These tasks are listed in the order of their execution.

1. Allocate Space for Internal Control Blocks.   First, space must be allocated in main memory for the file's I/O control block. Each and every file currently open in the system must have an allocated file control block. This is because an FCB is required in order to keep information critical to the correct processing of that specific file.

2. Get the Correct Volumes Mounted on the Device(s).   Second, if the user has specified a particular volume name, the basic file system must check the volume label against this name. If the names match, the correct volume has been mounted and processing can continue. If the names do not match, a message must be sent to the operator to mount the correct volume.

3. Locate the File on the Device.   Third, the BFS takes the device, user, and file names and concatenates them into a complete pathname to the file wanted by the user. Once the device is known by the BFS, it can read the directory listing on that device and see if the desired file is located there. If it is not there, the user either has made a mistake or someone has deleted the file. On the other hand, if the filename is found in the directory on the specified device, the location of the file is taken by the BFS from the directory entry. Note that not all systems construct their directories in the same manner. What is important to understand is that this key information is saved somewhere so that it can be retrieved easily when the file is being opened.

4. Allocate Internal Memory Space for I/O Buffers.   The BFS now knows the location of the file on the device. The next task to be performed is to allocate all internally required I/O buffers. This is done in a manner identical to the processing done as part of the CREATE_FILE request. At this time, the basic file system has established a logical connection between the user's program and the file itself (i.e., the location of the file is known, as are all of the file's attributes).

5. Protect against Unauthorized Users.   As part of the OPEN_FILE request, the BFS can check and see if anyone else on the system is using the same file. If yes, it is up to the BFS to guarantee that the users will not destroy each other's data.

6. Maintain a List of All the Open Files in the System.   After these tasks have been completed, the OPEN_FILE function has essentially completed. Still remaining is the returning of status to the user. What must be returned to the user is an indication that the request made on the BFS completed successfully or that it failed. With this knowledge, each user can take whatever corrective action is needed in the situation.

An important part of the code in the BFS relates to the processing of the various error conditions and exception conditions. For the OPEN_FILE command, we could encounter the following errors:

- File not found on the specified device and in the specified user account or directory. This could be because of an incorrectly specified filename or device identifier.
- File already in use by some other user application.
- Hardware error has occurred from which the BFS could not recover.

It is important that these exception conditions, as well as all the others, be processed in a timely manner.

In summary, an OPEN_FILE request is a subset of the processing done within the CREATE_FILE task. In both cases, the input parameters are validated. Also, in both cases, when the processing is completely done, the files are left in the open condition. Finally, in CREATE_FILE processing the information is gathered and then written out to the device. OPEN_FILE, however, reads back into memory the information written at CREATE_FILE time (see Figure 5-5).

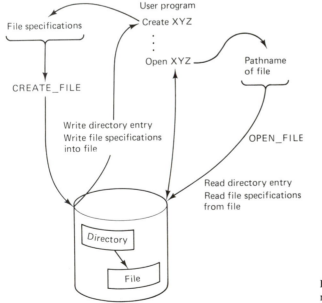

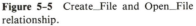

Figure 5-5 Create_File and Open_File relationship.

5.4.3 EXTEND_FILE Request

The purpose of the EXTEND_FILE function is to allow the user(s) to explicitly in crease the size of a file. If the user does not make an explicit call to EXTEND_FILE when the space in a particular file has been exhausted, the BFS may, depending on the capability of the system, *implicitly* extend the file on behalf of the user. This is done in order that the data not be lost, as well to be able to successfully complete the current request. Remember that the goal of a file system is to complete the processing of the data record, no matter what it takes to accomplish it.

What information will the BFS need to increase the size of a file for the user?

- Device and directory name where the file is located
- Name of the file
- Amount by which the file should be increased in size

The path to the device has been known since the file was first created or last opened. Thus we know the device and the location and size of the user's data file. Therefore, only the size of the extension is needed.

A user can request that a file be increased in size. How is this actually done, and what tasks must be performed to successfully complete the user's request? The work that must be done is as follows:

1. Validate the parameters in this request.
2. Check to see if there is enough room on this device to increase the size of the file by the requested amount.
3. If space exists, take the space from the medium's general space pool, and mark it in such a way that no other user can take this space.
4. Add the space to the file in question, and to the internal information kept on the file, so that can be correctly processed at a later date.
5. Return a success or failure status code to the user.

As part of the EXTEND_FILE request, certain errors will arise that must either be corrected or returned to the user. Following are the most typical error conditions that can be encountered:

- Device has no space available in which to extend the file.
- File was not previously OPENed, indicating that the user has inadvertently gotten the sequence of I/O processing out of order.

If we examined most higher-level programming languages, we would discover almost no mention of an EXTEND_FILE built-in request within the syntax of the languages. However, file extension can either be *explicitly* requested by the user via some other interface, such as a utility program, or *implicitly* done on behalf of the user by the BFS itself.

5.4.4 CLOSE_FILE Request

The purpose of a CLOSE_FILE function is to allow the user to deaccess, or stop using, the file, thereby allowing other users to access the file. To perform this function, the BFS need only know the name of the file to be closed.

To perform a CLOSE_FILE request, the BFS requires only an indication of which currently open file is to be CLOSEd. Once the BFS has the name of the file to be closed, it can perform the processing as follows:

1. Write Out Any I/O Buffers That Have Been Modified and Are Still in Main Memory but Which Have Not Yet Been Written Out to the Specified Device. There are several reasons this kind of function call is required, whether it is explicitly issued from the user's program or done implicitly for the user by the BFS. First, when a user explicitly CLOSEs a file, the BFS knows that the file is being released. Second, if the user program aborts, or simply fails to close all files, the file system must be invoked to close all the files on behalf of the user. This is accomplished by having the operating system call the file system whenever a job terminates, normally or abnormally. This action allows the BFS to effectively improve overall performance by delaying WRITE or output operations until the last possible moment.

2. Write Out Any Updated Information about the File That Would Be Useful or Required to Know in the Future in Order to Process the File Correctly. The BFS must write out any labels required if the file is a tape device. These labels serve to identify where the logical end of the tape resides so that when the tape is reread the next time, all the data, and only the data, can be successfully retrieved.

3. Release Any Internal Memory Space Dedicated to the Processing of That Particular File. The BFS can release any internal table or I/O buffer space which has been dedicated to this file. This frees up more memory for other uses.

4. Return Status to the User, Indicating Success or Failure. This allows the calling program to correctly resume processing.

If the BFS knows what file is to be closed, what kinds of exception conditions can arise during the processing of this function?

- The file to be closed was not currently open.
- Any of the errors that can occur on a WRITE_BLOCK operation could occur, since we are writing blocks back into the file.
- A hardware problem could occur that could abort the CLOSE_FILE processing.

These errors can occur, and the user must be notified of them when they do arise. In each case except for the WRITE_BLOCK errors, the BFS has nothing it can do to get around the problem. From a user perspective, if a CLOSE_FILE fails, it is typically not critical, since at most, only the unwritten records in memory have been lost, not the entire day's work. Although this is still painful to most users, the file has not been completed and can be accessed again tomorrow. Of course, this assumes that the hardware problems that arose did not destroy the user's files!

In summary, by requiring a CLOSE to be done, the BFS can gracefully release access to a particular file while ensuring the integrity of the data within the file.

5.4.5 DELETE_FILE Request

The function of the DELETE_FILE request is to "erase" or get rid of a specific file from the system. This occurs when the user no longer needs a particular file and wishes to reuse the file space for some other purpose. Note that the file space used by any file can subsequently be reused by other files. Thus it is important to have this capability.

We needed a lot of information to create this file and to "officially" incorporate the file into the computer system. How much data is needed to get rid of or delete this file? The following information is required:

- Device and user account name
- Filename

The input to this function is the pathname (i.e., device name, user name, and filename) of the file. Given this information, the BFS can locate and delete the specified file. Note that *unlike EXTEND_FILE, which could work only if the file was opened, the DELETE_FILE function will work only if the file is closed.* This is by convention, but it is reasonable since we would not want to delete a file when someone else was using it.

To delete a file from the system, the following tasks must be performed. Note that these tasks are the mirror image of the CREATE_FILE tasks. Since we are now logically removing a file from the system, we must undo everything that CREATE_FILE did to put the file into the system in the first place.

1. Validate the User's Input Parameters.   As was the case previously, all inputs to the basic file system must be validated for accuracy and completeness.

2. Return All the Space on the Media Taken Up by the File to the Space Pool on the Media.   Recall that when we created, or even extended, the file, we took space out of this pool, and now that we are deleting the file, we are returning the space taken. One of the tasks that the DELETE_FILE processing must do is to return all space freed up from the DELETEd file to some common pool of available space. It is this returning of space to a free-space pool that makes the space available for use by other programs.

3. Remove the File Name from the Directory Where It Resides.   To delete the file, we must remove its name from the directory entry. By so doing, no future scan of the directory will find the deleted file. Thus the purpose of this step is to remove the name of the file from the directory entry. This processing *physically deletes* the file from the disk.

On the other hand, we can *logically delete* the file by setting a flag byte, in the directory entry, to mark the file as having been deleted. Everything else in the directory entry remains valid, however. The major advantage of this approach comes when the file gets deleted by mistake. It is relatively easy to *undelete* the file by simply changing the flag that marked the directory entry as "deleted" to the normal state of being a valid file.

If a file is to be logically undeleted, it must be done immediately after the inadvertent deletion. If it is not done quickly, there is an ever-increasing likelihood that the blocks that belong to the file will be allocated to other users and to other files. At worst, this is a gamble to try and recover from a mistake relatively easily. In the best case, this can almost instantaneously restore a deleted file and avoid hours of work to regenerate the file.

4. Return Status to the User.   What can possibly happen while processing a DELETE_FILE request that could cause the request not to complete successfully? Virtually any of the following errors could occur:

- File could not be found, either because of an invalid file or user account name, or because the file never existed.
- Other users were currently active on the file.
- A hardware problem was detected.

5.5 BASIC FILE SYSTEM INTERFACE: BLOCK OPERATIONS

Block I/O is that part of the BFS interface that READs and WRITEs blocks of data to a device. The file operations just discussed prepared the file for use or stopped the file from being used. Here we discuss how the blocks of data actually get transferred to and from the device.

For each of the block operations to succeed, the user's file must have been prepared for access by the BFS. This means that the file must have just been OPENed or CREATEd. In either case, the file is ready for immediate processing by the user. It should be stated here that the BFS simply READs or WRITEs the blocks requested. *It does not understand the contents of the blocks.*

A block of data is the unit of data that is transferred to, or from, a device. The amount of data (i.e., the size of the block) is definable by the user. The larger the block, the more data that will be transferred in that I/O operation and the greater the performance of the program. This is true but must be taken from the perspective that the memory resources required to hold these blocks of data is not unlimited and should be considered to be a scarce commodity.

The blocks are READ or WRITTEN based on a block number specified by the user. The user specifies an LBN that the file system must convert to an actual physical block number (PBN). This block number is relative to the beginning of this specific file. Thus we have blocks 1, 23 and 799 within a given file. The calculation of how these logical block numbers get translated from a logical number to a physical block number is done within the BFS and is invisible to the user.

5.5.1 WRITE_BLOCK Request

The purpose of the WRITE_BLOCK function is to provide users with the capability of transferring data out of the computer's main memory and onto one of the devices connected to the system. The unit of data that gets read or written is called a block. The block can be of any size defined by the user. As a rule, the larger the block, the better the overall performance, but within the resource constraint that the main memory is available for general usage.

The information required by the BFS to successfully process a WRITE_BLOCK request consists of the following data:

- Number of the block to be written
- Address of the I/O buffer in main memory that contains the block to be written
- Size or amount of the block to be written
- Name of the status field into which the file system will insert the termination status of the I/O request

Since the BFS is simply a service routine, it will do what it is told to do by the user. Therefore, if these parameters are found to be valid, it is required that the BFS process the requested output operation.

The WRITE_BLOCK routine must perform the following tasks as part of the job of processing the request (see Figure 5–6):

1. Validate the input parameters.
2. Convert the logical block number to a physical device address.
3. Check if space exists in the file for this block.
4. If space exists, go to step 6.
5. If space does not exist in the file, extend the file. This is called an *implicit extend* of the file, since it is being done on behalf of the user and not because of an *explicit* user request.
6. Execute the WRITE_BLOCK I/O operation to the device.

   Reset the *buffer-modified* flag for that specific I/O buffer, since that block has now been written out to the device.

   When the requested I/O operation has completed, the basic file system must return the status of the just-completed I/O operation to the user's program.

This situation will most often occur when the entire file is not preallocated, and thus when the user wishes to write a particular block of data, the BFS has to check if the block exists in the file. If it does, the BFS will write out the block from

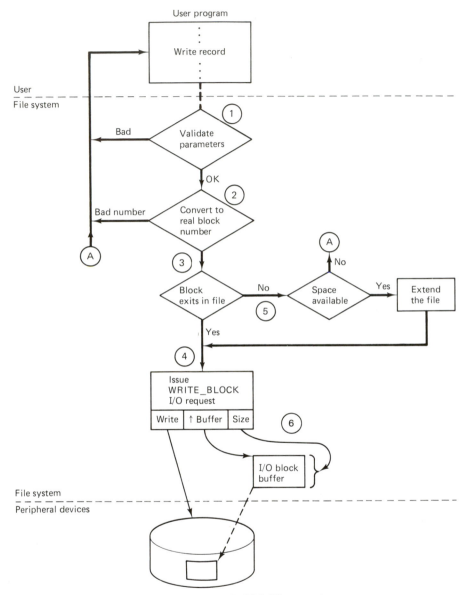

Figure 5-6 WRITE_BLOCK processing.

main memory to the device itself. On the other hand, if the block does not exist in the file, the block must be allocated. Thus the BFS must go through the space allocation process to add more space to the file.

Following are some of the errors that can occur while performing a WRITE_BLOCK operation:

- No space available for the operation to complete
- Hardware unrecoverable error has occurred
- Mismatch from READ after WRITE validation sequence

5.5.2 READ_BLOCK Request

The function of the READ_BLOCK routine is to transfer a specific block of data from the medium into main memory. Again, the unit of data transfer is the block. The information required to process the read request is as follows:

- Number of the block to be read into memory
- Address of the I/O block buffer in main memory into which the block will be read
- Size or amount of data to be read into main memory
- The address of a field into which the file system can store the status of the I/O request

The READ_BLOCK request performs exactly the opposite function to that of the WRITE_BLOCK request. This function is the means that users have at their disposal to transfer data blocks into main memory from a peripheral device. The steps required to perform this operation are as follows (see Figure 5–7):

1. Validate Input Parameters.   This step is always required to ensure that only valid requests get processed by any component of the file system.

2. Convert the Logical Block Number to a Physical Block.   This conversion is needed to allow the users of the basic file system to work with block numbers that are relative to the first block in a file. Since the basic file system can read a file's allocation definition, it is always possible for it to convert any logical block number into a specific physical block number on the device.

3. Read the Block into an I/O Buffer in Main Memory.   Once the block is found, read it into main memory.

4. Return Status to the User Program.   The only requirement on the block number parameter is that the block already exist in the file. If it does not currently exist, the block obviously cannot be read, and thus the user must be told that the block requested is invalid because it does not exist in the file. Otherwise, if the block existed, the user would be told that all was successful.

Some of the possible errors that can be encountered on READ_BLOCK operations are as follows:

- Read error detected by the device
- Invalid device block number requested
- Hardware failure detected

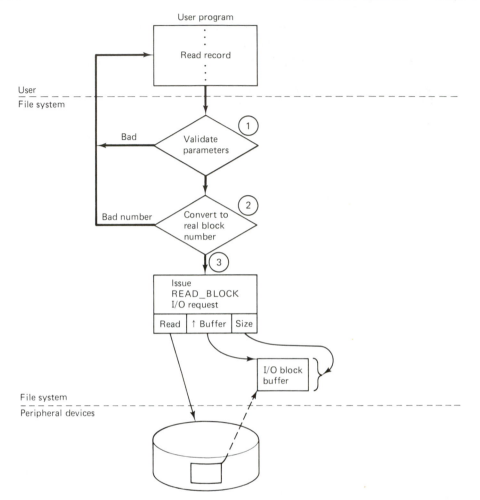

Figure 5-7   READ_BLOCK processing.

5.6 DATA FLOW

The basic file system is concerned with the transmission of data between the device and main memory (see Figure 5-8). Thus, when the user program makes a request to read or write a data *record,* it gets translated by the file system into READ_BLOCK or WRITE_BLOCK commands (step 1). If the user is writing a record, that data record is then copied by the access method from the user's record buffer into the I/O block buffer (step 2). Then the block I/O request is translated by the device driver into a specific sequence of device commands that will cause the target block to be accessed (step 3). If the user was reading a record, the target block is read from the disk and into an I/O buffer in main memory (step 4). The access method then locates

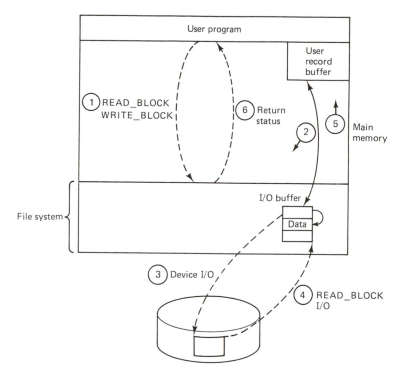

Figure 5-8 Data flow.

the record in the block and copies it back into the user's record buffer (step 5). In any case, when the operation has been completed, the user is given the completion status of the request (step 6). This information tells the user program whether or not the request was successful, and how much data was actually copied into the user's record buffer.

In summary, all blocks to be written out to a device are copied from an I/O buffer in main memory to the device. On read requests, the desired block is transferred from the device into an I/O buffer in main memory. What is important to understand is that the basic file system provides only the data transfer service to other users in the system. It does not understand any of the contents of the blocks it transfers.

5.7 PERFORMANCE CONSIDERATIONS

Since the basic file system is the lowest-level interface to the devices, how it performs its job can dramatically affect the overall performance of the system. For example, studies have been made which have shown that two-thirds of all I/O operations are *read* requests [4]. Therefore, a file system can improve performance most if it can figure out how to buffer the data blocks in such a way as to cut down on the *actual* number of I/O READ__BLOCK requests. In the chapters on disks and tapes as well as the following chapters, we discuss the performance criteria and attributes that must be considered when designing a file system.

5.8 IMPLEMENTATION REQUIREMENTS

Besides the DCT, which has been discussed in previous chapters, we now have need for an additional control structure called the file control block (FCB) (see Table 5–1). The purpose of the FCB is to hold all the information that relates to the file being processed. The FCB contains such information as:

- ID of the job being processed
- Filename
- File attributes defined when the file was created, as well as processing attributes that have changed since the file has been accessed (e.g., logical end-of-file marker)
- Address of the I/O buffer control table
- Address of the associated DCT

TABLE 5–1   FILE CONTROL BLOCK (FCB)

Header information	
Version ID	
Link to next FCB	
Status	
User information	
Job ID	Identification of job that is accessing this file (copied from UICB)
File information	
Volume name	Name of disk or tape on which this file resides
Volume sequence number	ID of the volume of the file that is currently mounted (tape only)
File name	User's name for this file
File size	Number of blocks, sectors, and so on
Physical end-of-file (PEOF)	Location of last block allocated to this file
Allocation type	Contiguous Noncontiguous Contiguous, if possible
Next block to allocate	The next free (i.e., unallocated) block in the file
Cluster size	Amount of space the file is to be extended whenever needed (in blocks, sectors, or tracks)

TABLE 5-1   (Cont.)

File information (cont.)

File organization	Sequential
	Relative
	Direct
	ISAM
	Indexed
	VSAM
	Multikey indexed
Block format	Fixed-length blocks
	Variable-length blocks
Maximum block size	Size of largest block in the file, also size of each of the I/O buffers (in bytes)
File status	File NOT open (i.e., closed)
	File currently open
Block count	Number of blocks written to or read from the file (tape only)

Record Information

Record format	Fixed-length records
	Variable-length records
	Undefined record format
Maximum record size	If FLR, this is size of every record in the file
	If VLR, this is size of the largest possible record in the file

Access-method-specific information

Logical end-of-file (LEOF)	Location of last data record written into this file

File system internal information

Address of IOBCT	Pointer to linked list of IOBCTs; set when file is first opened
Address of DCT	Link to DCT for the device on which this file resides

File-processing statistics

By referring to Figure 5–9, we can see how the basic file system ties together the control tables and I/O buffers which have been discussed previously. First (step 1), there is one file control block for each file currently OPEN in the system. In addition, there is one device control table (step 2) for every device in the system. The DCT also points to the queue of I/O requests that are waiting to be executed. This queue is known as the I/O request queue (IORQ) (step 3).

Associated with each device is the file structure on the device itself (step 4). This structure on disk consists of the allocation table and the system directory of files. This allows the basic file system to allocate space on the medium as well as

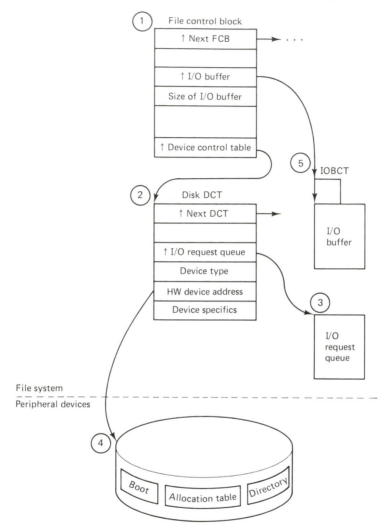

Figure 5-9 Control and file structures.

to locate files created earlier.

Finally, there are the I/O buffers (step 5) into or from which all data are transferred. These block buffers are, in turn, controlled by the I/O buffer control table (IOBCT) (see Figure 5–10 and Table 5–2). The IOBCT contains information that describes the current state and content of a specific I/O buffer. Thus there is one IOBCT per I/O buffer in the system, and it contains such information as the following:

- The *physical* and *logical* block numbers currently in the buffer, if any
- Address and size of the I/O buffer itself
- Flags that help the file system manage the I/O buffer

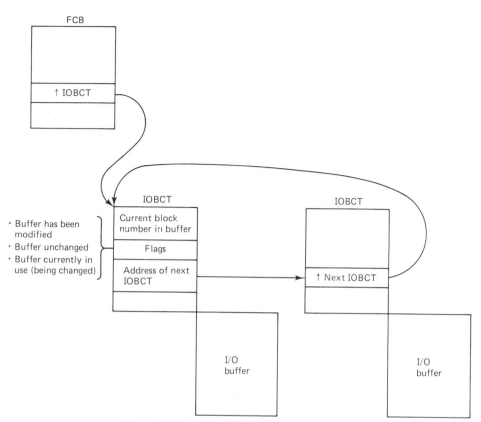

Figure 5–10 I/O buffer control table (IOBCT).

TABLE 5-2 I/O BUFFER CONTROL TABLE (IOBCT)

Header information

Version ID	Identifies which format this IOBCT conforms with; also allows for future expansion
Link to next IOBCT	All IOBCTs are kept in a linked list

Unique block identification

Device ID	Name of the device on which the block resides
Physical block number (PBN)	Actual physical location on the device of the block in the I/O buffer
Logical block number (LBN)	Number of block currently in the I/O buffer

Buffer information

Flags	Buffer is currently empty Block in buffer has been modified
Address of I/O buffer	Location in main memory of the I/O buffer into which the block will be read, or written
Buffer size	Length, in bytes, of the I/O buffer.

The management of these buffers is discussed in subsequent chapters. However, it is important to understand that all the control tables, I/O buffers, and so on, which the file system uses are linked together so that all the data can be used appropriately.

5.9 SUMMARY

In this chapter we have been introduced to the concept of a file system really consisting of several discrete components. The basic file system component serves as the primary interface with the external world of the peripheral devices. As such, its functionality was also discussed.

An important part of this chapter dealt with the processing steps that are required to perform very specific tasks, such as to read or write a block of data. This is critical, not because the steps must be cast in concrete, but to understand the impact of I/O operations on system performance. To do this, it is necessary to understand what the basic file system must do to completely process its requests.

KEY WORDS

Access methods
Basic file system (BFS)
Block operations
CLOSE_FILE
CREATE_FILE
Defaults
DELETE_FILE

EXTEND_FILE
File control block (FCB)
File operations
I/O buffers
I/O buffer control table (IOBCT)
I/O request queue (IORQ)
OPEN_FILE
READ_BLOCK
WRITE_BLOCK

SUPPLEMENTAL REFERENCES

1. Claybrook, Billy G., *File Management Techniques*. New York: John Wiley & Sons, Inc., 1983, Chap. 6. This book provides a rather detailed discussion of file system functionality, complete with tables and control block definitions.

2. Deitel, Harvey M., *An Introduction to Operating Systems*. Reading, Mass.: Addison-Wesley Publishing Company, Inc., 1984, Chap. 13. This is highly recommended reading. It discusses file systems from the point of view of their being integrated into an overall operating system environment.

3. Freeman, Donald E., and Olney R. Perry, *I/O DESIGN: Data Management in Operating Systems*. Rochelle Park, N.J.: Hayden Book Company, Inc., 1977, Chaps. 5–8. This

is another recommended reading. This book covers I/O control statements, device allocation, opening and closing files, and access methods from a different perspective.

4. Krastins, Uldis, "Cache Memory Quickens Access to Disk Data." *Electronic Design,* May 13, 1982, pp. 77–80. This is a short article on disk performance improvements that can come from caching the disk blocks.

5. Reece, Peter, "A Disk Operating System for FORTH." *BYTE,* April 1982, p. 322. This is a highly recommended reading. It is written from the perspective of designing and implementing an operating system. However, it does an excellent job of describing the file system that must be included in the operating system and how it might be implemented. It is also easy to read and understand.

6. Wiederhold, Gio, *Database Design.* New York: McGraw-Hill Book Company, 1977. This book discusses the functionality and performance aspects of file systems. It is very good on the critical performance issues that must be considered in the design of any file system.

EXERCISES

1. Select a high-level language of your choice (e.g., Pascal, COBOL, FORTRAN), and map the I/O capabilities that are provided into the file system functionality discussed in this chapter. Also describe the information that the language can provide the BFS from user-specified information.

2. Why is it important to *force* all users who want to perform I/O to go through the standard basic file system interface? Explain the advantages and disadvantages of doing this.

3. Assume that a user program attempts to open a file that does not exist. The file system *could* simply reject the request as an error, or the basic file system could just go ahead and create the file, under the assumption that if it did not exist, the user really wanted it created. Discuss the the benefits and drawbacks of each of these approaches.

4. Is it *really* necessary for a file to be open to explicitly extend the file, or is it simply a convenience for the file system to require this?

5. What would happen if two users tried to create a new file at the same identical time and in the same directory? Would the steps listed in the CREATE__FILE section be sufficient, or should the file system be concerned about processing for multiple users? What would/could happen to the directory or device allocation table in this case? What changes would you recommend?

6. Is it better for a user to have a file extended *explicitly* or *implicitly?* In your answer, consider the effects of cluster size, contiguity of the file, and performance.

7. The basic file system performs block I/O on behalf of all users. Is it necessary for the file system to know the *content* of the blocks it reads and writes? Explain why or why not.

8. Should the file system provide default values for fields not specified by the user, or should the request simply be rejected? Justify your answer.

9. If you were designing a file system and you could choose only one *delete* option (i.e., logical or physical deletes but not both), which would you choose? Why?

10. When a file is being created, should the file system complete the CREATE if all the file disk space requested by the user is not available? Justify your answer.

11. List five possible error conditions other than those discussed in the text that the file system should be able to detect and handle for the CREATE__FILE function.

12. Should a file system be able to explicitly detect and process all possible error conditions, or should it consolidate groups of similar errors into specific categories which it will then handle? Discuss the trade-offs in doing it both ways.

PROGRAMMING EXERCISES

1. Design and implement a disk directory structure and allocation system which emphasizes performance over the use of disk space. What changes would you make in your design if space utilization were the critical concern?

2. Given the solution to Programming Exercise 1, design an algorithm to allow a user to UNDELETE a file that has just been erased accidentally.

6

Basic I/O Supervisor

CHAPTER OBJECTIVES

When you complete this chapter, you will be able to:

- Understand how I/O requests are queued for a device
- Understand the key role of the job scheduler
- Understand the role of the resource manager relative to I/O
- Describe the concepts and functions of device drivers
- Understand I/O initiation and I/O termination processing

6.1 OVERVIEW

The basic I/O supervisor is the glue that ties together all the components of the file system and makes the system work (see Figure 6-0). As such, it is usually buried inside an operating system and is not clearly linked with the rest of the processing that the file system performs. Be that as it may, we separate out this component to make the overall I/O processing more complete and understandable.

Fundamentally, *the basic I/O supervisor is that component of the basic file system that is responsible for all I/O initiation and termination processing*. To accomplish this task, we need to develop several new control structures. In addition, we will need to link into the resident operating system as well as have an intimate knowledge of how the I/O portion of the computer works.

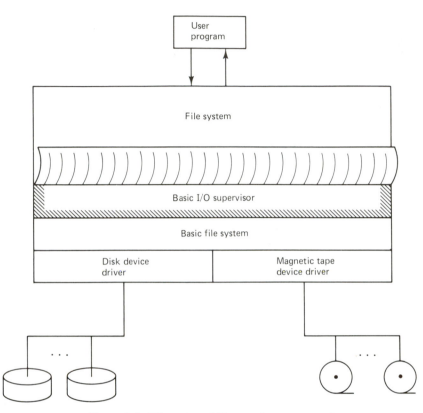

Figure 6-0   File system: I/O supervisor component.

6.2 BASIC FILE SYSTEM SUPPORT FUNCTIONS

Up to this point, we have discussed primarily the purpose and the function calls of a basic file system. In the process, we have skirted several key operational issues that are required to make it work correctly, such as:

- How is it determined which jobs get to run on the computer at any given time? This, in turn, affects how the devices on the system get allocated across all users.

- Since the BFS only reads and writes blocks, what piece of software exists that really understands how to get the devices to work correctly?

- How can a user request a specific device for a job being submitted?

- How is the space on the various media (e.g., disks) allocated among all the potential users on the system, and who ensures that no two users will ever be allocated the same space?

- The basic file system transfers data into and out of memory by utilizing main memory allocated as "I/O buffers." Where do these buffers come from, and how are they managed?

The answers to each of these questions resides in some piece of software that lies on the borderline between basic file system and operating system software. Since these routines are directly involved in making the I/O system work correctly, we will classify these software modules as low-level basic file system routines.

6.2.1 Job Scheduler

The function of a job scheduler is to select the next user or user job that can run on the computer. Although this is technically an operating system function, its impact on the BFS is such that we must discuss this routine. As part of the process of determining which job to run next, the scheduler must identify all, or as many as possible, of the resources that will be needed by each job. The resources used will usually consist of main memory, files, and devices such as disks and card readers or printers. If the resources required to successfully run the job are not available, the scheduler cannot, and will not, start that job.

The job scheduler gets its needed information (see Figure 6–1) from the program itself (a), the job control language (b) supplied with the program, operator commands (c) issued by the user, or by simply defaulting (d) to predetermined assumptions if all the data are not available.

Once the job scheduler knows all the requirements a user's job has in order to run, it can scan the job queue (e) looking for the next *possible* job that can be run. When it has made its selection, the scheduler will turn control of the CPU over to that job at the next opportunity to start a job. For example, it could be at the next time slice or when the current job stops when performing an I/O performing.

The role of a job scheduler has meaning only in a multiuser system. Most personal computers and workstations can run only one job at a time, although they can support multitasking. Thus whoever is currently running on the system "owns" everything in the system.

The job of the scheduler is to determine which jobs in the input queue of possible jobs *can* run. Thus the scheduler must perform the following tasks:

- Identify and allocate all needed resources for the entire job (e.g., main memory, devices).
- Set the priority of the job, based on key parameters, such as user-defined priority, CPU versus I/O-intensive jobs, or time scheduled to complete the job.
- Start the job.

The scheduler must ensure that all jobs having the necessary resources to run are indeed running on the system. Even though on most systems only one job can be executing or using the CPU at any time, it is up to the job scheduler to switch the CPU resource between the jobs that can run. This is called multiprogramming, or timesharing and results in multiple jobs sharing a single resource (i.e., the CPU) by rotating its use among the available jobs. Thus, based on the mix of jobs to be run, the scheduler always tries to ensure optimal use of the resources in the system. Next, let us discuss how some of the most critical resources in the system are managed.

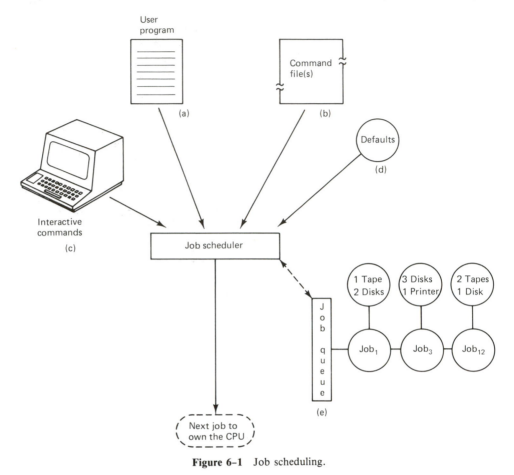

Figure 6-1 Job scheduling.

6.2.2 Resource Management: Main Memory

One of the most important resources within any computer system is the main memory in the machine. This is critical to the overall performance and throughput in the system because the amount of main memory is usually in short supply (i.e., more main memory is always needed than one actually has). While memory management, as this is frequently called, is part of the function of an operating system, we are concerned about that piece of memory management that relates to how memory gets allocated for I/O buffers and internal control information needed to perform I/O operations in an effective and efficient manner.

Most of the memory required by a file system is for the purpose of reading and writing blocks of data when requested by any user. Note that the term *user* can be the user, the user's application, or any other portion of the system software that needs to perform I/O operations. In other words, the user is that program which interfaces with the file system. For example, if we had a virtual memory operating system, the operating system itself would need to perform a large number of I/O operations to simulate a "larger" main-memory space available to a particular user or set of users. Specifically, the file system needs the following main memory allocated:

- I/O buffers in which to perform all I/O requests.
- I/O table space, into which we will allocate the control blocks discussed earlier. These tables contain all the information that the file system needs to keep track of to successfully process I/O requests.

What differentiates memory used for I/O purposes from all other memory? It is that the main memory I/O buffers must always be resident within the machine itself for the duration of the I/O operation. This is because when a device begins to transmit data into an I/O buffer, for example, it is impossible to stop the flow of data so that the operating system has enough time to get more memory. This typically occurs with programs in virtual memory or paging operating systems. *The key point is that the memory used for an I/O operation must be resident in the machine for the duration of the operation, regardless of how the rest of memory within the machine is managed.*

The main memory used for user control blocks, such as the FCB, does not need to be permanently in main memory. It just needs to be resident when that user is attempting to perform an I/O operation. On the other hand, the file system control blocks, such as the IORB, IOBCT, or DCTs, *must be memory resident* at all times. This is because these structures are used to manage all of the resources in the system (see Figure 6–2).

6.2.3 Resource Management: Devices

The second major resource that must be managed and controlled is the allocation of the peripheral devices attached to the computer. For example, an installation could have a system consisting of a CPU, main memory, card readers and punches, printers, disks, tapes, and supermarket optical scanners. *It is the job of the device resource manager to allocate or assign the devices to particular users.* This implies that the device resource manager must keep track of what every user "owns" and wants. When the job scheduler decides to run a job, it is the device resource manager that determines if the requested devices are available or whether they are being used by some other user.

The major point here is that there are software routines whose job it is to ensure that all the system resources are properly allocated, deallocated, and controlled. Next, it is important to understand that not all devices are created equal. Specifically, some devices can have only one user utilizing the device at a time. Examples of this type of device are card readers and printers. We do not want our listing or report to be intermixed with lines from someone else's reports. *These kinds of devices are said to be nonshared, or owned exclusively.* On the other hand, there are devices that multiple users can access "simultaneously." The primary example of this kind of device is a disk. *Devices that can support more than one user at a time are called shared devices.*

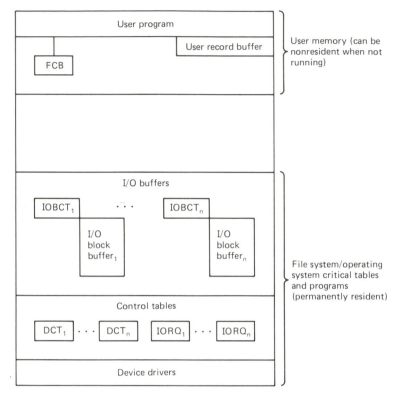

Figure 6-2   Main-memory utilization.

The distinction between shared and nonshared devices is important because a disk could have a hundred users simultaneously, each of whom believes that he or she owns the machine exclusively. For nonshared devices, the job scheduler must defer the allocation and running of a job until all devices are available. This could result in rather lengthy delays in the actual running of those jobs.

Finally, although we have implied it previously, the device resource manager must also know every device connected to the computer system. Then all devices can be properly allocated to the users of the system. This knowledge of all the devices that need to be managed usually comes from a procedure known as system generation. This procedure is run just after the hardware is installed. System generation is a software program that builds the necessary device and other resource configuration tables that will later be used by the file system and the resource manager. Thus, after a system generation, the resource manager will know every device connected to the system.

6.3 DEVICE DRIVERS

The role that device drivers play in any system is one of knowing precisely how to control and run every device connected to the system. This means that there is one device driver routine for every unique device type within the computer system (e.g., tapes, disks). It is the responsibility of the device drivers to ensure that I/O is performed correctly and efficiently. In addition, should an error occur, it is their responsibility to try and recover from the error.

The tasks performed by device drivers can be broken down into two rather distinct categories, that of starting I/O operations on a device (i.e., I/O initiation) and that of processing the completion of each I/O request (i.e., I/O termination) We discuss each of these in much more detail in the following sections. To perform this task, the *device drivers* must maintain I/O processing information in the device control table (DCT). This information must be maintained for each device in the system. The information saved can be described as follows:

- Status field
- I/O request type (i.e., read/write)
- Device-specific characteristics

6.4 I/O REQUEST QUEUEING

We can now write a program to command the device to do something for us. However, we have yet to discuss how to tell the device: ''Here's the I/O program, start executing it.'' This is where the true connection between the CPU and the external I/O devices takes place. Somehow we need to be able to execute an instruction that tells the device, and not the CPU, to start working.

On virtually every computer there is at least one such instruction that allows us to cross the line between the CPU and the peripheral devices from within a software program. On the large IBM machines it is the *Start I/O* (SIO) instruction. No matter what its name may be, its function is to take the I/O program or command and tell the device to begin its execution (refer to Figure 6-3).

In reality, however, we can start our I/O request only if there are no other requests from other users ahead of us. Typically, microcomputers have been single-user machines. Thus there can only be one I/O operation at any time. On the other hand, on more powerful micros, superminis, and mainframe computers, multiple users can be running on the machine at the same time. In these cases, the standard file system will act as the funnel to the various devices and will queue all incoming requests until the current requests complete.

There is typically one I/O request queue for each device connected into the sytem. In addition, there are several algorithms for queueing I/O requests. The algorithm chosen depends on the device type and the requirements for system throughput.

6.4.1 FIFO I/O Request Queues

In FIFO queues, *each incoming I/O request is inserted at the end of the queue of I/O requests*. When the current I/O operation for that specific device terminates, the *first* entry in the related I/O request queue is selected and initiated.

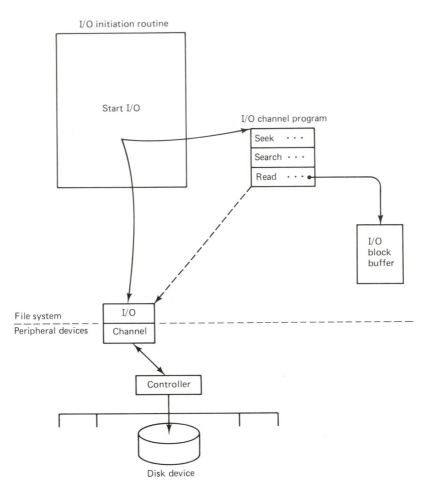

Figure 6-3 I/O channel program initiation.

In FIFO queues, all I/O requests are treated equally. There are no priorities or other techniques used to reorder the entries. The drawback to this algorithm is that if a high-priority event occurs, it cannot be processed until all I/O requests ahead of it in the queue have completed execution. Conversely, it gives every I/O request an equal chance to be executed.

6.4.2 Priority-Based I/O Request Queues

Here we add the concept of *job priority* into the queueing algorithm. The idea here is that there can be jobs running in the system that are more or less important than other jobs currently in the system. When a higher-priority job issues an I/O request, it should be executed ahead of any queued I/O requests of lower-priority programs.

The algorithm for doing this consists of a minor modification to the FIFO algorithm. Within any specific priority level, we have a FIFO queue. However, there are multiple priority levels supported in the queue.

150

The benefit of this technique is to differentiate between normal and critical jobs and thus give preference to the more important jobs. Conversely, a low-priority job is one that can run anytime there is CPU time available. For example, we could have a large-print job that we want done, but we only care that it is done by tomorrow. In this case, it will typically be run at night when there are no priority jobs in the system.

6.4.3 Device-Specific Queueing

For some devices, usually disks, there are other algorithms that attempt to make better use of the device (see Section 4.8). What is important to understand here is that it is possible to design a queueing algorithm that takes advantage of the mechanics of the device itself. Thus we can achieve a higher level of throughput on that device.

6.5 I/O INITIATION

Whenever a device is idle, the file system selects from the I/O request queue, the next request for that specific device and starts it execution. This sequence of events is known as I/O initiation (see Figure 6–4a) and consists of the following steps:

1. *Dequeue the next I/O request.* This selection will be based on the queueing algorithm implemented for the specific device type.
2. *Initiate the I/O request* on the appropriate device.

The I/O initiation routine dequeues an I/O request and initiates its execution on a device. This is because the I/O initiation routines are invoked only to start I/O operations. It is the responsibility of the I/O termination routines to determine that a device is now idle and thus I/O initiation can be called. Thus the I/O initiation and termination routines work hand in hand to keep a device working as much as possible. This increases the throughput of the device, and since I/O tends to be a system bottleneck, it also improves overall system throughput.

6.6 I/O TERMINATION PROCESSING

Now that we have successfully started an I/O request executing on a device, how can we tell when the I/O request has completed? How can the file system know when it can start that *next* I/O request against that device?

Over the course of the industry's history, many techniques have been used to accomplish this. For example, on some older computers, the file system software had to *poll* or request status from the device by effectively asking "Are you still busy?" questions. This status request is made repeatedly until the device responds "Not busy." Then the file system knows that the device has completed its work and is sitting idle

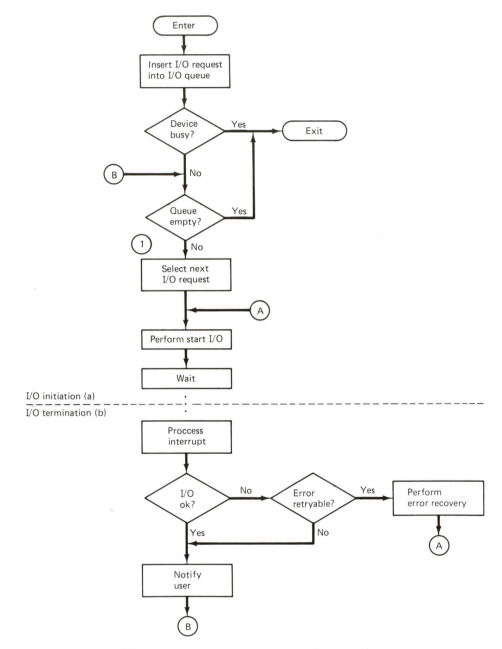

Figure 6-4 I/O initiation and termination processing.

waiting for the next I/O request to be submitted. The major disadvantage of this approach is that the file system had to spend much time polling for the device status when the same CP cycles could have been utilized more productively by user programs.

Eventually, the concept of *interrupts* was implemented on most machines. An interrupt is just what its name implies: namely, it interrupts (i.e., suspends) the currently executing program. It then calls the *interrupt handler* whose job it is to process the device interrupts.

To better understand the concept of an interrupt, let us use the telephone as an example. It would be silly for us to stop what we are doing every 5 minutes or so to run to the telephone to see if anyone is on the line. We need to know immediately when someone is calling us. How can this be accomplished?

The telephone rings loud and clear. The purpose of the ring is to *interrupt* us from what we were doing and force us to respond to the phone. We "process" the phone call by talking to the person on the other end of the line. We then hang up the phone when the conversation has completed. We have two choices. We can return to what we had been doing before the phone call, or we can go off and do a higher-priority activity that arose as a result of our telephone conversation.

In a similar manner, devices and interrupts to the system that interrupt the currently executing job. The file system then determines what the interrupt is for and processes it. Finally, the file system returns control to the job scheduler, whose job it is to determine the next task to execute. That task may be the job that was interrupted by the device, or it could be another job that has higher priority.

The function of the file system I/O termination routine is to perform the following tasks for all system and user programs that may be running on the machine (refer to Figure 6–4b):

1. Detect that an interrupt has arrived.
2. Determine which device sent the interrupt so that we can relate the interrupt to a specific I/O request.
3. Determine what kind of interrupt it is (i.e., is it a solicited or an unsolicited interrupt?)
4. Process the interrupt accordingly.
5. If error conditions were detected, perform the most appropriate form of error recovery.
6. Return the appropriate completion status of the I/O operation to the user's program via the file system interface.
7. Call the I/O initiation routines to select the next I/O request from the I/O request queue for this specific device and then initiate it.
8. Call the job scheduler to resume execution of the highest-priority program waiting to be executed. This may or may not be the job that was just interrupted.

As can be seen from this list, the amount of time this task can consume could be significant. This is one of the reasons for always trying to minimize the actual number of I/O requests that get made. We shall see in later chapters how we can accomplish this objective.

6.7 INTERRUPT HANDLING

An I/O interrupt notifies the file system when an I/O request has completed and therefore the file system no longer needs to probe the device for completion status. This not only saves time but also increases performance by freeing CP cycles that would normally have been spent probing a device for the status of completion, and returns these cycles to the user programs.

An I/O interrupt from a device provides two pieces of information to the interrupt handler. *First, it identifies the device that sent the interrupt.* This is needed to relate the interrupt to a specific device queue and thus to the job that requested the I/O operation.

Second, the interrupt returns data known as status information. These data tell the interrupt handler all the details regarding why the interrupt was sent. For example, a READ operation could have just successfully completed. On the other hand, it can tell the interrupt handler that an error has occurred. Here, the interrupt handler will have to examine all the status bytes to determine what the problem is and what can be done about it.

A signal sent as a result of an executing I/O channel program is called a *solicited interupt.* This is because we implicitly requested it by starting a channel program. However, there are occasions in which the file system will be interrupted that do not relate to an executing I/O request. These *unsolicited interrupts are called attention interrupts.* Both solicited (i.e., from an executing I/O request) and unsolicited interrupts must be processed completely by the file system.

6.7.1 Successful I/O

The completion of the execution of every I/O channel program or command is signaled by an interrupt. Not only does the interrupt signal error conditions, it also tells when all went well. The vast majority of I/O requests are completed successfully. Therefore, the interrupt handling is straightforward and fairly fast. For example, the processing steps for this condition are as follows:

1. Check that I/O was successful.
2. Determine from the interrupt information which device just had the successful completion.
3. Notify the calling program which requested this I/O that its request was successful.
4. Dequeue the next I/O request from that device's I/O request queue and initiate it.
5. Return to the *waiting* state until the next interrupt comes in and this routine is reawakened to process it.

If the control tables are setup to allow this module to quickly determine the device, IORQ, and requesting program, the time to process a successful I/O interrupt can be very brief. This is also one of the reasons that some information is duplicated in various tables—so that the number of references required to make decisions can be improved.

6.7.2 Exception Handling

If the user's I/O operation terminates unsuccessfully, it is up to the file system to determine the error condition. Also, it must try and recover from the failure. Recall that one of our early premises was that the file system should do whatever is necessary to try to successfully read or write the desired blocks (i.e., get the user's I/O request to succeed).

The basic file system must distinguish between normal error conditions and unexpected error events. Normal errors include such events as end-of-file and beginning-of-tape reached on a rewind. Unexpected events include all conditions in which the requested operation fails. For example, there could have been a READ error detected because of dirt on a tape, or a device was not powered-on (i.e., hardware failures).

Typically, more retries are performed when there is a failure in *reading* a data record than when a *write* operation fails. This is reasonable since one objective is to try and never lose data, and an inability to read data is equivalent to losing it. Alternatively, the file system should not try too hard to recover from a Write request. This is because the error could be an indication that the device, or medium, is truly failing. Therefore, the file system should avoid knowingly writing data records on a device or medium that is of questionable quality and reliability.

We cannot always detect errors when they occur during WRITE operations. However, there are techniques that can be tried. For example, we could perform a READ after a WRITE to verify that the WRITE operation wrote a record that can be read back. However, this slows down the execution of the job because of the additional I/O involved.

Alternatively, we can change the medium (i.e., replace the disk or tape itself). However, if we lose data, we will have a severe problem. To put this into proper perspective, suppose that the system could not read a record, and that record contained the data required to allow us to get paid. What if the error occurred on your payroll record?

An important part of exception processing is that the file system should take the time to record the relevant error statistics in a standard "error log" file within the system. Every piece of information that could be of use in the future should be recorded, since the data cannot be reconstructed later. However, the recording of this information takes time and will thus affect system performance. For example, the error data that should be maintained could include at a minimum the following items:

• The *identification of the device* on which the error occurred

- The *identification of the volume* that was installed in the device at the time of the error
- The *entire channel program or I/O operation that failed*
- All *error status* returned by the device and controller via the I/O termination interrupt
- The *number and type of retries performed,* including whether or not the retries were successful

The usefulness of these data will arise as part of the computer maintenance or preventive maintenance programs. If the service person can print out the error history of the devices in the system, preventive maintenance can be performed on the devices *before* they break down completely.

If a particular medium volume has had numerous errors, the files can be copied to another volume to minimize future errors due to media problems. The data recorded in the error log file can be invaluable in aiding the ongoing maintenance program of the machine. They can also be used as an indicator of which vendor products are reliable and which are not.

There are two kinds of solicited errors that can occur in day-to-day operations, unrecoverable errors and recoverable errors.

6.7.3 Hardware Unrecoverable Errors

These error conditions are, exactly as the name implies, unrecoverable. When the I/O interrupt status is sent into the file system, it may indicate that an unrecoverable hardware error has occurred. In these cases, there is little that can be done, short of shifting to another device or system. The file system must notify the user program that an unrecoverable error has occurred. Obviously, no more I/O requests should be initiated against this device until the error condition has been corrected. Finally, these kinds of errors should be written out into the system error log file.

6.7.4 Recoverable Errors

When the device error status indicates that the error condition was not due to a fatal hardware problem, some kind of error recovery can be performed. *Error recovery consists of the file system attempting to retry the failing I/O request in the hope that within the next n retries the request might succeed.* This would allow the user's program to continue, and possibly complete successfully, rather than aborting early due to an error.

The general error recovery processing steps are as follows:

1. Reposition the Media.   This step repositions the media to the same file block location that existed prior to the failing I/O request. This is required in order that we can retry the I/O operation that failed.

2. Retry the I/O Request.   Once we reposition, we can retry the entire user I/O request. Sometimes, simply retrying the operation can remove stray dirt or debris, and the I/O request can then succeed. Also, there are times when transient errors will arise that cannot be duplicated. Retrying may also get around these errors.

The number and kinds of retries that should be attempted are device specific and were discussed in Chapters 3 (i.e., tapes) and 4 (i.e., disks). However, all recovery attempts have a limited number of retries to balance the time it takes to perform a retry against the probability of success. Thus most retry sequences will have a limit of 10 to 20 retries before the file system gives up and classifies the error as being unrecoverable.

A second characteristic of recovery relates to how "intelligent" the device and its controller really are. Some devices can detect errors and send only those data to the file system. Other, more intelligent devices can actually attempt error recovery themselves, either by retrying the I/O operation or by correcting single-bit data errors on the fly. The file system must understand which kinds of devices and controllers it is dealing with so as not to replicate any portion of the recovery sequence.

3. Return Status to the User.   No matter what happens, the program that made the I/O request must be notified when the I/O request, and all its associated error recovery processing, has completed. If the recovery actions were successful, the user need only be told that the request was successful. The user does not need to know that error recovery was performed as part of processing the request. The file system needs to know and record the data in the system log file, but these data are of no use to a user's program. If error recovery fails, the user must be notified. Then it is up to the user's program to decide whether it can continue or whether it must abort.

6.7.5 Attention Processing

Attention interrupts are sent by the device or controller to notify the file system that something unrelated to an I/O request has occurred within the system. Attention interrupts from devices signal the file system software that, for example:

- A device has just been powered-on and is now available to be allocated and used.
- A device has just had a new volume mounted on it, and the device is now available to be used.
- A device has just been powered-off and will be unavailable for further use.
- The user just hit the "break" key.

In each of these cases, the device made a transition from a state of readiness to being unavailable, or vice versa. Thus attention interrupts signal the software about all device state transitions that occur within a system configuration. This is useful to the device resource manager, because this is the only way in which it can tell how many devices are connected and available to be used and which ones are not available.

An attention interrupt does not result in status being sent to a user's program. This is because a user program is concerned only with I/O operations and the resulting interrupts that are issued by the program itself. Since attention interrupts occur independently of I/O requests, no status information needs to be returned to any user's programs.

6.8 PERFORMANCE CONSIDERATIONS

The performance of the basic I/O supervisor is critical to the overall throughput and responsiveness of every computer system. The primary reason for this is that most systems are constrained by I/O (i.e., they are I/O bound). In other words, there are usually enough compute cycles available to process all the jobs. However, the jobs end up spending most of their time sitting idle while waiting for their I/O operations to complete.

What can be done? There is nothing that can be done about the devices themselves since they are mechanical in nature. New devices may come along, but relative to the performance of the CPU, devices will always be "slow." Thus it falls onto the file system software to perform efficiently and effectively under all circumstances.

What are the critical performance areas within the basic I/O supervisor? Fundamentally, there are the following three key areas in which performance must be measured.

I/O Initiation.   Since the device is sitting idle waiting for the next I/O request, the faster this component can dequeue a request and send it to the device, the less idle the time device will have. Therefore, a larger percentage of the device's operational time will be spent actually processing I/O operations, and thus the device will achieve higher levels of throughput.

Critical to this processing is the ability to scan an I/O request queue rapidly and to make a quick determination as to what the next request to select should be. The real objective here is to minimize the idle time of the device, not to make the most "optimal" selection possible. Thus set up the I/O queues in such a way that the next I/O to be executed can be determined quickly and chosen realistically.

It is also important to select the most appropriate queueing algorithm for a device's IORB. A poor algorithm will not take advantage of the mechanical characteristics of the device and will result in lower device throughout. This is critical since the major bottleneck in most systems is the amount of I/O that can be performed on behalf of user programs. The more I/O that can be accomplished, the greater will be the system's throughput. The queueing algorithm can play a significant role in the level of system performance achieved.

I/O Termination.   I/O termination processing takes a relatively large amount of time. This is because it must determine what device sent the interrupt and what the status of the interrupt indicates. If errors were encountered, error recovery may need to be performed. Finally, it must call the I/O initiation routine to dequeue and start the next I/O request for that specific device.

One of the ways to improve I/O termination processing as well as I/O initiation processing is to implement them in the assembler language of the machine. Although this tends to conflict with the trend toward higher-level languages, the performance issues are so critical that there is really no other choice.

Finally, the major I/O termination and initiation routines can be kept permanently resident in the memory of the machine. User programs can be read into memory on demand, but these routines are too important not to be there all the time. Although this affects the resident size of the file/operating system, the trade-off is being made for improved performance.

I/O Request Queue Algorithms.   There are many different algorithms that can be implemented to insert I/O requests into the proper queue and to select the next queue entry to process. There is a trade-off that must be made between the time it takes to make these selections and the real performance gain for the overall system. It is quite difficult to measure differences between algorithms on multiuser systems because the operating environment is constantly changing. However, the goal here should be to implement a *reasonable* algorithm, not the best or the worst. Then measure system performance with the available tools and tune the algorithm to minimize bottlenecks.

6.9 IMPLEMENTATION REQUIREMENTS

There was one major new control structure introduced in this chapter, the I/O request queue (IORQ) (see Figure 6–5 and Table 6–1). This queue, in whatever form it may take, needs to contain the following kinds of information:

- Link to the next IORQ
- Pointer to the entry currently being executed on a device
- Pointer to the last entry in the queue
- Maximum, if any, number of entries allowed in this queue
- Selection algorithm to be used in this queue (queues for different devices can use different algorithms)
- Current position, or location, on the device (e.g., track and cylinder)

TABLE 6-1   I/O REQUEST QUEUE (IORQ)

Header Information	
Version ID	
Link to next IORQ	All IORQs reside in a linked list
Status	No I/O request in progress
	I/O request in progress
	Waiting
Current position	Disk: track/cylinder/block
	number of current location
Queueing algorithm ID	Number of the queueing algorithm
	to be used on this IORQ
	1, FIFO
	2, Job priority
	3, Shortest SEEK first *(Continued)*

TABLE 6-1 (Cont.)

Header Information	
Point to first queue entry	
Pointer to last queue entry	
Pointer to active entry	I/O request that is currently executing
Flags	Currently moving inward (disk) Currently moving out (disk)
IORQ request entries	
Link to next entry	All I/O requests for a device are linked together
Address of FCB	Initiator of this I/O request
Job priority	Input to device I/O scheduling algorithm
Address of I/O request	Operation (e.g., read/write) Address of buffer Amount of data to be transferred
Queueing information	Data needed by the selected queueing algorithm, e.g.: Time in queue Number of times passed over

The foregoing information is kept for each device queue in the system. The following information is kept for every entry in each queue (i.e., per request):

- Address of channel program
- Priority of this job

The device control table (see Table 6–2) associated with this device also contains useful information needed for I/O processing, such as:

- Address of the I/O request queue
- Status of the current request
- Number of retires to perform
- Location of the system error log

Finally, the file system is responsible for the processing of the system error log file (see Table 6–3). This is a file into which the file system records all errors that occur within the system. Specifically, these include all read and write failures as well as attention interrupts which indicate that a problem has occurred at the device. Essentially, enough information should be saved so that anyone analyzing this file could determine what the error was and what was done to correct the problem.

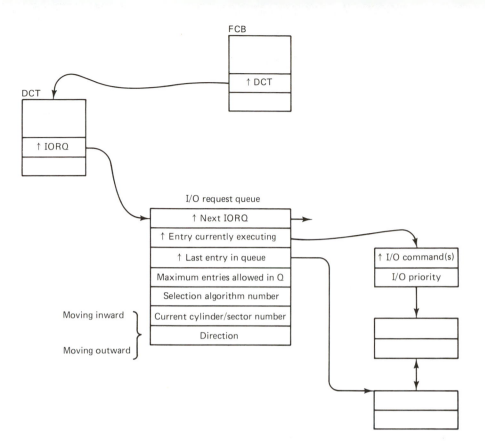

Figure 6-5 I/O request queue (IORQ) interrelationships.

TABLE 6-2 DEVICE CONTROL TABLE

Header information

Version ID
Link to next DCT
Address of IORQ   IORQ associated with this specific device

General device information

Device status
HW address of device
Volume name
Device type
Address of device driver

Exception-processing information

Address of system error log   Central file into which all errors are written
Maximum number of retries: device   Limit on number of retries
  positioning commands
Maximum number of retries: READs
Maximum number of retries: WRITEs
Number of current retry counter   For current error processing
Number of recoverable errors   Total number of errors detected and
                                          successfully recovered

---

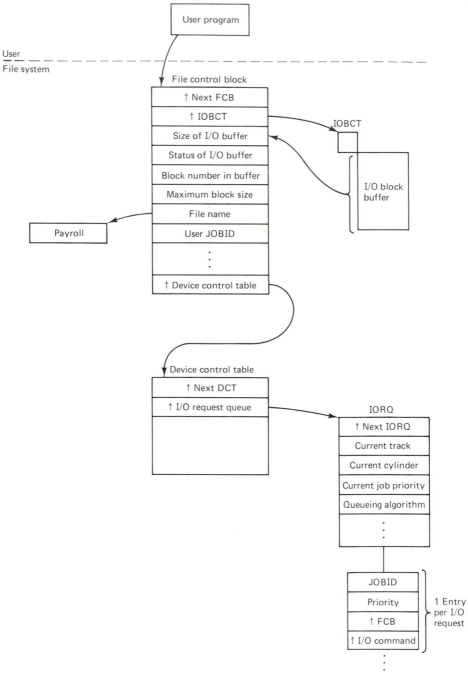

Figure 6-6 Basic file system control structures.

Figure 6–6 shows an updated picture of the overall internal data structures that the basic file system uses to do its work.

TABLE 6–3 SYSTEM ERROR LOG

Header information	
Version ID	
Device information	
Device type	Identifies which device has failed
Device address	Identifies specific device in the configuration of the overall system
Volume	Name of volume or medium that was on the device when the error occurred
Error information	
Channel program or I/O command that failed	Copy of the I/O operation that failed
Status	All I/O status returned by this exception condition
Type of retries performed	Reread, rewrite, and so on
Number of retries performed	How many times the recovery procedures had to be run
Status of retries	Was error successfully and fully recovered?

6.10 SUMMARY

In this chapter we have begun to tie together all the file system components that have been discussed so far. We have also introduced the important role that the basic I/O supervisor plays in the overall I/O operation in the system. What is important here is to understand that this part of the file system *must* be done efficiently and effectively. If it is not, there is almost nothing that the other components of the system can do to improve I/O performance.

KEY WORDS

Attention interrupts	I/O request queue (IORQ)
Device driver	I/O termination
Error recovery	Job scheduler
FIFO I/O request queues	Solicited I/O interrupts
I/O Interrupt	Unsolicited I/O interrupt
I/O initiation	

SUPPLEMENTAL REFERENCES

1. Comer, Douglas, *Operating System Design, the XINU Approach*. Englewood Cliffs, N.J.: Prentice-Hall, Inc., 1984, Chaps. 9, 11, 12. This recommended book has some very good descriptions of how pieces of the file system software could be designed and implemented. Chapter 9 is devoted to the interrupt processor. Chapter 11 talks about implementing device-independent I/O, and Chapter 12 has an implementation of a device driver.

2. Freeman, Donald E., and Olney R. Perry, *I/O DESIGN: Data Management in Operating Systems*. Rochelle Park, N.J.: Hayden Book Company, Inc., 1977, Chap. 9. Chapter 9 is devoted to a discussion of the tasks and responsibilities of the I/O supervisor. This chapter is also highly recommended for a different perspective on I/O software.

3. Lister, A. M., *Fundamentals of Operating Systems,* 2nd ed. New York: Springer-Verlag, 1979, Chap. 6. This text is a short, concisely written book on operating systems. The sixth chapter is devoted to I/O processing and contains a rather detailed description of the process.

EXERCISES

1. Pick any high-level language. Then, knowing what the information needs of a file system are, list the data that come from the programming language, the interactive system commands or job control language, and the data that must be defaulted.

2. Why must the block I/O buffers be resident in main memory all the time? What would/could happen if they were not resident?

3. Why is it important for a resource manager and job scheduler to understand the distinction between shared and nonshared devices?

4. Why do unsolicited interrupts exist? Why are they critical to the successful operation of the resource manager?''

5. How does the I/O termination routine know where to send the I/O completion status at the end of a requested I/O operation?

6. Should the I/O initiation and termination routines, as well as device drivers, be written in a higher-level language, or should they be written in assembler language? Explain the pros and cons of each approach.

7. What is the "best" queueing algorithm for a disk's IORQ? Justify your answer.

8. Is it possible for a user to completely bypass the file system and device drivers and to read or write directly to a device? If yes, what burdens fall on the user? If no, why not?

9. Should the file system retry write errors more times than read errors? Explain.

10. What file system structures must be kept resident in main memory? Explain what would happen if these structures were *not* kept resident.

PROGRAMMING EXERCISES

1. Design and implement an I/O request queueing algorithm for disks and one for tapes. How do these algorithms differ, and how are they alike?

2. Design and implement an I/O termination routine(s). Then simulate an I/O interrupt and demonstrate the processing performed by your module. Demonstrate how it handles both successful and unsuccessful I/O requests.

7

Logical I/O Concepts

CHAPTER OBJECTIVES

When you complete this chapter, you will be able to:

- Discuss in detail, the purpose and functionality of logical I/O
- Understand record buffering techniques and why they are critical to performance
- Discuss the critical aspects and trade-offs in I/O performance and how overall throughput can be improved dramatically without changing one line of code in the user's program

7.1 OVERVIEW

Logical I/O (LIO) is that part of the file system that allows user programs to access logical data records. Another term that we shall use for logical I/O is *access method* (see Figure 7-0). An access method uses the basic file system functions described in Chapter 5 to perform all its processing.

Basic file systems are never really seen by the average user. Typically, the file system and its associated capabilities are seen only through the window of the language selected. If the language offers a wide range of I/O capabilities, such as COBOL, the user can take advantage of a large portion of the file system. On the other hand, many languages, such as Pascal, have a bare minimum of I/O capabilities.

One advantage of LIO is that it allows the user to think in terms of the applica-

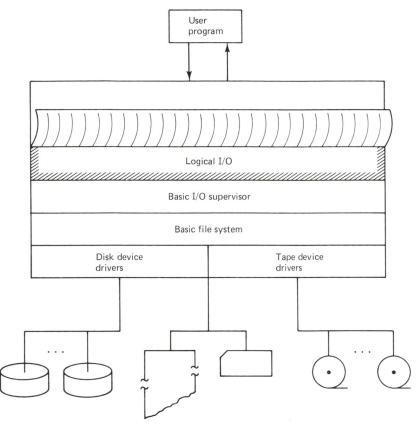

Figure 7-0   File system: logical I/O component.

tion to be performed, not in terms of how to interface the application to the system. Indeed, LIO allows the user to think in terms of *logical records* instead of the blocks that the basic file system processes. A record is much easier to understand, since it is easy to conceptualize an employee's record, a payroll record, a student's scholastic record, and so on. LIO allows users to think in the terms they understand best. LIO handles records and the basic file system processes blocks. The latter is known as *physical I/O* since it deals with the physical, or actual, reading and writing of blocks onto the various devices. LIO reads and writes records, whether or not a physical block had to be read or written at the same time. Thus LIO deals in user data records. Since the data records reside in blocks that must be read into main memory, all record I/O or logical I/O takes place within main memory. Thus logical I/O can be orders of magnitude *faster* than physical I/O since internal CPU speeds are significantly faster than device speeds.

The primary purposes of LIO are to provide the user with the following capabilities:

7.1.1 Standard Interface to Perform I/O

All languages, for example, should use the standard interface to perform all their I/O needs. In addition, should the user need to write programs in assembler language, the standard interface is both easier to code and easier to debug.

7.1.2 Standard Set of File Organizations

Why should users have to develop their own file system software when it is already available? A file organization is the way in which logical I/O or the access method organizes the data records in a file (e.g., sequential or indexed files.) By providing the capabilities of the most needed file organizations and capabilities, all users and applications can use the standard LIO facilities.

7.1.3 Generalized Data Management for All Users

Whenever a generalized piece of software is provided to users, there are usually negative comments about its performance and response time. This is essentially the trade-off that gets made between providing a lot of software so that many users can use it, versus tailoring the code to a specific purpose, with no exceptions allowed. Although somewhat slower than custom software, a generalized package will grow with the user as the needs and requirements expand over time.

7.1.4 Standard Interface to the World of Devices

Why should a user need to rewrite, or even modify, an application just because a new device was just about to be installed in the system? Users should be device independent and should let other software (e.g., LIO or the file system) handle all device specifics. Similarly, the user can be concerned with the problem to be solved and can leave the technical complexities of device specifics to the file system. Remember that one of our goals is to allow the user to focus on the application to be written and not have to be diverted by hardware technicalities.

In summary, LIO forms the standard interface between applications written in high-level languages and the file system/devices. As such, the LIO also serves to hide most, if not all, device specifics from the application, and thus the user really only needs to understand the application to be done.

7.2 FILE ATTRIBUTES

As we discuss the record operations supported by the access methods, there will be a core set of data that will be used over and over again. *This set of file information is known as the file's attributes.* These are the pieces of information that are absolutely needed by the access methods. Since these data are so important, they are written out and saved as part of the overall file structure so that they can be reread the next time the file is accessed. For example, the following list is a subset of the total realm of file attributes:

- *Filename:* How can we be sure that the proper file is being accessed?
- *File organization:* This tells the access method how the records are arranged within the file structure so that the records can be retrieved later.
- *Record format:* This reports whether the records written into the file were of fixed or variable length, so that they can be read and interpreted correctly.
- *Record size:* If the record format is fixed, this is the size of all records in the file. If the record format is variable in length, this represents the maximum length of any record in the file. This allows the access method to ensure that no record will ever get written into the file which conflicts with the file definition of the user. In addition, it allows the access method to read, write, and interpret the data correctly.
- *File size:* This is the amount of file space the access method has in which it can read and write records.
- *Block size:* This is how large every block in the file is, and therefore the AM can allocate I/O buffers large enough to accommodate the entire block.

This critical information is usually stored within the file itself. Thus we can locate a file's attributes by looking for them at a predefined location within the file. Alternatively, the attributes can be saved within the directory entry on the medium. For example, the directory entry for a file must, at a minimum, have the name of the file and its location. Other attributes could be stored either within the directory or in the file itself. In any case, it is important to understand what file attributes are and that they are stored at a prespecified location within the file or directory entry. Thus they can always be retrieved on as needed.

One last question: Can a file's attributes be changed after a file has been created and populated with user data records? Technically speaking, the answer is yes. Realistically, however, the time and processing effort required to do this would be enormous. The reason for this is that since all of the data records were inserted into the file by the old attribute values, they will now need to be reinserted by the new attribute requirements. Thus we will end up repopulating the entire file. This amounts to a full-blown file reorganization. Thus since attributes can be changed prior to a reorganization, it would perhaps be best if file attribute changes were limited to when the file gets created or reorganized.

7.3 DATA FLOW TO/FROM USER

One of the most important concepts to understand is the way in which the data flow from the device into the main memory of the CPU, and vice versa. This is critical to the overall understanding of I/O in general and to the actual number of I/O opera-

tions required to perform a task in particular. It is also an area that is usually misunderstood. Initially, let us examine some of the most fundamental concepts related
to I/O.

First, *the only way that data get transferred to or from a device is via an I/O
operation.* Within main memory, data are moved by using CPU instructions.

Second, *the only time when the data on the device are changed is when an output operation (e.g., WRITE, UPDATE, DELETE) is executed.* An input operation
(e.g., READ, READ_NEXT, or POSITION) never changes the data on the medium.
Therefore, if a user wishes only to read and examine the data but not change them,
only READ operations need be requested. The file system never needs to re-WRITE
the data since the data have not been changed.

Next let us trace through the flow of data as shown in Figure 7–1. First, the
user determines that a record is to be written out to the device. For the access method
to "retrieve" a data record, the user must copy the record into a user record buffer
(step 1). *This user record buffer is large enough to hold an entire record.* Next (step
2), the user issues the WRITE request by utilizing the appropriate syntax for the

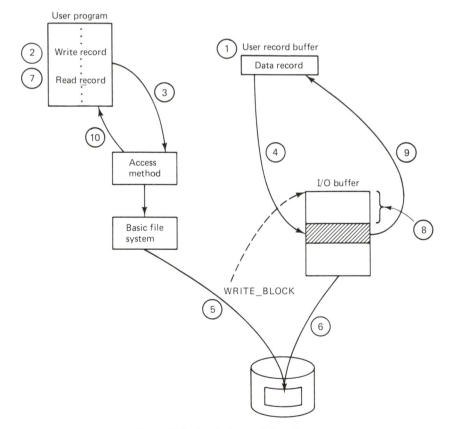

Figure 7–1   Logical record data flow.

language in which the program was implemented. This WRITE request passes control to the access method.

The access method (step 3) then takes the two input parameters—record size and address of the user record buffer—and locates the record to be written. Based on the particular file organization, the access method then determines the block into which the user's data record is to be written. If that block is currently residing in one of the current I/O block buffers, the access method does not need to go out to the device to reread the desired block into memory.

If the desired block of the file is not in main memory, the file system will be requested by the access method to read the block in the file and to transfer it into one of the I/O buffers in the main memory of the CPU. Once the block is in main memory, the access method is again given control in order to copy the user data record from the user's data record buffer into the appropriate area in the block. *This moving of the user's data record to the I/O buffer is known as the move mode of operation.*

There is also a locate mode of operation, in which time is saved by not actually performing the move of the user data record into the I/O buffer. Instead, the record is put directly into the I/O buffer by the user. To accomplish this operation, the user is given a pointer into the I/O buffer into which the record will be put. This is somewhat dangerous since if a mistake is made by the user, system data could be overwritten. Also, in modern machine architectures, the user is prevented from accessing critical system areas. When the record has been copied into the block in the I/O buffer (step 4), the access method will again call the file system to write the block back to the disk (step 5).

Only after the I/O operation transferring the block from the I/O buffer in main memory out to the media on the device has been completed has the user's data record actually been entered into the file itself. If the system should crash at any time after the I/O has completed, the data record will not be lost. On the other hand, should the system crash before the write I/O operation has completed, the user data record will be lost.

The final step in transferring data to a device (step 10) is for the access method to return the appropriate status back to the user's program. With this status information, the user can tell whether or not the data were successfully transferred to the device.

Conversely, if the user decided to read a record off the medium, the user must (step 7) issue the appropriate READ command in the application's implementation language. With this call, the user must pass to the access method the address of the user record buffer into which the access method will move the data record. Also, the user must tell the access method how large the record buffer is, so that only as much of the data record as is wanted by the user gets copied into the user record buffer. Note that no matter how much of a record a user may want, the access method reads into memory the entire block in which the record resides.

Once the desired block has been read into an I/O buffer in main memory, the file system returns control to the access method. It is then (step 8) up to the access method to extract the desired record out of the block of records in the I/O buffer and copy that record from the I/O block buffer into the user's record buffer (step 9). The access method will copy into the user's record buffer only as much data as was requested by the user.

After all of this processing has been performed, the access method returns status to the user (step 10). Then, and only then, is control passed back to the user's program. This is a major point to remember—that the user program is suspended until the desired record has been returned to the calling program. Thus the user's program is synchronized with the I/O request, or to put it slightly differently, *synchronous I/O* is being performed (see Figure 7-2a).

If control had been returned to the user's program before the I/O operation had been completed, the I/O and the program would be running in parallel. Therefore, by convention, we can say that *asynchronous I/O* is being performed (see Figure 7-2B). Most of the major high-level languages (e.g., FORTRAN, BASIC, COBOL, RPG) support only synchronous I/O. Therefore, the programs must sit idle waiting for an I/O operation to complete. This is critical to overall performance and throughput in that the more actual I/O operations that must be performed on behalf of the user, the more time the user's program simply sits and waits.

In summary, only I/O operations transfer data between the main memory of the CPU and the device itself. Similarly, CPU instructions only massage the data within the limits of the main memory of the machine. Also, note that the user deals with data records while the access method must take the user's data record and then map the specific record request into a series of block I/O calls to the file system. Again, the file system understands only block I/O; it does not understand the content of the blocks (i.e., the records contained within a block).

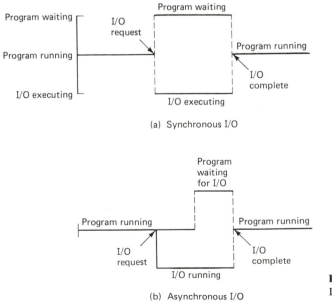

(a) Synchronous I/O

(b) Asynchronous I/O

Figure 7-2 Synchronous/asynchronous I/O processing.

7.4 I/O BUFFERING TECHNIQUES

I/O block buffers are contiguous areas of main memory dedicated to the transfer of blocks between a file and the memory in the machine. *An I/O buffer must be large enough to hold the largest possible block in the file being accessed.* Most files have fixed-length blocks, so that by reading the file attributes, the file system can determine how large to make the I/O buffers for that file. Note that there could be separate I/O buffers allocated for every file that is being accessed simultaneously. In this situation, the amount of main memory taken up by I/O buffers is directly related to the number of files that can be OPEN at any one time.

Alternatively, the file system could "own" all of the I/O buffers in the system and then share the available space with all users. This would optimize the use of main memory in the sense that dedicated space for each open file would not be required. Instead, only those files currently active (i.e., being used) will take up buffer space. This approach also permits *sharing* of files so that if two users want a record in the same block of a file, the first user will cause the target block to be read into memory. The second user will simply access the block already in the I/O buffer. Thus improved performance can be achieved.

On the other hand, having a central pool of I/O buffers owned by the file system has the drawback of space fragmentation. In other words, not all buffers need be, or will be, the same size. Thus, whenever space is needed, the file system may need to move buffers around in main memory to be able to allocate a new buffer large enough to meet the current request. One way to solve the fragmentation problem is to force all I/O buffers to be the same size. This *is* possible on those machines that have disks with fixed sector or block sizes.

There is another reason why I/O buffers are so important—to help improve overall system performance. This can be accomplished by cutting down the actual number of I/O operations that must be performed. In the example in the preceding section, once the user data record was copied into the I/O buffer, we had the file system immediately write the block to the device. In reality, this write of the block could have been delayed until more buffer space was needed. Then the block could be transferred to the device and the I/O buffer could be reused for some other block in the file. Conversely, if a record needed by a READ request already exists in an I/O buffer, there is no need to reread the block.

We can begin to see how we could cut down the number of actual I/O operations needed by a job, by allocating multiple I/O buffers to a specific file. Therefore, we can increase the chances that a desired block, or record, is still in main memory even though an I/O operation need not always be performed. In actuality, there is not an unlimited amount of main memory space available for I/O buffers, since there could be many files OPEN simultaneously and the user does not have an unlimited amount of memory. For example, most microcomputers have 64 to 256 KB of main memory, which is not very large once the operating system and the user applications get loaded into it.

Therefore, we have two conflicting choices: allocate as much memory as possible to I/O buffers to gain in performance; or because memory is very limited, do not allocate more than is really needed. What should we do? Basically, we should allocate whatever space we can to I/O buffers, no matter how limited. Then we should select the best algorithm for managing those buffers in order to gain the highest throughput possible. To accomplish this, we will examine two choices, single and double buffering. There are other buffering algorithms, but these are the most popular on machines of all sizes, from micro to mainframe.

7.4.1 Single Buffer per File

Whenever only a single buffer is allocated for I/O, it typically means that not much memory is available. Thus the space taken up by I/O buffers must be minimized. Specifically, what this means is that every READ_BLOCK or WRITE_BLOCK command will utilize the identical space in main memory. For example, in Figure 7–3, if the user wanted to either read or write a record, the access method must perform the following checks and tasks:

1. If the record that the user wants is located in the block that is currently in the I/O buffer, go to step 4.
2. Since the desired block is not now in the I/O buffer, the access method must read the block into the buffer. First, however, it must check to see if there are any data currently in the buffer that need to be written out to disk. If not, go to step 3. The access method knows this because whenever the user writes a new record and the access method copies it into the I/O buffer, it also sets an internal flag to remember the fact that new data have been moved into the buffer and have not yet been written out to the disk. *When data in an I/O buffer have been changed, the buffer is said to be modified, or dirty.* Conversely, when the block does get written into the file, the access method resets the flag.

    If data need to be written out, the access method must first write the data in the I/O buffer onto the medium. Only after this operation has been completed can the access method read the user's desired block into the I/O buffer in main memory.
3. If the needed block is not in the current I/O buffer, the access method goes out and reads into the main memory I/O buffer.
4. The desired block is now in main memory. If the request was to read the record, the access method copies the record into the user's record buffer and then returns to the user. On a write record request, the record is copied into the appropriate location in the I/O buffer.

Note that the user's program has been suspended while all this work has been taking place on its behalf. Thus the overall performance of the user's program can be affected adversely if much I/O needs to be performed. Also, all the I/O was performed in a serial sequential manner, meaning that each I/O operation had to wait until the current I/O operation completed.

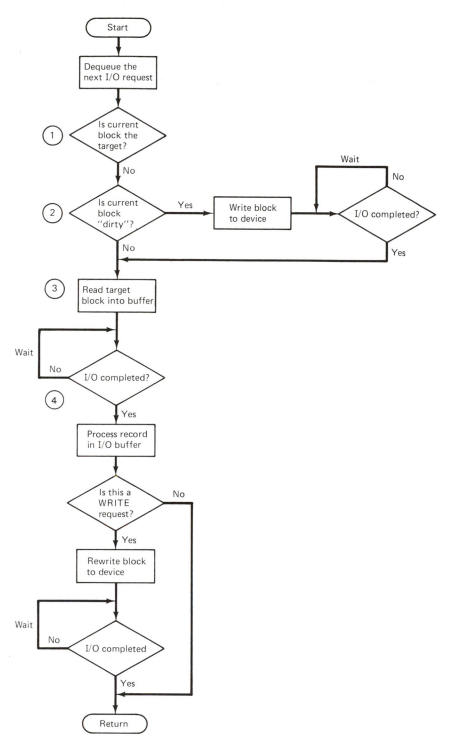

Figure 7-3 Single I/O buffer.

7.4.2 Multiple Buffers per File

The nonoverlapping of I/O, in the single-I/O-buffer case, is one of the major areas of performance degradation. For this reason, multiple buffers can be used to greatly improve a program's performance and responsiveness. *If two buffers are used, it is called double buffering,* a technique in common use today. The access method has a choice of which buffer to use for any particular request. Specifically, it can try to select a buffer that either has not been modified, thus requiring the buffer to be written back to the media, or the buffer containing the "oldest" data. In this manner, it is possible to eliminate much of the I/O delay of the single-buffer case.

If it is possible to predict the sequence of records the user will request, it might be possible to improve performance further. For example, if the user were sequentially reading and processing a payroll file, it might be possible for the file system to predict with a high degree of accuracy where the next record resides in the file. Given this advance knowledge, the file system could then read ahead of the user requests. Thus, when the user makes a request, the likelihood will be that the file system has already read that block into main memory. This approach, which is valid only when the file system knows that the user is performing sequential processing, is known as *anticipatory buffering.* For example, when a user opens a sequential file for reading, the file system *knows* that it can successfully utilize anticipatory buffering techniques to gain performance.

If a system had *n* I/O buffers available, it would be possible to have *n* I/O operations going on simultaneously on *n* devices. If *n* = 1, however, there can be only one I/O operation and all other I/O requests must wait.

As can be seen from Figure 7–4, the file system needs certain information in order to properly manage the I/O buffers. This information is maintained in a file structure known as the *I/O buffer control table (IOBCT)*. Specifically, the IOBCT contains the following data:

- Line to the next I/O buffer
- Control flags, such as *buffer modified* (i.e., dirty) or *buffer currently in use*
- Block number of the block currently in that I/O buffer

7.4.3 Blocking/Unblocking of Data Records

Record blocking is the process in which LIO packages more than one user data record into a single block. Record unblocking is the process by which LIO extracts a specific data record from a block containing multiple records. The blocking factor is the average number of user data records that can be inserted into a single block in the file.

To minimize the actual number of I/O operations that must be performed on behalf of the user, it is possible to place within a single block one or more user data records. Thus instead of one real I/O operation for every user data record in the file, there are only

$$\frac{\text{number of UDRs in file}}{\text{average number of UDRs per block}}$$

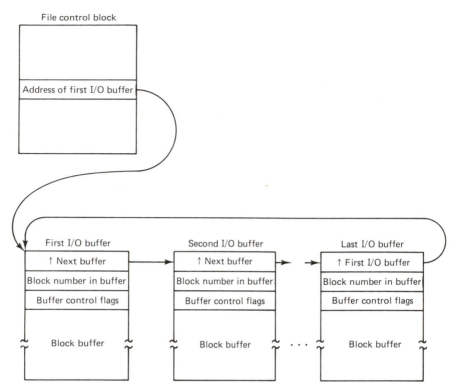

Figure 7-4 Multiple I/O buffers.

number of actual I/O operations. For example, assume that we had a blocking factor of 10. Then, 10 user data records, on the average, can be inserted into every block within the file. There will be only one-tenth of the actual number of I/O operations required than if the blocking factor been 1. In other words, the reading of just one block results in 10 logical data records being brought into main memory. Thus the user could then read 10 data records sequentially and never need to go to the device for data.

The calculation performed above assumes that the WRITE_BLOCK operation will *not* be performed until the I/O buffer is needed for some other block in the file. *This delaying of the WRITE_BLOCK operation until such a time as it is necessary to be done is sometimes called deferred writing.* There is a risk when this technique is used. Although the performance gained can be significant, it is possible to lose data records in the case in which the system crashes before the WRITE_BLOCK occurs. Then any new or modified user data records residing in that I/O buffer will be lost.

Although it is probably not a major task to regenerate these missing records, it can be a considerable problem. This is because the user programs returned *success* status codes immediately after their data records were copied into the block in the I/O buffer. Thus, from the user program point of view, all has gone well and no records have been lost. Therefore, the issue is not the reentering of the lost changes but the identification of which record changes did not get written into the file before the system went down.

The ability to block records can dramatically cut down the actual number of I/O operations required to complete a job. In actuality, the number of I/O operations is reduced by the following factor:

$$(\text{I/O reduction factor} =) \; \frac{1}{\text{average blocking factor}}$$

In turn, the job completes sooner, since I/O tends to be a major bottleneck to overall system performance. Blocking records is one of the key functions of the file system, as it improves overall system efficiency as well as overall performance.

It is the responsibility of the LIO routines to know how to add records into a block, and conversely, how to extract the correct record from a block. Since *blocking* is concerned with adding records to a block, we are really only concerned with output or write record operations. Conversely, *unblocking* deals with locating an already existing record so that it can be transferred to the calling program. Thus unblocking will occur only on input operations such as a read.

To better understand the concept of blocking and its counterpart, unblocking, refer to Figure 7–5. Before a user program can write a record, it must first copy the record into the user record buffer (step 1). Next, the user program must call LIO by issuing a WRITE command (step 2). The LIO routines then take the address and size of the user record buffer, which are parameters of the WRITE operation, and locates the data record to be written (step 3).

LIO now has the user's data record. The next step is for LIO to calculate into which block of the file the record should be added. This calculation is based on the way in which the records in the file are organized. The access methods discussed in Part III of this book go into considerable detail on how records can be organized and accessed. For now, just assume that the LIO routines must somehow determine the block in which the user data record belongs. Then LIO issues a READ_BLOCK command to read that block into an I/O buffer in main memory (step 4).

LIO now has the user's data record and the target block into which that record will be added. The issue is that there may or may not already be one or more data records in the target block. It is the task of LIO to be able to detect how many, if any, records are already in that block, as well as to determine precisely where in the block the new record belongs. For example, if we were adding record 5 to the block (step 5), it might logically exist after record 2 but before the record whose number is 7 (step 6). Thus LIO must not only locate where in the record sequence in the block the new record belongs, but it may also be required to move the other records around in order to make this happen (step 7). The result, however, is that all of the records in that block end up being in the correct order as required by the specified file organization.

How can LIO locate the records in the I/O buffer? If the file has fixed length records, LIO knows the size of all the records in the file. If we have variable-length

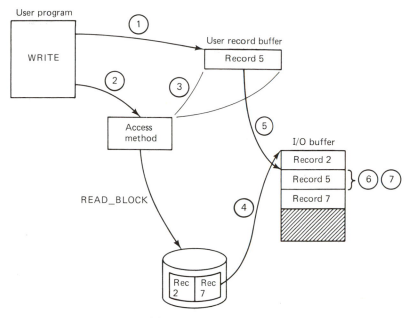

(a) Record blocking

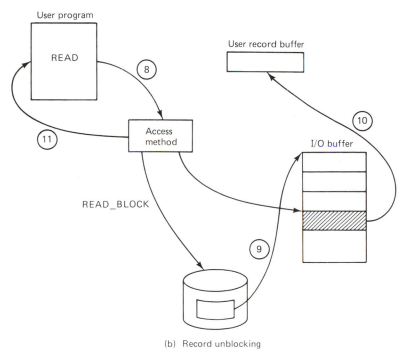

(b) Record unblocking

Figure 7-5 Record blocking and unblocking.

records, each record has a length field as a prefix to the data. Thus, again, LIO can skip over the records in the block. The only piece missing is how LIO can tell when there are no more records in a block. This is *file organization* specific and is dealt with in Part III. For now, assume that LIO can detect when there are no more records in a particular block.

In summary, given a user data record, LIO can locate the block in which the record belongs. It can then examine all the records in that block, if any, and determine where in the block the new record belongs. LIO can then move the records in the block around so that the end result is a block in which all the records are in the correct sequence.

Unblocking is the reverse of blocking. When the user makes a read-type request (step 8), LIO determines which block in the file contains the target data record. It then issues a READ_BLOCK (step 9) to bring that block into an I/O buffer in main memory.

Just as LIO could examine all the records in the block to determine where a new record must be inserted, it can also scan the data records in a block looking for the data record that was requested by the user program. When found, LIO copies the record into the user's record buffer (step 10). The final step is for LIO to return to the calling program two critical pieces of information. First, the program must be told how large a record was copied into the user record buffer. Second, the calling program must be told the status of the request (step 11).

In summary, the ability to block and unblock data records can have a dramatic impact on the performance of the system by cutting down on the actual number of I/O operations that are required to process a user request. There is a downside risk of possibly losing records in the case of a system crash, but if the ability of having deferred writing capabilities can be made optional for users, each system can have the performance and reliability levels that it needs.

7.5 FILE REORGANIZATION

There will be times when the responsiveness of the access method to a user request degrades to the point of being unacceptable. This happens because the number of actual I/O operations required to access a record for the user increases and therefore the amount of time it takes for the access method to respond to the user with the desired record also increases.

The primary reason for this change in response time is that as the file itself changes, because records are being added, updated, or deleted, the file structure changes to accommodate the activity. We will see this more vividly as we investigate a variety of access methods in the following chapters. For now, it is important to understand that as activity in a file increases, the file itself changes. These changes can adversely affect performance and responsiveness. *To restore the file to its most optimal structure, and therefore to improve its performance, the user needs to reor-*

ganize the file. The result of a file reorganization is a new file that has all deleted records and unusable space removed and the file rebuilt as optimally as possible. The following steps are required to perform a file reorganization:

1. Create a new file with the same file attributes as those of the original file. This empty file is therefore a mirror image of the original *master file* except that it has no data records in it yet. This new file is given a name that is not the same as the original master file's name.
2. Copy all the valid data records from the master file to the new file. This step skips over deleted records in order to end up with a "cleaned-up" file containing only currently valid user data records.
3. Compare the master file records against the records in the new file. This is done to verify that the data were copied completely and correctly.
4. Delete the master file, leaving only the new copy of the file.
5. Name the new file with the identical name of the just deleted master file. This is done so that all programs that access the file will not need to be changed because the file itself was changed.

Now, we have a new version of the file, except that the file structure has been optimized by eliminating wasted space and by rebuilding all structures. The performance of the file will be as it was originally.

How often must a file reorganization be performed? Sometimes never, sometimes nightly, depending on the structure of the file and the usage levels. What is important to understand is that over time, the performance of a file can change for the worse. It is equally important to know that the original performance levels can be regained by performing a file reorganization.

7.6 PERFORMANCE CONSIDERATIONS

For each of the file organizations that we will examine, the performance issue will be discussed. This is critical, since the user judges a product by its usability. Thus the product's performance and responsiveness are guaranteed to play major roles in the user's perception. We will now examine performance from several vantage points.

From the user's point of view, performance relates directly to the responsiveness of the user's program I/O calls (e.g., READ_BLOCK, WRITE_BLOCK). In particular, we will be looking at the performance of both random and sequential operations.

Random I/O (e.g., random read of a record) is important in applications that tend to be interactive, such as airline reservations, banking, and browsing through data bases. Waiting 3 minutes at a teller's window for account data to be displayed will generally be intolerable to a customer.

On the other hand, there are many applications that require every record in the file to be accessed sequentially. For example, each week an employer must calculate and print payroll checks for all employees. Again, the amount of time that it takes to run the job is important to the user.

We will also examine performance from the vantage point of how each access method really works, and therefore how we can take advantage of this by manipulating some of the characteristics that affect performance. For example, if we preallocate all the space for a file, we can improve performance by eliminating all system calls to extend the file. This, of course, assumes that the system supports this kind of feature. What is important here is that *performance hinges on the actual number of I/O operations that must be performed to get a job done*. Therefore, whatever can be done to cut down the number of I/O operations will improve performance.

Finally, as we investigate the design and implementation trade-offs that are made in each type of file organization, we can determine what kinds of applications would benefit by using a particular kind of file type. This is important, since the selection of the most appropriate file organization will to a large degree dictate the resulting level of performance as seen by the user.

In summary, when we discuss performance, we will be interested in the following key areas:

- Time to position to the target record
- Total number of I/O operations required to complete a request
- Method by which data records are being accessed (i.e., randomly or sequentially)
- The amount of main memory allocated to I/O buffers
- The amount of disk space used
- Any user response-time requirements
- Performance of READ, READ_NEXT, READ and then UPDATE, and WRITE record

7.7 DESIGN TRADE-OFFS

Although each of the file organizations that we will examine is relatively "standard" in how it works, we will investigate the trade-offs that were made to achieve the set of functionality given to the user. If we can understand some of the design issues, we will have a better idea of when to choose a particular file type for an application, and also when a specific file type is absolutely inappropriate. In addition, if we understand the design constraints, we can better understand the performance implications and what we can do about them.

Some of the file design issues that are discussed will be concerned with the following issues:

- The functionality available to the users
- The overall performance or the entire file system

- The amount of media storage required for a record as well as a file
- The time it takes to randomly read a record
- The time it takes to add a record to a file
- The time it takes to read the entire file sequentially
- The time it takes to reorganize a file as well as the frequency of reorganizations
- How easy it is to change any of the attributes of a file after the file has been created and populated with data
- What precautions are taken to protect the integrity of the data and to make the data secure from unauthorized users

The "answers" or results for each of the topics listed above will change depending on the kind of file organization selected.

7.8 I/O STATUS HANDLING

At the completion of every user I/O request, the access methods must return to the calling program the completion status of the request. The reason this is done is so that the calling program can determine whether the request that just finished completed successfully or not.

It is the job of the access method to map the status coming from the basic file system into a status that the user's program can understand. All high-level languages have some predefined status codes, such as for end-of-file. See Table 7–1 for the most typical status codes found in today's high-level languages. What this really means is that all of the status conditions detected by the file system must be mapped into one of the error codes defined by a particular language. It is the access method working with the supporting language run-time library that make this status mapping successful.

TABLE 7-1   I/O STATUS CODES

Status
I/O successful
End-of-file reached by a READ statement
Invalid key
Key sequence error
READ with duplicate key found
No record found
etc.
Record locked
Hardware Error
I/O Unsuccessful

a particular language. It is the access method working with the supporting language
run-time library that makes this status mapping successful.

7.9 IMPLEMENTATION REQUIREMENTS

Finally, we will discuss how the various access methods actually accomplish their work.
This is not being done only because it provides an insight into the internal workings
of a file system, but also to better explain the why and how of the functionality that
a file system provides to a user.

For example, how does the file system remember which blocks of a file are currently in main memory I/O buffers, or what the last record read was, so that when
the user says READ_NEXT record, the correct record can be retrieved?

In the single-buffer case, the access method can keep all of the necessary control information in the file control block. However, this becomes impossible once
multiple buffers are allocated and need to be managed. Thus we must keep this buffer control information as a prefix to each buffer itself. Therefore, there will always
be associated with each I/O buffer the data necessary to manage it. This buffer control information is maintained in the I/O buffer control table (IOBCT) (see Table
7-2) and can be summarized as follows:

- *Pointer:* indicates the next I/O buffer control block.
- *Control flags:* Modified, in use, and so on.
- *Logical block number (LBN):* identifies the block currently in the I/O buffer.

TABLE 7-2 I/O BUFFER CONTROL TABLE

Header information	
Version ID	
Link to next IOBCT	Pointer to next buffer
Unique block indentification	
Device ID	Name of the device on which the block resides
Physical block number (PBN)	Actual physical location on the device of the block in the I/O buffer
Logical block number (LBN)	Number of block currently in the I/O buffer
Buffer information	
Flags	Buffer is currently empty Block in buffer has been modified
Address of I/O buffer	Location in main memory of the I/O buffer into which the block will be read or written
Buffer size	Length, in bytes, of the I/O buffer

- *Device identifier:* needed because block 5 could be on any of the devices connected to the system.
- *Physical block number (PBN):* needed because the logical block number maintained above is only relative to a file. Thus many files can have an LBN of 5. However, the PBN uniquely identifies a particular block on a specific device.

Whenever the access method copies a data record *into* the I/O buffer, it must also set the "dirty" or "buffer modified" flag for that buffer. This is done so that the file system can know that that block will need to be written back to the device at some point.

It is also necessary to keep enough data to uniquely identify each and every block of data in the entire system. Thus the combination of device ID, PBN, and LBN is kept to uniquely identify a block in the I/O buffer.

7.10 SUMMARY

In this chapter the concept of logical I/O has been introduced. This is the area of a file system that affects just about every program that performs I/O, since it deals with data records, not with blocks of data records.

We also discussed the issue of a file's attributes. This is a critical area that must be clearly understood. It is the sole means that a file system has to ensure that all data records are written and read correctly, today and tomorrow.

Buffering techniques were also discussed. This is an area in which overall performance of programs can be greatly improved, because it allows logical I/O to cut down on the actual number of I/O requests that must be executed.

In summary, several of the major concepts and ideas concerning logical I/O and access methods have been discussed. We will begin to apply these concepts to specific applications in the chapters that follow.

KEY WORDS

Anticipatory buffering	I/O buffer control table (IOBCT)
Access method	Locate mode
Deferred writing	Logical I/O (LIO)
Dirty buffer	Master file
Double buffering	Move mode
File attributes	Physical I/O (PIO)
File reorganization	User record buffer (UBF)

SUPPLEMENTAL REFERENCES

1. ANSI, *American National Standard Programming Language COBOL*. New York: American National Standards Institute, Inc., 1974, ANSI–X3.23–1974. This is *the* standard for the COBOL language. As such it explicitly defines all of the possible conditions that the language can detect, as well as the complete I/O interface that it will support.
2. Hanson, Owen, *Design of Computer Data Files*. Rockville, Md.: Computer Science Press, Inc., 1982, Chap. 4. This book has a short discussion of various I/O buffering techniques.

EXERCISES

1. What is the function of logical I/O, and how does it differ from the function of the basic file system? Explain.
2. What criteria should be used to select which of the I/O buffers to select for the next I/O operation? Explain.
3. Why is it necessary to have a "buffer modified, buffer dirty" status flag for each I/O block buffer? What would happen if it did not exist?
4. Discuss the trade-offs between large blocking factors and main memory utilization. How should a user decide what blocking factor is best to use?
5. Examine the I/O status codes that are visible to you in your favorite programming language. Do you think it matters that all sorts of error conditions are mapped into that set? Are there any specific errors you would like to see but cannot because the language does not allow it?
6. Why is a "standard" I/O interface a benefit? Consider both the user's and system's points of view.
7. What should the file system do when a user tries to read a record that is *larger* than the user's own record buffer? Explain.
8. When should a user "reorganize" a file? What will happen if the user does *not* do this?
9. We have assumed that I/O buffers are dedicated to the user's job. What if, instead, they came out of a central pool of I/O buffers for the entire system? What would be the advantages and disadvantages of this approach?
10. Is the user aware that physical I/O is taking place? If not, why not? If yes, how is it visible?

PROGRAMMING EXERCISES

1. Design and implement an algorithm to manage four I/O buffers associated with a particular file. Take into consideration any differences that might exist between sequential and random I/O against the file. Also try and minimize the *actual* number of I/O operations needed to process the user's requests.

8

Access Method I/O

CHAPTER OBJECTIVES

When you complete this chapter, you will be able to:

- Describe the user-visible file and record operations as well as when and how each is used
- Understand the concept of a *current record* and how it is used by both the access method and the user's program
- Understand the internal control structures that are required to design and implement an access method
- Discuss the critical aspects and trade-offs in I/O performance and how overall throughput can be improved dramatically without changing one line of code in the user's program
- Discuss how access method I/O differs from basic file system I/O

8.1 OVERVIEW

In this chapter we discuss how an access method (AM) spans the gulf between the user and the file system in order to get the job done. To accomplish this objective, we must determine what kinds of operations users would like to be able to perform on records. Then we will examine how these requests can be mapped by the access method into a series of calls that are understandable by the file system.

The access methods form the standard interface between applications written in high-level languages and the file system/devices (see Figure 8–0). As such, the AM also serves to hide most, if not all device specifics from the application, and thus the user really only needs to understand the application to be done. In addition, the access method is able to provide user programs with more capability than the basic file system alone can provide. Thus, although many of the commands appear similar to the BFS commands, the user is really gaining the capability to work with records instead of blocks. The specifics of the access methods will become much clearer in Part III of the book. Finally, *the AM understands the content of the blocks that it passes to the file system to be read or written.* The file system, on the other hand, does not understand the content of the blocks that it reads and writes.

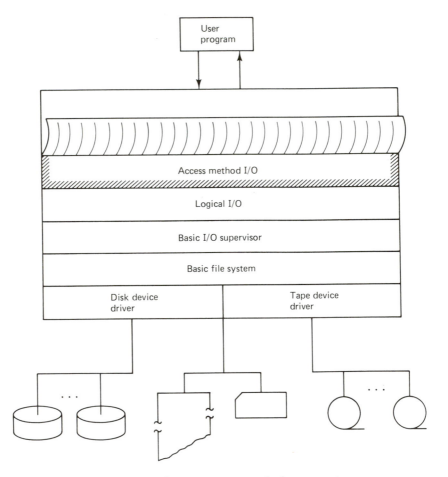

Figure 8–0   File system: access method component.

8.2 FILE DESIGN CONSIDERATIONS

How does an access method actually organize user data records within a particular file organization? What algorithms are used to insert new records and also to retrieve old data records? Each of the file organizations discussed in the rest of Part III uses different techniques and trade-offs. It is the purpose of this section within each chapter to discuss in detail how each file organization is designed.

8.2.1 File Attributes

In this chapter we discuss the file-organization-independent file attributes that are required to perform a particular function call. Then, in each of the following access-method-specific chapters, we discuss only those attributes and characteristics that are required over and above this norm.

For example, the standard set of file attributes might consist of the following items:

- Filename or pathname
- File organization type
- Record format and maximum record size
- Maximum block size
- File size
- File organization-specific information

It is the last item in the list above that will be discussed in some detail in each of the following access method chapters.

8.2.2 File Structure

To insert and retrieve user data records from a file, it is necessary to build enough file overhead or file structure to enable the associated access method to access the data records. This is similar to the overhead that the basic file system built on the disk or tape devices. On disk, the BFS built a boot block, a disk allocation table, and a directory structure. With this system overhead, the BFS was able to manage all of the users and all of the disk space efficiently and effectively.

This section in each of the unique access method chapters that follows will discuss what structure is built and why. With knowledge of the file structure, we will then be better able to understand the following characteristics of files:

- The performance characteristics of each file organization
- The space requirements for each type of file
- The benefits as well as drawbacks for each file organization

8.3 FILE OPERATIONS

What kinds of operations do users want to perform, and what kinds of file operations need to be supported? File operations operate not on the data records within the file but on the file itself. For example, we might want to *create* a file today and access or *open* it tomorrow. In addition, when we are done processing the file, we may want to cut the link to the file or *close* the file. Similarly, we may not always guess correctly how large the file will become. Therefore, we will want the capability of increasing the size or *extending* the file. Finally, at some point in the future, we may no longer need to keep it, and therefore we will want to get rid of or *delete* the file.

In the following sections we discuss the requirements and functionality of these file operations. As we proceed through this section, try to relate the functions and information requirements to the capabilities provided in one of the higher-level languages with which you are familiar. When you run across data that are not supported by the language, try to determine where the access method can retrieve the information. Finally, compare these access method file operations against those performed by the basic file system.

8.3.1 Create File

The purpose of the CREATE function is to allow users to create brand-new files. Before any records can be written into a file, and before any records can be read from a file, the file must first be created. How can a file be created? What does it mean to create a file? If we examine most high-level languages, the capability of creating all but the most simple sequential files is just about nonexistent. One of the reasons for this is that the languages were defined with a particular audience in mind.

COBOL was designed for efficient business applications. These applications tend to perform many I/O operations. Thus the COBOL I/O support is fairly extensive. FORTRAN was targeted at scientific and engineering applications that require many calculations and few I/O operations. Thus the FORTRAN language supports a very restricted set of I/O operations. Given this situation, most systems provide users with utility programs that interactively request all the data needed to create a file, and then it goes off and creates the file itself.

What information is needed to create a file? In addition to the information needed by the BFS CREATE_FILE function, all of the following data are needed:

- Device/user name or pathname
- Filename
- File size
- File organization
- Block size
- Record format
- Maximum record size

- File-sharing information
- File-organization-specific data

Next, we discuss step by step the tasks performed by the CREATE function.

1. Validate All Input parameters.   Within a data management system, we must never create a file that cannot be used because the user parameters are incorrect, or worse, correct but inconsistent. At the successful completion of the CREATE request, the user must be assured that the file is ready for use. Therefore, the job of the access method is to ensure, to the best of its abilities, that the input parameters are consistent and correct. For example, if a filename was not supplied, how could the user identify and locate the file tomorrow? Also, it is wrong if the block size specified for the file is smaller than the record size, because a block must be able to contain an entire record.

2. Call the Basic File System's CREATE_FILE Function.   The heart of CREATE processing requires that the correct disk or tape be mounted in the device, the name of the file be added to the directory, and disk space be allocated to it. These are the primary functions of the basic file system CREATE_FILE routine. In addition, the I/O buffer(s) must be allocated and initialized. The size of each I/O buffer is determined from the block-size input parameter.

3. Perform File-Organization-Specific Processing.   In virtually every file organization, there is something "nonstandard" that must be done in order to properly CREATE the file. In this section we discuss those things that must be done for each file organization over and above the standard processing. For examples, labels could be written onto tape files.

4. Write Out the File's Attributes.   As part of the CREATE processing, information must be written onto the medium in order for the file system to locate the file and to read and write the blocks within the file. In addition, information must be written out in order for the access method to be able to manipulate the records within the file. The basic file system deals only with the blocks in the file, but the access method must deal with the records within the blocks.

For the access method to be able to manipulate the records, it must know the record's format and size as well as other file-organization-specific data. The file organization, record format, and record size are attributes of the file that the access method must have in order to operate on the records correctly. Therefore, this information must also be written to the file. In fact, the overall set of file attributes, as these parameters are really known, include all the important information about a file that is needed to be able to process the file correctly, such as:

- Filename
- File organization
- Block size
- Record format

- Record size
- File size
- File organization specific data

The question is: Since it is so important, where is this information written? *The file system can record these data virtually anywhere, as long as they can be readily retrieved whenever they are needed.* The two easiest places to record the data are either as part of the file's directory entry or within the file itself. The directory entry is acceptable for standard data required by all file organizations, but when we get to file-specific information, we begin to run into complications of size of entry, as well as directory search performance degradation issues. Therefore, we will adopt the convention of putting only a minimal amount of data into the directory entry and the rest of the file attributes into the file itself (see Figure 8-1). For example, in the directory entry we could store the following information about the file:

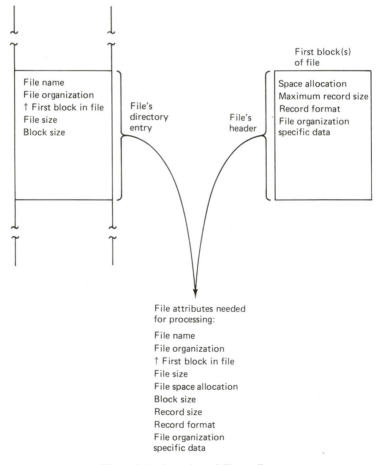

Figure 8-1 Location of file attributes.

- Filename
- File organization
- Address of first block in the file
- File size
- Block size

Then, within the file itself we could store the "nonstandard" data, such as:

- File space allocation
- Maximum record size
- Record format
- File-organization-specific data

The rationale for this split is to put into the directory entry only those data that might be reasonably useful when not accessing the file. After all, if we were going to access the file, it would not really matter much where the data had been stored, since we would have to retrieve them anyway. However, if we wanted to request a directory listing, it might be useful to have some of the data about the file displayed without taking the performance penalty of accessing the file.

Where in the file do we write the attributes? By convention, we can record them in the first n blocks of the file. Why? Because at create time, there are no records in the file yet, and thus the first block in the file will always be available. Also, it is an easy convention to remember and the file system does not need to go looking through the file to find the attributes.

5. Return Status and a File Identifier to Calling Program.   This is the last step in the file CREATE process. The *file identifier* is required so that the user can read and write to many different files at the same time. The file identifier allows the user to uniquely specify which of the current files the record operation is to be performed on. It is always necessary to notify the calling program whether or not the request that was made completed successfully or whether it encountered errors. Only when the calling program is told that the operation completed successfully can the program assume that records can now be written into the file.

Unsuccessful CREATE requests could have failed for any number of reasons, such as:

- Invalid create input parameter (e.g., no filename specified).
- No space available to create the file on the medium selected.
- File already exists on the medium with the same name. In this case either we gave an incorrect name, or the file had already been created by someone else.

What is important to remember is that the access method is the interface to the user application programs, and status must always be returned to the user's program.

In summary, we have seen that the access method (AM) CREATE function greatly overlaps the basic file system's CREATE_FILE operation. We can summarize this as follows:

AM CREATE = (BFS CREATE_FILE) + (AM-specific processing)

At the completion of the CREATE processing, the file has been completely built and is left open for the user to write and read records.

8.3.2 OPEN File

The purpose of the access OPEN function is to allow users to access files that have been previously created within the system. If the file has already been created, all a user wants to do is to read and write the records within the file. Thus the appropriate access method call is to open the file for processing.

On the other hand, some high-level languages do not provide the capability of allowing a user to create a new file. Instead, they allow the user to *open* a file. If the file does not exist, it is assumed to be a user request to create a new file.

In any case, the OPEN request formally connects the user's program with a file. The information required to OPEN a file can be specified as follows:

- Device/user name or pathname
- Filename

In addition, users are allowed to open the file under certain user-defined constraints. Specifically, users can request the following:

- OPEN for *input* only (i.e., the user will perform only READ type operations)
- OPEN for *output* only (i.e., the user will only WRITE to this file)
- OPEN for *input and output* (i.e., the user wants to be able to perform all types of record operations on this file)

It is again up to the access methods to ensure that only those record requests that conform to the mode under which the file was opened are actually processed. All other requests must be rejected as errors.

All other attributes of the file were specified at file CREATE time. Thus, with the complete pathname to locate the file, the file system can then retrieve the file attributes that were written at the time the file was built.

All the information written out as part of the CREATE processing is read back as part of the OPEN processing. This is because the OPEN task must bring the file system and access method back up to the level that existed just after the file had been created. Therefore, the processing of the OPEN operation is as follows:

1. Validate Input Parameters.   This essentially corresponds to the same step in the CREATE processing. However, the input parameters are somewhat different since we no longer need to specify all the file attributes; we need only find and read them back. How can we find the location of the file, and then its attributes? All that is required is the file, or more specifically, the pathname. With these data, the file system can read the directory entries until it finds a matching name. It can then read the attributes into memory, where the access method can copy them into the preallocated file control blocks.

Thus the only parameter that needs to be validated is the file's pathname. If that is correct, the file can be found, and all the other parameters or attributes can be read from the file itself. This is a critical point. We could have let the user respecify all of the file's attributes. However, it is the job of the access methods to guarantee that data are never destroyed within the file and that the records can always be successfully read and written, barring hardware problems.

If the user must specify the file's attributes each time, what if the user makes a mistake? What if there are 200 users each wanting access to the same file? What is the probability that all of those 200 users will supply the file attribute data with no errors? It is simply not worth the risk to the data within the file. The file system and the access methods should only trust the person who had the responsibility of creating the file and defining all of the file's attributes. If the person who created the file was wrong on one or more of the attributes, there is nothing that can be done, short of recreating the file. But if there is a conflict between the attributes recorded in the file and the attributes passed by a user of the file, there is no choice but to take the attributes that were written into the file itself. Also, remember, that all records written into the file were written according to the attributes defined within the file, so they really cannot be changed on the fly.

2. Call the Basic File System's OPEN_FILE Function.   As part of the OPEN processing, the access method must ensure that the file is ready for the user to access the records in it. First, the access method must check the volume label to ensure that the correct volume has been mounted on the device. Remember that file "abc" can reside on multiple volumes (e.g., backup versions). Thus it is critical that the *correct* volume be mounted and verified by the access method. Then, and only then, can processing continue.

Next, the access method must determine the size of the blocks in the file from the file attributes. Then it must tell the file system to allocate one or more I/O buffers large enough to contain the largest block in the file. Once this has been done, I/O can be done by the file system to read or write any block in the file on behalf of the user.

The next function that must be performed is to allocate mainmemory space for the FCB. Then the access method must copy the relevent file attributes into the FCB for future use.

Each of these functions is performed by calling the OPEN_FILE routine in the basic file system. Like the CREATE processing, a fair amount of the processing overlaps with that of the basic file system processing.

3. Perfrom File-Organization-Specific Processing.   Although the OPEN process is much more standard across the set of file organizations, there are still certain unique things which must be done at OPEN time for particular file types. It is the purpose of this section to highlight all file organization specific processing which is over and above the standard processing. Typically, at the completion of OPEN processing, the access methods set the current record pointer to point to the first user data record in the file. This is done so that the user can immediately execute a READ or READ_NEXT operation and have it succeed.

4. Read the File's Attributes.   Now that the control blocks and I/O buffers have been allocated, it is necessary to access all of the attributes of the file. These characteristics can be read both from the file's directory entry and from the file itself. These attributes are then copied into the various control blocks within the file system.

5. Return Status and the File Identifier to the Calling Program.   Again, as with the CREATE request, the calling program must be informed as to whether or not the request was completed successfully. If it was, the user can assume that reading and writing of the records can begin immediately. If there was an error, the user must determine the next course of action. In any case, it is up to the user to determine what to do next.

An OPEN function call can fail for a variety of reasons, such as:

- File cannot be found in the location specified by its pathname.
- File was found, but the current user does not have sufficient access rights to use the file.
- Unrecoverable hardware problems were encountered.

Also, the OPEN function returns to the calling program a file identifier, which uniquely identifies this specific file among all the files that are currently OPEN on the system.

In summary, an OPEN request is very similar to the basic file system's OPEN_FILE function. The access method OPEN can be viewed as follows:

AM OPEN = (BFS OPEN_FILE) + (AM-specific processing)

As was the case with the CREATE function, if the OPEN is successful, the file is left in a state in which the user can then access the data records.

8.3.3 Close File

The purpose of the CLOSE function is to allow users the opportunity to deaccess, or stop using, a particular file. After a user has processed the records in the file, there needs to be some way to tell the access method "I'm done." This is one of the tasks of the CLOSE request. When this function is invoked, the access method knows that its sole responsibility is to ensure that the file is deaccessed correctly in such a way that no records are lost or destroyed. The only input required is the unique file identifier that was returned by the file system by the CREATE or OPEN functions. To accomplish this task, the CLOSE routine performs the following tasks:

1. Write Out Any Remaining Data Still in I/O Buffers.   Sometimes, as we shall soon see, the records and blocks in a file are not actually written back to the file until they have to be. This cuts down on the actual number of real I/O operations performed and therefore improves performance. On the other hand, it then forces on the CLOSE routine the responsibility to ensure that any data not yet written into the file actually get transferred there. In this manner, no records will be lost and performance will be improved.

To perform this function, the access methods must maintain enough internal control information to know the following:

- What I/O buffers are in main memory?
- Who owns the data in the I/O buffers?
- Which I/O buffers have been modified?

2. Perform File-Organization-Specific Processing.   This step mainly involves ensuring that all critical file-processing information has been written out into the file. Although this may be the case in most situations, there will arise cases in which the data are not rewritten until the file is closed in order, for example, to improve performance. Trailer labels on tape could be written out now, for example.

An access method might need to write out the following kinds of information:

- File-processing statistics
- Current end-of-file or last block used
- Current physical end-of-file

By saving these data, each access method will then be able to successfuly re-OPEN the file later and correctly process all of its data records.

3. Call the Basic File System CLOSE_FILE Function.   The purpose of this call is to allow the basic file system to clean up its tables, as well as to be able to deallocate any main memory that was used in support of the processing of that file. Also, the basic file system will write out all blocks in I/O buffers which have been modified since the last write of the buffer.

4. Return Status to the Calling Program.   This is done for the same reasons as mentioned previously. It is brought up here again simply to help drive home the importance of notifying the calling program of the status (i.e., success or failure) of the completed request.

It is possible for a CLOSE function to encounter errors and thus not complete successfully. Typically, these kinds of errors are easy to fix, such as:

- File to be CLOSEd has never been OPENed.
- File I/O errors encountered when writing the I/O buffers out into the file.
- Not enough space on the medium to write out all of the modified I/O block buffers.

In summary, the CLOSE operation is almost the exact inverse of the processing that is performed at OPEN time. Also, it is again worthwhile to view the CLOSE function in the following perspectives:

AM CLOSE = (BFS CLOSE_FILE) + (AM-specific processing)

It is worth noting that if a user fails to issue the CLOSE request before finishing execution of the program, it is the responsibility of the access method to perform the proper processing *as if the user had specifically requested a close operation to be performed.* This is needed as a safeguard against potentially losing data in the file. Also, there could have been a bug in the user's program, but the user is not yet aware that a problem exists. Remember, the file system and access method must always work together to ensure that the correct processing gets done, whether or not the user program is "correct."

8.3.4 Extend file

The purpose of the access method EXTEND file function is to allow user programs to increase the size of a file. This is essentially the same function as that provided by the basic file system EXTEND_FILE function. It is redone here to present to users a consistent access method interface.

The inputs to the EXTEND file function are as follows:

- Unique file identifier
- Size by which file is to be extended
- Contiguous allocation required, or not?

The processing that the EXTEND function performs is similar to the processing done by the other access method file operations.

1. Validate All Input Parameters.   First, all input parameters are validated.

2. Call the Basic File System EXTEND Function.   Then, if all is well, the basic file system EXTEND_FILE function is called to physically extend the file by the amount requested by the user program.

3. Perform File-Organization-Specific Processing.   While the processing required for each file organization that is unique is minimal, there will be cases in which the EXTEND processing *will be* access method dependent. For example, with the more complex file organizations such as VSAM, space might be allocated for very specific uses within the file itself, as opposed simply to adding to a pool of space usable anywhere in the file structure.

4. Return Status to the Calling Program.   Finally, status is returned to the calling program to indicate whether or not the file was extended successfully. As is usually the case, it is possible for the EXTEND function not to complete processing correctly. Some of the reasons for this conclusion are as follows:

- Not enough total space available on the device.
- If contiguous was requested, there might not be enough contiguous space available on the device.
- Some systems have a preset maximum number of times in which to EXTEND the file. This is typically done to prevent the case of a runaway program taking more and more room on a disk.

Thus the access method EXTEND processing can be summarized as follows:

$$\text{AM EXTEND} = (\text{BFS EXTEND\_FILE}) + (\text{AM-specific processing})$$

8.4 RECORD OPERATIONS

Once we have managed to gain access into the file via an OPEN or CREATE request, the file is left in a state such that records can now be processed. Therefore, in this section we examine the various record operations that users might like to perform. Before we do that, however, let us first look at three concepts that are important to an understanding of access methods in general: the concepts of *record access modes, record currency,* and *end-of-file.*

Record addressing algorithm(s).   Once the file structure is built and the proper file attributes have been written into it, how are the data records accessed? In this section of each chapter we discuss how records can be inserted into and retrieved from the file. Specifically, given a particular file organization, how can we both sequentially and randomly access individual data records within the file?

Record access modes.   Whenever a user wishes to access records in a file, it is usually done in one of two ways, *sequentially* or *randomly.* These are called *access modes.* In *sequential access mode, the user tells the access method that the records will be requested in the same order in which they exist in the file.*

For example, reading sequentially could retrieve the records in *chronological* order or in a predefined *ascending key sequence.* Thus the user will read data records 1, 2, 3, and so on, until either the last record in the file has been accessed or until the last record needed by the program has been read. Note that when records are read sequentially, the only information the access method requires is to know where in the file to start reading the records. After that, the user simply requests the next record. The access method understands that this means the record immediately following the last record given to the user.

In random access mode, the user effectively relates to the access method the fact that the records will not be read in any predetermined sequence, and in fact, they will be read randomly. Thus the user may read records 5, 186, 1, 9608, and 444. For the access method to know which record to read next, the user must always supply a *key,* such as a record number, from which the access method can determine the exact record desired.

Record currency.   It is critical that the access method remember precisely where the last record read was located. For example, in sequential access mode, if we knew where in the file the last record read was, it would be a simple matter to reposition to that location and then get the very next record in the file. *The identification of the last record successfully read is known as the current record pointer (CRP), and the record itself is called the current record (CR)* (see Figure 8-2). We will discover in the next several sections how valuable the CR and CRP are. For now, just understand that the current record position and current record are important pieces of data that the access method must remember. Also, since the file system works only in blocks, and not records, the file system does not need to remember anything about CRs or CRPs. Finally, it is important to understand that the current record and the current record pointer are set only on input (i.e., READ, POSITION) requests, not on output (i.e., WRITE, DELETE, UPDATE) requests (see Table 8-1).

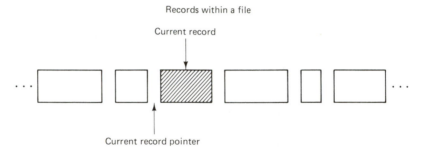

Figure 8-2   Record currency.

For the purposes of this book, we will adopt the COBOL standards for the modification of current record pointers. This means that only input operations (e.g., READ, READ_NEXT, and POSITION) will be able to set the CRP. Output operations (e.g., WRITE, UPDATE, and DELETE) will not modify the current record or the current record pointer.

TABLE 8-1   CURRENT RECORD POINTER STATES

Current record before Operation	Record operation	Current record after operation
Not applicable	POSITION	Changed to point to record retrieved
Not applicable	READ	Changed to point to record retrieved
Must be valid	READ_NEXT	Changed to point to next record retrieved
Not applicable	WRITE	Unchanged
Must be valid	UPDATE	Unchanged
Must be valid	DELETE	Unchanged

Logical end-of-file.   This is an important concept to understand since it is a critical indicator to the access methods. *The logical end-of-file condition indicates that while reading the records sequentially within the file, there are no more user data records left in the file.* Thus we are at the logical end-of-file.

Note the difference between *logical* and *physical* end-of-file. *Logical end-of-file indicates that there are no more user data records left in the file.* Not all of the blocks in the file need to contain data records. Thus a program could reach the logical end-of-file and there could still be space available in the file itself. On the other hand, *physical end-of-file indicates that there are no more allocated blocks left in the file* (see Figure 8–3). In other words, the program has used all the blocks that were allocated to the file. Thus the file is physically out of blocks, or at physical end-of-file.

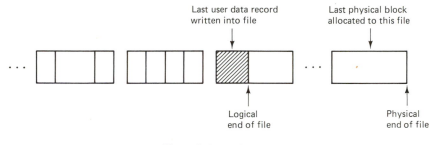

Figure 8–3   End-of-file.

This condition cannot be reached while randomly accessing the data records. This is because when we randomly try to fetch a record, it is either in the file or not found. The record being accessed could actually be past the end-of-file, but the proper response to the random read would be *record not found.*

8.4.1 POSITION to Record

The POSITION command allows a user to position to a particular valid record in a file, but not to actually read the record into the user's record buffer. For example, the user may just want to determine whether or not a particular record exists. The way to do this is via the POSITION request. This is similar to the START verb in COBOL. Alternatively, the POSITION command can be used to position to a specific point within the file so that the user can then sequentially access the data records starting at that point in the file. The inputs required by this record operation are as follows:

- The unique *file identifier* that is associated with this file
- The *key* that identifies the record desired
- Key search criteria, such as:
    - Locate an *exact* key match in the file

— Locate a record that has a key *equal to or greater than* the search key

— Locate a record that has a key *greater than* the search key

- A *status field* into which the access method can store the termination status for this I/O request.

To successfully POSITION to a specific record in a file, the access method must determine in which disk block the target record resides. Then it must read that disk block into an I/O buffer in main memory. Once in memory, the access method must search the block to find the location of the record requested by the user.

The steps required to successfully process a POSITION request are as follows.

1. Validate Input Parameters.   This step is always required in order to catch errors *before* they get into a file.

2. Convert Key to Actual Disk Address.   User programs always work in terms of records or record keys when they are accessing a file. This is done because it is easier for the user program to understand and relate to the data in a file than to how a file is constructed or accessed. It is the task of the access method to convert a record address, or identifier such as a key, to a block address within a file. The basic file system then converts the block address, which is relative to the first block *of the file,* to a real disk address.

3. Call the Basic File System's READ_BLOCK Function.   The block identified by the calculation in step 2 must then be read into an I/O buffer in main memory. The only exception to this is when that specific block is already in an I/O buffer in main memory. It is the function of the basic file system first to check the I/O buffers to see if the target block already resides in memory. If it does, no additional I/O need be performed, and thus performance, as seen by the response time of the request, will be dramatically improved.

4. Perform Access-Method-Specific Processing.   Once the target block has been read into main memory, the access method must then search the block for the specific record that was requested by the user program. The precise technique for doing this depends on the file organization and is thus file specific. We discuss this topic in more detail in the chapters that follow. However, the POSITION command always locates the *first* valid record that matches the search criteria. This means that it will skip over all records that meet the criteria but are marked as having been deleted.

5. Set Current Record Pointer to Target Record.   The POSITION command changes the value of the current record identification. Thus a successful POSITION will force the current record to be updated to reflect the record just POSITIONed to. An unsuccessful POSITION operation will cause the current record to be marked as invalid.

Note that the block containing the target record must have been read into one of the I/O block buffers. Then the data records in that block must be searched according to the specified search criteria. Thus, even though the block is read into main memory, no data record is copied from the I/O buffer into the user's record buffer.

6. *Return Status to the Calling Program.* After every operation, status must be returned to the calling program. A POSITION function can either succeed or fail. If it fails, it can be for a number of reasons, such as the following:

- Record identified by *key* could not be found.
- Input key value was invalid.
- Target record has been locked by another user, thus preventing us from accessing it.

In summary, the outputs from the POSITION function are as follows:

- The current record is reset to the record just POSITIONed to.
- The user data record buffer is *not* changed.
- The I/O buffer holds the block from the file that contains the data record the user wanted to POSITION to in the file.
- Status is returned to the calling program.

The POSITION processing can be summarized as follows:

AM POSITION = (BFS READ_BLOCK) + (AM-specific processing)

8.4.2 READ Record

Up to this point we have not discussed how the user could request a copy of a record in a file. *The READ record operation requests that a record in the file is to be read into the file system I/O buffer, and then the record is to be copied into the user's record buffer.* To be valid, the user must have opened the file for either *input only,* or for *input and output* processing. The inputs to the READ request are as follows:

- Unique *file identifier*
- The *key* that identifies the data record wanted
- A key search criterion, as defined in the POSITION command
- An address of the *user record buffer* that holds the record to be READ
- The *size* of the user data record buffer
- A *status field* into which the access method can return the final status of the request

Again, the key is the identification of the record within the file so that the access method knows which record the user wants: for example, the record whose key was my employee number or student ID. We will discuss keys in greater detail when we talk about the specific access methods.

What is the difference between the POSITION command and the READ command? The READ command reads the record into main memory and then copies it into a user data record buffer. On the other hand, a POSITION command only reads the block containing the data record into main memory. POSITION does *not* copy the record into a user record buffer.

The processing steps required to perform a successful READ request are as follows:

1. Validate the Input Parameters.   Again, catch all errors now, before they can make it into the file and corrupt the data.

2. Call the Access Method POSITION Function.   Before a user data record can be retrieved, it must be located within the file itself. This is precisely the function of the POSITION function.

3. Copy the Record from the I/O Buffer into the User Buffer.   Unlike the POSITION function, which does not give the calling program visibility to the target record, the READ function actually copies the target record from the I/O buffer to the user data record buffer. Thus a successful READ operation gives the user a copy of the desired record to work with.

We need to be careful, however, as to how much of the data record is to get copied into the user record buffer. First, if the record is equal to or larger than the size of the user data record buffer, only the *record buffer size* amount of data can be copied. This is true even if the data record is longer than the buffer supplied by the user.

In the case in which the data record is shorter than the user data record buffer, the entire data record is copied from the block in the I/O buffer into the user data record buffer. In no case is more data copied into the user's buffer than is requested by the user in the buffer-size parameter.

4. Return Status to the User Program.   A READ command has status conditions that are almost identical to those of the POSITION command. This is because the majority of the processing is performed by that command function. There is, however, an additional error condition that can arise.

If the data record is *larger* than the user buffer size, the calling program must be told that it did not receive all the information in the data record. It is up to the calling program to determine whether or not this is an error and what needs to be done about it. However, it is the responsibility of the access method to inform the calling program whenever it has not been given all the data it could have received.

The outputs from a successful READ command can be summarized as follows:

- Current record reset to the record just READ.
- I/O buffer contains the block that holds the data record just READ by the user.
- Data record copied from the I/O buffer *into* the user's own record buffer.
- The size of the data record copied into the user's buffer is returned to the calling program.
- Completion status is returned to the calling program.

The READ command processing can be summarized as follows:

AM READ = AM POSITION + (copy record to data record buffer)

At the completion of both the READ and POSITION commands, one of the I/O buffers in main memory contains the block that holds the record just accessed. This is important, since if the next record that is requested resides in this same block, there is no I/O operation involved in accessing that record. This is because the basic file system checks all I/O buffers for the desired block *before* it attempts to perform an actual I/O operation. In this manner, performance can be improved substantially.

8.4.3 READ_NEXT Record

We said earlier that the user could specify a record access mode of sequential access. If not done explicitly, it can be done with this command. *The READ_NEXT opera-tion requests that the access method get the next logical data record following the current record that was read or positioned to via the READ or POSITION commands* (see Figure 8-4). Depending on the type of file organization, the *next* record in the file could be the next record in the block or the next record in ascending key sequence. It is up to the access methods to determine how to locate the "next" record. To allow READ_NEXT commands, the file must have been opened in either the *input only* or the *input and output* processing mode. The inputs to the READ_NEXT request are as follows:

- Unique *file identifier*
- The *address* of the user record buffer into which the data record will be copied
- The *size* of the record buffer
- A *status field* into which the access method can store the completion status of the request

Note that there is no input *key* parameter. This is because the READ_NEXT command tells the access method to go get the next logical record following the last record given to the user, wherever it is. How does the access method know where to get the next record? It goes to the current record pointer, which points to the last record successfully read or positioned to, and then finds the next record in the file.

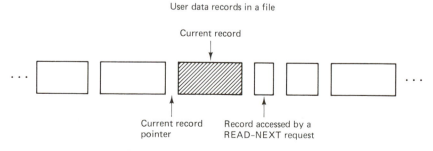

Figure 8-4   READ_NEXT processing.

Thus the CRP is used to locate the next record when the file is being processed in sequential access mode.

To read all of the user data records in a file, we would need to write a small loop of READ_NEXT requests. This would continue until the end-of-file condition had been reached. Note that the end-of-file is really a *logical end-of-file (LEOF) since it only indicates that there are no more data records left in the file. Physical end-of-file indicates that there is literally no more space available on the medium at all (see Figure 8–5).*

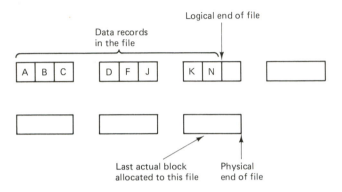

Figure 8-5 READ_NEXT error conditions.

In summary, the difference between the READ and the READ_NEXT commands is that a READ can *randomly access any data record* in the file. A READ_NEXT can only access the *next logical record* in the file.

The processing steps for READ_NEXT are identical to those for READ. However, what is different is how each access method determines where the *next* data record in the file is located. In addition, there are several error conditions that can arise here that cannot be seen elsewhere, such as:

- Logical end-of-file reached. This condition simply states that there are no more user data records in the file
- The current record identifier is not valid. Thus the access method cannot position to the logically next record in the file.

The outputs from a successful READ_NEXT operation are as follows:

- The current record is reset to the record just accessed.
- An I/O buffer in main memory holds the block of the file that contains the data record just read.
- The data record is copied from the I/O buffer into the user's record buffer.
- The length of the data record is returned to the calling program.
- The completion status of the READ_NEXT is returned to the calling program.

The READ_NEXT processing can be described as follows:

AM READ_NEXT = AM POSITION + (copy record into record buffer)

Again note that the READ_NEXT function is almost identical to the READ function. The only difference is that the READ is used to *randomly* access any record in the file. READ_NEXT can only sequentially access the next logical data record in the file.

8.4.4 WRITE Record

The WRITE record command allows the user to add a new record into the file. The WRITE command is the only way in which a user can add new records into a file. It is also the only way in which the file system or access method can tell that a new record is being added to a file, as opposed to simply changing an old version of a record. To allow WRITE operations on the file, the user must have opened the file for *output* or for *input and output*. Its input parameters are as follows:

- Unique *file identifier*
- The *key* that identifies the user data record to be written into the file
- The *address* of the user record buffer that contains the record to be written
- The *size* of the data record in the user record buffer
- A *status field* into which the access method can pass back the completion status of the request

Here *key* tells the access method where to put the record in the file. Depending on the file organization, the records could go in sequentially, by record number, or by a key such as name, ID, and so on. An important point to remember is that no matter where we currently are in the file, *the access method will always place new records into their proper location as determined by the file organization.* The reason for this is that if the records are inserted into the file by the proper algorithm, the access method can later retrieve those same records by the same algorithm.

The WRITE record request implies that a *brand new record* is being added into the file (see Figure 8–6), not an old one simply being changed. This is an important distinction, since the access methods must be able to tell whether a request is adding a record to the file or simply changing an already existing record.

Note that since we are writing into the file, space on the device must be available into which data records can be written. There will be occasions in which all the space in the file has been used and the user requests that one more record be written into this file. In this situation, the access method can call the file system to increase, or EXTEND, the size of the file. This is called *an implicit extension since it is being done on behalf of the user and without an explicit user request.* Some file systems will not perform an implicit extend, so that the WRITE request would then fail. However, philosophically speaking, an access method should always try to successfully

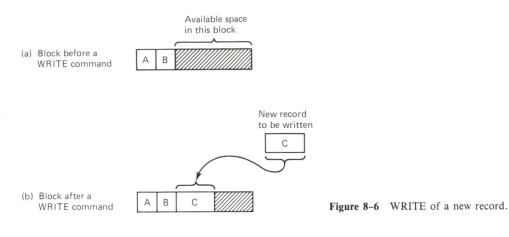

Figure 8-6   WRITE of a new record.

complete the user's requests. Why? Because to fail on the WRITE says that data that should be in the file are not, because we knew what needed to be done and we chose not to do it. Again, the overall file system should be concerned with the data, not over how much work or code it might need to accomplish the task.

The processing steps required to perform a WRITE operation are as follows:

1. Validate Input Parameters.   This is done to ensure that only correct input data are processed.

2. Convert Key to Valid Disk Address.   This step may require multiple reads in order to eventually arrive at the target block. In any case, the user provides a logical record identifier which the file system must convert into a physical device address.

Also, the target block is read from the device. This is done because the target block may indeed already contain data records. Thus this new WRITE is just a matter of adding the new record into this block. Also, if this block is already in an I/O buffer in main memory, the actual I/O operation is not performed because the latest version of the block is already in memory.

3. Perform Access-Method-Specific Processing.   Once we have arrived at the target block, the access method must decide whether or not the user data record can actually be inserted into that specific block. Depending on the access method, a variety of responses could occur if there were no room for the record at that location. This condition is known as a *collision. A collision occurs whenever a record cannot be inserted into a file where logically it should go.* For example, the target block may already be filled with data records. Then what?

4. Extend the Size of the File, If Necessary.   It may be that there is no space available in the entire file for this record. The choice then is whether to extend the file for the user. This step, and the preceding step, work hand in hand to get the record successfully processed. This step is split out individually to highlight the fact that the file may need to be extended.

5. *Copy User Data Record into New Target Block.* Once a block has been found that has enough room for the data record, it must be copied from the user record buffer into the I/O buffer.

6. *Re-write the Target Block into the File.* Once the record has been copied into the target block, it is necessary to rewrite that block into the file. This WRITE operation may take place immediately, or it may be delayed until that I/O buffer is needed for another block.

The block in the I/O buffer may or may not be written back to the device at this time. It all depends on whether or not the file system is using a *deferred writing* option to help improve performance. *Deferred writing is the situation where the file system delays writing of a block to a device until that specific I/O buffer is needed for some other purpose.* Then and only then will the file system write that block out to the device. The expectation here is that the user will process multiple records in that particular block, so why continually reread the same block? This action should, in turn, improve overall performance. Should the next request from the user also read or write a record that requires this same block, the file system does not need to reread the block.

7. *Return Status to the Calling Program.* If the WRITE operation fails, it can be for a variety of reasons, such as:

- File cannot be extended and there is no room in the file for the user data record.
- Another record with the same *key* may already exist in the file. It is up to the access method to determine whether to allow this condition to occur.
- Hardware failure detected.

The outputs of the WRITE function can be listed as follows:

- The block in which the data record is to be written into has been read into an I/O buffer in main memory.
- The data record is copied from the user's record buffer into the proper location in the block in the I/O buffer.
- The I/O buffer is marked as *modified* or dirty.
- Completion status is returned to the calling program.

Finally, the WRITE operation does not modify or change in any way the current record or the current record pointer. The WRITE operation can be summarized as follows:

$$AM \ WRITE = POSITION + (\text{copy data record into I/O buffer})$$
$$+ (BFS \ WRITE\_BLOCK)$$

The POSITION command is needed in order to locate the target record and to read it into an I/O buffer in main memory. The WRITE_BLOCK command is needed to rewrite the modified block back into the proper place in the file.

8.4.5 Update Record

When the user wants to add a new record into the file, the WRITE record request is issued. However, what if the user simply wants to change or modify a record that already exists in the file? *The purpose of the UPDATE record command is to allow the user to change, or modify, a record that already exists in the file.* To accomplish this, the user must issue an UPDATE record request. Also, the user must have opened the file for *input and output*. No other open mode is valid, since in order to UPDATE a record the user must first have read that data record. Note that to the access method, a new record is distinguished from a change of an old record by the command issued, either a WRITE (i.e., a new record) or an UPDATE (i.e., a change of an old record).

The input parameters to the UPDATE request are as follows:

- *File Identifier*
- The *address* of the user record buffer that contains the updated data record
- The *size* of the data record in the record buffer
- A *status field* into which the termination status can be stored

Again, note that no record key or identifier has been specified. The reason for this is that the access method will modify only the *current record*. This also means that to UPDATE a record, the user must have previously issued a successful READ, READ_NEXT, or POSITION request, since only these operations set the current record pointer.

Technically speaking, it is possible to randomly modify a record in a file without having read the record. However, one of the responsibilities of the access method is to protect the integrity of the data as much as impossible. When records are randomly changed without having read them first, how can the user know that the correct record was changed? For example, what if there were 2057 SMITHs in a file. Which of those records would be changed via an UPDATE operation?

Since the record is being changed or modified, it is reasonable to expect that the record size might also be changed. In fact, the record could either get larger, stay the same, or decrease in size if the record format were defined as variable length. This is important, since not all file organizations allow all these possibilities to occur, and therefore the access methods must be sensitive to the constraints and the objectives of each file organization.

The processing steps involved in updating a record that already exists are almost identical to the steps involved in the WRITE processing. This is because the target block *and target record* must be read into main memory first (see Figure 8–7a). Then, instead of copying a new record into the block, the updated record *replaces* the old record in the block (see Figure 8–7b).

The error conditions that can arise are somewhat different from the WRITE command. For example, some of the UPDATE errors that can occur are as follows:

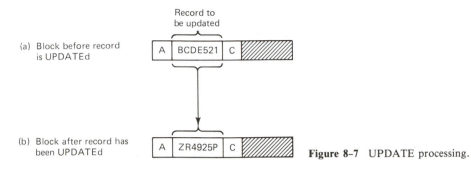

Figure 8-7 UPDATE processing.

- Record to be UPDATEd does not exist in the file.
- The *key* of the UPDATEd record has been changed, and this file organization does not allow keys to change.
- The UPDATEd record has increased in size, and there is not enough room in the file for the UPDATEd record.

The results of a successful UPDATE operation can be described as follows:

- Current record is not changed.
- Modified record copied from the user's record buffer and into the I/O buffer containing the target block.
- Status is returned to the calling program.

As was the case with the previous operations, the BFS WRITE_BLOCK operation may not actually take place at this time. In summary, an UPDATE of a record consists of the following operations:

$$AM\ UPDATE = POSITION + (\text{copy modified record into I/O buffer})$$
$$+ (BFS\ WRITE\_BLOCK)$$

Note that the formulas for WRITE and UPDATE are nearly identical. This is because both operations write out modified versions of a record to the file. In the case of a WRITE, it is an entirely new record. For UPDATE, it is an old record that has been modified in some manner.

8.4.6 Delete Record

On occasion, a user may want to get rid of a record that already exists in the file. *The DELETE record command allows the user to logically delete records that currently exist within a file.* To be allowed, the user must have opened the file for both *input and output* processing permitted. The input parameters to this function are as follows:

- The *file identifier* for this particular file
- A *status field* into which the end result of the request can be stored.

An important point is again raised here, as the identification of the record being deleted is not specified explicitly by the user. This is analogous to the way in which the UPDATE command worked, namely that the record being operated on is defined by the current record pointer. Thus the record being DELETEd is the current record. This is done for the same reasons mentioned previously. Therefore, to DELETE a record, the user must have had a previously successful input operation on that specific record.

Records can be either logically or physically deleted from a file. Records can be physically deleted by having the file system compress them out of the block in which they were located (see Figure 8-8a). This is done by shuffling all the records in the block to overlay the space used by the deleted record (see Figure 8-8b).

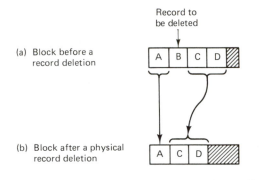

(a) Block before a record deletion

(b) Block after a physical record deletion

Figure 8-8   Physical DELETE of a record.

Records are logically deleted by setting a *flag byte* which indicates that the record has been deleted and is no longer logically present (see Figure 8-9a). Thus if someone tries to READ that record, the request will fail since the record no longer logically exists within the file. The benefit of logically deleting a record is that the record still exists in case it is ever needed (see Figure 8-9b).

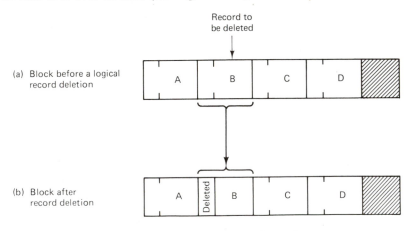

(a) Block before a logical record deletion

(b) Block after record deletion

Figure 8-9   Logical deletion of records.

What could we do if we accidentally deleted the wrong data record? If we logically deleted the record, we could easily undelete it. Although this is usually *not* part of an access method's functionality, it is available to a user if special programming is done to take advantage of it. On the other hand, if we physically removed the record from the file, our only alternative would be to restore the record from some past backup tape. This would not only take a considerable amount of time, but the restored record may not reflect the latest changes made since the last backup was performed. Also, when we consider performance, it is much faster simply to mark a record as being logically deleted.

The end result of the processing performed by the DELETE operation results in the following:

- The current record is marked as being logically deleted from the file.
- The current record remains unchanged.
- Status is returned to the calling program.

The DELETE function can be viewed as logically consisting of the following I/O requests:

$$\text{AM DELETE} = \text{POSITION} + (\text{set deleted flag on record})$$
$$+ (\text{BFS WRITE\_BLOCK})$$

The DELETE processing is identical to the UPDATE processing. In each case, they write out modified records to the file. However, the modification that DELETE makes is simple to turn on the *record deleted flag*.

Finally, why should an access method prohibit *random* record deletions? It is technically possible to design and implement a DELETE function that would randomly delete any valid user data record in the file. The only interface requirement would be the addition of a *record number* or identification of the record to be deleted. The access method could then read the block containing the record, locate it in that block, and mark it as deleted.

The primary reason random deletes are being prohibited in this discussion is that they are extremely dangerous. For example, how can the user program *know* that the record being deleted is the correct one? Which record should be deleted when the user program requests ''SMITH'' to be deleted and there are 1000 SMITHs in the file? On the other hand, if the user program is forced to read the target record first, the user has the capability of verifying which record is to be deleted.

8.5 PERFORMANCE CONSIDERATIONS

8.5.1 General Issues

The performance characteristics that are important to file processing are discussed in more detail in the specific access method chapters. However, we should begin to appreciate the performance differences, as well as requirements, for the file operations as well as for the record operations.

Finally, if there is a choice between doing some processing task in *either* the file or record operations, it would be perferable to perform the work during the file operation processing. This is because the file operations tend to be requested much less frequently. Thus a slight performance hit there would not appreciably affect overall processing time for the job (refer to the 80/20 rule which was discussed in Chapter 1).

8.5.2 File Population Techniques

Although not usually thought of as an access method issue, there is a serious problem related to how long it takes to insert all of the user data records into a file. This process, known as *populating the file*, can take a considerble amount of time for some file organizations. In this section in each of the access method chapters we discuss issues that are relevant to that specific file type.

8.5.3 File Reorganization

Over a period of time, the performance of a file can degrade. This can happen for a variety of reasons, such as:

- The file contains many deleted records.
- Many records have been added to the file since it was originally populated. Thus many records are not located in their most ideal places in the file.

What has really happened is that every record in every file has a very specific location where it should be written. This is the primary record address in a file. However, as records get added and deleted over time, there will be an increasing number of times when a record cannot be placed in its target spot (e.g., perhaps there is no more room in the target block). Therefore, the access method is forced into alternative algorithms in order to successfully write the record into the file. This exception processing always takes more time than it would take if the records went into the primary part of the file. Thus, over time, performance gets slower and slower. To correct this situation, the file must be reorganized.

File reorganization is the procedure performed to recreate a brand new file that has the same file attributes as the original, yet has all records in their most optimal locations. The processing steps involved in a file reorganization are as folows:

1. Create a New Temporary File with the Same File Attributes. The purpose of this step is to create a mirror image of the original or master file. The only difference is that the user could change the amount of space allocated to the file so that all records could be held in a more contiguous allocation.

2. Copy All User Data Records to Temporary File. Basically a program is written which reads all the records in the original master file and then writes each record into the temporary file. This is *not* a file copy. This copy is performed by using the record operations of the related file organization.

What really occurs is that the access method can end up writing all the current records in the master file into their proper locations in the temporary file. Thus the end result is a more optimally built file structure. Once again, performance will be restored to its original levels. However, over time, as records again get added and deleted, performance will begin to degrade. For some applications and file organizations, file reorganizations can be required every night or every week. In other cases, file reorganizations are never needed. It all depends on the file organization selected and the activity within that particular file.

3. Verify that the Temporary File Is OK.   Once all the data records have been written into the temporary file, it is necessary to verify that the new file is readable. This is an important step, because once we decide that the temporary file is valid, we will then delete the original master copy. If the temporary file subsequently becomes unreadable, we will be forced to go through a difficult file reconstruction process.

4. Delete the Original Master File.   This step can occur only after we are sure that the temporary file is readable. The original master file is being deleted because it is no longer required, and we also do not want any confusion as to what the latest version of the file really is.

5. Rename the Temporary File to the Original Master File's Name.   The purpose of this step is to make the new file appear to all programs as the original master file. The only difference is that the file has been reorganized and thus users should notice improved responsiveness.

In summary, a file reorganization reconstructs the entire master file in such a way that user programs do not actually know that a change has occurred. Yet performance and space utilization should be noticably improved.

8.6 DESIGN TRADE-OFFS

8.6.1 General Issues

In discussing the various access methods, it will be necessary to discuss the *costs*, as well as the *benefits*, of each. In addition, how a file is structured may vary depending on whether the application machine is a mainframe, minicomputer or microcomputer. Thus it is critical to understand what trade-offs can and should be made under varying resource configurations.

Another issue that will be discussed is the space versus performance trade-off. When space is important, performance will be affected, and vice versa.

8.6.2 File Size Calculations

Since files take up disk space, it is important to understand how to calculate how much space a particular file will take. It is fairly straightforward to calculate the amount of space the user data records will take up if we know the following:

- The expected number of data records that will exist in the file
- The average number of data records that will fit per block in the file
- The average size of each block in the file

There is, however, a further complication. Each file organization has associated with it some additional space requirements. This additional space is to allow the access methods to be able to correctly process all the data records. Thus each access method must write certain additional information into the file to enable it to process successfuly. This is effectively the *overhead* of the file. As the file organizations become more complicated and the capabilities provided to the user program increase, the larger the associated file overhead will become.

8.6.3 Costs versus Benefits

While each file organization has its good attributes, they each have drawbacks. It is important to understand what these costs and benefits are to make reasonable choices for file organizations for specific applications. What matters is the functionality and performance required by the user application, as well as any space constraints that may exist.

8.6.4 Mainframe versus Microcomputers

Today all users have a wide range of machines from which to chose. Each category of machine, based on price or performance, has different needs and capabilities. Thus it is important to select file designs or file organizations that enhance the capabilities of the chosen machine. Similarly, it is important that a file organization not require capabilities that a particular machine cannot provide.

It is the purpose of this section of each of the following chapters to investigate what, if any, features a particular file type has that may have a bearing on how well it will perform on a given machine.

8.7 IMPLEMENTATION REQUIREMENTS

One of the critical tasks that this section of each of the access method chapters will discuss is to describe both the control structures required by the access method to perform its work and the content of each of the control structures.

For the user program to communicate with the access methods, it is necessary to establish an interface structure. *The user interface control block (UICB) will serve as the interface between the user program and the access methods.* The user program, or the language run-time libraries on its behalf, must stuff the appropriate parameters into the UICB prior to any access methods calls. They must also examine the UICB for I/O request completion status after the access methods have finished with the request. The UICB contains the following fields (see Table 8-2):

- Address of user record buffer
- Size of the user record buffer
- Address of the associated file control block (FCB), which is filled in by the OPEN processing within the access methods

TABLE 8-2 USER INTERFACE CONTROL BLOCK

Header information	
Version ID	Identifies which format this UICB conforms with; also allows for future expansion.
Address of next UICB	Link all UICBs for user
User status	I/O successful
	HW unrecoverable error
	End-of-file
	Record not found
	Invalid key
	Space not available
	Invalid filename
File information	
Job ID	Unique ID of job accessing this file
File name	Name of the target file
File organization	Sequential file
	Relative file
	Direct file
	Indexed file
	ISAM file
	VSAM file
	Multikey indexed file
Address of FCB	Set when file is OPEN
Record information	
Record format	Fixed-length records (FLR)
	Variable-length records (VLR)
Record structure	Spanned records
	Unspanned records

TABLE 8-2 (Cont.)

Record information	
Record access mode	Input operations only
	Output operations only
	Input and output operations
Operation being requested	CREATE, OPEN, CLOSE
	READ, READ_NEXT, POSITION
	WRITE, UPDATE, DELETE
Access mode	Sequential, by ascending key
	Sequential, by chronological order
	Random by key valve
	Dynamic (i.e., both sequential and random access to be done)
Address of user record buffer	Location in memory where to get or put data for the user
Size of user record buffer	Number of bytes long
Target record size	Actual amount of record copied into URB by file system
Block fill percentage	Amount of file's data blocks to be filled with records (default = 100%

- Record access mode, such as input only, output only, or both input and output operations
- Status field used to return status to the calling program

There is a second major structure that can now be defined. When a file is created, all of the critical attributes of the file are written out into the file header block. This is done so that when the same file is subsequently opened, all of these parameters can be retrieved. *The block into which the important file attributes get written is called the file header block.* In reality it may consist of more than one block in the file, depending on all of the features supported by a particular file system. The contents of the file header block are as follows (refer also to Table 8–3):

- Volume name
- File name
- File organization type
- Record format and maximum record size
- Block format and maximum block size
- Key definitions for those files that have user defined keys

The access methods maintain these fields and more, in order to always be able to correctly process the records in the file. For data integrity reasons, users have no access to the file header block.

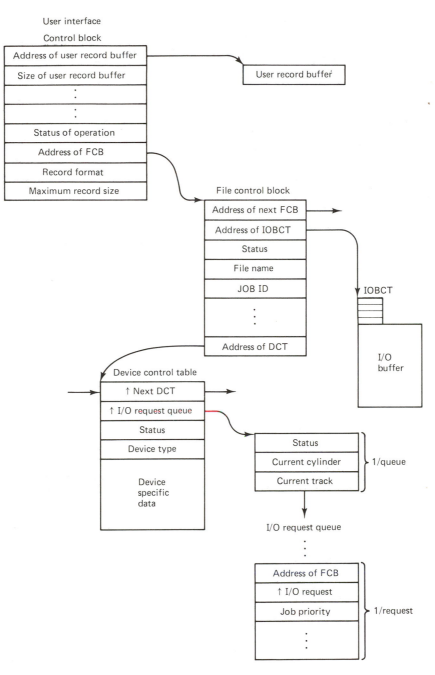

Figure 8-10 File system control structures.

The relationship between all the control blocks designed so far is shown in Figure 8-10. The FCB and the UICB could indeed be merged into one structure. They are split here because of the logical difference in the commands in which they are used (i.e., the FCB for file and record operations and the UICB for interfacing with the user).

TABLE 8-3 FILE HEADER BLOCK

Header information

Version ID	Identifies which format this header conforms with; also allows for future expansion
Date/time created	When was file created
Date/time last modified	When was file last changed
Link to next FHB block	All blocks making up the FHB are chained together

File information

Volume name	Name of disk or tape on which this file resides
Volume sequence number	ID of which volume of the file is currently mounted (tape only)
File name	Name of the file, same as in the directory entry, can be used for recovery
File size	Number of blocks, sectors and so on
Allocation type	Contiguous Noncontiguous Contiguous, if possible
Nest block to allocate	Number of the block that can be allocated next
Cluster size	Amount of space the file is to be extended when needed (in blocks, sectors, or tracks)
File organization	Sequential Relative Direct ISAM Indexed VSAM Multikey indexed
Block format	Fixed length blocks Variable length blocks
Maximum block size	Size of largest block in the file; also size of each of the I/O buffers (in bytes)

TABLE 8-3 (Cont.)

File information

Block count   Number of blocks written to or
                                                                            read from the file (tape only)

Record information

Record format   Fixed length records
                                                                         Variable length records
                                                                         Undefined record format

Maximum record size   If FLR, this is size of every record
                                                                            in the file
                                                                         If VLR, this is the size of the
                                                                            largest possible record in the file

Access-method-specific information

Logical end of file   LEOF

File-processing statistics

Number of read operations   These data can provide useful
write operations   information as to when the
update operations   user's file should be re-
delete operations   organized; they also tell how
errors successfully   the file is being
   recovered   processed
Number of
   file extensions performed

8.8 SUMMARY

In this chapter we have learned what each access method interface is to the users of the system. It is important to be able to differentiate the file operations (i.e., CREATE, OPEN, DELETE, EXTEND, and CLOSE) from the record operations (i.e., READ, READ_NEXT, WRITE, UPDATE, and DELETE). It is also important to understand how each of the access method functions gets its work done by mapping the required tasks into a sequence of basic file system commands (refer to Figure 8-11).

Finally, this chapter did not get too specific relative to "AM specific processing." This is because we cover this in depth in the remainder of the book. The purpose of this chapter was to introduce the concepts and features of an access method in order to set the stage properly for Part III.

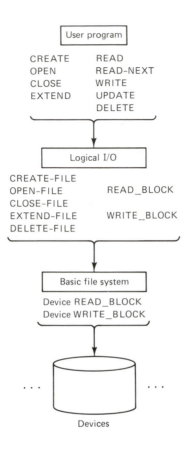

Figure 8-11   LIO-to-BFS function mapping.

KEYWORDS

Access Modes
CLOSE file
CREATE file
Current record
Current record pointer
Deferred writing
DELETE record
Extend file
File identifier
Logical DELETE (LEOF)
Logical end-of-file (LEOF)

OPEN file
Physical DELETE
Physical end-of-file (PEOF)
POSITION record
READ_NEXT record
READ record
UPDATE record
WRITE record

EXERCISES

1. What is the function of an access method, and how does it differ from the function of the basic file system? Explain.

2. When a file is OPENed, the access method reads in the file attributes and copies then into the FCB. Also, the access method could have visibility to some of the attributes that the user may have defined in the application program being run. This is quite typical, for example, in programs written in COBOL. Then:
   (a) Should the access method check to see if the user specified attributes match identically the attribute of the file?
   (b) If the attributes did not match, what should the access method do next?

3. What should be done when a file is not closed properly by the user prior to the job's termination? What can and what should be done?

4. When a record is read that is longer than a user's record buffer, not all of the data record can be copied back to the user. Therefore, should the user be notified that the read request was successful, failed, or whatever? Explain your answer.

5. Most higher-level languages (e.g., COBOL, FORTRAN, Pascal) only allow sequential files to be created. How can a user then go about creating other file types, such as indexed files? Explain your proposal.

6. Why are some of the file's attributes kept in the directory entry, whereas others are maintained in the file's header block? Would it be reasonable to keep all attributes in the directory entry? Explain.

7. An OPEN function *assumes* that the file being opened already exists. If the file does *not* exist, would it be acceptable for the file system simply to go ahead and create the missing file? Explain.

8. As part of the CLOSE function, the I/O buffers are written back to the file.
   (a) Must *all* buffers be rewritten or only those that have been changed?
   (b) How can the file system know when a block in an I/O buffer has been changed?

8. Why does a file system need a "current record pointer"? Is it possible for the file system to successfully process all read and write requests *without* having the concept of a current record pointer? Explain.

10. If a user successfully makes the following I/O requests, after the last request has been successfully processed, what record does the current record pointer point to?

    - READ record 5
    - READ record 27
    - UPDATE record
    - READ record 18
    - WRITE record 93

PROGRAMMING EXERCISES

1. Select one of the access method file operations, such as CREATE. Design and implement that function.

2. Select one of the record operations, such as READ_NEXT. Design and implement as much of this procedure as is currently possible. What problems do you expect to run into? Why?

Part III

Access Methods

In this section of the book we discuss a variety of access methods. The obvious reason for doing this is to describes the various file structures that are common today. However, one of the main themes of this section is to highlight the differences between the structures and some of the trade-offs that were made in selecting one of these designs.

It is important to know a particular file design and how things are done, but it is equally important to know why designs were done the way they were. Then, when it is time to either design our own file system or to select one to be used in an application, we will know what to consider in making this critical choice.

In Part III we therefore discuss designs ranging from simple sequential files, to random access files, and all the way to multikey indexed files. As you read these chapters, keep in mind the costs and benefits of the file organizations already studied. This will help you to analyze the next file type from the perspective of what the new design is trying to accomplish.

9

Sequential Files

CHAPTER OBJECTIVES

When you complete this chapter, you will be able to:

- Describe the functionality, costs, and benefits of sequential files
- Design the structure of a sequential access method and know the kinds of information that be maintained in internal tables

9.1 OVERVIEW

A sequential file is a file in which a data record is stored immediately following the previous record (see Figure 9-0). Since there is no attempt to make a relationship between where a record is located in a file and the record itself, the sequential file becomes device independent. In fact, sequential files are the only file organization that can reside not only on disks but also on tapes, printers, card readers, or any other type of device. One of the major reasons for investigating the sequential file first is that the major design ideas, which are the foundation for each of the other access methods, can be discussed much more easily since this file organization is one of the simplest file types to understand.

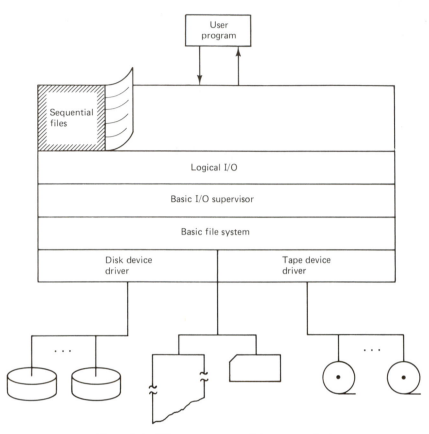

Figure 9-0   File system: sequential access method.

9.2 FILE DESIGN CONSIDERATIONS

In a *sequential* file organization, the records are inserted into the file in order by *time of arrival, that is, in chronological order. Thus records are added at the logical end-of-file (see Figure 9-1).* Regardless of how the records are inserted into the file, there is *only* sequential access to the records. It is not possible to randomly retrieve a specific record without having previously read all preceding records in the file.

9.2.1 File Structure

There is really only one file structure of a sequential file, the sequential file structure. The sequenced sequential file is a special case of this file structure. *A sequential file, also known as a serial sequential file, is made up of user data records, each of which has both a predecessor and a successor record* (see Figure 9-2). In such a file, each record is adjacent to the next and previous records in the file. Also, new records

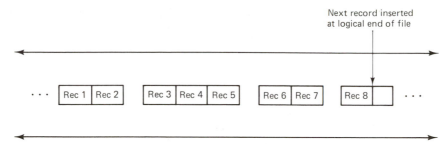

Figure 9-1   Sequential file organizations.

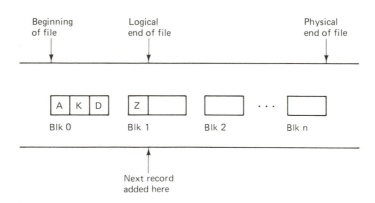

Figure 9-2   Serial sequential file.

can be added only at the logical end of the file. A tape file is a sequential file, as is a deck of cards.

Each block in a sequential file is packed with records and written out to the file. Then the next block in the file is filled with user data records. In this manner, all the blocks in the file can be filled with data records. Note also that there is no implied ordering of the data records except by time of arrival.

Given this file structure, we can conclude that a user will only be able to access the data records sequentially. There will be no random access to the data records.

9.2.2. Record Addressing Algorithms

Whenever an access method is requested to read, add, or change a record in a file, it must always know beyond any shadow of a doubt where to put or find the target record. In the case of sequential files, we have two questions to deal with:

- Where in the file are new records added?
- How do we find the next record being read?

In the sequential file, *all records are added at the logical end-of-file* (see Figure 9–2). Thus whenever a user program issues a WRITE record request, the access method must *know* enough to write it after the last valid record currently in the file.

When a user program is reading records, which record gets read? Again, our range of choices and possibilities is severely limited. In a sequential file, the user programs can read only the *next record* in the file. Since all records are back to back in the blocks of the file, it is a matter of skipping past the current record and picking up the next data record. Thus to read a particular data record, it is necessary to read all the data records that precede it in the file.

In summary, the sequential file access method adds all records at the logical end-of-file and reads all records sequentially. In addition, there is no possibility of randomly reading or randomly writing a record without reading over all the records that come before it in the file.

9.2.3 File Attributes

In addition to the standard file attributes discussed in Chapter 8, the only major file attribute that is specific to this type of file is the *file organization* attribute. This must be declared by the user to be *sequential*. All other attributes, such as record format, are standard (see Table 9–1).

TABLE 9–1: SEQUENTIAL FILE ATTRIBUTES

Attribute	Setting
Required	
File Organization	Sequential
Filename	name of the user file
Maximum Record Size	user definable
Can be Defaulted	
Volume Name	
File Size	
Block Format	
Block Size	
Record Format	

9.3 FILE OPERATIONS

As with any file organization, users will want to perform operations on *files* specifically, as opposed to just the data records themselves. These operations are discussed in detail in this section. In particular, we will be concerned with the CREATE function, since from this we can understand in detail what the file structure of a sequential file consists of. In general, however, the amount of processing required by the file operations in a sequential file is minimal.

9.3.1 CREATE File

The purpose of the CREATE function is to physically create a brand new file (i.e., one that does not currently exist). This means that if we tried to create a file that already existed, the CREATE function should fail. Since we discussed in Chapter 8 the standard tasks performed by CREATE, only those unique or specific to sequential files will be discussed here.

The only real file structure consists of writing the file attributes into the file's header block. Specifically, those attributes that identify this file as being a sequential file are as follows:

- FILE_ORGANIZATION must be set to *sequential*.
- DEVICE_TYPE can indirectly declare the file as being sequential in nature since the only file type allowed on nondisk devices is a sequential file.

All the other file attributes (i.e., filename, record format, maximum record size, file size, block size) are still written into the file's header, but they do no uniquely identify the sequential file type. If these are not specified by the user, the file system can set predefined default values (see Table 9–1). Once these attributes have been written into the file, the sequential file create is essentially complete (see Figure 9–3). No records are added to the file during a create call, so that at the completion of

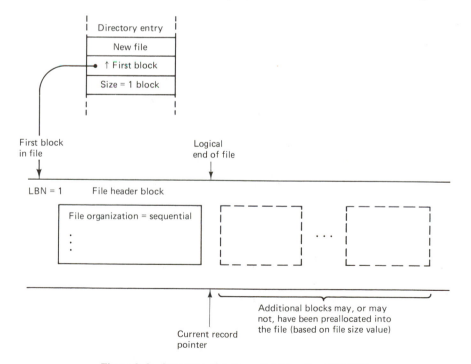

Figure 9–3   Structure of a sequential file after CREATE.

the CREATE request the file is completely empty. However at the completion of the CREATE function, the file is left open and can be accessed by the user.

9.3.2 OPEN File

An OPEN request establishes a link to a file that currently exists. If the file does not exist, the OPEN function should fail. The only information needed to open a file is the filename and the device on which the file resides. With these data, the basic file system can locate the file's header block. Since OPEN request processing is largely independent of file type, a file's header block can always be located because it is always in a standard location within the file. Once the header block is found, the rest of the file's attributes can be read into main memory and copied into the internal tables of the access method and basic file system. In particular, the major attribute read is the *file type*. Once this is known, the appropriate file organization access method can be invoked to process the file correctly for the user.

9.3.3 CLOSE File

When the user has completed doing everything desired against this file, the file can be deaccessed. This is accomplished by the use of the CLOSE function call. The CLOSE processing is the inverse of the OPEN processing. In particular, CLOSE deallocates main-memory space, rewrites the file's attributes in case one (i.e., at logical end-of-file) or more of them has been changed, and then releases the remaining file control blocks and buffers still in use by this specific task.

9.4 RECORD OPERATIONS

Whereas the file operations for a sequential file do very little sequential file specific processing, the record operations are much more aware of the file type being sequential.

Record access modes.   The only access mode that is valid for a sequential file is sequential access. This means that to access a particular record in the file, it is necessary to sequentially access all of the records that precede the desired record in the file. Thus to read the fifty-first record, a user would need to read the first fifty in order to be correctly positioned to read the fifty-first record. Random access to user data records is not supported.

9.4.1 POSITION to Record

The question here is: Where in a sequential file is the next logical record? The POSITION function must be able to locate every record. It is able to do this because the current position within the file is identified by the *current record pointer*. For example, in Figure 9–4, the last record read was "H," so the current record points to it.

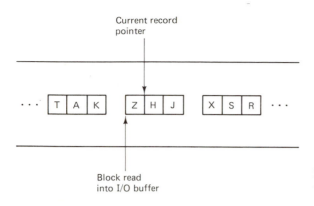

Figure 9–4 Inputs to POSITION function.

A subsequent POSITION command would then start at the current record and scan forward looking for the next valid record in the file (i.e., "J"). Note that we can only perform sequential positioning within the file. We cannot position to records outside the file or randomly access records within the file.

After successful completion of either a CREATE or OPEN function call, the access method positions itself to the first record position in the file (see Figure 9–3). This is done so that if the next request made is a WRITE call, the access method can simply write the block at that predefined location within the file. Once there is one record in the file, the access methods will always remember the location of the last record written so that new records can be added to the file.

9.4.2 READ Record

Since the READ function is also a *random* record operation, we must disallow this function call when the file organization is sequential. What should be understood here is that even though the user may, or may not, know which function calls are allowed for a particular file organization, it is always up to the access method to know absolutely what function calls are valid in order to protect the integrity of the data within the file.

9.4.3 READ_NEXT Record

Records in a sequential file can be accessed sequentially via the READ_NEXT function. For this function to work successfully, there must be a valid current record pointer within the file. From this pointer, the access method can reposition, and move forward in the file to find the next valid user data record. For example, in Figure 9–4, the current record is "H." A READ_NEXT would therefore return to the record "J" to the user's program and the current record pointer would be adjusted to point to that record. Another READ_NEXT would need to read in the next physical block of the file in order to access the next data record, namely "X."

Both the CREATE and OPEN functions set the current record pointer to the first possible record in the file at the completion of their processing. This is done so that if the very next user request is a READ_NEXT command, it can be processed successfully.

   If a user wants to read all the records within a file, a series of READ_NEXT requests would need to be issued until all records have been read (i.e., the end-of-file condition has been detected). In any case, the performance of a READ_NEXT request is very high, since the access method knows exactly where to look for the next record. If it is in the block currently being accessed, the access method merely copies the data record from the I/O buffer into the user's record buffer. There is no I/O involved at all. The worst case is when the access method must go out to the device and read in another block of the file. Thus the maximum number of I/O operations required is 1, and the minimum number of I/O operations is just 0.

9.4.4 WRITE Record

To *add* a new record into the file, the WRITE function is provided. The key to adding records to a file is to always *know* where to put each record so that it can be retrieved successfully. *Since this is a sequential file, all records are added at the file's logical end-of-file.*

   As can be seen in Figure 9–5, in the case of a sequential file the record is added immediately after the last record (i.e., after "B") that currently exists in the file. This location is known by the access method and is kept by the AM in an internal control table known as the file control block (FCB). After the record has been written into the file, the internal LEOF pointer is updated so that any write requests in the future will be processed correctly.

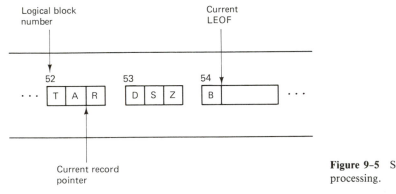

Figure 9–5 Serial sequential WRITE processing.

9.4.5 UPDATE Record

An UPDATE operation changes or modifies a record that *already exists* in the file. To modify a currently existing record, the access method must find the record in the file itself.

   For a sequential file, the block containing the record to be changed must be found and then read into one of the I/O buffers in main memory. This is done when a user requests a POSITION or READ_NEXT request. The original version of the record is copied from the I/O buffer into the user's record buffer, where it can then be modified.

After the user has modified a data record, an UPDATE request is issued. The access method then copies the user's record from the user's record buffer back into the correct position within the I/O buffer. Then the entire block can be rewritten into the file. Since the records in a sequential file are written one right after the other, there is no wasted space between the records in the file. This means that if all the user wanted to do was to add some new fields to a record, thus increasing the length of the record, the access method must reject the request.

Updated records that are the same as or smaller than the original record can be correctly processed since there is always enough room in the block (see Figure 9–6a and b). However, if the UPDATED record is *larger* than the original record, space may or may not always be present (refer to Figure 9–6c). Thus it could be possible for some UPDATEs to work while others could fail. This would provide the user

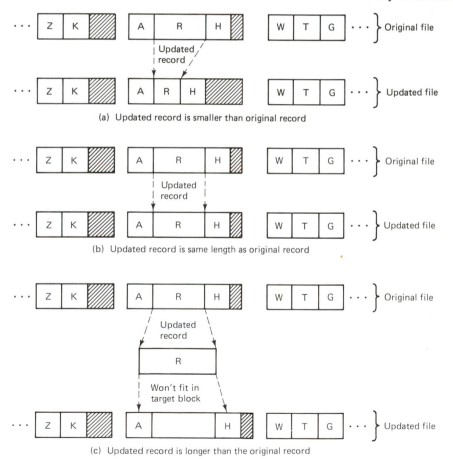

Figure 9–6   Sequential file UPDATE processing.

with an inconsistent and unpredictable interface. Therefore, by convention we shall prohibit UPDATE operations on sequential files that *increase* the length of the original record.

Although a sequential file can reside on almost any medium, not all of the access method functions are available for all devices. For example, UPDATE cannot be performed if the file is on a tape. This is due to hardware constraints of the tape drive being unable to rewrite a block that already exists on the medium without potentially destroying the following block. It is up to the access method to know not only the type of file organization, but also the type of device on which the file resides in order to process the data records correctly.

9.4.6 DELETE Record

A DELETE request logically deletes the specified record from the file. DELETE processing is very similar to the processing done in support an UPDATE request. Specifically, the AM must locate the most current version of the record by the methods described earlier. Then the access method must logically delete the record, in the I/O buffer, by turning on a *deleted* flag in the record itself (see Figure 9–7). This logically marks this record as having been deleted. However, the record will not actually be deleted from the file until that specific block has been rewritten back into the file itself.

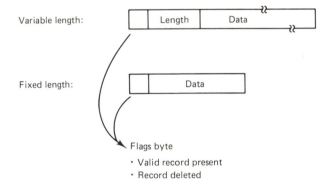

Variable length: | | Length | Data |

Fixed length: | | Data |

Flags byte
· Valid record present
· Record deleted

Figure 9–7   Sequential file Record formats.

The actual data record is never physically deleted, but instead, it just marked as being logically deleted. Given the constraints of being able to WRITE only at the logical end-of-file, and device limitations (e.g., tape), it is not feasible to physically free up the space of a deleted record for future use. Thus the space can only be reclaimed when and if the file is reorganized.

As was the case with UPDATE, DELETE is not available for sequential files on tape. These functions are essentially identical with respect to the I/O involved, and thus the same restrictions hold.

9.5 PERFORMANCE CONSIDERATIONS

To a large extent, the performance of a sequential file is directly related to the number of *blocks* in the file, not the number of *records* in the file. This is because time is consumed only when the next block in the file must be read or written. Thus the blocking factor, or average number of user data records that can fit within a block in the file, is one of the most critical factors for achieving high performance in sequential files.

For example, if one file had a blocking factor of 10 while another file had a blocking factor of only 1—and they both had the same number of records in the file—the first file could be read in order of magnitude *faster* than the second file. This, of course, assumes that the increased internal memory space is available for I/O buffers.

9.5.1 I/O Buffering Techniques

In a sequential file, we can access the records only by reading all the blocks in the file. Thus, without the capability of random access to individual records, it is important to try and improve overall performance and responsiveness as much as possible. One of the most common ways to accomplish this feat is to enhance the I/O buffering algorithms in order to minimize the actual number of I/O operations (see Chapter 7).

9.5.2 File Population Techniques

It is very straightforward to populate or add records to a sequential file. Since there is no ordering of the data records, and since all new records are written at the logical end-of-file, file populating is just the writing of the records into the file. Not all data records need exist before the file is populated, since all new records are written at the logical end-of-file, no matter when they are added into the file.

In summary, the concerns about how we actually populate a file with user data records is a negligible issue for sequential files. In future chapters, as we discuss more complicated file organizations, the file population issue gets to be critical.

9.5.3 File Reorganization

Sequential files never really need to be reorganized. Why? The reason for this is that a file need to be reorganized only when the processing of the data records slows down so much as to degrade overall performance. When a file gets reorganized, it runs faster.

In the case of a sequential file, there is no explicit or implicit ordering of the data records. Thus the records are always "in sequence by time of arrival." The only time when a reorganization of a sequential file might help is if there were a high proportion of deleted data records in the file. If performance is adversely affected because of the need of the access method to skip over so many deleted data records, a file reorganization would be beneficial.

9.6 DESIGN TRADE-OFFS

One of the skills that we must develop is that of being able to analyze a given situation and to determine the best solution to the programming problem at hand. One of the key pieces of any solution is the selection of the file types that would be best suited to the application. This choice must take into consideration the *functionality and performance* capabilities of the file organization, as well as other factors. Therefore, let us now examine the costs and the benefits of the sequential type of file organization, so that it will become much clearer what criteria to use when making the file-type selection.

9.6.1 File Size Calculations

The key to calculating the size of a sequential file is to be able to determine the number of blocks that will be required to contain the expected number of data records. For these calculations, if the record format is variable, assume an average-sized record. If the records are fixed length, the exact record size can be used. Then the average number of data records per block, or the blocking factor, can be calculated. Once this is known, the major unknown variable is the number of records expected to exist within this file. Let us assume the following:

R = average record size

B = average size of the blocks in the file

M = expected number of data records in the file

Then the number of records per block, *n,* is

$$N = \frac{B}{R}$$

The number of blocks in the file, *F,* is found as follows:

$$F = \frac{M}{N} + 1$$

Note: The "+ 1" is needed to account for the file header block.

This calculation does not take into consideration interrecord gap sizes or any other device overhead. It simply calculates the number of blocks that a sequential file will require. This is important, because as we progress to the more complex file organizations, the amount of access method *overhead* can become a significant portion of the entire file.

9.6.2 Costs versus Benefits

All file organizations have their individual strengths and weaknesses. It is important to understand what these trade-offs are in order to make the most appropriate judgment calls when selecting a file organization to do a particular job (see Table 9–2).

TABLE 9–2 SUMMARY OF SEQUENTIAL FILE ORGANIZATION CAPABILITIES

Function	Capability supported?
Functionality	
READ-sequential	Y
-random	N
WRITE-sequential (at EOF)	Y
-random	N
UPDATE-in place	Y
-change length?	N
DELETE-logical	Y
-physical	N
READ_NEXT	Y
Performance	
READ_NEXT	High
READ_NEXT entire file	High
WRITE a record	High
#I/O's to READ a record	0–1
#I/O's to WRITE a record	0–2
Costs	
File structure space utilization	High
Supports multiple users reading and writing	N
Risk of data lost	Low
Devices supported: Disks	Y
Tapes	Y
Printers	Y
Cardreaders	Y

Costs

- The records are not ordered in any specific sequence.
- There is *no random access* into a sequential file in order to retrieve a particular record without reading all the records in the file that precede it.
- There is no real update or delete of user data records, except possibly for those files that reside on disk.

Benefits

- These files are compatible with all device types, unlike most other file organizations, which are supported only if the files are on disk.
- There can be very fast *sequential read/write* performance. In fact, the performance or response-time measure for sequential record access is usually defined in terms of a sequential file on disk.
- The sequential file type makes the best utilization of the space on the medium in the device. This is because there is almost no file structure overhead in a sequential file. Thus the space a file consumes is mostly taken by user data records, not by "system overhead."

9.6.3 Mainframe versus Microcomputers

A sequential file has within it very little access method and file structure overhead. Indeed, it has the very least of all the file types that are discussed in this book. Therefore, file space utilization is not really an issue for sequential files. Conversely, when space utilization is a critical issue, sequential files must be considered, all else being equal.

Performance, however, can vary widely depending on how many I/O buffers can be allocated per file. On mainframe computers, there is usually a large amount of main memory available. Therefore, it is somewhat easier to allocate additional I/O buffers on mainframe computers than it is on microcomputers.

9.7 IMPLEMENTATION REQUIREMENTS

To perform all of the correct processing of the data records, it is necessary for the sequential access method to keep track of a variety of information. In addition to the information discussed in Chapter 8, the access method must maintain the following information in the file control block (see Table 9–3).

TABLE 9-3   FILE CONTROL BLOCK: SEQUENTIAL FILES

Header information

Version ID
Link to next FCB
Status

User information

Job ID
I/O mode

File information

Volume name
Filename
File size

TABLE 9-3 (Cont.)

File information

Physical end-of-file (PEOF)	Location of last block allocated to this file
Allocation Type	
Next block to allocate	The next free (i.e., unallocated) block in the file
Cluster size	
File organization	Sequential
Block format	
Maximum block size	
File status	

Record information

Record format	
Maximum record size	
Access mode	Sequential, by ascending key

Access-method-specific information

Logical end-of-file (LEOF)	Location of last data record written into this file

File system internal information

Last successful operation	READ, READ_NEXT, WRITE, UPDATE, DELETE, POSITION Index number
Current record pointer	Block number Current record size Offset in block to record (sequential only)
Address of IOBCT	
Address of DCT	

File-processing statistics

Number of read operations
Number of write operations
Number of update operations
Number of delete operations
Number of errors successfully recovered
Number of file extensions performed
Number of block splits performed

Logical and physical end-of-file.   The logical end-of-file (LEOF) is needed for two reasons. First, all new records are written at LEOF. Therefore, to know where to add the new records, the access method must keep track of where LEOF is after every output operation.

Second, LEOF is needed to stop READ_NEXT processing after the last valid data record has been read by the user program. If this field were not maintained, the access method could not know where the last valid record was in the file. Therefore, potentially invalid information could be passed back to the user as read data.

Physical end-of-file (PEOF) is needed to ensure that no block is accessed that does not already exist in the file. When all blocks have been used (i.e., current block is PEOF block), the file must either be extended or the user must be notified that no more space is available.

Next block to allocate.   Whenever a new block is required, the sequential file access method will try and allocate it. The way it does this is to check this field against the physical end-of-file value. If they are not the same, the access method can allocate this block. Finally, it must increment the "next block to allocate" field to represent the next available block in the file.

File organization.   This must be set to *sequential* in order for the correct processing routines to be invoked.

Last successful operation.   To process all records requests successfully, the access methods must keep track of the last successful record operation. For example, if the last successful operation was a POSITION, a subsequent READ_NEXT must read the record positioned to, not the following record.

Current record pointer (CRP).   The function of the CRP is to allow the access method to keep track of where it is currently reading data records in the file. The CRP consists of the following information for a sequential file:

- Block number containing record last successfully accessed
- Byte offset in block to the *beginning* of the last record read

With the foregoing information kept up to date, the access method will always know where it is in the file. More important, it will know the starting location in the file at which to begin looking for the next data record in the file.

In addition to the file control block information, it is necessary to understand the correct format of all the data records in the file. As can be seen in Figure 9–7, all records have a single *flag byte* prefix appended. The purpose of the flag byte is to be able to maintain the current status of every data record in the file. Thus the flag byte can contain the following indicators:

- This data record is *valid*.
- This data record has been *deleted*.

As we progress through the other file organizations, there will be more flags or indicators that will need to be maintained. The format of the fixed- or variable-length records is the same as discussed in Chapter 1, with the addition of the prefix flag byte.

Note that the fields in the FCB are almost identical to the fields in the file header block. The reason for this is that the internal structures must contain all the necessary information to manage the file properly. The access method gets this critical data from the file header block. It then copies the data into the FCB or the key descriptor blocks (see Table 9–4).

TABLE 9-4   FILE HEADER BLOCK: SEQUENTIAL FILES

Header information

File information

Filename	
File size	
Next block to allocate	Number of the block that can be allocated next
Cluster size	
File organization	Sequential
Block format	
Maximum block size	

Record information

Record format
Maximum record size

Access-method-specific information

Logical end-of-file	LEOF

File-processing statistics

Number of read operations	These data can provide useful information as
Number of write operations	to when the user's file should be re-
Number of update operations	organized; they also tell how the file is be-
Number of delete operations	ing processed
Number of errors successfully recovered	
Number of file extensions performed	

9.8 SUMMARY

In this chapter we have discussed in detail our first file organization and access method. Although sequential files are by far the simplest file types, they do raise several important points. For example, the requirement to maintain correct processing information in the file control block is critical. In addition, the how the current record pointer is used is critical to successful processing of the data records in the file.

What we also learned was that this file organization had both good and bad points. These are important to understand, since when an application is being designed, a file type must be selected that is compatible with the needs of the application.

KEY WORDS

Logical end-of-file
Sequential file
Serial sequential file

SUPPLEMENTAL REFERENCES

1. Freeman, Donald E., and Olney R. Perry, *I/O DESIGN: Data Management in Operating Systems.* Rochelle Park, N.J.: Hayden Book Company, Inc., 1977, Chap. 11. This text has a rather complete description of sequential files and how the processing is performed.

2. Johnson, Leroy F., and Rodney H. Cooper, *File Techniques for Data Base Organization in COBOL.* Englewood Cliffs, N.J.: Prentice-Hall, Inc., 1981, Chap. 3. This chapter gives a good perspective of sequential files from the perspective of a COBOL program. This is important because many of the features in access methods are not directly visible in all the higher-level languages. It also shows how the COBOL language syntax can be related to the various access method parameters required.

3. Toby, J. Teorey, and James P. Fry, *Design of Database Structures.* Englewood Cliffs, N.J.: Prentice-Hall, Inc, 1982, Chap. 12. There is a rather thorough discussion of performance in sequential files, including many interesting formulas. In addition, there is a discussion of a variant of the sequential file type discussed in this book, the linked-sequential file organization.

EXERCISES

1. In this chapter only sequential files were discussed. However, it is possible to implement an *ordered* sequential file, otherwise known as a *keyed sequential* file. In this case, the records are inserted in order by some key field. Additions must be placed into a second *log file*. Discuss in detail how records would get added, deleted, and updated in such a file organization.

2. Discuss the costs and benefits of a sequential file type that allowed *spanned records* to exist. Be sure to discuss performance, file-size implications, and record operation processing.

3. It is possible to UPDATE a record in a sequential file? Explain your answer.

4. Although we discusssed only sequential access to records in a sequential file, and specifically prohibited random access to records, is there any way in which random access to the user data records could be provided to the user? If so, explain how it could be done and what limitations or restrictions would have to be imposed on the user. If not, explain why not.

5. List the actual I/O operations that would be needed to for a user program to read and update a single record in a sequential file. Assume that the target record resides in the next physical block in the file.

6. If the user in Exercise 5 had really wanted to delete the record, not update it, what differences would there be in the actual number of I/O operations required to complete this task? Explain.

7. When a sequential file is opened, the access method reads in all of the file's attributes from the file's header block. Wouldn't it be easier simply to require the user to supply all of these parameters at OPEN time? Explain the risks involved in each approach.

8. If a user issues a READ_NEXT request and the current record pointer is not valid, what should the file system do? Explain.

9. When the logical and physical end-of-file markers are identical, can any more records be added to the file? If yes, explain how. If no, explain why not.

10. If the file organization is not specified at the time of the CREATE request, would it be acceptable for the file system to assume that a sequential file should be created (i.e., it is the default file type)? Explain your answer.

PROGRAMMING EXERCISES

1. Design and implement an algorithm to manage a variable number of I/O buffers. The algorithm should allow the user to request that a specific number of buffers be allocated to a job.

2. Select one of the sequential file record operations and design and implement the function.

10

Relative Files

CHAPTER OBJECTIVES

When you complete this chapter, you will be able to:

- Describe the differences between a sequential file and a relative file
- Understand the structure of a relative file and its use of fixed-length cells
- Understand the concept of record hashing algorithms and how they are used to access specific records
- Understand the trade-offs of disk space utilization for functionality and performance
- Calculate the size of a relative file and be able to determine the overhead within the file structure

10.1 OVERVIEW

In Chapter 9 we discussed sequential file organization. Sequential files, however, have several major problems. For example, records can be added only at the end of the file, and it is impossible to *randomly* access individual records without reading all records preceding it in the file.

If it is acceptable to restrict the user's files to random access devices only, we can design a file organization that has the speed and functionality of a sequential file but eliminates the problems that are inherent in sequential file design. This second file type will be known as the *relative file organization* (see Figure 10–0).

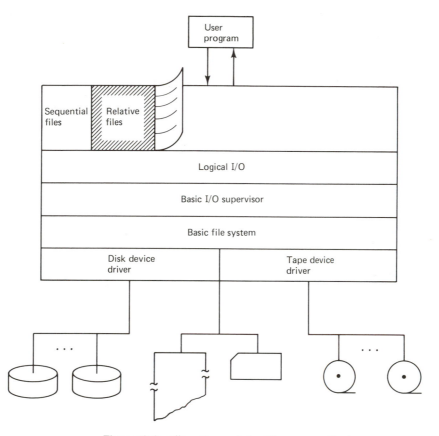

Figure 10-0 File system: relative file access method.

10.2 FILE DESIGN CONSIDERATIONS

A relative file is a file in which any individual record can be accessed directly or randomly. In fact, any record in the file, no matter how large the file is, can be accessed in a maximum of a *single* I/O operation. In addition, any record can be updated or deleted, including the changing of the updated record's length. However, to provide this functionality to the user, the file system/access method requires that *relative files exist only on random access devices (e.g., disks)*. Finally, unlike sequential files, not all records need exist in a relative file at any given point in the life of the file.

10.2.1 File Structure

As can be seen in Figure 10–1, a relative file is made up of *fixed-length* blocks. Inside each block are *fixed-length cells*. Each cell can hold just one user data record and each cell must fit completely within a block (i.e., cells cannot span blocks). Just as

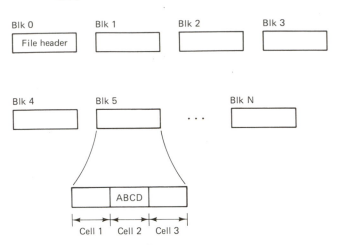

Figure 10-1 Relative file structure.

a higher blocking factor in a sequential file improved performance, the more cells that can be completely contained in a block, the better will be the performance of a relative file. Indeed, cells are fixed-length containers within a block, much as an egg carton has a dozen fixed compartments each capable of holding only one egg.

The cell size is based on the *maximum*-size user data record. Therefore, any cell can hold any size valid data record. However, not every cell needs to contain a data record. One of the problems with a sequential file is that all records must be added at the end of the file. In a relative file, a record is placed in whatever cell is associated with the record of the target record.

Each data record must have associated with it an integer key value that will be used both to add the record into the file, and to read the record out of the file. In the next section we discuss how the access method converts the integer key into a precise block and cell number within the entire file. Note, however, that the integer key is *not* physically part of the data record itself. Thus the responsibility falls on the user to make the correct association between data record and key value.

The *first block* of the relative file is the *file header block* (FHB). It contains information that allows the relative file access method to process the data records correctly within the file.

In summary, a relative file consists of fixed-length blocks that contain fixed-length cells. Each cell is capable of holding just one data record, no matter what the record size is.

10.2.2 Record Hashing Algorithm

The key to locating or addressing an individual record is the record's own *record number* (see Figure 10–2), which is unique within the file. This uniqueness is an explicit design decision, not because it is technically impossible to do it otherwise.

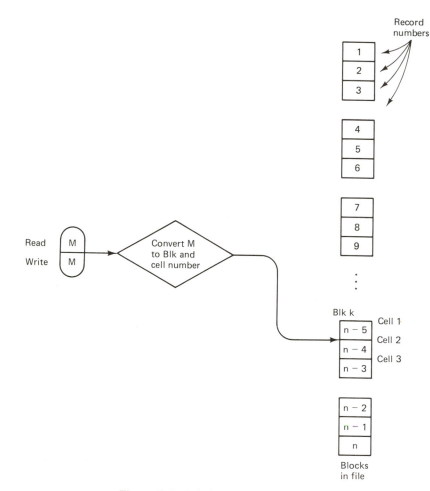

Figure 10-2   Relative file hashing algorithm.

The records in a relative file are numbered from 1 to n, where n is defined to be the highest possible record number in the file. More specifically, one or more data records may fit within a block. A block is divided into one or more fixed-length cells each large enough to contain the largest possible record, including record overhead. Thus there is one preallocated cell for every possible record in the file. The user data records must fit within a cell and cannot overlap between multiple cells. Therefore, the cells themselves are numbered from 1 to n whether or not a particular cell contains a valid user data record. When the user defines a relative file, one of the parameters that can be set is n, known as the *maximum record number* (MRN). MRN is the highest possible record number that the relative file access method can accept as being valid.

The formula for locating the cell into which a record belongs can be shown as follows. If

$$0 = \text{block number of file header block}$$
$$x = \text{number of cells per block}$$
$$r = \text{target record number}$$

then

$$\text{block number} = \text{integer}\left(\frac{r - 1 + x}{x}\right)$$

$$\text{cell number in block} = 1 + \text{mod}\left(\frac{r - 1 + x}{x}\right)$$

Thus, to lcoate any record in a relative file, the access method must first convert the record number into a block and cell number within the file. Then at most one I/O operation will have to be performed in order to read the target block into main memory.

If only a small percentage of cells actually contain a valid user data record, the file is said to be sparsely populated or nondense. On the other hand, *if most of the cells contain valid user data records, the file is said to be densely populated.*

10.2.3 File Attributes

The critical file attributes that must be specified at file creation time which are unique to relative files are as follows.

File organization.   This must be declared as being a *relative file.*

Record size.   Whether the record format is fixed or variable, *this parameter will determine the size of the fixed-length cells that will hold each individual data record.*

Cell size.   Although this is *not* a file attribute in the strictest definition of the term, it is important to the correct processing of a relative file. *Cell size is fixed in length for a file and equals the maximum record size plus record/cell overhead, such as the record length and flag byte (see Figure 10–3).* The cell size is fixed for the entire file. Every cell is large enough to hold the largest possible record in the file. Cell size is not a user-definable file attribute because the access method can always calculate it from the user-defined *record format* and *maximum record size* parameters.

Block size.   *The block size parameter dictates the size of the blocks that get read or written to the file.* In particular, the block size divided by the cell size determines how many cells will fit in each block of the file.

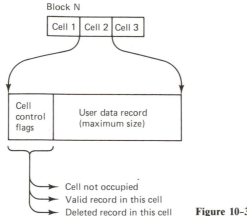

Figure 10-3   Format of a record cell.

A comparison of block size versus the cell size will highlight how well those two parameters were chosen. If there is a good fit between the number of cells that can fit within a block (i.e., not much space left over and thus wasted in every cell), the space utilization of the file will be high. On the other hand, if there is much space left over in which one more cell just will not fit, the size of the file will be increased and the space utilization will be low. The best possible cell–block size combination is one in which the block size is an *exact* multiple of cell size. Then *no* space is wasted in any block.

File size.   *This parameter determines both the initial size of the file, in blocks, and the highest possible record or cell number that can exist without extending the file to make the file even larger.* This parameter is important to performance, since the more time the file needs to be extended to add a new record, the longer the user's program will take to run.

Maximum record number (MRN).   *The MRN is the highest possible record number that can exist within the file.* It is set so that the access method can check record numbers for validity. The file size discussed above may or may not be large enough to hold all the user data records, up to and including the record whose number is equal to the maximum record number. If the file size is not large enough, the access method can implicitly extend the file whenever required, until it is large enough to hold the record whose number equals the maximum record number. After that there is no need to extend the file, since no valid record can be inserted into the file if its record number exceeds the MRN.

All the other file attributes (e.g., filename) are still required in order to properly define the file. However, the processing is the same for all file organization types and will not be discussed again in this chapter.

10.3 FILE OPERATIONS

With the exception of the CREATE file operation, the other file operations perform similarly for all file types. Although each function does have some unique processing to perform for a specific file type, most of the processing is really file organization independent. This is not true in the case of CREATE, since one of its most important functions is to build the file structure that is unique to each file organization.

10.3.1 CREATE File

The output of the CREATE file function is a file structure built according to the definition of the file organization selected by the user as one of the file's attributes. Now let us walk through the specific steps that the relative file access method goes through in order to CREATE a relative file. The other steps in the CREATE process that are common to all file organizations were discussed in Chapter 8.

1. Initialize All Record Cells. When a file is first created, there are no valid user data records in it. Since in a relative file each record occupies a specific cell within a block, the only way in which the access method can tell whether a valid record is present is if one of the flags at the beginning of each cell marks the cell as being empty, occupied, or deleted. Therefore, at create file time, the access method must write all the allocated blocks into the file and then must mark every record cell as being empty (i.e., no valid record present).

Even though this process seems long and involved, it can actually be made quite straightforward. Consider for a moment what would happen if the I/O buffer in main memory were cleared to binary zeros. Also, what if the flag byte in each cell had been defined such that a byte equal to zero could be interpreted as meaning that there is not, and never has been, a valid user data record in this particular cell? Then all the relative file access method needs to do is to write out this same buffer into every block within the file. When this process has been completed, every block within the file would have been initialized and every record cell would have been marked as being empty.

2. Write File Attributes into File Header Block. Finally, it is necessary to save enough data about the file to process it successfully tomorrow or next year. This information consists of the file attributes discussed in previous chapters as well as relative file specific parameters. In addition to the standard set of file attributes, the access method will write out the following data:

- Maximum record number allowed into the file
- Block size

With this information plus the file's attributes written into the file header block, at any future time the file can be opened and successfully processed by the access method.

10.3.2 OPEN File

The OPEN file task is almost opposite to the CREATE file task, in that the CREATE file processing writes the critical data to the disk file and the OPEN file processing reads the critical data from the file header itself (see Figure 10–4, step 1). Once all these important data have been read into an I/O buffer in main memory, the access method proceeds to copy them from the I/O buffer into its internal table structures (step 2). Then the relative file access method has enough data on which to successfully process all requests made against the file. Once this has been accomplished, the user has established an access path to the designated file.

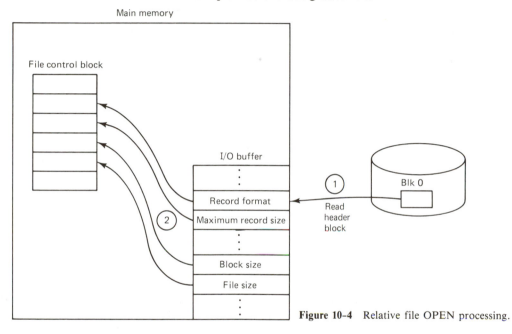

Figure 10-4   Relative file OPEN processing.

10.3.3 CLOSE File

There is virtually nothing specific to relative files that is done as part of the CLOSE file request. As is the case for previous access methods, CLOSE writes out any dirty buffers in main memory, deallocations internal control blocks and I/O buffers, and returns status back to the calling program. Fundamentally, the CLOSE file processing is simply a way of undoing what was done at OPEN file time.

10.4 RECORD OPERATIONS

The relative file record operations are really a superset of the record operations supported by the sequential file access method. Specifically, in a relative file, the user will gain the ability to randomly read or write any record in the file without accessing all the preceding records in the file. In addition, the user will gain the capability of being able to UPDATE and DELETE records.

Record access modes.   *A relative file access method supports both sequential and random access modes.* Thus the user can randomly access any record in the file, as well as sequentially read back all the records in the file, or any other combination of these modes. The way the access method can tell whether the request is for sequential or random access is by implementing two distinct calls to the access method by the calling program. Specifically, a READ record call will indicate that this is a *random* record operation. On the other hand, a READ_NEXT record indicates that this is a sequential request and that what the user wants is the next valid record in the file.

10.4.1 POSITION to Record

The function of the POSITION to record function is to locate a specific record within the file. The user data record itself is not copied out of the I/O buffer and into the user buffer. The only input required is the number of the user data record within the file that the user wants.

The actual processing performed in order to POSITION to the desired record is as follows:

1. Convert the record number supplied by the calling program into block and record-within-block numbers by using the hashing algorithm described earlier.
2. Check to see if the needed block already exists in an I/O buffer currently in main memory. If it does, go to step 4.
3. READ in the needed block from the disk file.
4. Locate the cell within the block that should contain the record wanted by the calling program. This can be done, since the access method already knows the cell size and therefore can locate the calculated cell number within the block just read.
5. Examine the flags byte, which is the first byte of the cell. If no flags are set, no record has ever existed in that cell, and the access method must return a *record not found* error message to the calling program. If the *record deleted* flag is set, the record once existed but no longer does. Thus the access method must again return the *record not found* error message. Finally, if the valid record flag is set, the access method knows that a valid record exists within the cell. Thus the POSITION operation is now complete.
6. Return the success status to the calling program.

If the operation is successful, the current record pointer is set so that the access method can remember where in the file the user is currently processing.

Sometimes the POSITION request does not succeed because of some kind of error condition. Following are some of the errors that can arise:

- *Invalid record number:* This is another way of saying that the record number supplied by the user is not valid for this file (i.e., it could be larger than the maximum record number, etc.).
- *Record Not Found:* The record number provided by the user was valid for this file, but the cell that was mapped by the record number-to-cell number conversion algorithm did not contain a valid user data record (i.e., the cell was empty). Remember that each cell has a flag byte to indicate the presence or absence of valid data records within a record cell.

Whenever one of these conditions arise, it is up to the user to determine what the user's program should do next. It is the responsibility of the individual access methods to notify the user, via status returned, of these exceptions. The user must then decide what action will be taken next.

10.4.2 READ Record

The READ record operation randomly retrieves the desired user data record from the relative file. In addition, it reads the block into the main memory I/O buffer and then locates the desired record within the I/O buffer and copies it into the record buffer specified by the calling program.

The random READ and the POSITION commands are very similar. The only difference is that the READ command actually copies the specified user data record into the user's record buffer, and POSITION does not. After the completion of a successful READ, the current record and the current record pointer are set to point to this record.

To process a relative file READ request, it is necessary to perform the following two steps:

1. POSITION to the target record.
2. If successful, copy the user data record from the appropriate cell into the user's record buffer.

What is important to realize here is that unlike a sequential file, it is now possible for the user program to try to READ records that do not currently exist in the file. It is up to the access method to determine whether a valid data record currently exists and to take the appropriate follow-on action.

10.4.3 READ_NEXT Record

The READ_NEXT record operation retrieves the next valid record in the file, wherever it may be located. In a sequential file, the next record is always the next *physical* record within the file itself. All records are valid. However, in a relative file, we are guaranteed only that the record *cells* exist. As we discovered in the READ section, a cell may or may not actually contain a valid data record. Therefore, how can the relative file access method locate the next valid record and return it to the calling program?

Note that there is no record number specified for the READ_NEXT request. The access method knows where to start looking for the next record because it has the starting position identified within the current record pointer. From that position within the file, the access method performs the following tasks:

1. Examine the cells, if any, that come *after* the current cell within the block in the I/O buffer to see if any of them contain valid records. If one of the follow-on cells within the current block contains a valid record, that record is copied into the user's record buffer, and the operation is complete. Go to step 4.

2. READ the blocks that follow the current block. Scan every cell within each of the blocks searching for a valid data record. The access method may READ one or many blocks from the file before it finds a valid record to return to the user. *If* a record is not found, go to step 4. Else, copy the newly located record from the cell within the block in the I/O buffer to the user-specified record buffer. Go to step 4.

3. If no valid record is found, the READ request will eventually hit the physical end-of-file. If this occurs, it means that there are no more valid records within the file and the user should be notified that the end-of-file was reached.

4. Return the appropriate status message to the calling program.

There are two important points to remember here. First, *the READ_NEXT operation can only return valid data records to the user.* Thus the access method must be able to determine whether a record is present and valid, present but deleted, or simply not present. Second, even though the user thought that only one I/O operation might be needed to access the desired record, in actuality, many I/O operations could occur. Thus unless the data records were dense, it is impossible to predict how long a READ_NEXT request will take to process. What the user will see will be an occasional fast response (i.e., dense files; see Figure 10-5a), in cases in which the next record resided in the I/O buffer currently in main memory. Also, the user will occasionally see very long response times in cases in which the access method has to READ and search many blocks in the file looking for the next record (i.e., non-dense files; see Figure 10-5b).

10.4.4. WRITE Record

The purpose of the WRITE record operation is to add a new user data record into the relative file. The record number is not physically part of the record itself. Thus it must be specified as part of the request. It is up to the user to remember the relationship between the record number assigned to a record and the content of the record

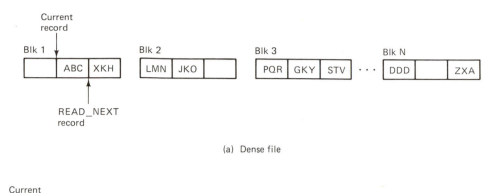

(a) Dense file

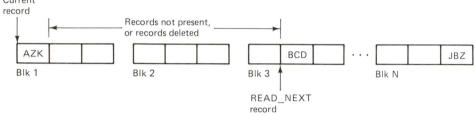

(b) Nondense file

Figure 10-5   READ_NEXT processing.

itself. This is required so that the user can later retrieve the desired record via its record number.

The processing that must be performed to add a record into a relative file is as follows:

1. Calculate the block number and cell number within that block in the file into which the record should be added (see Figure 10–2). Every record has a unique cell within the file to which it belongs. That cell is calculated from the *integer record number* of the user data record itself.

2. Issue a POSITION request to access the target block and cell.

3. Locate the cell within the block that will hold the record and examine the flag byte for that specific cell.

4. If the flag byte indicates that there is no valid record currently in that cell, copy the new record from the user's record buffer into the cell location of the block in main memory. Then set the *valid record exists* flag within the cell's flag byte to indicate that the cell is now occupied.

    If the cell is marked as containing a *deleted* record, what should be done? A deleted record is not a valid data record. It once was, but it is no longer valid. Therefore, if a new record is being written into this cell, the WRITE should be allowed to proceed.

    On the other hand, if the flag byte indicates that a valid record does currently exist in that cell, the WRITE request should fail. Why? Because a WRITE request adds a new (i.e., not currently existing) record into a file. If the cell is occupied, a record exists with the identical record number, so the addition of the new record must fail. Recall that in a relative file the record numbers are unique. Thus records with duplicate record numbers *cannot* exist. On the other hand, this means that a cell is always guaranteed to be available for every record in the file.

5. Return the appropriate status message to the calling program.

After successful completion of the WRITE operation, a new record has been added to the relative file. Also, the current record pointer has, by convention, been left unchanged from whatever state it was in prior to the WRITE operation.

Something happened in the foregoing sequence of events that never occurred in a sequential file—addition of a new record can fail. In a sequential file, new records are always added at the logical end-of-file. The only limiting factor is having enough available space. In a relative file, it does not matter whether or not the space is available. What matters is whether or not there is another record in the file with the identical record number. If a record does exist like this, the WRITE can fail, since records must have *unique* record numbers.

Could something else be done to get the new record added to the file (i.e., not to fail the WRITE request)? As a matter of fact, there are some things that could be done and we investigate them in subsequent chapters. For now, relative files are defined to have unique record numbers, so there is nothing that the access method can do to successfully add the record into the file.

Finally, note that the WRITE processing will perform *at most two I/O operations,* one to READ in the desired block from the file and one to WRITE the changed block back into the file itself. If the block already resides in memory, zero I/O operations would be required since the record could be copied into the block and not immediately rewritten to the file. Thus WRITE performance in a relative file is very fast and very consistent. This is in stark contrast to the unpredictable performance of the READ_NEXT operation.

10.4.5 UPDATE Record

The UPDATE record operation changes a user data record that already exists within the relative file. The record that is changed is the current record, which is also identified by the current record pointer. In other words, the record to be UPDATEd is the last record that was successfully retrieved via a POSITION, READ, or READ_NEXT record operation.

Like the READ_NEXT operation, there is no record number specified by the user. The relative file processing specific to the UPDATE operation is as follows:

1. If the record is of variable length, ensure that the length of the UPDATEd record, which is contained in the first two bytes of the user record buffer, is equal to or less than the *maximum* length allowed. If it is, go to step 2, else return an invalid-record-length error message to the calling program.

2. Check to see if the required file block is currently in an I/O buffer in main memory. If not, read the block into main memory.

3. Copy the modified user data record from the user record buffer into the cell designated by the current record pointer.

4. Make sure to set the cell flags to show that a valid record exists within the cell (this should, indeed, already be set).

5. Return a successful completion status message to the calling program.

The output of the UPDATE is twofold. First a record that previously existed in the file has been modified, including a possible length change. Second, the current record pointer is left valid and unchanged.

Since the current record pointer identifies where in the file the record must be placed, the task of the UPDATE processor is minimal. Note that an UPDATE operation can be extremely fast. If the desired block is in the main memory, and if the writing of the blocks back to the file is delayed until the block is forced out, the UPDATE operation will require one internal memory move and *zero* I/O operations. The worst case is that the UPDATE process will take two I/O operations. Therefore, the responsiveness and performance of an UPDATE is predictable and consistent.

10.4.6 DELETE Record

A DELETE record request against a record in a relative file completely removes a currently existing (i.e., valid) user data record from the file.

The result of the DELETE is to logically remove the user data record from the file. By this is meant that the record is not physically erased and removed from the file. Instead, the flags byte at the beginning of the cell containing the record to be deleted is marked *record deleted.* This not only saves processing time but also allows for *UNDELETEs* to take place should a record be inadvertently deleted. To undelete the record requires only the record number to locate the particular cell within the file. Then the flag byte in the cell is changed to state that the record is now valid. This function is not normally provided in general-purpose access methods, but it is possible to write these kinds of recovery routines.

10.5 PERFORMANCE CONSIDERATIONS

As we have already seen, the performance of POSITION, READ, WRITE, UPDATE, and DELETE is predictable as well as very good. On the other hand, the performance of READ_NEXT can vary widely depending on whether the file is sparsely or densely populated. Thus overall, performance is good.

There are, however, two areas in which performance improvements could be made. First, at CREATE time all the allocated blocks within the file are initialized and written back into the file. Second, the selection of block and cell or record size can have a dramatic impact on performance.

Performance at CREATE time is not a big issue, since a file is created only once. However, there is a question of how much of a file should be preallocated at CREATE time. This preallocation quantity has two effects on overall performance. First, the more blocks in the file, the more they have to be preinitialized, thus making the CREATE process vary in time according to the size of the file. However, the more blocks that are preinitialized, the fewer file extensions that will need to be performed during WRITE operations. Thus WRITE performance will be improved. Since users perform many more WRITEs than CREATEs, it is better to pay the penalty at CREATE time.

Next, if READ_NEXT performance is important to an application, the user should attempt to create and populate a *dense* relative file. This means that most cells in the file will contain a valid user data record. Thus it will minimize the delay in searching for the next valid logical record in the file, while making better use of the space in the file.

Finally, the selection of block and record/cell sizes can have a dramatic effect on performance. First, if the sizes are not consistent, there will be wasted space in every block. This, in turn, requires more disk space being spread over more cylinders. This means more SEEKs, and therefore poorer performance. Also, the more cells that can be made to fit within a block, the fewer I/O operations need to be performed. Again, like the blocking factor for sequential files, performance can be changed dramatically simply by changing the number of cells that can fit within a block. One caution, however: Main memory also tends to be in limited quantities in microcomputers. Therefore, by selecting an arbitrarily large block size, one could actually adversely affect overall system performance. Thus the file designer must be aware not only of the possible application requirements, but also of the target machine constraints.

10.5.1 File Population Techniques

In some file organizations it is important to populate the file with all the known records in a particular sequence. A relative file has no such requirement, since there is a preallocated cell for each possible record in the file. Thus it does not matter when a particular record is added to the file. Indeed, both the relative and sequential files are the easiest files to populate with data since it does not matter what the incoming record sequence is.

10.5.2 File Reorganization

A file reorganization is required only when the access times for the typical record operations get unacceptably long. This usually occurs when records get added to the file in locations that are not the most optimal.

In the case of a relative file, records are *always* added in their correct locations (i.e., cells) within the file, or else the WRITE will fail. Similarly, all UPDATEs and DELETEs act on the user data records in their proper cells. Thus no matter how many changes may occur within a relative file, all the valid records are always in their correct cell. Therefore, file reorganizations in the traditional sense are never required.

A relative file may, however, be reorganized if it has been frequently extended in order to successfully complete WRITE requests. In this case, the blocks within the file extensions may not be contiguous with the original main file or even with themselves. This could cause an increase in the number and length of SEEK operations needed to get to the track and cylinder on which the desired block is located. This, in turn, will have a negative impact on the overall performance of the job. To improve the performance, the file needs to be remade in a contiguous extent of blocks on the disk.

To reorganize the file, a new temporary file must be allocated, preferably requesting a contiguous set of blocks. The file is initialized by the CREATE function. Then the user data records are simply copied from the original file (i.e., READ or READ_NEXT) and written into the new temporary file (i.e., WRITE). When done, a comparison can be made to ensure that all records were copied successfully. If so, the original file can be deleted and the temporary file renamed to the same name as that of the original file. Performance should improve due to the minimization of file fragmentation on the disk.

10.6 DESIGN TRADE-OFFS

One of the key elements in the design of a relative file is the use of fixed-length cells, whether or not the user data records are of fixed or variable length. The argument can be made that space on the disk medium is wasted when variable-length records are used. Also, users are being "fooled" into thinking that variable-length records will save space, whereas in reality they will not.

First, one of the goals of the file design is to provide the user with the functionality and performance required by the application. In the case of the relative file, the user has gained the ability to randomly access *any record* in the file. Also, UPDATE and DELETE are fully supported and performance is consistent and very good. Therefore, from the user point of view, the relative file access method provides much more functionality than does the sequential file organization.

Second, even though the cells are fixed in length, a simple calculation *with no I/O required* could determine the block and cell of the desired record. This would be impossible if the cells themselves were not of fixed length.

Finally, by allowing the user to select either fixed- or variable-length record formats, the user gets to make the choice of which format is best for the user application being run. Thus the user gets to work within the specifications that are best for the application, and the access methods get to provide the level of support and performance required.

To summarize:

- The user can select the most appropriate record format for the application.
- The access method can provide the user with the capability of being able to

randomly access any record in the file, as well as being able to update and delete records.

- Performance is dramatically improved over sequential files because records can be fully UPDATEd, and records can be added at any time anywhere in the file.

10.6.1 File Size Calculations

How large is a relative file? The formula for making this calculation is as follows:

M = highest record number excepted in the file

B = block size

C = number of cells per block

N = number of blocks in the file

$$C = \frac{B}{\text{maximum record size} + \text{cell overhead}}$$

and therefore

$$N = \frac{M}{C} + 1$$

The result is the number of blocks allocated to a file. The value of C should equal or be very close to an integer value. Anything outside this range means that in addition to the cell overhead, there will be wasted space in every block in the file. Since the person who creates the file can select the block size as well as maximum record size, it is up to that person to choose these parameters carefully and wisely.

10.6.2 Costs versus Benefits

While the relative file has many advantages over sequential files, it still has some drawbacks. Since it is important to understand a particular file organization's strengths and weaknesses, they are listed below for the relative file (see Table 10–1).

Costs
- Relative files are restricted to *disks*.
- It is sometimes difficult to associate a unique integer key value with every record that might go into the file.
- If the records are nondense (i.e., sparsely populated), disk space utilization is poor.
- READ_NEXT performance in nondense files is unpredictable and slow.

Benefits
- There is minimal file overhead in a relative file.
- There is *fast* random access to any record in the file (i.e., a maximum of zero to one I/O operations)

- Any record can be written to, updated, or deleted very rapidly (i.e., a maximum of one to two I/O operations). Thus the amount of time required to process a request is small, so the risk of possible data loss is also low.
- UPDATEs can change the length of the record, including increasing its length.
- Relative files *never* need to be reorganized.
- The user has both *random* and *sequential* access to the data records in the file.

TABLE 10-1   COMPARISON OF RELATIVE FILE CAPABILITIES

Function	Sequential files	Relative files
Functionality		
READ		
-Sequential	Y	Y
-Random	N	Y
WRITE		
-Sequential	Y	Y
-Random	N	Y
UPDATE		
-In place	N	Y
-Change length	N	Y
DELETE		
-Logical	Y	Y
-Physical	N	N
READ_NEXT	Y	Y
Single key retrieval	N	Y (integer)
Performance		
READ_NEXT	High	Low→high
READ	N/A	High
READ_NEXT: entire file	High	Low→high
WRITE a record	High	High
Number of I/Os to READ a record	0–1	0–1
Number of I/Os to WRITE a record	0–2	0–2
Costs		
File structure space utilization	High	Low→high
Devices supported		
Disk	Y	Y
Tape	Y	N
Other	Y	N
Risk of data loss	Low	Low
File needs frequently to be reorganized	N	N

Note: Y, yes; No, no; N/A, not applicable

10.6.3 Mainframe versus Microcomputers

With wider use of microcomputers, a concern became their relatively small amounts of disk storage. Even though the size of this external storage is growing rapidly, it is still dramatically smaller than the space available on minicomputers and mainframes. What this means is that space is at a premium. Therefore, unless we know for sure that all the space preallocated to a relative file will indeed be used, we should probably preallocate fewer blocks and accept the effect on future WRITE performance. In this case, where we have both I/O and disk space constraints, we need to spread the risk between the two. In the standard design, we attempted to minimize the number of actual I/O operations almost to the exclusion of considering the impact on disk space. This was because on the larger machines there is less constraint on space. On micros, however, we need to be more sensitive to disk space issues.

10.7 IMPLEMENTATION REQUIREMENTS

A relative file, although fairly straightforward, still has more file system overhead requirements than does a sequential file. In this section we discuss both the *on-disk file structure requirements* and the *internal control structures* that must be maintained in main memory.

10.7.1 File Header Block

The function of a file header is to hold additional processing information that the relative file access method needs to process data records correctly. The file header is the first block of the file and is usually a preset standard length so that the access method can always allocate an I/O buffer large enough to read it into memory. This is very similar to the processing of tape labels, where each label is 80 bytes long, no matter how large the other blocks in the file are. These data are in addition to the information that is normally written into the file's directory entry (e.g., filename, location). The additional information required is listed below and must be maintained in the file's header block (see Table 10–2).

Record format and maximum record size. These fields are required in order to calculate the correct cell size. The maximum record size *plus* all record overhead (e.g., the length field on a variable-length record) becomes the real cell size.

Block size. Given the cell size calculated above, the block size allows the access method to determine how many cells exist per block in the file. This information is needed for the hashing algorithm to work correctly.

Maximum record number (MRN). This value, if set, tells the access method what record numbers are to be considered invalid. In other words, any number equal to or greater than the MRN is invalid.

TABLE 10-2 FILE HEADER BLOCK: RELATIVE FILES

Header information

Version ID
Date/time created
Date/time last modified
Link to next FHB block

File information

Volume name
Filename
File size

File organization	Relative
Block format	Fixed-length blocks
	Variable-length blocks
Maximum block size	Size of largest block in the file; also, size of each of the I/O buffers (in bytes)

Record information

Record format	Fixed-length records
	Variable-length records
	Undefined record format
Maximum record size	If FLR, this is size of every record in the file
	If VLR, this is size of the largest possible record in the file
Maximum record number	Relative files only; if set, this is the highest record to be allowed in the file

Access-method-specific information

File-processing statistics

Number of read operations	These data can provide useful information as to when the user's file should be reorganized; they also tell how the file is being processed
Number of write operations	
Number of update operations	
Number of delete operations	
Number of errors successfully recovered	
Number of file extensions performed	

The relative file FCB and FHB are shown in Tables 10-2 and 10-3.

10.7.2 Cell Format

A cell is fixed in size and can hold just one user data record. All cells in a file are of the same fixed size. The algorithm for calculating the size of a cell is basically as follows:

$$\text{(size of largest possible user record)} + \text{(record overhead)}$$

TABLE 10–3　FILE CONTROL BLOCK: RELATIVE FILES

Header information

Version ID
Link to next FCB
Status

User information

Job ID
I/O mode

File information

Volume name	
Filename	
File size	
Physical end-of-file (PEOF)	
Allocation type	
File organization	Relative
Block format	
Maximum block size	Size of largest block in the file; also, size of each of the I/O buffers (in bytes)
File status	

Record information

Record format	
Maximum record size	If FLR, this is size of every record in the file If VLR, this is size of the largest possible record in the file
Maximum record number	Relative files only; if set, this is the highest record to be allowed in the file.
Access mode	

Access-method-specific information

Cell size	Relative files only

File system internal information

Last successful operation	
Current record pointer	Record number
Address of IOBCT	
Address of DCT	

File-processing statistics

Number of read operations
Number of write operations
Number of update operations
Number of delete operations
Number of errors successfully
　recovered
Number of file extensions performed

This overhead consists of a *flag byte* which must be appended to all data records. The function of this flag byte is to indicate whether a valid record exists within that specific cell. More specifically, the flags that can be set can be defined as follows:

- No data record is present in this cell (i.e., cell is empty).
- A valid data record resides in this cell.
- A deleted data record occupies this cell.

With all of the foregoing information, cell size can be calculated as follows:

- For *fixed-length records:*

$$\text{cell size} = 1 + \text{fixed-length record size}$$

- For *variable-length records:*

$$\text{cell size} = 3 + \text{maximum record size}$$

For variable-length records, the three-byte overhead consists of the two-byte record length field plus the one-byte flag field.

If the record format is of fixed length, the largest record possible is equal to the record size defined when the file was created. Conversely, if the file supported variable-length records, the largest user data record possible would be equal to the largest variable-length record permitted to be in the file. Again, this size is the maximum record size defined when the file was created.

10.7.3 Current Record Pointer

The current record pointer points to the last record that was successfully READ, READ_NEXT, or POSITION'd to. It is the unique identifier of a data record. Therefore, in a relative file, the current record pointer (CRP) consists of the following information:

- Block number containing the data record
- Cell number containing the data record

Although each of these can be calculated from the record number, they are both kept in order to avoid the recalculation.

10.8 SUMMARY

In this chapter we have learned how to organize and access user data records in a manner different from that in a sequential file. In so doing, we got around many of the constraints of the sequential file. On the other hand, we had to make other trade-offs in the design of the relative file, which raises design issues that are addressed in subsequent chapters.

KEY WORDS

Cell   Maximum record number (MRN)
Dense file   Sparsely populated file
File size

SUPPLEMENTAL REFERENCE

1. Johnson, Leroy F., and Rodney H. Cooper, *File Techniques for Data Base Organization in COBOL*. Englewood Cliffs, N.J.: Prentice-Hall, Inc., 1981, Chap. 5. This chapter contains a rather complete discussion of the way that COBOL uses relative files. It also contains several sample programs that indicate the system within COBOL that is available to the business programmer.

EXERCISES

1. Given that a sequential file and a relative file each contain the *same* records, if you want to sequentially read all the records in the file, would the *sparsely populated* relative file processing be faster, slower, or about the same as the serial sequential file? Explain your answer.

2. Given the same situation as in the first exercise but with a *densely populated* relative file, would relative file processing be faster, slower, or about the same as sequential file processing? Explain why.

3. Assume that a user tried to randomly READ a record whose record number would have placed the record beyond the physical end-of-file. What kind of error message should be returned to the user? Explain why.

4. List the file attributes of a relative file. Then discuss how you would choose the most appropriate attribute values for a user who had a mainframe computer. How would your recommendations change if the user had only a microcomputer? Explain.

5. How many fixed-length records can fit within one block? How many variable-length records can fit within a single block? Explain.

6. Given the following data:

Block size	= 100 bytes
Record format	= Variable length
Maximum record size	= 25 bytes, including overhead
File size	= 10 blocks
Maximum record number	= 75
File header	= block 1
File contains records: 1, 3, 5, 7, 26, and 32	

In what block, and in which cell within that block, would record 11 belong?

7. Given the file description above, in what block and cell would record 38 belong?

8. If record 3 was READ and then record 28 was WRITTEN, which record would be retrieved by the following READ_NEXT operation? Explain your answer.

9. Given the following sequence of operations on the file described in Exercise 6, what record will be UPDATED?

    READ   record 7
    WRITE   record 29
    READ_NEXT
    UPDATE

    Explain.

10. Assume that the block size is 100 bytes and the cell size is 33 bytes. How many blocks will be needed if the largest record number written into the file is 10,000? What would happen to the size of the file if the cell size was really 34 bytes? Explain why there is such a difference between the two file sizes when the access method itself has not changed.

PROGRAMMING EXERCISES

1. Design and implement the CREATE function for a relative file.

2. Design and implement the POSITION function. This requires the design of the hashing algorithm, as well as the setting of the current record pointer, and so on.

11

Direct Files

CHAPTER OBJECTIVES

When you complete this chapter, you will be able to:

- Describe the differences between a relative file and a direct file and know when each should be used
- Describe several additional kinds of hashing algorithms, as well as the cost and benefits of each
- Understand the concept of collisions, how they are caused, and what can be done about them
- Understand the concept of overflow areas within a file and why they are needed
- Understand more about record keys, what they are, and how they can be used

11.1 OVERVIEW

A direct file organization is one in which the user can randomly access any record in a disk file simply by hashing a key value into a disk file address (see Figure 11-0). This is very similar to the relative file structure discussed in Chapter 10. However, the direct file type attempts to overcome some of the shortcomings of the relative organization, while providing more functionality and performance. It might be helpful to recall the strengths and weaknesses of the sequential and relative file organizations, in order to have a clearer understanding of why the direct file is designed the way it is.

270

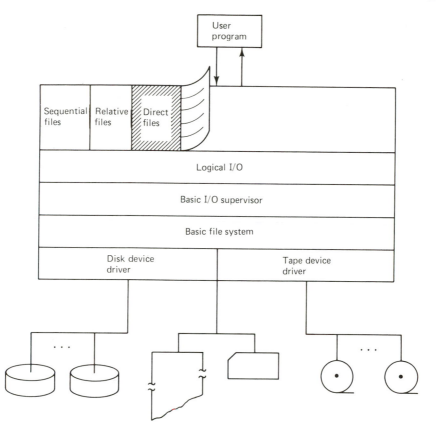

Figure 11-0   File system: direct access method.

11.2 FILE DESIGN CONSIDERATIONS

One of the major drawbacks to using a relative file organization is that it is often difficult to create a reasonable relationship between the integer-only key and the record itself. For example, there are not many applications today in which the keys on which we need to access data occur in an orderly, sequential manner, such as 1 to *n*. Thus, unless the application maps closely to an integer key, the relative file type would be difficult or impossible to use.

The direct file organization solves this difficulty by allowing the user to specify *any* type of key, alphanumeric or otherwise. Therefore, the user can work with keys that make sense for the application and still retain the random access capabilities of the relative file.

Finally, there is the problem with relative files that enough space must be allocated to the file to hold the block with the highest potential record number. Thus, if a user writes record 1 million as the first record, it is required that enough blocks be added to the file to hold not only the target record, but all records of lower key values. Not only is this potentially a major waste of disk space, but it is also a performance loser.

11.2.1 File Structure

A direct file, when viewed by the underlying file system, appears as a series of fixed-length blocks on the disk medium. However, as with the other file organizations, the access methods build a file structure within the blocks of the file that is completely invisible to the basic file system. In the case of the direct file organization, all of the blocks in the file are of fixed length.

The amount of space allocated to the direct file at CREATE file time is critical, since this file size then becomes part of the record hashing algorithm. This is because the hashing algorithm tries to place all records within the bounds of the file's allocated space. This original space allocated is known as the *primary data area*. Any data record that cannot fit within this area must be placed in *overflow area* for that target block.

Records are inserted or retrieved from the file by running the user-defined record key through a hashing algorithm whose output is the number of the block within the file that holds the target record. Unlike the relative file structure, *direct has no fixed-length record cells* and no preallocated location in the file where every record will be copied. Direct does, however, always hash the same record keys to the same block numbers. Thus a single block in a direct file can contain one or more records with the identical key value (refer to Figure 11–1). Thus, unlike the wasted space in a relative file that had empty cells, the direct file will fill the block with whatever records map into that block, irrespective of position within the block.

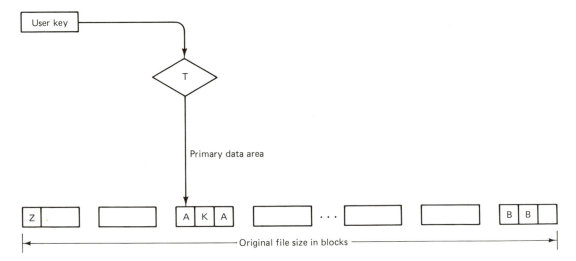

Figure 11–1 Direct file organization.

All records within a block are physically adjacent to each other, just as they were in the sequential file. In a direct file there is an additional exception condition that could never occur in the relative file—collisions. In a relative file each data record had one and only one cell in which it could be placed. If it did not fit there, the record could not be added to the file. In a direct file, there are no cells. If the block in which a record is to be placed is full, the new record is forced to spill over into the overflow chain linked to that specific block.

However, there is a cost involved with the direct file organization. To provide a random access type file with better space utilization, it is necessary to give up the functionality of being able to read sequentially through the file. This is required because in a direct file there is no concept of a predecessor/successor record relationship. In a sequential file every record had a predecessor and successor record relationship, with the exception of the first (i.e., no predecessor record) and last (i.e., no successor) records in the file. In a direct file, there is no such relationship, since the records are inserted by their key value only, with no implicit, or explicit, ordering performed within the file itself. Note that it is theoretically possible to perform a sequential read by calculating all of the possible key values in ascending sequence. However, this would be an extremely tedious and time-consuming task that has no guarantee of success.

11.2.2 Record Addressing Algorithms

One of the major advantages of a direct file over a relative file is the ability to specify any type of key to identify the record. Therefore, the user can select the key that is best for the task at hand, and not be forced into choosing from a list of options selected by the program itself. Also, in the case of the direct file, *the key is physically part of the data record itself* (see Figure 11–2). Although that figure shows the key field as the first field in the data record, in actuality it can be any field or series of consecutive bytes in the record.

User data record

| Employee number | Last name | First name | Address | Department | . . . |

Key

Figure 11–2 Record and its key.

There are many hashing algorithms that can take a key and convert it into a physical file address where the desired record is located. We shall examine three of these techniques. The principal fact to remember here is that we can hash to where the record should be, but the record may or may not be in that specific block. Thus we may have to take alternative actions to locate the actual record. The three types of hashing techniques to be discussed here are as follows:

- Key hashing
- Linear search
- Overflow search

As we examine each of these techniques, we should try and determine the costs and benefits of the various techniques used compared with what occurs in the other file organizations.

Key hashing.   *Hashing is a technique of taking a key supplied by a user program and converting it into a block number in the file which should include the target record, if it exists.* The primary item used to locate a record is the hashing of the record's key. The access method knows where to locate the key in the record because this was defined at CREATE time and recorded in the header of the file. For example, in the case of the relative file, we converted (i.e., hashed) a record number into a file address at which the record was located. Similar algorithms can be developed for direct files.

First, however, there are some criteria with which the hashing algorithm must conform:

- The size of the file is fixed. Therefore, the major goal of a hashing algorithm must be always to produce record addresses spread over the entire length of the file but never outside the file limits. Thus the hashing algorithm must have access to the file size parameter in the file's header.

- The ordering of the user data records within the file can be specified by the user. For example, the hashing algorithm could try and maintain the data records in *key* sequence. Thus the records with low keys will be placed toward the beginning of the file, and records with high keys will tend to be placed in the latter part of the file. On the other hand, the hashing algorithm could try to spread the records throughout the file in as many unique locations as possible. There are many, many hashing algorithms available which distribute the records within the file.

When the user requests that a record either be read or written, the access method must first extract the key from the user data record (see Figure 11–3, step 1). Next, the key is passed to the appropriate hashing routine to calculate where in the file the record should be located (step 2). The output from the hashing algorithm is a block address within the file itself which should contain the desired record (step 3). Then the direct file access method goes out and reads that specific block of the file into one of the file's I/O buffers in main memory (step 4). Once the designated block has been placed in memory, the access method must determine whether this is the block in which the record resides or can be placed. The following steps describe the possible actions that could occur once the block determined by the hashing algorithm has been read into memory.

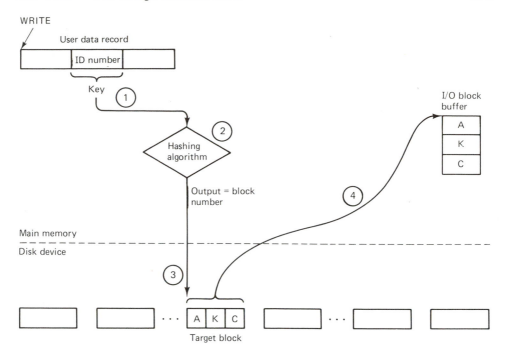

Figure 11-3   Record hashing algorithm.

If the user is trying an input operation (i.e., READ-type request), the following decisions must be made:

- Does a record exist within the designated block with a key that is identical to the key specified by the user? If it does, copy that record into the user's record buffer.

- If the desired record does *not* exist within the block and *the block is full,* the access method must search further for the record. This event, called a collision, will occur whenever more than one record can occupy the same block within the file such that the desired record cannot fit in that specific block. The question then arises of where to look next for the record. Recall that in the relative file, a record either exists in the designated cell or it does not. In either case, the relative file access method does not search further for the record.

- On the other hand, *if the record is not found and the block is not full,* there is no need to search further (i.e., the record does not exist in the file).

Collisions.   The direct file is the first file structure studied where space for the data record is not guaranteed to exist in the primary data area. Recall that in a sequential file the records are always added at the end of the file. In a relative file, there are preallocated cells for each data record. Now, in direct files, there is only the target block in which the record *should* be inserted. However, there is no guarantee that space will always be available in that block.

Whenever the desired record is not found in the hashed block, a collision is said to occur. When this happens, the access method must then revert to other techniques to locate the requested record. Specifically, we could choose to perform any of the following techniques to try to locate the record:

- Rehash to another location within the file by using *another* hashing algorithm.
- Perform a linear search from the hashed block forward, examining each block for the desired record.
- Scan down the overflow chain, if one exists.

Rehash to New File Address. Using this approach, the access method simply rehashes to another file address (see Figure 11–4), hoping that at the new location the record can be found. The problem with this approach is that if the record is not

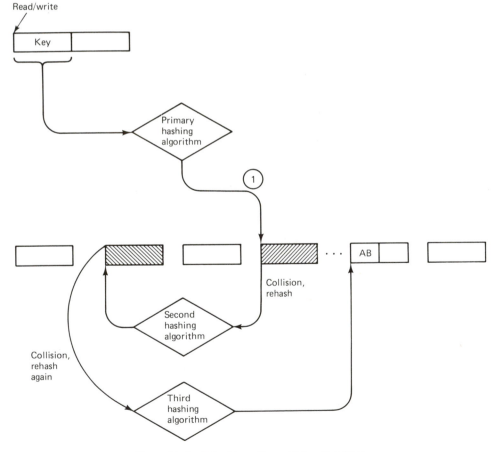

Figure 11-4 Rehashing after collision algorithm.

located at the new address, another hashing algorithm must be tried. Thus we would potentially require many different hashing algorithms under the assumption that many collisions could occur. Also, in the end, we may never actually find the record, because it may never have existed. Therefore, the performance of this approach is questionable unless it can be determined that no more than one or two rehashes would ever typically take place.

Perform a Linear Search for the Record.   Using this approach, the access method would start from the designated block calculated by the primary hashing algorithm, and then begin sequentially searching, block by block, the succeeding blocks of the file (see Figure 11-5). This is done in the hope of finding the record placed somewhere further on in the file.

The benefits of this approach are that it does not require multiple hashing algorithms and that it is simple to implement. However, the drawbacks are similar to those of the rehashing technique. First, the record may not be found prior to arriving the end of the file. Therefore, much I/O time could be spent only to determine that the record does not exist. Second, the amount of time it would take to perform this scan is totally unpredictable.

Utilize File Overflow Areas.   The real disadvantage of the preceding two techniques is that their performance is poor and completely unpredictable. The real issue,

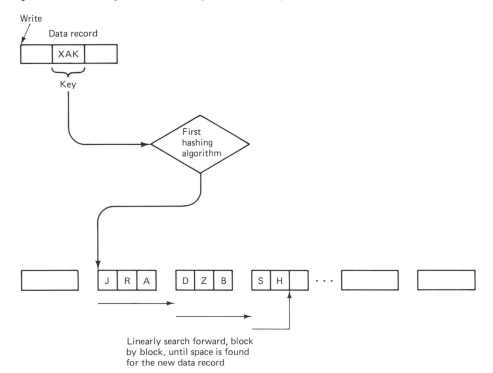

Figure 11-5 Linear search after collision.

then, is whether we can provide the functionality required and do it in a somewhat more predictable and consistent manner. One technique that can be used is to implement overflow areas within the file. *An overflow area is simply a specific area of the file to which the access method can go whenever a collision occurs.* An overflow area can be designed in many different ways. For example, there could be an overflow area for every block within the file, or there could be a common area allocated as the overflow area for the entire file (see Figure 11-6). The latter approach is best since it tends to make more efficient use of the space on the disk.

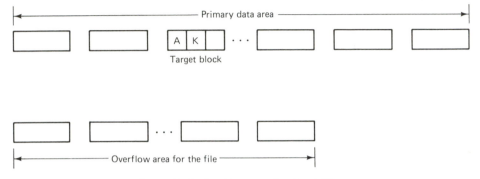

Figure 11-6 Overflow area for direct files.

Now, let's investigate how the access method would handle a collision given that overflow areas were implemented within the file structure (refer to Figure 11-7).

1. After the collision is detected, check to see if an overflow chain currently exists for this block. If it does not and if the user is reading a record, the record does not exist within the file. This is determined from the fact that the record is not in the designated block and that there are no other records associated with this block because there is no overflow chain established for this particular block. Therefore, in these cases the performance is high because there is not endless searching of other blocks in the file.

2. If the operation requested by the user was a WRITE request, the record must be added into the file. Since the designated block is full, or at least cannot hold the new record, an overflow chain must be created (step 1). First, a block must be allocated from the file's overflow area. Next, that block is linked to the designated block within the primary data file. This is done by updating the overflow chain pointer field in the designated block and then rewriting that block to the file. Finally, the record is inserted into the overflow block and that block is rewritten into the file.

3. If an overflow chain *does exist* from the designated block, the access method need only scan the blocks associated with that specific overflow chain, and not be concerned with other blocks in the file (step 2). An overflow chain is simply a linked list of blocks originating from the block designated by the file's hash-

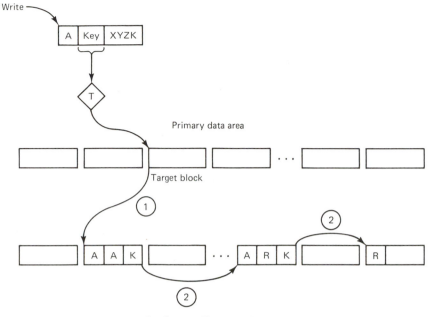

Figure 11-7 Block overflow chains.

ing algorithm. Therefore, what now happens is a linear search of the chain until either the record is found or the end of the overflow chain is reached. If the size of the file and the efficiency of the hashing algorithm are consistent with each other, the length of any particular overflow chain should be relatively short. Thus, with only a small number of block reads, the record will either be found or the search will be terminated.

The overall benefit of an overflow chain is that the follow-on searching of blocks within the file can be limited to those blocks that could contain the record. The effectiveness of an overflow chain is completely determined by the ability of the hashing algorithm to spread the records "evenly" throughout the file so that there is minimal concentration of records in any specific block. Should that occur, the longer the overflow chain would become, and the longer it would take to process a request from a user.

What we have now seen is that there is not a unique place within a direct file for every record in the file. The cost of this is that if the record does not exist within the block pointed to by the hashing algorithm, responsiveness and performance may well become unpredictably slow. On the other hand, by not allocating space for every possible record, more efficient use is made of the file's disk space. Thus if we know that there will be about n records in the file, we can preallocate space for these n records. If, by chance, there are more records or if the incoming sequence of record keys does not match the assumption used in the hashing algorithm, then, and only then, will alternative actions be required (e.g., overflow chains).

11.2.3 File Attributes

In addition to the standard file attributes such as filename, the critical attributes for direct files are as follows:

File organization.   This attribute must be set to identify this file as having the direct file structure.

File size.   Unlike most file organizations, which can arbitrarily expand the file whenever required to do so, the direct file cannot. The reason for this is that the primary hashing algorithm will always attempt to produce a record address within the bounds of the file. Thus if the file size changes, the algorithm must change and the records that exist in the file will no longer be accessible. This is because the algorithm that added the records to the file has now been changed. Consequently, the records will no longer be retrievable.

This is a very critical point. Since the hashing algorithm must know the file size in order to produce its output, the initial calculation of the size of the file ultimately determines the effectiveness and performance of the file organization. Therefore, a system administrator should exercise great care when calculating the optimal size for a direct file organization.

In summary, the initial size of the file is the most critical attribute after file organization. *This is because the hashing algorithm(s) will always try to place a record within the bounds of the initial file size.*

Block size.   The size of the file and the average number of records that can fit within a block are completely dependent on the specified block size. Care should be taken in specifying this value, since overall performance is heavily dependent on this parameter.

Key position and size.   The input to the hashing algorithm is the record's key. In the relative file, the key was an *integer* value and it was never physically part of the user data record. Now, for a direct file, which can have keys of almost any variety, the key is defined to be located within the record itself. Key position and size of key tell the direct file access method where to find the key and the size of the key. Note that it will be assumed here that the key is one contiguous string of bytes within the data record. It should, however, be understood that a key could be made up of parts of multiple noncontiguous fields within the data record. If this were the case, all the key sizes, locations, and data types would need to be declared by the user.

Key data types.   Since the key is embedded in the user data record itself, the access method must be able to process the key successfully. Thus it must know the data type of the key so that the correct compares and hashing can be performed.

In most cases, the key will either be alphanumeric or just alphabetic. However, there could be situations in which other data types could be selected for key fields, such as EBCDIC, ASCII, packed decimal, and so on.

Key attributes.   If we allow the user to define the fields that are to be considered key fields, we give the user the capability of changing those key values. In the relative file case, the keys are record numbers that cannot be changed as part of an UPDATE operation. However, direct file keys are embedded in the data record itself and are thus visible to the user and capable of being modified at any time.

This is important to the direct access method, since all records are inserted into the file by their key values. Thus if a key value changes, the access method must process the record accordingly. In other situations, the user may want to specify that a key can never be modified, even by accident. It is up to the access method to detect these changes and prohibit them from getting into the file.

The method by which the user specifies whether or not a key can be changed or duplicated is by specifying the attributes of the key field. Specifically, the user can select from the following list of attributes:

- Key fields can be changed.
- Key fields cannot be changed.
- Duplicate records with the same key value can exist in the file.
- Keys cannot be duplicated in the file.

The user can select any combination of key change and/or key duplication desired. However, if the option to allow keys to be changed is selected, duplicate records must also be allowed. This is because it is quite possible that a key can be changed and not inserted into the file because a record already exists with that key in the file. To stop this condition, the access method prohibits the combination of keys can change but not duplicate.

11.3 FILE OPERATIONS

As we did with the access methods discussed previously, in this section we discuss the file operations that are applicable to the direct access method. Since the common processing was discussed in Chapter 8, this section, as well as the following section on record operations, will be limited to those features and tasks that are unique to the direct file type.

11.3.1 CREATE File

To CREATE a direct file, the file system needs to know the set of file parameters that uniquely identify this as being a direct file organization. When the user CREATEs a direct file, all the standard file processing and validity checking is performed, as discussed in Chapter 8. The work done specifically because this is a direct file organization is simpler than the work done to create a relative file. Specifically, the tasks that need to be performed because this is a direct file are as follows:

1. Initialize the Blocks Allocated to the File. In this case, all the blocks allocated to the file, including provisions for an overflow area, must be preinitialized to a known value such as nulls or binary zeros. The reason for this is that the direct file access method must be able to tell whether a record exists in the file. If the blocks were not initialized, the access method could be mislead by the data left behind in the blocks from times past. Therefore, it is always best to initialize the blocks to a known and detectable state.

Note, that unlike the case of the relative file, there is no concept of fixed-length cells. In a direct file organization, the records fit back to back within a block. The block into which a record is inserted is determined by the result of the file's hashing algorithm.

2. Allocate the Overflow Area. If the user has specified an allocation size for the overflow area, allocate it now. Alternatively, we could preallocate a standard amount of space based on some percentage of file size, for example. Or we could simply ignore the issue of the overflow area until it is needed.

3. Write All File Attributes into the File Header. This is similar to what occurs in the other file organizations. What is particular to the direct file here is the fact that several new file attributes must now be written into the file header. Specifically, the key location, size and data type, and size of overflow area must be recorded in the file header. As can be seen, more and more information that is critical to the successful processing of the records in the file must be added to the file header. To look at it another way, how could the direct file access method successfully access the records in the file tomorrow if this information had not been written into the file header when the file was created?

11.3.2 OPEN File

For a user to OPEN a direct file, only the pathname for the file need be specified. This allows the file system to locate the file, if it exists, and then to complete the process of OPENing the file. The tasks that must be performed to OPEN a direct file are almost identical to those required to OPEN a relative file. Specifically, the I/O buffer(s) must be allocated in main memory, as well as the internal control blocks needed to keep track of the processing of the file. In addition, the file attributes must be read from the file's header block, which by convention is always assumed to be the first block in the file.

11.3.3 CLOSE File

To CLOSE a direct file is identical to the processing required to CLOSE a relative file. Essentially, all blocks still residing in the I/O buffers that have not yet been written to the file must now be written out. In addition, all buffer and internal table space must be deallocated and status returned back to the calling program. At the completion of the CLOSE processing, the file system is no longer aware of the file and will not be until the file is OPENed again.

11.4 RECORD OPERATIONS

The most important processing that a user wants to perform against a file is to access the records in the file itself. As a group these are known as the file's record operations. In this book, we have standardized the functions that a user can perform across all the file organizations. What is important here is that we understand the idiosyncrasies of each file type so that we can really understand the processing that occurs on behalf of the user.

Record access modes.   The sequential file allows the user to access records any way the user chooses, as long as it is sequential. The relative file expands the user's capabilities by allowing both sequential and random access to records. The direct file organization modifies this to allow the user to randomly access any record in the file by any key type the user chooses to use. However, by so doing, it becomes impossible to also allow the user sequential access, by ascending key values, to the same data. Thus, in a direct file, the user gains flexibility in defining key values, but loses the capability to access the records sequentially by key.

However, if it is desired simply to access all the records, no matter in what sequence they may be, it could be possible to support a direct file READ_NEXT capability. This would be accomplished by starting at the current record position and taking each of the records within that block and all following blocks in the file. This would take the records in physical block sequence, not key sequence. This capability is most useful in file recovery situations where a piece of a file or its disk has been clobbered and an attempt needs to be made to retrieve as much data as possible.

Although this may seem restrictive, we must recognize that a file organization is designed to accomplish a set of goals and objectives. It is almost never a goal that the organization be a superset of all previous file designs. Therefore, for users who want random access via user-definable keys, the direct file fulfills the bill. For users who require sequential access to data records, another file type must be selected.

Record currency.   The current record in a file identifies to the access method the location of the last record successfully accessed by the user. To make this more precise, it is the last record successfully read that then becomes the current record. This, of course, assumes that there are no intervening read failures.

In a sequential file the current record consists of a block number and an offset within that block to the record itself. The relative file changed this somewhat by making the current record the block number and the cell number within the block. Since there was only one record per cell maximum, this was sufficient to uniquely locate and identify every record in the file.

In the direct file, there are no record cells. Also, since there can be several records within the block, there must be some way in which to uniquely identify each record. The way this is accomplished is to define the current record in a direct file as follows:

- The block number containing the record
- The key value in the record
- A unique record number within that block of data

The key is needed because the records in the block do not appear in any particular order other than first in gets the next available slot. Similarly, the block number is needed to specify where in the file the particular record exists.

Finally, there is a unique record ID associated with each record. For example, if there were four records each having a key of "ABC," how can the access method distinguish among them? It can if each has a unique identifying ID. Therefore, once the block is located, the direct file access method must scan each record in the block by comparing the search key of the desired record against other records in that block. If duplicate keys are not allowed, the block number and key value uniquely identify any user data record.

11.4.1 POSITION to Record

The purpose of this function call is to locate the specific record wanted by the user's program. The actual processing performed to POSITION to the desired record is as follows:

1. Find and convert the key supplied by the user into block and record-within-block numbers by using the hashing algorithm described earlier.
2. Check to see if the needed block already exists in an I/O buffer currently in main memory. If it does, go to step 4.
3. READ in the needed block from the disk file.
4. Scan the block just read into an I/O buffer for a record with a matching key value. If found, set the current record pointer to reference this record. If not found, check if an overflow area is linked to this block. If there is no overflow area, the record does not exist in the file. If an overflow chain exists, walk down the chain, repeating steps 3 and 4 until the record is found or the chain is exhausted.
5. If a record is found, examine the flag byte, which is the first byte of the record. If the *record deleted* flag is set, the record once existed but no longer does. Thus the access method must return the *record not found* error message. Finally, if the record has not been deleted, the user data record can now be copied from the appropriate block residing in the I/O buffer in main memory to the user-specified record buffer.
6. Return the success status to the calling program.

The time it will take to locate that record can be defined to be as follows:

$$t_{loc} = t_{hashed\ block} + t_{scan\ overflow\ chain}$$

Whenever a record is to be located, the first attempt is to see if the record resides within the block within the primary file pointed to by the output of the hashing algorithm. If it does exist there, there is no need to search further.

On the other hand, if the record is not located in the primary file, the access method must resort to other algorithms to search and locate the data record. It is this processing that can be open-ended and unpredictable. This is why having an overflow area can improve overall performance, since the chain can be made to contain only those records whose keys hashed to the same identical block in the primary file. Thus unrelated records will not be read or searched.

11.4.2 READ Record

The random READ of a record consists of two processing tasks:

- POSITION to the record.
- Copy the record from the I/O buffer into the user's record buffer.

POSITION processing was discussed in the preceding section. The only additional processing required to complete the random READ is the record copy. In each case (i.e., POSITION or READ), the current record and current record pointer are identical. Also, the performance of the READ request is directly related to the overall performance of the POSITION function. The time it takes to perform an in-memory copy of a record is negligible compared to the I/O required to locate a record within the file.

11.4.3 READ_NEXT Record

As stated previously, the direct file organization does not support the capability of sequentially accessing the records by ascending key values within the file. Consider for a moment what would be required to provide this feature to the user. Given any key value, what is the next sequential key value? Since the records are not physically in sequence by ascending key, the only way to get the record with the next higher key in the file would be to increment the current key value to the next possible value. Then the access method would have to attempt to READ that record. If it did not find that record, it would again have to increment the value of the key and retry the READ record operation. This processing could take an enormous amount of CPU and I/O processing time and end up producing few, if any, results.

Alternatively, this could be done by starting at the current record and simply taking the next record in that block. When the last record in the block has been taken, all records in the associated overflow area are then accessed. Finally, when all records connected to that block have been accessed, the next physical block in the file is read and processed in a similar manner. The problem with all this is that although it retrieves all records in the file, it reads them in no particular order.

11.4.4 WRITE Record

The WRITE record operation *adds* a new record to the direct file. Unlike the WRITE in the case of a relative file, there is *no* record key specified by the user. Why is this? Recall that when the file was defined, the user had to declare the key location and key size within a record. That definition is the only definition that the access method can trust, since the file was built to those specifications. Since the key information was recorded in the file's header, during the OPEN process, these attributes were read into memory and saved within an internal information table. Therefore, when a WRITE request comes along, the direct file access method knows where in the record to look for the key.

The process of adding a new record into the direct file is straightforward if there is room in the block calculated by the hashing algorithm. More specifically, the steps that must be taken to insert a new record into the file are as follows:

1. Hash the Key to a Specific Block in the File.   Here the access method extracts the key from the record that resides in the user record buffer address. This key is then passed on to the hashing algorithm in order to calculate where in the file the record should be inserted. This designated block is then read in an I/O buffer in main memory.

2. Scan the Block for Available Space.   If duplicate record key values are not allowed, search the block first to see if there already exists a record with an identical key (see Figure 11–7). If there is not and if there is no overflow area, it must be determined whether there is space in the block for the record.

If there is an overflow area associated with this block, the entire overflow chain must be searched to see if there is a record that already exists which has an identical key. If there is a matching record, this WRITE must be aborted and appropriate status returned to the calling program.

If duplicate key values *are allowed* in the file, simply search the block or overflow area for available space. When some is found, add the new record to that block.

3. Insert Record into Designated Block.   If there is enough space within the block, copy the record into the next available free space in the block and go to step 5. If there is not enough space available, or if there is an overflow area, go to step 4.

4. Search for Available Free Space.   The overflow chain must be walked until the end is reached. Then the record can be added to the end of this chain. Note that if the record does not fit in the last block of the chain, another block is added to the chain.

If, on the other hand, the overflow area is maintained as a linked list in ascending key sequence, the record is still added at the end of the chain. However, it is then linked back into the overflow chain in its proper sequence.

5. *Return Status to the Calling Program.*   At the completion of all access method calls, status must be returned to the calling program. Depending on whether the operation was successful, the calling program can react and process accordingly.

What we have seen here is a series of tasks that must be performed to add a new record into the direct file. However, unlike the case of the relative file, the record may not always fit in the primary file; indeed, it may need to be pushed off into an overflow area. What this means, in turn, is that for the first time, the performance of a WRITE operation is now unpredictable. If all goes well, it is fast. If a long overflow chain must be searched, the processing time will be long. In the file organizations discussed subsequently, we will see this phenomenon over and over.

11.4.5 UPDATE Record

The UPDATE operation changes a record that currently exists in the file. The record that is to be modified is identified by the current record pointer. If it is valid, the UPDATE can take place. The steps involved in the UPDATE processing are listed and discussed in the following paragraphs:

1. *Check for Valid Current Record Pointer.*   The current record pointer should have been set by the preceding successful READ or POSITION request. If the CRP is not valid, the request must be rejected with an appropriate error message returned to the calling program. On the other hand, if the CRP is valid and the block is currently in an I/O buffer in main memory, proceed to step 2. If the CRP is valid but for some reason the block is not currently in main memory, READ the block back into an I/O buffer.

2. *Determine If UPDATED Record Will Fit into Block.*   If the record format of the file is of fixed length, the UPDATEd record will always fit. In this case simply copy the UPDATEd record from the user's record buffer over the old record located in the block in the I/O buffer.

If the record format is variable and the size has not been changed, proceed as in the previous paragraph. Conversely, if the record length has been *decreased,* copy the record into the block as described above (see Figure 11–8a). Then compress all the records following the UPDATEd record in the block down to the end of the record. This makes available more space within the block by forcing the records to be back to back.

If the record format is variable and the UPDATEd record has been *increased* in length, proceed as follows. If there is still enough room in the block to accommodate the increased size of the modified record, move the records in the block in such a manner as to open up a window within the block that is large enough to contain the modified record. When this has been accomplished, copy the newly changed record from the user record buffer into this window in the block.

Finally, if the record will not fit within the block, compress that record out of the block by moving the other records over the old record. The resulting block

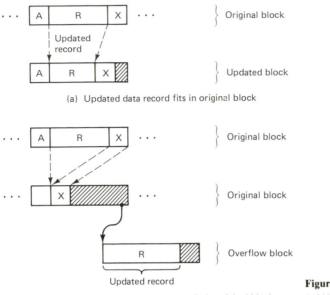

(a) Updated data record fits in original block

(b) Updated data record does not fit in original block

Figure 11-8 Direct file UPDATE processing.

should now contain only the other records in the block, and the UPDATEd record is now gone. Next, search the overflow chain until the end is reached. Then add the record just as if it were a brand-new record (see Figure 11–8b).

The time between the compressing out of the original version of the record and the rewriting of the updated version of the record in another block in the file is the window of risk for data loss. Should the system fail anytime during that period, the user data record would be lost. This is because it has been removed from one block and has not yet been reinserted into another block in the file. It is the responsibility of the file system to minimize the time the data are at risk. In this case, the access method could delay rewriting the old block until the new block containing the updated record was ready to be written into the file. Then the access method could write those two blocks back to back. Thus the window of opportunity for data loss is kept at a bare minimum.

3. Return Status to the Calling Program.   Whether a success or failure, always tell the calling program what happened.

The processing described above can be made much more complicated if we considered all the possible cases, such as updating a record located in the middle of an overflow chain. However, it was intended here to convey a flavor of the processing required and to leave it to the reader to consider all the remaining possibilities. There is one more case, however, that should be discussed since it brings out some important processing considerations.

We have implicitly assumed here that the record being UPDATEd was the last record READ or POSITIONed to by the last successful operation. Thus we needed only to "overlap" the old record with the new version and the UPDATE was accomplished. However, *what if the user gives us a modified record in which the key has also been changed?* Then what must be done? In the relative file we never have this case since keys are not part of the record and thus can never be changed by the user. What can, and should, be done?

First, the "old" version of the record must be deleted from the file. Then the modified version of the record, with the new key value, must be added back into the file. Thus an UPDATE with a key change can be viewed as follows:

$$\text{UPDATE}_{\text{key change}} = \text{DELETE}_{\text{old record}} + \text{WRITE}_{\text{new record}}$$

With all of the exception conditions that can occur, it may be possible to end up with a situation in which the old version of the record has been deleted, only to find out that the new version cannot be added to the file. For example, if the new key is not unique and duplicates are not allowed, the WRITE would fail. Also, if there were no more room available on the disk for the new record, the WRITE would also fail. In any case, we could end up actually losing a record from the file, instead of modifying a record.

To minimize the possibility of this happening, it is possible to sequence or stage the processing in such a way that the record is never lost. However, the risk is that there could end up being two copies of the record in the file (i.e., the old version and the new version). This could occur if we delayed the deletion of the old record until after the insertion of the new record. Then, before we could delete the old record, the system crashes. Alternatively, we could save a copy of the old record in memory, so that if an error occurs on the WRITE portion of the UPDATE, the old version of the record could be reinserted into the file. In any case, the processing algorithm can be extremely complicated.

11.4.6 DELETE Record

The processing required to delete a data record from the file is identical to the processing performed in a relative file. Specifically, once the record has been read (see Figure 11-9a), the access method must set the *deleted* flag in the record within the block. Then it must rewrite that block back into the file to make the delete "official" (see Figure 11-9b).

There are other considerations, however. The space taken up by a deleted record can be physically deleted and reused by the WRITE routine when it is looking for space into which the new record can be written (see Figure 11-9c). Also, if the records have been deleted from the primary data area, should the access method pull one or more data records from out of the overflow area and move them into the primary data area? There are no easy answers to these questions. Technically, the access method could perform this localized space optimization. However, is it worth the time and effort to perform this task?

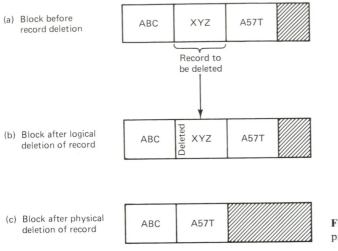

(a) Block before record deletion

(b) Block after logical deletion of record

(c) Block after physical deletion of record

Figure 11-9   Direct file DELETE processing.

11.5 PERFORMANCE CONSIDERATIONS

The key to overall performance is the calculation of the size of the file. This is dependent on the average number of data records that can be held per block within the file. It is this calculation that determines how many record collisions are likely to occur. This, in turn, will determine how many records will fall off into the overflow area and thus directly affect overall performance. Calculation of the file size depends on being able to accurately predict how many records will be in the file at any time. In many cases, this is difficult to predict accurately. When this is the case, file reorganizations become an accepted practice in order to tune the file structure for its best levels of performance.

Another way in which performance of READs can be improved is by ordering the overflow chains by ascending key. This also means that the output or WRITE operations will take longer to complete. However, it means that READ operations can stop searching for a record as soon as the key they are searching for is less than the key in the next record in the overflow chain. Again, it boils down to a trade-off between the time to WRITE or add records to a file and the time to READ the records back. In many, if not most applications, records are READ many more times than they are written. Therefore, it can be concluded that READs should be optimized for performance at the expense of WRITE operations.

11.5.1 File Population Techniques

Like the case of the sequential and relative file organizations, there is no particular requirement as to the ordering of the data records in order to populate the data file. This is because records are added to the direct file by a key specified by the user.

11.5.2 File Reorganization

Is it ever necessary to reorganize a direct file? The key to the answer is to understand when, and under what conditions, a file reorganization is needed.

First, it is required whenever the response-time performance degrades to such an extent that it becomes unacceptable to the user community. Second, a file reorganization is useful if there have been many DELETEs in the file and the logical record deletion strategy has been followed. In this case, a file reorganization would get rid of all the deleted record space and thus increase the possibility that more of the valid records could end up being placed in the primary file as opposed to an overflow chain.

We can conclude from the paragraph above that file reorganizations scan and will occur with DIRECT files. The steps to reorganize the file are the same as for any other file type:

1. Create an identical temporary file.
2. Copy the records from the old file to the temporary file.
3. Verify that all records were copied correctly.
4. Delete the original file.
5. Rename the temporary file to the same name as the original file.

The result of all this processing is a new file with all the deleted records removed completely. In fact, if a recalculation was done to determine how many valid records were still in the file, the primary file size could be reset in the temporary file. This would gain the distinct advantage of having all the records end up in the primary file after the file reorganization.

11.6 DESIGN TRADE-OFFS

To gain the random access capability via user-definable keys, the design of the direct file type has to be compromised in several areas. In this section we discuss these and other details of the direct file organization.

11.6.1 File Size Calculations

Since the original size of the direct file plays an important role in the record addressing algorithm, the file size parameter should be calculated with some degree of care. Also, since data records map into target blocks, not cells, it can be fairly difficult to calculate the potential size of the file if the records ae of variable length. However, it is possible to get a fairly accurate estimate of file size by first estimating the average number of data records that can fit within a single block. Once this has been determined, estimate the total number of records likely to exist at any one time in the file itself. The combination of these two numbers can give the user a first-guess estimate of how large the file should be initially.

The next step is to estimate how many records will be *added* to the file over its lifetime. Next, determine how many extra blocks this will take and add this figure to the file size just estimated. The result is the user's initial best guess of what the file size should be.

Thus the steps required to calculate the size of a direct file are as follows:

1. Calculate the Average Number of Data Records per Block.   With fixed-length records this calculation is trivial. On the other hand, if the file has variable-length records, it is necessary to make a rough estimate of what the average number of data records per block will probably be.

2. Estimate the Anticipated Number of Records in the File.   This may or may not be an easy task. In any case, include some additional records to allow for expected future expansion.

3. Calculate the Number of Blocks in the File.   From the numbers in the first two steps, calculate the number of blocks the file should be allocated.

4. Add in Some Number of Blocks to Be Used As the Overflow Area.   We can estimate the amount of space needed in the overflow area by projecting how many additional records will be added to the file over its lifetime. The result, added to step 3, gives the user an estimate of the amount of space to allocate to the specific file.

11.6.2 Costs versus Benefits

As with any design, there are trade-offs that are made in the design and implementation of the direct file organization. Table 11–1 summarizes some of these compromises compared with both sequential and relative files.

Costs
- Keys must be unique. Although it is possible to support nonunique keys, the overhead required makes this added functionality very expensive.
- There is no way the records can be read sequentially by key. It is possible just to start at the first block and extract all the records. Then READ the next block and retrieve all its records, and so on, until all records have been retrieved. However, the records will not be in sequence by key.
- The user cannot request records within a range of key values. For example, retrieve all the records that have a key value greater than *nnn*.
- Overflow areas are required so as "always" to have a place to add records into when the primary file space gets used up.
- If a record resides in an overflow area, the time it takes to retrieve that record can vary greatly. It is totally dependent on the length of the overflow chain of blocks.

On the other hand, the picture is not totally bleak. Some of the benefits of a direct file organization are listed below.

TABLE 11-1   COMPARISON OF DIRECT FILE CAPABILITIES

Function		Sequential Files	Relative Files	Direct Files
	Functionality			
READ	– Sequential	Y	Y	N
	– Random	N	Y	Y
WRITE	– Sequential	Y	Y	N
	– Random	N	N	Y
UPDATE	– in place	N	Y	Y
	– with length change	N	Y	Y
DELETE	– logical	Y	Y	Y
	– physical	N	N	Y
READ_NEXT		Y	Y	N
Single-key Retrieval		N	Y (integer)	Y
Unique key required		—	Y	N
	Performance			
READ_NEXT		High	Low-High	
READ		N/A	High	Low→High
READ_NEXT-entire file		High	Low-High	—
WRITE Record		High	High	Low-High
#I/O's to READ record		0–1	0–1	0–N
#I/O's to WRITE a record		0–2	0–2	0–N
	Costs			
File Structure Space Utilization		High	Low-High	High
Devices Supported:				
Disk		Y	Y	Y
Tape		Y	N	N
Other		Y	N	N
Risk of Data loss		Low	Low	Low-Medium
File needs frequent Re-Organizations		N	N	Y
Overflow Areas required		N	N	Y

Benefits

- It takes zero to two I/O operations to READ or WRITE any record in the primary area of the file. This is not only fast but is consistent and predictable. Both aspects are important to users.

- Any data type can be selected by the user for the key. This allows the user to select the best key data type for the application to be run.

- Unlike some file organizations, there is no index to transverse in order to access a record. An index adds processing time to most user I/O operation requests.

- Space does not need to be preallocated for all the possible records that may ever exist within the file. This makes better use of the disk space than the relative file provides.

11.6.3 Mainframe versus Microcomputers

Whereas a relative file tends to waste space on the disk, the direct file makes optimal use of the disk space. Thus the direct file can be used in both micro and mainframe systems with a high probability of success. The only drawback on micros is that the performance of the I/O devices tends not to be very high, so the overall responsiveness of a direct file may vary depending on the environment within the overall system.

11.7 IMPLEMENTATION REQUIREMENTS

The direct file has added the concept of keys being embedded within the data record itself. Since it is critical for the access method to be able to tell where in each record to look for the key field, it becomes important to store this additional information within the header of the file. Thus the following information, in addition to the standard set of data, is saved in the *file control block (FCB),* the *file header block (FHB),* or the *key description block (KDB)* in main memory:

- Offset in record to the key field
- Size of the key field
- Data type of the key field
- Record hashing algorithms being used
- Technique to be used in processing overflow areas

    In addition, the current record pointer (CRP) has also been modified as follows:

- Block number of the target block
- Key value identifying the record
- Unique record ID of record in that specific block

    The updated FCB, FHB, and KDB for direct files are shown in Tables 11–2, 11–3, and 11–4. The user interface with the access methods is the *user interface control block (UICB).* Table 11–5 shows what information the file system expects the user to pass to it in the UICB in order to correctly process all the user requests. Finally, the interrelationship among all of these structures is shown in Figure 11–10.

TABLE 11–2 FILE CONTROL BLOCK: DIRECT FILES

Header information

Version ID
Link to next FCB
Status

User information

Job ID
I/O mode

File information

Volume name
Filename
File size   Number of blocks, sectors, and so on
Physical end-of-file (PEOF)
Allocation type
Next block to allocate
Cluster size
File organization   Direct
Block format
Maximum block size
File status

Record information

Record format
Maximum record size
Access mode   Random
Address of key definition Block   Location where file's keys
                                         are all defined
Number of keys defined   How many keys are defined for
                                         this file

Access-method-specific information

Logical end-of-file (LEOF)
Location of overflow area   Direct and ISAM only
Size of overflow area   The size of the overflow
                                         area in blocks, sectors,
                                         tracks, or cylinders
Next overflow block to   DIRECT and ISAM only
  allocate

File system internal information

Last successful operation
Current record pointer   Block number
                                       Index number
                                       Key value

TABLE 11–2 (Cont.)

File systems internal information

Address of IOBCT
Address of DCT

File-processing statistics

Number of read operations
Number of write operations
Number of update operations
Number of delete operations
Number of errors successfully
  recovered
Number of file extensions performed

TABLE 11–3 FILE HEADER BLOCK: DIRECT FILES

Header information

Version ID
Date/time created
Date/time last modified
Link to next FHB block

File information

Volume name	
Filename	
File size	Number of blocks, sectors, and so on
Allocation type	
Next block to allocate	
Cluster size	
File organization	Direct
Block format	
Maximum block size	

Record information

Record format
Maximum record size

Access-method-specific information

Logical end-of-file	
Address of file overflow area	DIRECT and ISAM only
Size of overflow area	DIRECT and ISAM only
Next overflow block to be allocated	Next block to be assigned in the overflow area

Keyed access methods only

Number of keys defined for file	Tells number of entries that follow

TABLE 11–3 (Cont.)

Key descriptions: one per key defined
  in file

Index number	Number of the index to which these data apply
Key location	Offset in bytes to beginning of the key field in the data record
Key size	Length of key in bytes
Key data type	Alphanumeric or other
Key attributes	Keys must be *unique*
	Keys may be *duplicated*
	Keys *can change*
	Keys *cannot change*
Hashing algorithm number	Direct files only

File-processing statistics

Number of read operations	These data can provide useful information as to when the user's file should be reorganized; they also tell how the file is being processed
Number of write operations	
Number of update operations	
Number of delete operations	
Number of errors successfully recovered	
Number of file extensions performed	

TABLE 11–4 KEY DESCRIPTOR BLOCK: DIRECT FILES

Header information

Version ID
Link to next KDB

Key information

Index number	Number of the index to which these data apply (0, primary key; 1, first alternate key; . . . *n*, last alternate key)
Key location	Offset in bytes to beginning of the key field in the data record
Key size	Length of key in bytes
Key data type	Alphanumeric or other
Key attributes	Keys must be *unique*
	Keys may be *duplicated*
	Keys *can change*
	Keys *cannot change*
ID of hashing algorithm	Allows user to select which algorithm is to be used in a DIRECT file

TABLE 11-5 USER INTERFACE CONTROL BLOCK: DIRECT FILES

Header information

Version ID
Address of next UICB
User status

File information

Job ID
Filename
File organization   Direct
Address of FCB

Record information

Record format
Record structure
Record access mode
Operation being requested
Access mode   Random by key value
Address of user record buffer
Size of user record buffer
Target record size
Address of search key buffer   For keyed access methods only
Size of key   Length of key in key buffer
Key definition   Full key in key buffer
                                               Partial key in key buffer

11.8 SUMMARY

In this chapter we discussed the design trade-offs of the direct file organization. We have seen that direct files have capabilities that sequential and relative files do not possess. On the other hand, direct files lack a critical characteristic of sequential files—sequential access to the data records. This trade-off is acceptable if the user does not require sequential access to the data records. There are many applications that fit this category, so direct files can provide a very feasible solution to a user's problems.

Since file structures are becoming more complex, as are internal control structures, Figure 11–10 shows how the old tables (e.g., FCB, UICB) are linked together with the new structures added in this chapter (e.g., KDB).

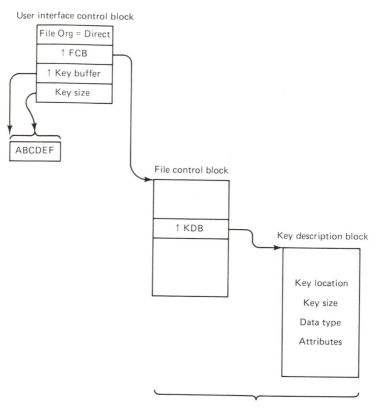

Figure 11-10   Direct file control structures.

KEY WORDS

Collision	Key size
Key data type	Linear search
Key hashing	Overflow chain
Key position	Overflow search

SUPPLEMENTAL REFERENCES

1. Freeman, Donald E., and Olney R. Perry, *I/O DESIGN: Data Management in Operating Systems.* Rochelle Park, N.J.: Hayden Book Company, Inc., 1977, Chap. 13. This chapter discusses how direct files form a different perspective on performance and design issues. It is useful as a second reference on direct file organization.

2. Wiederhold, Gio, *Database Design.* New York; McGraw-Hill Book Company, 1977, Secs. 3-5, 4-6. These sections are valuable in that they not only discuss direct files, but also deal with multikey direct files. It is interesting to see how the design changes when there is more than one key to be dealt with.

EXERCISES

1. List four data types that might be assigned to a key in a direct file. For each data type, discuss costs, benefits, and applicability.

2. When might the *linear search* collision algorithm be a better solution to the collision problem than overflow areas?

3. Direct files allow data records to be physically deleted from the file. Discuss two benefits and two risks involved with providing this capability.

4. We have assumed that the keys are made up of a contiguous set of bytes in the user's data record. This limits what the user can and cannot use as key values for a file. An alternative is to allow the user to define the components that the file system then gathers up and makes into a key value. Discuss the impact of noncontiguous key values on the design and implementation of internal data structures as well as on disk file structures.

5. List three situations in which the user would not want to allow a data record's key value to be changed in an UPDATE operation.

6. What are the advantages and disadvantages of allowing multiple data records to exist in a file with identical key values?

7. Assume that a file has variable-length data records. What should the file system do if a user requests a record to be written that is not long enough to contain the entire data record? Explain.

8. What guidelines would you give a user who wanted to know how direct file reorganizations could be minimized or eliminated?

9. The file header block contains a variety of processing statistics. What statistics do you believe should be kept for the direct file organization? Explain.

10. Should the user be notified when a record gets forced into the overflow area? If yes, how would you implement this notification? If no, why not?

PROGRAMMING EXERCISES

1. Design on algorithm that would allow users to access *multiple records with the same key value.*

2. Design an algorithm for UPDATING a record that has its key changed by the user. Try to minimize the time interval in which, if the system crashed, the record would be lost or duplicated. What effect will your algorithm have on the performance of the UPDATE operation as seen by the user?

3. Design an algorithm and file structure for a multikey index direct file.

12

Indexed Sequential Files

CHAPTER OBJECTIVES

When you complete this chapter, you will be able to:

- Understand the concept of an index structure and how it is used to locate records within the file
- Describe the trade-offs among ISAM, direct, relative, and sequential files, and when each should be used
- Describe in detail the use of cylinder and track overflow areas and their impact on performance
- Describe how records get inserted into an ISAM file and later retrieved
- Describe the performance characteristics of ISAM files
- Understand the *two* types of records that exist in index files

12.1 OVERVIEW

Although ISAM is fairly dated and has been replaced by updated designs by many of the software vendors, it does provide valuable insight into how to design a much more complex file organization.

In Chapter 9 we learned that the sequential file organization provides sequential access to records, but not random access. The relative file organization, discussed in Chapter 10, gives the user rapid random access as well as sequential access. However, the keys used consist of simple integers and are difficult to relate to many applications. Keys are made much more usable in the direct file organization discussed in Chapter 11. However, to achieve its design goals, the user has to give up sequential access to records.

In summary, each of the file organizations discussed earlier give the user much of what was wanted, but not all. ISAM thus becomes the first file organization that provides the user with the capability to access records either sequentially or randomly. In addition, the user may define realistic keys that are consistent with the application job.

An ISAM file maintains the user data records in sequence by ascending key value (see Figure 12-0). In addition, there is an index structure built on top of the data so that the data records can be accessed randomly by key value. Thus a user can have both sequential and random access to any data record in the ISAM file.

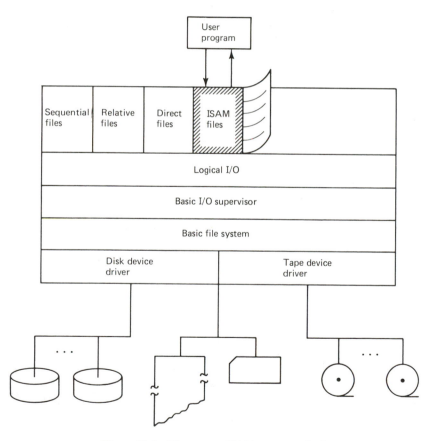

Figure 12-0   File system: ISAM access method.

12.2 FILE DESIGN CONSIDERATIONS

The question now is: How can we design and implement an access method that allows both sequential and random access to user data records? This file type must still give the user an acceptable level of performance so that there will be some motivation to use it.

12.2.1 File Structure

An ISAM file structure is shown in Figure 12-1. It consists of a sequential file of data records kept in sequence by ascending key value, and the index structure sits on top of this ordered file. The index subdivides the ordered sequential file by key ranges. Block 2 in Figure 12-1 subdivides blocks 4, 5, and 6 into three distinct key ranges. Thus block 5 contains all records with key values greater than "AB" and less than or equal to "BA." We can achieve random access by walking down the index, or sequential access by stepping through the ordered sequential file.

It might be easiest at this point to think of an index as the card catalog in a library. The cards in the catalog point to various locations within the library, effec-

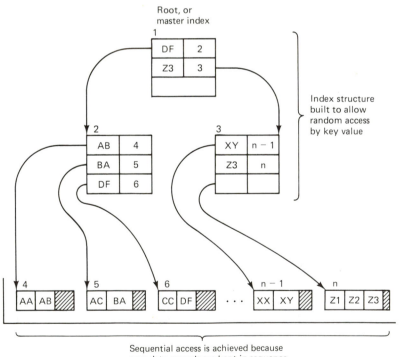

Figure 12-1 Conceptual view of an ISAM file.

tively subdividing the library into smaller and smaller areas. At the lowest level, there is a pointer to the book itself.

Alternatively, consider an example of an index in this or any other book. It consists of many key words, which are sorted as an entire unit (see Figure 12–2). To locate a particular key word, it is necessary to scan the headings at the top of each page until you have found the page on which the target word might reside. Once there, we scan down each word until we either find what we are looking for or discover that it is not there.

Index entry (read "key value")	Entry location (read "file location")
Access modes	p.52
Alternate track	p.113
Cell	p.416
CREATE_FILE	p.197
Direct file	p.465
File activity ratio	p.28
.	
.	
.	
Synchronous I/O	p.219
User record buffer	p.356
Write-protect	p.93
Write-ring	p.280

Figure 12–2   Book index structure.

If found, we must take the page numbers on which that word is referenced and go directly to those pages. This is exactly what happens in an indexed type file as the file system searches each index block until it finds the index record that points to the track on which the target user data record might reside.

Figure 12–3 shows roughly how an ISAM file is constructed and the multiple levels that exist within the index structure. These are discussed in more detail in the sections that follow.

Master index structure.   *The master index is the highest-level index structure within each index and contains pointers to the next lower level of the index, known as the cylinder indexes (see Figure 12–3a).* In actuality, the master index is the top of the index structure and is known as the *root of the index*.

A file can have more than one index, but only one copy of the user data records. *The index that is ordered in the same key sequence as the data is called the primary index, and access is via the primary key. All other indices, in which the indexes are ordered in a different sequence from the data records, are called alternate, or secon-*

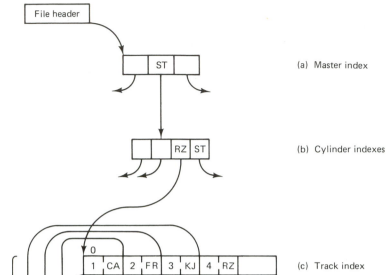

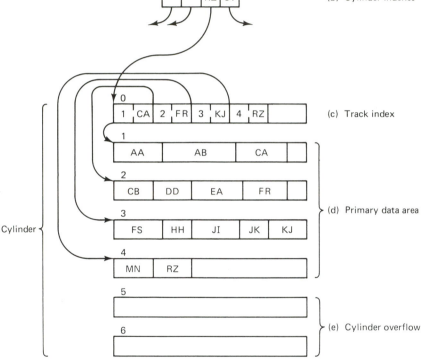

Figure 12-3 ISAM file structure.

dary, indices. Similarly, the keys in the data records used to access those indices are called alternate, or secondary, keys.

The master index serves as the starting point for randomly locating any user data record in the entire file. An index record contains the following information:

- Cylinder and track number, which points to another track in the file, whether it be another index track or a primary data record track
- Key containing the highest possible key in any record on that track

Cylinder index. The master index points to the cylinder indexes on each cylinder of the file. *The cylinder index further subdivides an ISAM file to the granulari-*

ty of what user data records exist within a particular cylinder (see Figure 12–3b).
Thus, if 20 cylinders contained user data records, there would be 20 cylinder index
records. Each record would contain the value of the highest key that resides on that
target cylinder. Each cylinder index may contain pointers to other cylinder indexes,
or at the lowest level in the index they could point to the track indexes on the cylinder
itself. The records in the cylinder index contain the following:

- Cylinder number
- Highest key of any index record in that cylinder

If the file is very large, we could end up with multiple cylinders of index records.
Therefore, the master index will begin to subdivide the cylinder indexes, and the
cylinder indexes will further subdivide the file down to the level of a cylinder that
contains user data records. Note that a master index and a cylinder index have identical structures. The only difference is the name. The reason for this is that it is useful
to differentiate the top or highest level of an index structure from all other elements
in the structure. Therefore, since the master index represents the highest level of the
index tree, all searches begin there.

Track index.   Once we get down to the cylinder that contains actual user data
records, we need to be able to locate specific user data records without having to
read all the tracks on that cylinder. What we need is to know where the user data
records are located. This is accomplished via the track indexes. *A track index contains one index record for each track on a specific cylinder. Each index record identifies a particular track within the cylinder, and the highest key value on that track
(see Figure 12–3c).* Therefore, each record in a track index contains the following
information:

- Track number within the cylinder
- Highest key value of any user data record on that track

Thus if we walk down the index structure from the master index through the
cylinder index(es) down to the track index, we can pinpoint the exact track within
the file where the user data record we want is located. Again, it is necessary to emphasize that we only know where in the file our record *could* exist. We do not know
that it *does* exist. We will not know that until we scan the track identified by the
associated track index record.

Primary data area.   *The set of tracks containing the user data records, and
pointed to by the track index records is collectively known as the primary data area.
All user data records reside in the primary data area (see Figure 12–3d).* All blocks
not included in the primary data area are either index blocks (i.e., file structure
overhead) or overflow area blocks.
    *The user data records in the primary data area are always kept in sequence by
the primary key.* Even if we add records to the file, the records on the designated

track are resequenced so that the key values are kept in ascending order. Reordering is performed even if it means that some records are pushed off the primary track into an overflow area.

Once the file is initially populated, the track indexes have been set and cannot be changed unless the file is reorganized. This means that the high key value for each track in the primary data area has been "cast in concrete." Thus, even though there could be room on other tracks, all data records will be forced to the track that includes that record's key value. Therefore, only some tracks might be forced into overflow areas, while others are left with room to spare.

Cylinder overflow areas.   In the relative file organization, there is always a guaranteed place in the file for each unique record in the file. In the direct file organization, this is no longer the case, so there had to be some mechanism by which these exception conditions could be processed. Thus it used the overflow area technique to accommodate this.

In the ISAM file structure, there can be a cylinder overflow area, as shown in Figure 12–3e. *A cylinder overflow area consists of one or more tracks within a cylinder. These tracks are dedicated to handling all overflows from the primary data tracks within that specific cylinder only.* Thus when a primary data track on that cylinder does not have enough room for a new record, one or more records must get pushed off onto an overflow track on the cylinder. This is the escape hatch that the access method has to enable it to process each record request to successful completion.

The user data records in the cylinder overflow area are linked to each other by ascending key value. The primary data track, in turn, is linked to the first data record in the overflow area that was pushed off that track.

File overflow areas.   Sometimes, the cylinder overflow area fills up. What happens when a record that belongs on that cylinder does not have enough space anywhere in the primary or cylinder overflow area? There is one last escape valve, the *file* overflow area.

The file overflow area is designed to handle the overflow from all the cylinder overflow areas in the file (see Figure 12–4). Thus, when a record does not fit in either its target primary data track or the associated cylinder overflow area, it is necessary to move the overflow into the *file* overflow area. When the file overflow area is filled, no more user data records can be added to the file until it is completely reorganized. This is because the size of the file, and all its overflow areas, is defined when the file is created.

Search algorithms.   Since the keys in the index are in sequence, we must search the index records by comparing the index record key value against the key value supplied by the user. We know that we have located the correct index entry when the key value in the user's data record is *less than or equal to* the key value in the index record. This means that if the record is to be found in the file, it must be located

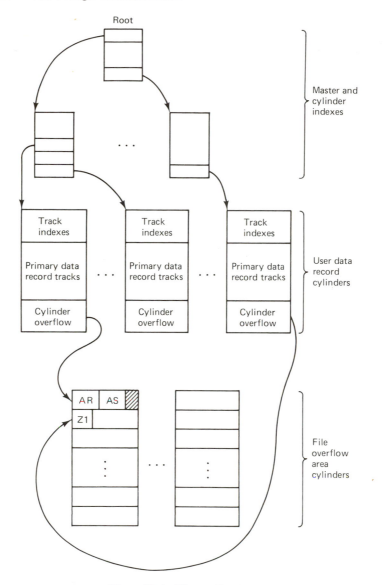

Figure 12-4   File overflow area.

on the path pointed to by the associated index record. We need only follow that path to find the user data record. Note that we only know where to *look for* the record, not whether the record itself actually exists.

Tree walking, the ability to walk down an index until the data record has been found, is a critical piece of any file system. Therefore, let us now discuss in some detail what tree walking is all about (see Figure 12-5).

First, the key must be extracted from the user data record or from a key buffer

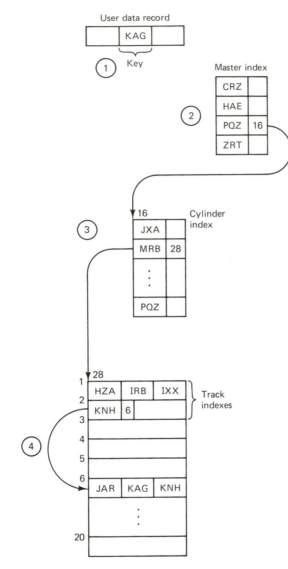

Figure 12-5   Walking an index tree.

filled in by the user program (step 1). Then the master index must be read into an I/O buffer in main memory.

Second, the key value supplied by the user, in this case "KAG," must be compared against each key in each of the index records (step 2). What we are searching for is the single index record that fulfills the following search criteria:

user key value ≤ key value in index record

This is because the index records partition the file into specific key ranges, and each index record contains the *highest possible* key in the partition of the file to which the index record points. In the example, the only index record that meets this criterion is the index record whose key is "PQZ." That index record then points to block 16.

Third, the file system must read block 16 into an I/O buffer in main memory (step 3). We are now positioned at the next lower level of the index structure. Again, it is necessary to scan all the index records in this block looking for the index record that meets the criterion defined above. The only index record in block 16 that meets that criterion is the record with a key value of "MRB" which points to block 28.

The files system then takes this link and reads in block 28. This just happens to be the track index. The file system then searches that block for the index record that matches our "less than or equal to" criterion. There is only one such index record, and it has a key value of "KNH" (see step 4).

Finally, the file system looks at track 6 and searches the track for a user data record that matches the key value originally requested by the user.

Note that in reality, there could be multiple levels of cylinder indices that must be walked through before arriving at the track index. What determines how many levels of index must be transversed is both the number of user data records in the file and the track and cylinder capacities of the device that holds the file.

12.2.2 Record Addressing Algorithm

In both the relative and direct file organizations, we had to hash a key to a *particular block address* in the file in order to locate where the user data record resided. Thus, for all file types discussed so far, all records can be retrieved only by calculating the physical block address of the record in the file. ISAM, however, is the first structure in which a key value is used to walk down an index structure to find the location of the desired record. Notice that the time it takes to hash a key is significantly faster than the time it now takes to read and scan multiple index blocks. Thus to gain sequential and random access to records, we are now paying the price of lower performance for random record addressing.

The principal mode of addressing records in an ISAM file is through the use of the key field, which is embedded within each of the user data records. By knowing the value of the key, ISAM can walk down the index tree structure directly to the specific track in the primary data area on which the record resides, if it exists.

However, unlike the records in a direct file, the records in an ISAM file are physically maintained in sequence by primary key. What this allows the ISAM to provide the user is the capability of doing exact, generic, and approximate key searches. Until now, we have implicitly performed *full key exact* searches. However, with ASCII keys it is possible to perform other kinds of searches as well.

A generic key is simply a partial key. In other words, if a key was defined to be eight characters long, a generic, or partial, key would be defined as the first *n* characters of the key field. Generic keys are equal to the full key value when *n* equals the key size. This means that the user need only specify the leading characters to access a record.

An approximate key search can be done with full or generic key values. By requesting an approximate key search, the user is really saying: "Find me the *first record* that has a key value greater than or equal to, or just greater than, a specified key value." In this manner, it does not matter whether or not a record with an exact match exists in the file. The user is really requesting the first record in the file that matches the key search criteria. Given the volatile nature of some kinds of files, it is a major benefit not to force users to know the exact key value in order to run an application successfully.

Direct files do not have the capability of performing generic or approximate key searches. These capabilities require that the user data records be in sequence by ascending key value. Otherwise, it would be almost impossible to implement these features. Since direct files are not kept in that required sequence, these features are not available to their users.

Finally, we have assumed that there is never more than one user data record in the file with the same identical key values. In fact, in the relative file, a matching record number causes the user's request to be aborted abnormally. In the ISAM file organization, we will continue to assume unique key values for user data records. This is done by convention only, as it is certainly technically feasible to allow duplicate key values within a file. However, the ANSI COBOL standard requires unique primary key values, so we will adopt the same convention for the ISAM organization.

12.2.3 File Attributes

The file attributes that are important in an ISAM file are very similar to those for a direct file. The reason for this is that both file types provide the user with random access to the data records by user-definable keys. The fact that ISAM also provides the capability to sequentially access the data records is a file structure design issue, not a file attribute issue.

File organization.   The only way that the file system can know that it is to create an ISAM file is if it is told to do so by the file organization defined by the user. Thus the user must set the file organization equal to ISAM.

File size.   In an ISAM file there are really two entities that together make up the size of the file. First, there is the estimated size of the actual user data records and the associated primary index structure. Second, there is the estimated size of the cylinder overflow area and/or the file's overflow area. As with the direct file, if the ISAM access method cannot find space available in the primary index or data set, it looks for available space in one of the overflow areas. These file sizes parameters are critical because the ISAM file cannot be extended; it can only be reorganized.

Block size.   The block size is the same for all blocks within the file. Thus both index and user data records will be written into the same-size blocks. What this means is that the block size chosen by the user must take into consideration both the average size of a user data record and the size of an index record. If these sizes are chosen well, a block size can be selected that will not waste much space no matter if it is used within an index structure or as part of the blocks holding the user data records.

Key position, size, and data type.   The only way the ISAM access method can locate a record is via the key value. Therefore, to locate the key, the user must declare not only where within the user data record the key begins, but also how long, in bytes, the key will be. From this size declaration, the access method knows how large all the index records will be, as well as where to look for the key when given a data record. The data type of the key is needed for the file system to correctly sequence the data records in the file.

12.3 FILE OPERATIONS

We will now examine in detail the ISAM-specific processing that the file operations perform. Remember that the standard tasks are still performed (see Chapter 8). What is important in this section is the processing that the CREATE operation must perform. ISAM is the first file structure in which there is really a different file structure that must be built. It takes time to accomplish a ISAM CREATE, due primarily to the complexity of the CREATE function and to the sheer number of I/O cells that must be performed to CREATE a complex file structure.

12.3.1 CREATE File

The CREATE file function is consistently the most complex of the file operations, since the file structure must be built from scratch. An ISAM file structure is also the first file type in which it is necessary to construct an index structure on the disk itself.

As we proceed through all the steps it takes to build an ISAM structure, it can be asked why so much work is being done at file CREATE time. In other words, why not push off as much of the work load as possible until that particular feature is required? Fundamentally, this ends up being the technical decision of the project leader of the ISAM development project. However, a file is CREATEd only once, whereas record operations will occur over and over throughout the lifetime of the file. Thus it is preferable to take the time once, at CREATE file time, to perform as many tasks as possible. Users understand that the time it takes to CREATE a file may be fairly substantial, so their intolerance for slower performance is muted. However, if we had pushed off some of the work to the various record operations, CREATE would be faster and the performance of their record functions would become unpredictable. Thus, from a user perspective, it is better to do as much as possible at CREATE file time.

Next, we will go through the steps required to CREATE an ISAM file.

1. Create the File's Header Block.   The file header, for an ISAM file, contains not only the standard information, but the key information as well. There is another piece of information that it might be useful to keep: the block number of the start of the master index and overflow areas. Sometimes this value is known by convention:"The master index will always begin in block 2 of the file." However, there are times when an explicit declaration of where the master index resides is required. If this is the case, put the block number of the master index into the file's header. Thus we can not only CREATE and OPEN files, but we also save all critical data needed to correctly process the records in the file.

2. Build the Master Index.   The size of the master index is usually defined to be *n* tracks or cylinders long. The user determines this value by calculating how many user data records will probably exist in the file, and then work backward to determine the size of the indexes, in particular the master index.

The ISAM file is tightly coupled to the capacity of the disk. This dependence is a two-edged sword. On the one hand, it allows the user to highly optimize the file structure. On the other hand, it forces the user to know too much about the technical details and design of the disk itself. Also, it means that if a new disk were to be rolled into the machine room at night, all these calculations would have to be redone to match the new disk's track and cylinder capacities. Later in this chapter we discuss in detail how to calculate the exact size of a file, given the estimated number of user data records expected to populate the file.

If we assume that the user had declared the number of tracks to allocate to the master index, it is the job of the CREATE function to create the master index structure. It does this by allocating the number of tracks or cylinders defined by the user, and logically assigns them to be the master index.

Next, the ISAM access method must make sure that the master index is empty. It does this by writing "empty" records the size of an index record throughout the master index. In fact, it writes one record for each cylinder allocated to the cylinder index. The key value inserted into each of these records is the highest possible key value allowed. The pointer field in each of these master index records would contain the cylinder number of each of the cylinders in the cylinder index. Thus a record is prebuilt which points to each of the cylinders at the next lower level within the index tree structure.

3. Build the Cylinder Index.   Each index record in the master index contains a pointer to each of the individual cylinder indexes. In fact, there is a one-to-one correspondence between records in the master index and the number of cylinders in the cylinder index.

The index records in the cylinder index must be preinitialized in an analogous manner. Thus there is one index record built for each cylinder containing a track index. Indeed, in large files, the cylinder index could point to another level of cylinder indexes. If this were the case, we would simply repeat the processing done previously.

The records in the cylinder index eventually point to the cylinders that contain the user data records, not the index data records. What the cylinder index records really accomplishes is to identify the highest possible user data record key in that cylinder. Thus the file can be split among many cylinders by knowing the highest possible key in each cylinder.

4. Build the Track Index.   The processing to create the track index is identical to the processing done to build the cylinder indexes. Now, however, there is one track index record per track on that cylinder which contains user data records. Thus the track index records further subdivide the cylinder by knowing the highest possible keys on each track. Once the appropriate track index record is located, the access method knows that the record it is searching for must be on that track, the track's overflow area, or the user data record does not exist.

5. Primary Data Area.   The tree-structured index has been built with dummy entries which will force future WRITE operations to follow the correct path through the index. At the bottom of the index structure is the user data area. All the index tracks and cylinders are overhead in the file. After all, the user is really concerned only with allowing enough space for the user data records. Therefore, when the file has been created and the user examines the total file size, it will be considerably larger than the actual amount of space needed to hold the user's data records. This difference is the overhead of the particular file structure utilized.

A sequential file effectively has zero overhead. A relative file has some, due to the fact that space needed to be allocated for every cell within the file, whether or not a valid user data record was present. In a direct file, the only overhead is the fact that the file has to be preallocated to a user-definable size in order for the hashing algorithm to work. If eventually all of the primary space is filled, there will be no overhead in a direct file. The overflow area in a direct file is not allocated until required, so it cannot be considered overhead.

The primary data area tracks will contain all the user data records. Should space ever be exhausted, an overflow area will take up where the primary data tracks leave off. Thus the overflow area can be considered to be a logical extension of the primary data area track.

To summarize ISAM CREATE processing, the following tasks are accomplished:

- The file header block has been written with all the file's attributes.
- The master index has been built with one index record for each cylinder needed for the cylinder index.
- The cylinder index has been built with one index record for each lower-level cylinder index.
- In the lowest-level cylinder index, there is one index record for each cylinder containing the primary data areas in the file.
- The track indexes have been built on all cylinders containing primary data areas. There is also one index record for every track in the primary data area on that specific cylinder.
- The cylinder and file overflow areas have been allocated.

12.3.2 OPEN File

An ISAM file can be OPENed for access by retrieving the file attributes and allocating the I/O buffers and internal table space needed to process successfully. The file attributes can be retrieved by reading into main memory the file header. In this critical block are all the data the access method needs to process the ISAM records properly. To improve performance, these attributes are copied from the file header block into internal control tables which will be resident in main memory for the entire time that the file is kept open.

For performance reasons, the OPEN processing could arbitrarily read into one of the I/O buffers the *root block or master index* of the index structure. The root block is the highest-level block in the index. It is the very first block in the index structure. The reason for doing this is that all random operations into an ISAM file must begin their searches at the top or root of the index. If we preread this block into memory, we can simply leave it in main memory waiting for the first record operation from the user. We will later see how performance can be improved by other techniques of using multiple I/O buffers to contain critical index blocks.

12.3.3 CLOSE File

When a file is CLOSE'd, the same kinds of processing occur independent of file type. What is peculiar to ISAM is that multiple I/O buffers could have been used. Thus each of these buffers must be examined to see if any of them contain updated information that has not yet been written into the ISAM file on the disk. If any fit this criterion, the CLOSE processing must ensure that each unwritten block gets rewritten back into the ISAM file.

This brings up an important point. The more I/O buffers we allocate to an ISAM file, the higher the performance level is likely to be. The flip side of this is that the buffers are not written back to the file until the I/O buffer space is needed by a future request. Thus there is an interval during which the I/O buffers can contain a new record that has not yet been written to the file. However, from the perspective of the user's program, OK status has been returned so the records *must* have been physically written to disk already. If the system should crash during this interval, all updated records in the I/O buffers in main memory will be lost.

12.4 RECORD OPERATIONS

The record operations for ISAM are the same as for the access methods discussed previously. However, now the performance characteristics of each function becomes much more critical. This is because an ISAM file structure has an index tree that must be dealt with. Therefore, in each of the record operation sections, we will delve into the performance side of the operation in much greater detail than we have in the past. It is important to understand in detail what is consuming the time for each operation. Because then, and only then, can we take the next step, which is to analyze how performance can be improved. In fact, it is important to understand that *most record operations can take from 1 to n actual I/O operations to complete.*

Record access modes.   An ISAM file provides the user with two access modes. First, there is *random access* to any record in the file. This is provided by the POSITION, READ, and WRITE operations. Second, the user has the capability to *sequentially access* the records in the file through the READ_NEXT operation. These run-time record options are specified by the user or the language run-time library in the user interface control block, which is the user interface to the file system.

Record currency.   The current record is set whenever an input operation completes successfully (i.e., POSITION, READ, or READ_NEXT). In file types discussed earlier, the current record always ended up pointing to a block within the primary data area of the file. With ISAM, we have a file type that has a potentially large amount of file structure overhead. Therefore, where should the current record point? The current record relates to the last user data record, not an index record. Therefore, the current record will always point into the primary data area or the overflow data area of the file. It will never address any record or block within the index structure.

The format of the current record, as kept by the ISAM access method procedures, contains the following fields:

- *Key* of the data record
- *Block number* of the block that contains the user data record

The block number allows the access method to randomly access the specific block, or cylinder and track, that holds the record. Once that block is in an I/O buffer in main memory, the access method can search the block for a record that has an identical matching key field. Once it finds a record with a matching key, the search stops. This is an important point to consider, because it says that *the keys in an ISAM file must be unique.* As we shall see when we discuss the other forms of indexed files, there is a way around this restriction. However, for the purposes of discussing ISAM, we shall follow the convention of requiring unique record keys.

12.4.1 POSITION to Record

The POSITION operation is a *random* record operation which positions to a particular record in the file. There is no user record buffer declared, since in a POSITION operation the user data record is *not* copied into the user's record buffer. The POSITION operation sets the current record pointer to a specific record within the file.

To perform a POSITION request, the following tasks must be performed in sequence.

1. Walk down the Index Tree to the Target Data Block.   Starting at the root of the index, walk down the tree. To do this, each index record in an index block must be examined until an index record is found that has a key value that is *greater than or equal to* the user's key.

Several points must be considered here. First, the amount of time it takes to locate the block containing the target user data record depends on the number of index blocks that must be read into main memory. Thus, if nine blocks must be read and searched in the I/O buffers in main memory, nine I/O operations must be performed.

Why is this so important? In a relative file, when we hash to a particular block, only that block has to be read into an I/O buffer—only one I/O operation to read any block, and therefore any record, in the entire file. In the ISAM example mentioned above, there were nine I/O operations just to walk through the index, plus a tenth I/O operation to read the data block in the primary data area. Thus to randomly read a single record, an ISAM file is an order of magnitude slower than a relative file. This is just an example, but ISAM will always be slower than either relative or direct files in performing random reads.

2. Read the Block Containing the Target Record.   Once we have reached the lowest level of the index (i.e., the track index record that points into the primary data area), we must actually read that block into an I/O buffer in main memory.

3. Search the Block for a Record with a Matching Key.   Just because the user wanted to read a record with a particular key value does not mean that the record exists in the file. Thus once we have the primary data area block in memory, we know only that if the record exists, it must be in this specific block or its associated overflow chain.

The data block is searched, record by record, in a manner similar to the way an index block is searched. Each user data record in the block is searched for a key that is *identical to the user supplied search key.* If a match is found, we have the record and the current record is set to this block number and key value.

If no matching key is found, the access method must check to see if there is an overflow chain associated with this block. This is determined by information the access method records within the block itself. If there is an overflow chain, each block in the chain must be read and searched in a manner identical to the way the primary data block was read and searched. If a matching record is found, the current record is set appropriately.

If the record is not found either in the primary data area block or in its associated overflow area, the operation is terminated. Then an "unsuccessful" status message is returned to the calling program.

It is critical to understand the number of I/O operations that are performed in order to get the target record read into an I/O buffer in main memory. This number can be calculated as follows:

$$\text{number of I/Os} = (\# \text{ I/Os}_{\text{search index}}) + (1 \text{ I/O}_{\text{read data block}})$$
$$+ (\# \text{ I/Os}_{\text{search overflow area}})$$

If we count every block that must be read into an I/O buffer in main memory in order to perform a key search, the real cost in time can be calculated. If we then take this total number of I/Os required and multiply it by the time it takes to SEEK to and SEARCH for each block, we will know precisely how many milliseconds, or whole seconds, it will take to perform an average random read within an ISAM file.

12.4.2 READ Record

The READ record operation randomly accesses any record in the ISAM file. The READ operation is the same as the POSITION operation except that the READ goes one step further and copies the user data record from the block in an I/O buffer in main memory into the user data record buffer specified in the call.

All the processing that the READ must perform is identical to what POSITION must do. However, once the record has been successfully located in a block in main memory, the READ specific processing takes place. There are several paths that the processing can take, depending on the relative size of the target record.

The performance of the READ request can be written out as follows:

$$t_{\text{read}} = t_{\text{position}} + t_{\text{copy record}}$$

The time to copy the record from the I/O buffer in main memory into the user record buffer is simply a *move* type of CPU instruction, not an I/O operation. Thus the move time is negligible compared to the I/O times involved in the operation. Therefore, the performance of the READ request approximates the performance of the POSITION request.

12.4.3 READ_NEXT Record

The READ_NEXT operation locates the next record, in sequence by primary key within the ISAM file, and transfers the record into the user record buffer. Since the data areas of the file are known, and since the data areas are implicitly linked together, it is *not* necessary to walk down the index tree on a READ_NEXT command.

There is no key supplied here because the position of the record in the file is identified by the current record pointer. This was set by the previous successful READ, READ_NEXT, or POSITION operation. Therefore, since the records in the ISAM file are kept physically in ascending key sequence, the READ_NEXT request must start at the current record pointer (see Figure 12–6b) and then retrieve the next record in the file.

The performance of the READ_NEXT operation can be very fast, indeed. *If* the next record in the file is located within the same block as the current record, the record can be copied out of the block in the I/O buffer in main memory and directly into the user record buffer. Thus zero I/O operations need to be performed. Conversely, if the current record was the last record in the block, the access method must perform an I/O read operation to get the next block in the primary data area in the

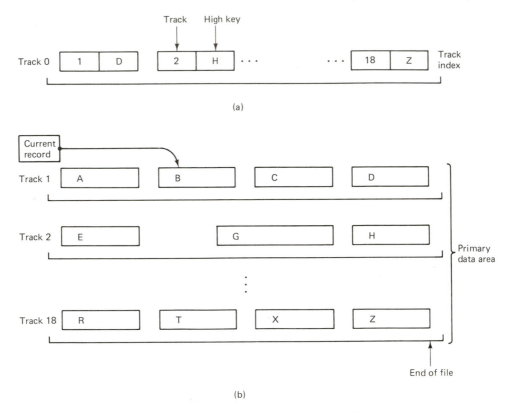

Figure 12–6　ISAM READ_NEXT processing.

file. In summary, the READ_NEXT operation can take either zero or one actual I/O operations, depending on whether or not the next record is in the current I/O buffer.

Another aspect of performance is how it compares among the various file organizations. This is important because users need to know on what basis to select one file organization over another. The fastest way to read records out of a file sequentially is by using a sequential file. However, a sequential file does not allow the user random access to records. An ISAM file, however, allows random access to the user data records. Also, if the file was populated in an optimal manner, the performance of sequentially reading all the records will be almost exactly equal to the performance of a sequential file. This is because when the records are read sequentially in an ISAM file, the index is completely bypassed. Thus the end result is what amounts to an ordered sequential file.

When a random READ occurs, and the record is not in the file, the status returned to the calling program indicated "record not found." This can never occur with a READ_NEXT, because this operation does not depend on a specific key value, but instead on the key sequence in the file. However, when the last user data record in the file has been read, what happens to the next READ_NEXT operation? No record is found, because there are no more records. This exception condition is known as "end-of-file." Most programming languages make provisions for the detection of this specific condition. To put this another way, there are no more records in the file because we are positioned at the *end of the file (see Figure 12-6b)*.

12.4.4 WRITE Record

The WRITE operation adds a new record into the ISAM file by utilizing the primary key value. This operation is easily the most complicated of all the record operations, because the user data record must be inserted into the file at the correct location and in the correct key sequence.

The key of the record is *not* specified by the user. Recall that the location and length of the key within the data record itself was defined at file CREATE time. These file attributes are the only ones used by WRITE to insert a record into the file. All the records are inserted into the file by using the same insertion criterion, by taking the key value from the user data record itself. In this manner, the access method can guarantee that the records are not only inserted correctly, but that the records can later be retrieved successfully.

The processing that the WRITE operation must perform can be formulated as follows:

$$t_{\text{write}} = t_{\text{position}} + t_{\text{add record}}$$

Thus the time to WRITE a record into the ISAM file is equal to the time it takes to POSITION to the track into which the record's key would be in proper key sequence. To this time we then must add the time it takes to add the record to the file. Next, we discuss the steps required to add the record to the file.

1. Determine If the Record Can Fit within This Block.   We know from walking down the index structure that we have reached the specific track in the primary data area into which the record must be added. However, we do not yet know whether the track is empty or full, or whether there is an overflow area associated with this track. We do know that the highest possible key value in this track, and its associated overflow chain, if any, is greater than or equal to the new record's key value.

Therefore, we must scan the track to see if there are any records with a higher key value (see Figure 12-7a). Since the records are kept in physical sequence by ascending key value, if we find a record with a higher key in the primary area track, we know that the new record must be inserted prior to any records with higher key values (see Figure 12-7b). Of course, if we happen to find a record with an identical key value, this WRITE must be terminated, since the keys must be unique.

If the record is to be inserted into this track and if there is enough room, the record can be rewritten to the file and a "success" status returned to the calling program.

If there is not enough room on this track, we must deal with the overflow situation. Since the records are kept in physical key sequence within a block, one or more records *with higher key values* must be pushed out of the primary data block and

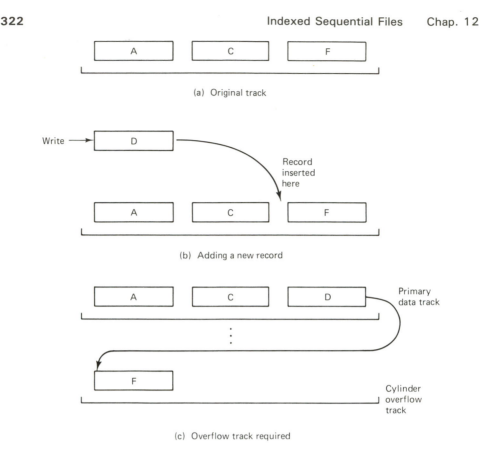

Figure 12-7   Adding a record to a track.

into the overflow area (see Figure 12-7c). Note that there is the special case in which the new record is the high key in the track and there is not enough room in the block. In this case, the new record is the one that is pushed into the overflow chain.

12.4.5 UPDATE Record

The UPDATE operation modifies a record that already exists within the ISAM file. The user's record buffer contains the modified record. There is no key specified because the access method will extract the key from within the data record itself. The record size is needed in order that the access method can know how much data lies within the user's record buffer. For fixed-length records, the length is obviously known. However, this is a required field for variable-length record files.

When an UPDATE is performed, *it is the responsibility of the access method to guarantee that the user has not modified the key within the data record.* Although it is technically possible to change a record's key, by convention we will prohibit this capability within an ISAM file. How does the access method tell if the user has changed the record's key? It is done by comparing the newly modified record's key, in the user's record buffer, against the original key in the original record in the block in the I/O buffer in main memory. If there is a mismatch, the user has changed the key and the UPDATE operation will be terminated.

The key validation is critical for the following reasons. The access method must guarantee that all records inserted into the file are retrievable and valid. This means that all the records must be inserted into the file based on the value of the record's key. During an UPDATE operation, the modified record simply replaces the original record in its original file location based on its original key value. It is not inserted into the file by key as it is in the WRITE operation. Therefore, if the user changes the key value, that record will never be retrievable because it does not reside at the correct key sequence location within the file.

The performance of an UPDATE operation relates directly to whether or not the record can be reinserted into the same track as the original record without other changes to the track. This will occur naturally when the size of the UPDATEed record is equal to or less than the size of the record it is replacing. In fact, even if the modified record is larger, if room is still available in the track, the other records can be shuffled within the track to make room for the larger record.

A problem arises when the modified record is larger than the record it is replacing and there is not enough available unused space within the track. When this occurs, one or more data records at the end of the track (i.e., the records with the highest keys on the track) will need to be moved off the track and into the overflow chain. When this occurs, the UPDATE processing will take a substantially longer time to complete.

One other point is worth mentioning here. Since we do not allow the user to change the primary key, no changes in the index tree structure will be necessary, because no key changes have occurred. This makes UPDATEing much faster than WRITEing even though both operations write new records into the file.

12.4.6 DELETE Record

The DELETE operation logically deletes a user data record from an ISAM file. The record to be deleted is the record identified by the current record pointer. Thus the record to be DELETEed has just been sucessfully accessed by a READ, POSITION, or READ_NEXT operation. No key is needed because the current record pointer identifies the record sufficiently well. If the current record pointer is not valid or does not exist, the DELETE operation will be abnormally terminated.

The way in which the record is deleted is simply by setting a flag within the record overhead to indicate that the record is no longer logically accessible. This is faster than actually erasing the record from the file entirely. It also allows the user to "undelete" the record in case of a major error.

The DELETE operation is very fast to complete. The reason for this high level of performance can be summarized in the following formula:

$$t_{delete} = t_{set\ delete\ flag} + t_{re\text{-}write\ record}$$

The time to set the delete flag in the I/O buffer is negligible since it is a simple CPU instruction only. Thus the time to DELETE a record is in direct proportion to the time it takes to re-WRITE the record into the file. We do know, however, that the DELETE operation has none of the complications of variable record sizes that UPDATE has. This is because the DELETE operation never changes the length of the record. It only sets on a flag in a field that already exists. Thus the deleted record can always be copied back into the exact spot on the track from whence it came.

12.5 PERFORMANCE CONSIDERATIONS

Since the performance of sequentially processing the records in an ISAM file approaches the high level of a normal sequential file, there is not that much that can be done to improve the performance even more. However, one of the techniques that can be used is to allocate additional I/O buffers so that the access method can perform "read-ahead" of the primary data area records. This has the effect of anticipating the user's next request and thus can already have the next block read into an I/O buffer in main memory by the time the user gets around to needing its records.

The second major area for potential high payback in performance is to populate the file optimally. This means that all of the file parameters, such as primary data area size, block size versus record size, and so on, are calculated such that there is no overflow area used when the file is initially being populated with data records. Sequential performance through a file with no overflow areas to be accessed is significantly higher than sequentially accessing a file that has many overflow areas. This is because, with no overflow areas, all records are physically on the primary data tracks of the file. Thus it is necessary only to read the primary data tracks one right after the other. Whenever overflow areas are needed, the records are no longer physically maintained in a linked list, by key sequence, in the overflow chain itself. Thus the record processing reverts to randomly accessing the records in the overflow area until the end of the overflow chain has been reached.

The major area for performance improvements is in the random accessing of the data records. In other words, whenever it is required to start at the top of the index and walk down the tree to locate the record, the overall performance gets much slower. Therefore, how can we improve performance of the random operations to an ISAM file?

We can save one or more I/O operations by allocating internal buffer areas large enough to hold at least the top level of the master index. This saves at least one I/O operation for every random request processed. If more space can be allocated to hold larger chunks of the index, more I/Os will be saved, and the performance will continue to improve.

Finally, several things need to be said about performance of ISAM files on microcomputers. These machines typically have devices that are much more restricted in data capacity and performance than similar devices on the larger machines. Therefore, it is even more critical to design the ISAM files correctly. This means that the file CREATE parameters should try to minimize the need for overflow areas. In addition, it may be useful to rebuild (i.e., reorganize) the file more frequently to keep the number of overflow areas, as well as wasted space taken up by deleted records, to a minimum. It is easier on the larger machines to "waste" disk space and not be hurt.

12.5.1 File Population Techniques

The way in which a file is populated with user data records is critical to the performance that can be achieved from the file itself. The objective in populating an ISAM file is to end up having created zero overflow areas. If done incorrectly, all the records within the file could end up in a single overflow chain (see Figure 12–8). First let us examine the correct way to populate an ISAM file, and then look at some of the poorer ways of accomplishing the same task.

At the completion of a CREATE operation, there are no user data records in the file. As we insert records in the file, the search path down the index always takes

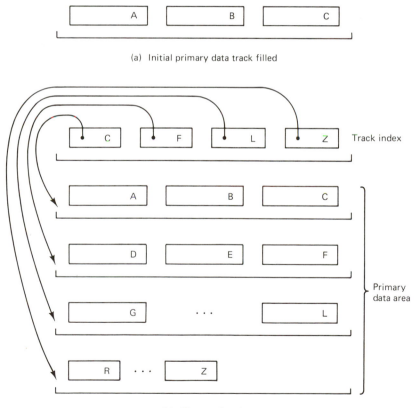

Figure 12–8 Populating ISAM file with sorted data records.

the less-than-or-equal-to path to the primary data block. If, and only if, the incoming data records have been presorted in ascending key sequence, the records will be added to each track one right after the other. When the end of a track has been reached, the track index record that points to that track will be updated to reflect what is now the official high key of that specific track. Thus track 1 (see Figure 12–8) has an associated index record with a key of "C." Then another track index record will be created to point to the next track in the primary data area. This processing will continue until all records have been inserted into the file.

Note that the high keys for each track (i.e., the key values set in each track index record for each track in the primary data area) are set during the original population of the file and can never be changed except by performing a file reorganization (refer to track 0 in Figure 12–8). This means that if the records come into the file in a sorted sequence, the high keys will be set as well as possible.

On the other hand, if the incoming records are not presorted by primary key value, the high key values put into the track index records could simply be all wrong. Consider the file in Figure 12–9. If we inserted records with keys of "Z," "X," and "V" before the primary data track was filled, the high key of the primary data track would be "Z" (refer to step a), and the track index record created for this track would contain a key of "Z." Since this is the high key in the file, *all other records will have*

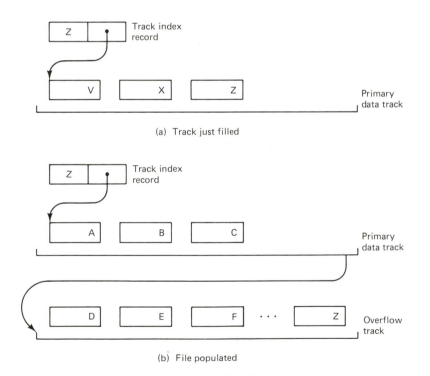

(a) Track just filled

(b) File populated

Figure 12-9 Populating ISAM file with nonsorted records.

keys less than or equal to "Z." Therefore, all records put into the file will be forced onto that track or into its overflow area, whether or not there is space available in the rest of the primary data area (refer to step b).

   The lesson to be learned here is that the performance of accessing records within a file can vary dramatically without changing one line of code in either the access method or user program. In summary, the most critical step in performance is to select the best combination of file size, allocation, block size, and record size possible within the constraints of the system on which the application is being run.

12.5.2 File Reorganization

When the ISAM file is first created and populated with user data records, there are no overflow areas. Thus random access to any record amounts to walking down the index tree until we find the pointer to the track on which our data record may reside. Whether or not the record is on that designated track, our search effort is finished at that track.

   However, as we add, change, or delete records in the file, more and more records are pushed into overflow areas. Thus not only must we walk down the index to find the record, but now we also need to walk down the overflow chain to find the record. This additional processing not only consumes more I/O operations to read the additional blocks, but performance begins to degrade rapidly as the search paths become ever longer. When the performance of the file accesses becomes relatively unacceptable, it is time to reorganize the file. What a reorganization accomplishes is to rebuild a brand new file containing only current valid user data records. In addition, if space is allocated properly, all the records will now reside in the primary file, and the overflow areas will again be empty. Thus we will once again be able to randomly access any record in the file without needing to resort to searching an overflow area. It is like giving a car a well-deserved tune-up. After the rework has been done, the car should again perform significantly better than before.

   The steps needed to reorganize an ISAM file are about the same as for a DIRECT file:

1. CREATE a temporary file with the same attributes, other than perhaps file size, as the original master file.
2. Copy all valid records from the master file into the temporary file.
3. When done, validate that the new file contains the correct number of records and that the file is readable.
4. If all is well, delete the master file, and rename the temporary file back to the same name as the original master file.
5. Now, from a programming point of view, nothing has been changed. However, structurally, the new file is "cleaner" and will provide a higher level of performance to the users.

This completes the file reorganization process. Note, however, that the file may not be identical. It is always a good idea to reexamine the file size and overflow area allocations whenever an ISAM file is reorganized. This is because we ideally want the new file to have all of its user data records in the primary file and none in the overflow areas.

12.6 DESIGN TRADE-OFFS

There is a tight coupling between the file structure of an ISAM file and the disk device on which it resides. To provide the user with both random and sequential access to the data records, an index structure had to be implemented. This is pure overhead from the user's point of view. Yet the index overhead can result in taking up a considerable amount of disk space. The easiest way in which to minimize the impact of this structure is to select record size, block size, and key size very carefully. The end result of these parameters dictates how the index will be built and how large it will become.

12.6.1 File Size Calculations

Since the ISAM file is closely tied to the disk's characteristics, it is important to be able to calculate precisely how much space is needed for both the data and the index. To perform this calculation, the following steps must be performed.

1. Estimate the Number of User Data Records in the File.   The basis for all file-size calculations is the estimate of the number of data records expected to exist in the file. The accuracy of this estimate will determine the potential level of performance when accessing this file.

2. Estimate the Size of the Average Data Record.   Between this and the item above, we can easily calculate the total amount of primary data area disk space required for *user data records only*.

3. Calculate the Number of Tracks Needed to Hold the Data.   Since the ISAM file is closely linked to the structure of the disk, this calculation will tell how many tracks on that disk are needed for data records.

4. Calculate Number of Cylinders Needed for Data.   Allowing for the track index and cylinder overflow area, this calculation tells how many cylinders will be needed to hold all of the expected data in the file.

5. Calculate Number of Cylinder Indexes Needed.   Since each data cylinder has associated with it an index record, we should now be able to calculate how many index records will be needed to point to the data cylinders. From this calculation we can calculate how many tracks will be needed to hold the cylinder indexes.

6. Calculate Size of Master Index.   Since there must be one index record in the master index pointing to each of the tracks holding the cylinder indexes, we now have all the data needed to determine the size of the master index.

7. Calculate File Size.   Sum all of the foregoing calculations to arrive at the estimated size of the file.

Although this may seem somewhat tedious, it is important to understand how to make this calculation.

12.6.2 Costs versus Benefits

As with any file organization, there are many costs and benefits associated with using this file type. Just what are these benefits and drawbacks as related to the ISAM file structure? (See Table 12-1.)

TABLE 12-1:   COMPARISON OF ISAM FILE CAPABILITIES

Function		Sequential files	Relative files	Direct files	ISAM files
		Functionality			
READ	- Sequential	Y	Y	N	Y
	- Random	N	Y	Y	Y
WRITE	- Sequential	Y	Y	N	N
	- Random	N	Y	Y	Y
UPDATE	- in place	N	Y	Y	Y
	- with length change	N	Y	Y	Y
DELETE	- logical	Y	Y	Y	Y
	- physical	N	N	Y	Y
READ_NEXT		Y	Y	N	Y
Single key retrieval		N	Y	Y	Y
Unique key required		—	Y	N	Y
		Performance			
READ_NEXT - one record		H	Low-High	—	H-M
- entire file		H	L-H	—	H-M
READ		—	H	L-H	M-L
WRITE		H	H	L-H	L-M
#I/O's to READ record		0-1	0-1	0-N	0-N
#I/O's to WRITE record		0-2	0-2	0-N	0-N
Dependent upon order records, get written into file?		N	N	N	Y
		Costs			
File Space Utilization		H	L-H	H	M
Devices Supported: Disk		Y	Y	Y	Y
Tape		Y	N	N	N
Other		Y	N	N	N
Risk of Data Loss		L	L	L-M	L-M
File needs frequent reorganization		N	N	Y	Y
Overflow areas required		N	N	Y	Y

Costs
- File structure is closely tied to the disk structure.
- The user is forced to know too many details in order to use this file organization.
- The overhead of the ISAM file is higher than any of the preceding file types.
- If records are forced into an overflow area, performance becomes erratic and unpredictable.

Benefits
- The user gets both random and sequential access to the data records.
- The user can define "English" keys, not just integers as was case in the relative file.
- The sequential READ_NEXT performance is just about as fast as the sequential access of a sequential file.
- Approximate key searches are possible to locate records in the file.

12.6.3 Mainframe versus Micro Computers

Although ISAM files have typically been built on large mainframe machines, they are also feasible to build on microcomputers. The large amount of file structure overhead required to support the record access can have an extremely negative impact on the normal micro user. Therefore, it ISAM is used on a microcomputer, file reorganizations will need to be performed more frequently in order to free up unused space on the disk.

12.7 IMPLEMENTATION REQUIREMENTS

With the ISAM file type, we have just added another degree of complexity to the file structure issue. The UICB and KDB requirements defined in Chapter 11 for direct files also holds for ISAM files. In addition, the following information in the FCB and FHB is needed to process an ISAM file successfully (see Tables 12–2 and 12–3). Specifically, we must add:

- Type of overflow areas in use (i.e., cylinder or file overflow areas).
- Size of each type of overflow area, if each declared.

TABLE 12–2 FILE HEADER BLOCK: ISAM FILES

Header information

Version ID
Date/time created
Date/time last modified
Link to next FHB block

File information

Volume name
Filename
File size
Allocation type
Next block to allocate
Cluster size
File organization   ISAM
Block format
Maximum block size

Record information

Record format
Maximum record size

Access-method-specific information

Logical end-of-file	
Address of file overflow area	DIRECT and ISAM only
Size of file overflow area	DIRECT and ISAM only
Next overflow block to be allocated	Next block to be assigned in the overflow area

Keyed access methods only

Number of keys defined for file	Tells number of entries that follow

Key descriptions: one per key defined in file

Index number	Number of the index to which these data apply
Key location	Offset in bytes to beginning of the key field in the data record
Key size	Length of key in bytes
Key data type	Alphanumeric or other
Key attributes	Keys must be *unique* Keys must be *duplicated* Keys *can change* Keys *cannot change*

TABLE 12-2 (Cont.)

File-processing statistics

Number of read operations	These data can provide useful infor-
Number of write operations	mation as to when the user's file
Number of update operations	should be reorganized; they also
Number of delete operations	tell how the file is being processed
Number of errors successfully recovered	
Number of file extensions performed	

TABLE 12-3 FILE CONTROL BLOCK: ISAM FILES

Header information

Version ID
Link to next FCB
Status

User information

Job ID
I/O mode

File information

Volume name	
File name	
File size	
Physical end-of-file (PEOF)	
Allocation type	
Next block to allocate	
Cluster size	
File organization	ISAM
Block format	
Maximum block size	
File status	

Record information

Record format	
Maximum record size	
Access mode	
Address of key definition block	Location where file's keys are all defined
Number of keys defined	How many keys are defined for this file

Access-method-specific information

Logical end-of-file (LEOF)	Location of last data record written into this file
Location of overflow area	Direct and ISAM only
Size of overflow area	How large the overflow area is in blocks, sectors, tracks, or cylinders
Next overflow block to allocate	DIRECT and ISAM only

TABLE 12-3 (Cont.)

File system internal information

Last successful operation

Current record pointer   Block number
                                          Index number
                                          Key value

Address of IOBCT
Address of DCT

File-processing statistics

Number of read operations
Number of write operations
Number of update operations
Number of delete operations
Number of errors successfully
  recovered
Number of file extensions performed

- Logical end-of-file indicating the last used block in the file for user data record storage.
- Next block to allocate in the file, whether for an index block or for a user data record block.
- Key size, location, and data type.

These "attributes" help to define more precisely what the internal state of affairs within the file really is. Without these data, the access method would have no way of knowing what blocks have, and have not, already been assigned to some use.

12.7.1 File Structures

To create an ISAM file, it is necessary to build the index and data records in such a way as to be usable tomorrow. Thus the following record structures are needed:

Index records.   The master and cylinder index records must have the following information:

- The *high key* of the next-lower index track
- The cylinder and track of the next index track

Track index records consist of the following information:

- The *high key* of the primary data area track
- The track number of the primary data area track

The format of the user data records remains the same as before.

12.8 SUMMARY

ISAM is the first, but not the last, of the more complex tree-structured file organizations to be discussed in this book. It is the first file organization that has two record types, the index records and the user data records. What this means is that the file structure requires more file system "overhead" to provide functionality for the user.

Also, for the first time, performance has become an important issue. This is because of the large number of I/O operations that are needed to write records into the file as well as to read them out of overflow areas.

Finally, more and more technical details are being required from the user in order to take advantage of a particular file organization. With ISAM, the user needs a thorough knowledge not only of the internal ISAM file structure, but also of the specific disks on which the files will reside. This can be a major issue, especially on microcomputers being used by business, which are much less technical.

KEY WORDS

Alternate index	Primary data area
Approximate key search	Primary index
Cylinder index	Primary key
Cylinder overflow area	Root index block
File overflow area	Secondary index
Generic key	Secondary key
Overflow area	Track index

SUPPLEMENTAL REFERENCES

1. Claybrook, Billy G., *File Management Techniques.* New York: John Wiley & Sons, Inc., 1983, Sec. 3.4. This short section has PL/I example programs which access ISAM type files. This is interesting because the only programs that are usually demonstrated with ISAM are COBOL programs. Thus a different perspective of language I/O can be seen here.

2. Hanson, Owen, *Design of Computer Data Files.* Rockville, Md.: Computer Science Press, Inc., 1982, Chap. 7. This chapter provides a thorough and detailed description of ISAM files and everything you ever wished to know about them.

3. Johnson, Leroy F., and Rodney H. Cooper, *File Techniques for Data Base Organization in COBOL.* Englewood Cliffs, N.J.: Prentice-Hall, Inc., 1981, Chap. 9. As stated above, the typical example of ISAM programming use is with COBOL. This book gives the COBOL implementation of how to access and use ISAM files.

EXERCISES

1. Why is ISAM so closely tied to the hardware capacities of disk devices? Is there any way to uncouple this link and still have sequential and random access to data records?

2. Explain how the ISAM file is built if the records enter the file in *reverse* key sequence (i.e., highest key first, lowest key last).

3. If all the user data records resided in the primary data area tracks (i.e., no overflow), how would you compare the performance of READ_NEXT with that of a sequential file? Explain your answer.

4. How many copies of the user data records exist in an ISAM file? Why?

5. Why is an ISAM WRITE performance potentially much slower that a WRITE to a relative file?

6. Is READ performance consistent, or does it vary depending on the size of the file? Explain.

7. What difference, if any, is there in the number of *actual* I/O operations required to UP-DATE a record and those needed to DELETE that record?

8. If you were a system administrator charged with specifying the file attributes of an ISAM file, how would you go about deciding what attribute values to select (e.g., record size, key location, size)?

9. Calculate the size of an ISAM file with the following attributes:

Block size	Fixed at 100 bytes
Track size	1000 bytes
Number of tracks/cylinder	Four
Record format	34 bytes (including all overhead)
Key size	10 bytes
File size	1000 user data records

10. In the file defined in Exercise 9, how many tracks are there in each of the following?
    (a) Master index.
    (b) Cylinder index.
    (c) Track index.
    (d) Primary data area.

PROGRAMMING EXERCISES

1. Design in detail an algorithm that walks down the index structure of an ISAM file to the exact record requested by the user.

2. Design an algorithm to insert user data records into the correct primary data area track. As part of this algorithm, provide support for cylinder and file overflow areas.

13

Indexed Files

CHAPTER OBJECTIVES

When you complete this chapter, you will be able to:

- Describe how indexed files differ from ISAM files
- Describe how indexed files avoid the problem of overflow areas
- Define the format of user data records and index records
- Begin to understand the concept of file structure overhead and be able to calculate exactly how much structure there is in a file
- Describe the performance characteristics of an indexed file versus an ISAM file

13.1 OVERVIEW

With the ISAM file structure, the user gains the capabilities of being able to perform both sequential and random access to the data records within the file. However, there are several shortcomings of the ISAM design. First, before the file is created, the user has to determine how large the index, overflow, and primary data areas will be. If the calculations are wrong, for whatever reason, the file has to be recreated and repopulated. No real damage is done, but a lot of time is wasted.

Second, ISAM, as do direct files, utilizes overflow areas as an escape valve. When there is no space available in the primary data area for the record, overflow areas can always be used. This allows many operations to complete successfully, but it also slowly begins to adversely affect the performance and responsiveness of the system.

Third, the file structure is closely tied to the configuration of the device on which it resides. Thus all space calculations have to take into consideration the amount of data that can fit on one of the tracks or cylinders. If the user wants to switch devices, these calculations all have to be redone and the file reorganized.

In summary, although ISAM gives the user new capabilities, it also forces the user to know and do a lot of things with which the user is not very familiar. ISAM files tend to be created by trial and error or by experience. Therefore, the question really becomes whether it is possible to come up with a file type that provides the capabilities, yet has none of the impact on the user? The answer is the indexed file discussed here (see Figure 13-0). Again, pay close attention to how the indexed file is able to provide these capabilities. More specifically, what are the trade-offs that are being made in the indexed file organization?

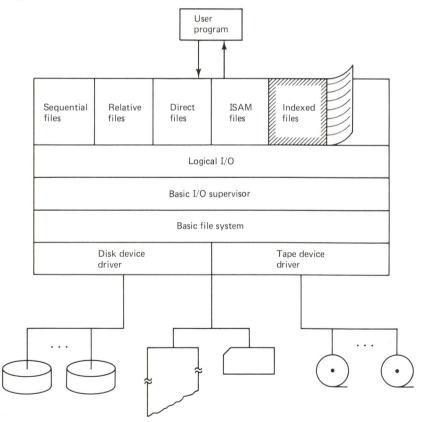

Figure 13-0   File system: indexed access method.

13.2 FILE DESIGN CONSIDERATIONS

We now begin to examine another method of designing "indexed" support, one without all the constraints of ISAM. Again it must be stressed that designs of file access methods, as well as those of other software products, consist of trade-offs, constraints, and performance goals. To achieve our objectives for the indexed access method, we will be making a different set of trade-offs than we made when we discussed the designs and implementations of the other access methods. It is important to understand what these trade-offs are in order to have a better insight into what the costs and benefits of the design will end up being.

13.2.1 File Structure

An indexed file organization is one that provides the user both sequential and random access to data records. In addition, unlike ISAM, data records are not kept in ascending key sequence; rather, the index records are maintained in strict ascending key sequence.

The file shown in Figure 13–1 shows an indexed file structure. *The levels of a file structure represent the number of layers in the index that must be transversed to go from the root index block to the user data records.* Level 0 always contains the user's data records, and levels 1 to *n* are always levels within the index structure.

The root of an index is the single block sitting at the highest level in an index structure. The root block is pointed to by the file header block so that the file system

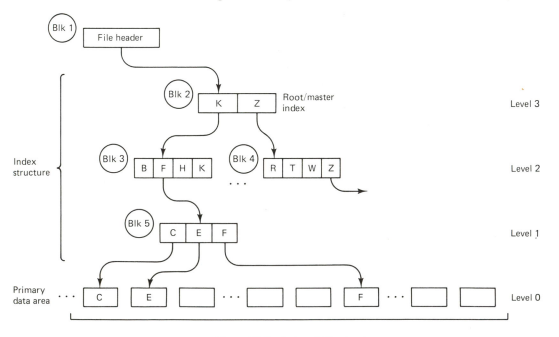

Figure 13–1   Indexed file structure.

can always know where the root of the index is located. The root block is always the starting block to be searched when a random operation is being performed.

The structure of an indexed file organization is shown in Figure 13–1. There is still an index tree structure that bears a strong relationship to the ISAM index structure. However, there is no longer any concept or constraint of *master indexes, cylinder indexes,* or *track indexes.* In addition, what is of great significance is the fact that there also is no overflow area in the entire file.

What this restructuring means is that while we still utilize an index structure to randomly access records in the file, we have managed to get rid of all the adverse costs of ISAM files:

- By having no predefined master, cylinder, or track indexes, we have relieved the user of the burden of calculating index sizes in advance of putting records into the file.

- The size of the index and data areas are no longer tied to a specific device type. Recall that in an ISAM file, in order to precalculate index sizes the user had to know what kind device the file would reside on. More specifically, the user had to know the exact track and cylinder data capacities. Since in an indexed file this precalculation is no longer required, it also means that the user does not need to know the technical details of the device in order to construct and use the file.

- By eliminating the concept of an overflow area, the indexed file organization can provide a more consistent level of performance and responsiveness than could ISAM.

On the other hand, to make these file organization improvements what trade-offs did we have to make? Fundamentally, only two trade-offs were made and they are closely related:

- *The user data records are not maintained in sequence by ascending key values.* Specifically, the data level of the file is simply a sequential file. All new records get added to the end of the file. We could get rid of overflow areas because, in effect, the free space at the end of the file functions is a large virtual overflow area, just as in the case of the serial sequential file. A record can always be added to the file at the logical end of file, unless there is no more space on the disk itself.

- By maintaining the data records in time sequence of arrival, as opposed to ascending key values, the only way the index structure can locate a record as if *there is one index record per user data record at the lowest level in the index* above the data level. Thus the tree that gets searched in an indexed file is identical to the ISAM tree except that at the lowest index level there is one index record per user data record. In ISAM there was one index record per track no matter how many records were on the track.

  What's the difference? ISAM indexes at the lowest level of the index will be significantly smaller than for the similar level in an indexed file. A larger index means that the file takes up more space on the disk medium. Also, it means that sequential access of records within the file will be slower than the ISAM level of performance. The reason for this is that in an indexed file there is always a pointer to the block containing the record. In effect, every time a record is accessed, there is one additional level of indirection that an indexed file must go through that an ISAM file does not have to accept.

Finally, by having record pointers rather than block or track pointers, sequential access of all the records in the file will at best be equal to that of an ISAM or sequential file, and could be worse. Thus one of the trade-offs being made here is that to achieve the other gains, what had to be given up was having as high a level of sequential performance as ISAM has. This is important to know, because there are applications that require rapid sequential access of all the records in the file.

In a manner similar to what was done in the case of ISAM, records can be *randomly* or *sequentially* accessed. Random access is performed by taking the user-supplied key, either from the record itself or directly from a user-supplied parameter, and walking down the index structure. The search must start at the root or top of the index, and proceed down the structure as was discussed in Chapter 12.

The primary difference from the ISAM case is that when the index tree search arrives at the last index block before reaching the data level, in the case of ISAM we have a high-key value and a track number containing that key. Then we locate that track and search for the record we want. In the case of an INDEXED file, level 1 of the index contains a pointer to the block that contains the record. Note that there is a one-to-one relationship between records in the file and index records in level 1 of the index. In other words, there is one index record for every user data record in the file. In the case of ISAM, there was one track index record for each primary data area track in the file.

Sequential processing is also slightly different in design and performance. Since new records are always written to the end-of-file, the associated level 1 index record must point to where the record is located in the file. However, the index records are maintained in order by ascending key values. In summary, ISAM maintains the user data records in ascending key sequence, while indexed keeps the lowest level of the index in sequence by key value.

13.2.2 Record Addressing Algorithms

Sequential access is accomplished by going across level 1 index records and fetching the associated user data record from the pointers in the level 1 index records. Random access is accomplished by walking down the index structure until the level 1 index record is found that points to the user data record wanted.

Collisions.   One of the most significant problems that ISAM files have is that whenever a record does not fit into the block where it should, one or more user data records are forced into the file's overflow area. It was a design goal of INDEXED files to try to avoid the use of, and requirement for, an overflow area in every file.

Overflows are prohibited by always writing new records at the end-of-file position. As long as there is room on the disk itself, there will always be room for the additional data records.

There is, however, another problem that is new to this file organization. As we just stated, all data records are written at the end of the file. However, in the *index blocks* we can have situations arise in which a new index record is needed and yet there is no room in the block. What then happens is a procedure known as splitting.

Block splitting.   *Block splitting is the process in which the contents on one full block are spread over two blocks to make room for more records.* In Figure 13–2a there is a filled index block into which a new index record "L" needs to be inserted. Remember that every user data record added to the file requires a related record in level 1 of the index. Furthermore, all index records are maintained in sequence by ascending key value. Thus it becomes necessary to shuffle the index records to get all the keys in proper sequence.

First, a new block is allocated and initialized. Then a set of records from the original index block are copied into the new index block. There are many algorithms for determining what set to copy to the new block, but here we shall copy roughly half the records. Then we must link the index blocks together (see Figure 13–2b).

We have just split an index block. What we are really doing is *dynamic reorganization* of the file so that the file structure is always correct and optimal. However, there is still one major step yet to be done. Since each index block is pointed to by another index block on the next higher level in the index (see Figure 13–2b), we must still do two things. First, we must find the index record that points to the index block (block 32) that just split. Its high key value still reflects the old high key of block 5. Thus we must now change that index record to contain the new high-key value of the old block 5 in this case "K"). Second, we have added a new index block to the structure and it has no index record pointing to it. Thus we must add a new index record to point to the new block 32 with the correct high-key value, "P."

Once the foregoing processing has been completed, we have rebuilt the index structure point once again to all index blocks correctly. What should be obvious now is the amount of time a simple WRITE can take if there is no room in the index block to add another record.

It is important to note that *only the index blocks will ever need to be split.* The data level blocks will never split because the data records are always written at the logical end-of-file, and they are not forced to be maintained in ascending key sequence.

13.2.3 File Attributes

The file attributes that are required to completely define an indexed file are almost identical to those specified for an ISAM file. The only major change is an internal structural modification, not a completely different file organization.

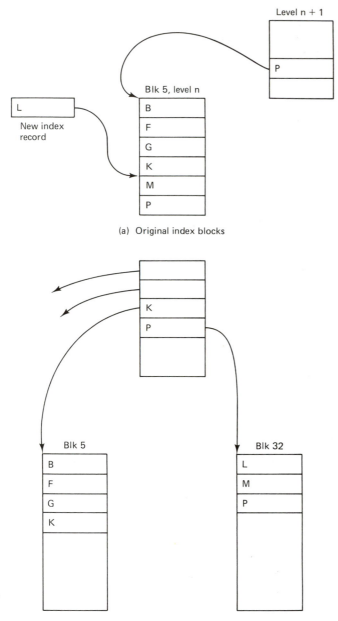

Level n + 1

Blk 5, level n

| B |
| F |
| G |
| K |
| M |
| P |

L

New index record

(a) Original index blocks

| K |
| P |

Blk 5

| B |
| F |
| G |
| K |

Blk 32

| L |
| M |
| P |

(b) Index blocks after split

Figure 13–2 Index block splitting.

342

File organization.   At file CREATE time, the file organization must be declared to be *indexed* type.

File size.   Unlike ISAM, which forces the user to know file size, cylinder and track capacities, and so on, an indexed file type only needs to know file size to be successful. In fact, this parameter is not needed at all, since if space is no longer available, the basic file system can perform an extension to the file itself.

Block size.   All blocks will be written out to the file in blocks that are exactly block size in length.

Key position and key size.   As with the ISAM and direct file organizations, the indexed access method must know where the key is and how large it is. By convention, we will again require the key to be physically contained within the body of the record.

Key data type.   In most situations the standard key data type will be ASCII. Why? Since the key values come from within the data records themselves, it is easiest for the user to manipulate English-like key values than other key data types. However, allowing other data types to be specified does allow for potential future requirements.

13.3 FILE OPERATIONS

Since we are implicitly building a file system and access method package that presents a consistent interface to the user community, the file operations will remain the same as before. The exception will be the CREATE processing that must be performed. Since we are now creating a different file structure, the CREATE file processing must also be different.

13.3.1 Create File

The purpose of the CREATE task is to build enough of the file structure so that records can be added, deleted, or updated successfully. Therefore, at CREATE time the first index block is initialized, as is the very first data block. In effect, we have built a two-block index structure. However, let's proceed in the sequence in which the processing itself would be performed (see Figure 13–3).

1. Allocate Initial Blocks for File.   What is required in every indexed file? We will always need a file header, an root index block, and a block for user data records. With these three blocks, we have a minifile that will allow us to add as many records to the file as are ever needed.

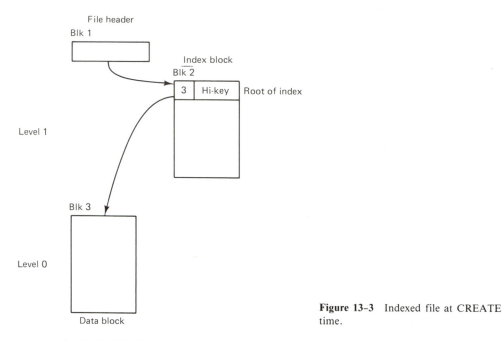

Figure 13-3 Indexed file at CREATE time.

2. Prebuild First Index Record.   Since the index records always point either to the next-lower level of the index or to a specific data record, we must build at least one index record. Here we can build an index record that has in it the *highest possible key value*. In addition, we can set it to point to the first data block. We always walk down the index by using the criterion that the user's key be less than or equal to the key value in the index record. Therefore, if we initialize the index record in the root to the highest possible key value, we will force all records to be inserted into the first data blocks (refer to Figure 13-3). Thus we have a data block ready to be used and an index structure initialized for any record operation.

3. Build an Empty Data Block.   The existence of an index record in level 1 of the index does not guarantee that the record exists; we can just build an empty data block. Thus if someone actually wanted to READ the record with the highest possible key value, the access method would walk down the tree, find the index record at level 1, and read the block pointed to by that index record. It will then search that block for a match on key value. In this case, no match will occur since the record does not exist. However, the important thing is that the structure has been built and does work.

13.3.2 OPEN FILE

The OPEN file process is similar to that performed in the other access methods. This is because the OPEN process really only reads in data from the file's header and performs some memory allocation for tables and buffers. Thus most OPEN processing is file organization independent.

13.3.3 CLOSE FILE

The function of the CLOSE request is to ensure that all modified blocks currently in main memory get written into the file. In addition, main memory space allocated to control blocks and I/O buffers must get released back to the operating system resource manager. These are standard functions of CLOSE. Unique INDEXED file processing is not required.

13.4 RECORD OPERATIONS

To continue to provide the user with a common I/O interface, the calls to the indexed access method are the same as the calls to any of the other access methods that we have studied thus far. However, the internal implementation of these functions does change with each access method. In this section we discuss the indexed access method specific processing. Pay close attention to how this processing differs from the work that was performed within the other access methods.

Record access modes.   The indexed access method supports both sequential and random access of user data records. With sequential access it is possible to provide the user with the capability of specifying how the records should be retrieved. More specifically, the user can request the following:

- Sequential access by ascending key value.
- Sequential access in chronological time sequence of being added to the file

The former is achieved by walking through the level 1 index blocks and taking the pointers to the various data records. The latter is processed by walking through the level 0 data blocks, since new records are always added at the end-of-file position.

In random access mode, the index structure must be transversed from the very top of the index. However, unlike the ISAM case, the lowest level of the index contains a pointer directly to the user data record itself. Thus random access performance is very consistent since the number of levels in the index from the root to the data is the same for all user data records in the entire file.

In the ISAM case, the lowest level index blocks point to the track on which the target user data record might reside. Since there is no overflow area to concern us, once we get the pointer in the index to the data record, we know that the record will be there. In ISAM, the record might be there or in the overflow chain. Thus the performance of random operations in an indexed file tends to be more predictable and consistent from day to day.

Sequential access to the user data records is where the major difference between ISAM and indexed algorithms occurs. In the case of ISAM, the index record references a track on which the target record will reside. Once positioned to that record, sequential reading of the records is simple. ISAM merely takes the next record on that track.

Indexed files have no concept of ordering user data records by some key value. However, in an indexed file, the level 1 of the index is maintained in key sequence but not the data records. Therefore, to sequentially process the data, it is necessary for the access method to sequentially scan the level 1 blocks for the next available record pointer (see Figure 13–4). Therefore, sequential accessing of an indexed file results in one level of indirection to go from the level 1 pointer to the data record itself. ISAM, on the other hand, would know immediately where the next entry for a record was unless there was an overflow area involved.

There are several ways in which we can search for particular data records or classes of records. As with ISAM files, we can again search for *exact, partial,* or *approximate* key values.

In summary, random access is more predictable and faster in indexed files. On the other hand, the sequential accessing of the data records is faster in the ISAM case (assuming no overflow areas being used) than in the indexed file case.

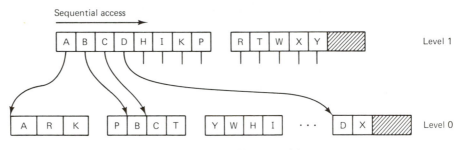

Figure 13–4   Indexed file sequential access.

Record currency.   Given the fact that we now have both data blocks and index blocks, what is the current record pointer? *For INDEXed files, the CRP points to the level 1 index record associated with the target user data record.* This is the first case in which the record pointer did not physically point to the data record itself. However, this is done to allow the access method to more optimally process both random and sequential requests for data records.

13.4.1 Position to Record

The POSITION request can be used to locate any specific record in the file without actually causing that data record to be transferred from the I/O buffer in main memory into the user's record buffer.

The user supplies only a key value to the POSITION command. This is all of the information needed to locate where within the file the record should be and then to specifically locate the target record.

It is important to understand the tasks performed here since similar sequences are repeated over and over as part of the other function requests.

1. Walk down the Index Structure.   Starting at the root of the index, walk down the tree structure until level 1 of the index has been read into main memory. When this occurs, that block must be scanned to see where the target record is located.

In the ISAM case, the only way to tell whether a target record exists in the file is by scanning the entire track or until the keys of the records get to be higher than the key of the target record. However, in an INDEXED file, we can tell immediately whether the record has ever existed in the file. This can be done based on the fact that there is one level 1 index record for every user data record in the file. Thus if no level 1 index record is found with a matching key value, we know that the record does not exist in the file. *Indeed, the record has never existed in the file.* Therefore, the search for the target record can stop at that point in the processing.

2. Read the Block Containing the Target Record.   Once the pointer to the target record has been retrieved from the level 1 index block, the POSITION module must randomly read the block in which the target record resides.

3. Scan the Target Block for the User's Data Record.   Once the block containing the target record has been read into an I/O buffer in main memory, it must be searched for the presence of the target record itself. If the record exists, it must be in this block due to the fact that the record pointer was put into the index. Even if the record has been deleted, we will still find the record in this block.

4. Return Status to the Calling Program.   Once the record has been found, one of two conditions must exist. First, the record is currently valid. In this case, status is then returned to the calling program, effectively stating success (i.e., the record has been found and is valid).

The second condition that can arise is that the record is found but has been flagged as having been deleted. If the user requested an exact match, the access method must return a failing status message to the calling program. However, if an approximate match was requested, the access method must return to the level 1 index block from which it retrieved the target record's pointer and then select the next pointer in the current, or next, block. In other words, the access method is proceeding to reselect for the next valid record following the target record. The processing then proceeds as in the steps above until either another valid record is found or until the file's end-of-file condition is reached.

Upon examining the number of actual I/O operations required to perform a POSITION request, it becomes obvious why the operation takes so long. First, there is one I/O operation for each block per level in the index. If the depth of the index was 5, five I/O operations had to be performed to get to the pointer to the target user data record. Therefore, the complete operation requires at least six I/O operations. More would be required if the record was not found and a generic search had been requested. In the RELATIVE file case, we could randomly READ any record in the entire file in a maximum of one I/O operation. Therefore, in this example, random READs into an indexed file would be six times slower than in a relative file.

In summary, positioning to a record in an indexed file consumes much more time than it does in a relative file. One or more of these I/O operations could be avoided with multiple I/O buffers and an intelligent I/O buffer management algorithm. The point is, however, that to provide the user with increased functionality over, say, the relative file case, the cost will be in time.

13.4.2 READ Record

The READ request is really the POSITION request with the option of requesting that the actual user data record be copied from the I/O buffer into the user's record buffer. There is a straightforward formula that conveys the READ processing function:

$$t_{\text{READ record}} = t_{\text{POSITION}} + t_{\text{copy record}}$$

Since the copy record function is carried on completely within the CPU, this time is negligible compared to the time it takes to POSITION to the data record. Thus in terms of performance, the READ operation approximates the POSITION function.

13.4.3 READ_NEXT Record

READ_NEXT provides the user with the capability of accessing the data records in the file in a particular sequence, such as ascending key value or chronological order. READ_NEXT sequential processing walks through the level 1 index blocks, since that level of the index contains one valid pointer for each valid record in the file.

13.4.4 WRITE Record

The WRITE operation adds new records into the file. The WRITE operation processing is getting more and more complex, as the file structures in which it must operate are also becoming more complicated. The other side of the coin, however, is that the amount of functionality being provided to the user is also increasing.

In no case is a key value ever given as input to this function. The reason for this is that since the records are inserted into the file based on the value of the key contained in the record, the only key that can be trusted is the key within the record. Consider, for example, what the ramifications would be if the key supplied by the calling program were different from the key contained within the data record. How could that record be retrieved if it was inserted via the wrong key?

Let us now proceed to walk step by step through the process of inserting a new user data record into an indexed file.

1. POSITION to the Index Block Containing the Target Key Value. To insert a new record into the indexed file, it is necessary to locate the precise level 1 index block in which the record pointer must be inserted. This is done by performing a POSITION request, except that instead of stopping at the user data record position, the search is stopped at the level 1 index block of record pointer.

2. Search the Index Block for a Matching Key Value.   Since a WRITE operation adds a *new* record into the file, the access method must first check to see if there is a record currently in the file which has the same key value. If there is another such record, the current WRITE request must terminate. If there is no matching key value, it continues.

3. Add the Data Record at the Logical End-of-File.   Now that we know that the key value is unique, we can add the record into the file. Since the access method has within its control structures a pointer to the logical end-of-file, we can now read that block. Once in an I/O buffer in main memory, the record can be inserted into the block. If there is not enough room in the block, a new block is allocated, LEOF updated, and the record is copied into the block and written back to the file.

Why did we not simply add the index record first and then go down and insert the user data record? There are at least two reasons why it was done in this particular sequence. First, it is the job of the access method to guarantee the integrity of the data within the file. If we had written the index record containing a pointer to the record first, what if the system had crashed? We could have found the record in the index and then gone off and retrieved the target block only to discover that the record did not exist. Since by design, the record's existence is known by whether or not there is an index record in the lowest level of the index which has a matching key value, we immediately have an exception. More specifically, we can no longer assume that the index is correct. To circumvent these inconsistencies, it is best to write the data record first. Then if the system crashes, the worst that has happened is that some extra space has been taken up.

Second, had we written the index record first, what if the logical end-of-file block did not have enough room for the target data record? The problem now is that the index record still points to a block that does not contain the record. To get around this difficulty, we could then go back and update the index record. All of this rework can be avoided by simply waiting until the exact block number that will hold the data record is known and available. Then rewrite the index record in its proper location.

4. Add an Index Record in Proper Key Sequence.   To insert a data record into the file, there must be an index record at level 1 which points to the data record. Therefore, add an index record that points to the new data record and has the key of the new data record.

If there is not enough room in the index block for another index record, we will need to split the index block into two index blocks, as discussed earlier. In any case, at the completion of the WRITE operation, the index structure is always organized and sequenced correctly.

13.4.5 UPDATE Record

Whereas the WRITE operation was long and complicated, the UPDATE operation is much more straightforward. An UPDATE request causes a current record in the file to be modified and then rewritten back into the file.

The user buffer contains the modified record. The value of the current record pointer is the specific identifier of the record within the file. If there is no valid current record pointer, the UPDATE operation will terminate.

The key value under which the record will be reinserted into the file is questionable. Do we use the key value of the record last READ (i.e., the key value of the operation that set the current record pointer), or do we use the value of the key in the modified record? To answer this question, we must first determine whether we should allow the user to modify the value of the key on an UPDATE request.

If, by convention, we declare that the key value cannot change during an UPDATE request, it is up to the access method to verify that the key has not been changed. If the user modified the key, the UPDATE operation must be terminated with no change to the file. In this manner, we are allowing the user to change any field within the record as long as the key is not modified. On the other hand, what happens if the access method allows keys to be changed?

To understand the difference between these two options, let us first walk through the UPDATE operation in a file that does not allow the keys to be changed during an UPDATE operation. Then we will discuss the effect of changing the keys.

UPDATE with no key changes allowed.   The first check that the access method must perform during UPDATE processing is whether or not the user has modified the key value. If the key has been changed, the UPDATE request is immediately terminated, with an appropriate error message returned to the calling program.

If the key value has not been changed, the length of the modified record must be checked. This is needed only in the case of variable-length records. If the record has decreased in size or remained the same length, we know that the record will still fit in the slot from which it came. Therefore, the access method can copy the modified data record back into the proper block in the I/O buffer and then rewrite the block to the file.

On the other hand, if the size of the record has been increased, the access method has to determine whether there is enough room in the current block to hold the increased size. If there is room, the processing of the record continues as described in the preceding paragraph. However, if there is not enough room in the current block, the access method must determine where it can find the space for the record (see Figure 13–5a).

Where is there always space available? All new records are written at the logical end-of-file. Therefore, we could simply treat the newly updated record as a new record and add the updated record to the logical end-of-file. By doing this, however, we give ourselves the problem of having two records in the file by the same key value. How can we solve this problem?

After adding the record to the end-of-file, we go back into the index and change the associated index record to point to the new location of the record (see Figure 13–5b). Then, as far as the index structure is concerned, there is only one record in the file that contains that key value. To complete the processing, the access method

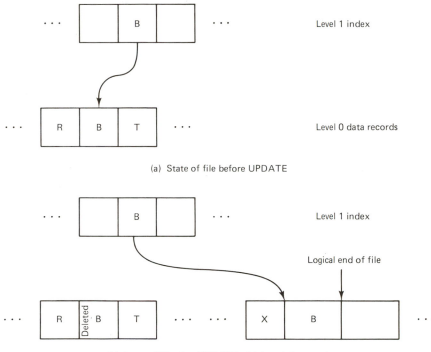

(a) State of file before UPDATE

(b) State of file after UPDATE with length increased

Figure 13-5 UPDATE with increased record size.

must go back to the original record that was UPDATED and mark it as being deleted. This block is then rewritten back into the file so that there are no longer two data records in the primary data area with the same key values. The reason for this cleanup is really for recovery purposes should the index ever become destroyed. We could then go into the data level and retrieve all of the valid data records.

In summary, if keys are not allowed to be changed in an UPDATE operation, the associated level 1 index record will never need to be modified. The only exception to this is if the data record is forced to move to the current end-of-file because it increased in size. Then the index record has only its block pointer updated to where the data record now resides.

UPDATE with key change allowed.   If we allow the value of the key to be changed by the user, the processing described above is made somewhat more complicated. Briefly, the following steps must be performed (see Figure 13–6).

- Check to see if the new key value exists within the file. If it does, abort the operation.
- Delete the index record that contains the old key value (step 1). This is done

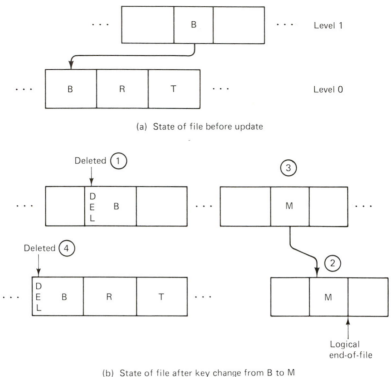

(a) State of file before update

(b) State of file after key change from B to M

Figure 13-6   UPDATE with key change.

to maintain the integrity of the file structure if the system should crash before the processing is completed.

- Add (i.e., WRITE) the record back into the file under its new key value. This is identical to the WRITE processing, since from the index structure point of view, we are indeed adding a new record (step 2) into the file. This includes the building of a new index record (step 3) and inserting it in the correct index block and in the correct sequence in that block.

- If successful, go back and mark the original user data record as deleted (step 4). This task is done last in case there are problems. If the system crashes and the index is not usable, a scan of the data blocks can retrieve the valid data records. The original record is the valid record until the new record has been fully added to the file.

In summary, if the key value is allowed to be changed, the UPDATED record with the new key value is added to the file as if it were a brand-new record. The old record is not fully deleted until the access method has completely inserted the new record into both the index and data levels of the file structure. Note the amount of time and all the processing that must occur just to allow the user to change a key value. That is not the real issue, however. The question is whether or not the user needs the ability to change keys. Then it is up to the user to do so cautiously, or the response times will degrade enormously.

13.4.6 DELETE Record

The DELETE operation logically deletes a record from being accessed in the file. The record to be deleted is identified to be the record defined by the value of the current record pointer. If there is no current record pointer, the DELETE processing will terminate immediately, with no changes made to the file.

If there is a valid record to be deleted, the processing consists simply of turning on the delete flag associated with the record. This prohibits further access by the primitives POSITION, READ, or READ_NEXT.

It can be asked why the index record itself is not deleted. Then, when the tree is transversed, we would save the one additional I/O operation needed to access the data record only to discover that the record had already been deleted. It can be done either way. The fastest method is simply to flag the data record as deleted and return to the user. Then if the sequential performance ever degrades to being unacceptable, the file can be reorganized to clean out the deleted records.

Alternatively, the associated index record could be deleted from the file. The user data record always needs to be flagged as having been deleted so that any sequential scan of level 0 would not read the record and assume that it was still valid. Again, it is a design question, not an implementation issue.

13.5 PERFORMANCE CONSIDERATIONS

Since applications tend to utilize INDEXED files frequently, it is important to understand the issues surrounding performance and what can be done to improve performance. The WRITE operation is consistently the record operation that takes longest to complete. This is because it must physically add a record into a preexisting file structure. Recall that the key to overall performance is directly related to the number of actual I/O operations that must be performed. How many are performed to add a record in the case of an indexed file?

Number of I/O Operations	Description
$+n$	There is one I/O operation for each level in the index that must be performed in order to walk down the index structure.
$+1$	The target block for the data record must be read into an I/O buffer in main memory. If the data record fits, our search is done. However, if the record does not fit we must perform the following steps:

Number of I/O Operations	Description
$+m$	Number of I/Os required to allocate a new block to the file.
$+1$	Write the block containing the new data record back into the file.
$+i$	Add the index record into the proper key sequence in the index. This will take one or more I/O operations depending on whether there is room in the index block to hold a new record. If there is room, one additional I/O is needed. On the other hand, if there is no room, a new block must be allocated to the index (1 to n I/O operations). Then the index records must be resequenced so that the resulting series of index blocks, including the new block, contain index records that are in ascending key squence (maximum of two I/O operations).
$+x$	The performance issue is further compounded if the index block splitting causes further block splitting at one or more of the higher levels in the index (see Figure 13-7). If this occurs, then *at each level* I/O operations will be required to allocate a new block to the index, as well as I/O operations to write all the new blocks back into the file. Note that the data record level never has a block split, since the user data records are always added at the end of the chain.

As can be seen from the table, the number of I/O operations that takes place on behalf of a seemingly simple user request can be quite large. This is what accounts for the variance in speed, or response time, from the vantage point of the user. These ''hidden I/O operations'' are the cause of the performance questions.

The most critical aspect that determines performance is the number of levels in the index. This value effectively constrains the highest possible level of performance, since it requires that many I/O operations to walk the entire tree. The number of levels is related directly to the size of the block, user data records, and key size. The more records, either user data records or index records, that can fit within a block, the shorter the index path will eventually become.

A second consideration concerned with performance relates to the number and usage of the I/O buffers in main memory. The more that exist, the more frequently used blocks can be saved within one of the buffers and need not be reread upon each user request. The amount of main memory allocated to I/O buffers will have an effect on the amount of real memory that is used up. However, if memory is no great problem, it is better to allocate somewhat more I/O buffers than is considered normal.

Finally, the performance of READ_NEXT is less than the sequential reading of all the records in a sequential file. If READ_NEXT processing is frequently performed by the user, the user must consider several other alternatives. For example, if all the indices fit within one or more cylinder's on the disk, the access method might just consider the storing of the information in the index in a contiguous set of cylinders to minimize seek time.

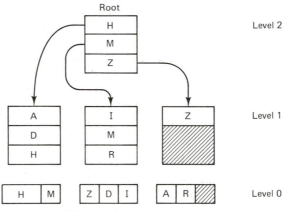

(a) File before insert of a data record

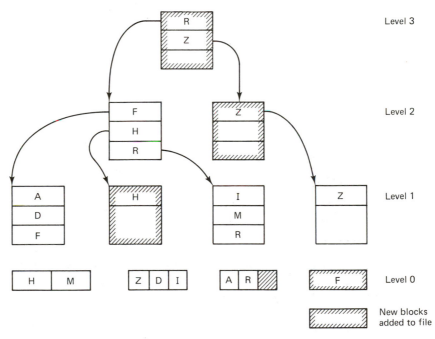

(b) File after insert of key of F

Figure 13–7 Indexed file worst-case insert.

13.5.1 File Population Techniques

With an indexed file, it is not necessary to add records to the file in a specific sequence. The reason for this is that the index structure will always be dynamically rebuilt if any changes are required. This is a dramatic change from the ISAM file, where if we guess wrong on the index structure we have to recreate the entire file.

However, there are ways in which the performance of the file population process, as well as space utilization, can be improved. Remember that whenever a new data record gets added to the file and thus an index record must get added into level 1 of the index, block splitting can occur. Since this is a time-consuming process, it would be beneficial if most of this overhead could be avoided. It can if, and only if, we sort all the data records by ascending primary key values. Then, as the file is populated, there will be zero block splits—only new blocks being added to the existing level. Another benefit of this procedure is that the index blocks at level 1 will be filled about the same. Thus space within the index will be better utilized.

13.5.1 File Reorganization

Why do we have to occasionally reorganize direct and ISAM files? Fundamentally, there are two reasons:

- Whenever the number of valid user data records in the file's overflow area gets high, the performance as seen by the user gets to be unacceptable. Reorganizing the file gets rid of the overflow areas and thus the level of performance improved.

- The second reason relates to the fact that there is no easy way in which to reclaim deleted record space. Applications that delete a lot of records will end up with a much larger file size than would be the case if only valid records were in the file. Therefore, by reorganizing the file, all the "lost" space due to deleted records is recaptured. This also tends to improve performance because the file is smaller, thus cutting down on the number of SEEKs required.

Indexed files have no overflow areas, and therefore the first reason does not apply. However, since records are always added at the logical end-of-file, there is no attempt to reuse deleted record space automatically. Therefore, the second reason applies directly to indexed files, perhaps even more so than any of the other file types that have been covered so far.

How can the user know when there are a lot of deleted records in the file? There is really no easy way to find out other than to write a special utility program to examine all records in the file. Since this type of program is not usually supplied by the vendor of the product, the user would have to write this utility program. Alternatively, if the user knew approximately how many records should be in the file at any time, the user could calculate the potential size of the file and compare that size against the current size of the file. If there is a dramatic difference, perhaps a reorganization should be done. At a minimum, the user could then determine how many records were currently in the file and what percentage of the old file consisted of deleted records.

13.6 DESIGN TRADE-OFFS

An indexed file represents an improvement over the other file organizations discussed so far in that it offers more functionality to the user's program than do any of the other file organizations. However, this gain is not without its costs and side effects.

13.6.1 File Size Calculations

To calculate the number of levels that will be generated, we need to proceed through the following steps:

1. Estimate the number of user data records that will be in the file over the period of your choice.
2. Estimate the size of the average user data record, including all access method overhead.
3. Calculate the number of blocks required to hold the estimated number of user data records calculated in steps 1 and 2. This calculation defines the estimated total number of blocks required in the primary data area of the file.
4. Given that there is one index record per data record in the file, estimate the total number of level 1 index blocks required to hold the pointers to the data records. This will define how large the lowest level of the index must be.
5. Since above level 1 there is just one pointer record for each block in the index, calculate how many blocks will be needed in all of the remaining levels of the index structure. Stop when there is only one index block on a particular level, because that is then the root block of the index structure.
6. Once the foregoing calculations have been made, the size of the target file is known. If the block size or record size is changed, recalculate the size of the file to see what effect the change has had.

13.6.2 Costs versus Benefits

As happens whenever trade-offs have to be made, there are always some gains as well as drawbacks. Table 13–1 compares the indexed file organization with the other file types discussed so far in this book.

Costs
- Sequential access to the records is slower than in a sequential file.
- The amount of space taken up by the index is larger than in an ISAM file, since there is one index record for each user data record in the file at level 1.

Table 13-1: COMPARISON OF INDEXED FILE CAPABILITIES

Function	Sequential Files	Relative Files	Direct Files	ISAM Files	Indexed Files
Functionality					
READ – sequential	Y	Y	N	Y	Y
– random	N	Y	Y	Y	Y
WRITE – sequential	Y	Y	N	N	N
– random	N	Y	Y	Y	Y
UPDATE – inplace	N	Y	Y	Y	Y
– with length change	N	Y	Y	Y	Y
DELETE – logical	Y	Y	Y	Y	Y
– physical	N	N	Y	Y	—
READ_NEXT	Y	Y	N	Y	Y
Single key retrieval	—	Y	Y	Y	Y
unique key required	—	Y	Y	Y	Y
Performance					
READ_NEXT – one record	H	L–H	—	M–H	M–H
– entire file	H	L–H	—	M–H	M–H
READ one record	—	H	L–H	L–M	L–M
WRITE one record	H	H	L–H	L–M	L–M
#I/O's to READ record	0–1	0–1	0–N	0–N	0–N
#I/O's to WRITE record	0–2	0–2	0–N	0–N	0–N
Dependent upon order records got written into file?	N	N	N	Y	N
Costs					
File Space Utilization	H	L–H	H	M	M
Devices Supported: Disk	Y	Y	Y	Y	Y
Tape	Y	N	N	N	N
Other	Y	N	N	N	N
Risk of Data Loss	L	L	L–M	L–M	L–M
File Needs Frequent Re-organizations	N	N	Y	Y	N
Overflow Areas Required	N	N	Y	Y	N
#Index records of level 1	—	—	—	1/trk	1/data record

Benefits
- An overflow area is never used.
- Random access performance is consistent and predictable from a user point of view.
- Both rapid random access and reasonable sequential access to the data records are provided.

- Keys may be allowed to change in an UPDATE operation.
- The file structure is dynamically built and grows dynamically as the file expands.

13.6.3 Mainframe versus Microcomputers

The primary concerns of micro users are the limitations of available disk space and CP cycles (i.e., the processing power of the microcomputer). The indexed file does have associated with it a sizable amount of file structure overhead. However, it provides the user with the capability of both random and sequential access to the user data records. Since the index dynamically reorganizes itself, the path to a specific data record is always kept optimal. Thus the indexed file structure is fairly well suited to microcomputer environments.

The mainframe computer world tends to be less limited in disk space, and the processing power of the computers tends to be quite high. Therefore, indexed files provide users with a significant piece of functionality without apparent negative effects.

13.7 IMPLEMENTATION REQUIREMENTS

As our file structures become more and more complex, it is necessary to examine more of the structural details to see how the access method can be implemented. Here we examine the file structures required of the indexed file.

13.7.1 File Header and File Control Block

The file attributes must be written into the file header from the file control block and associated control blocks in order that the file may be processed successfully after it has been created. In addition to all the file attributes that ISAM has, we are going to add several more (see Tables 13–2 and 13–3).

Block number of the root of the index.   This parameter is required for the access method to know where in the file the top level of the index resides. This value is not user definable but is determined when the file is created. Part of the processing done during a CREATE is to initialize the index and data blocks. By convention, the access method assigns block numbers to the file header, root of the index, and the first data block. However, when the file is later accessed, the access method has no way of knowing where the root of the index is (we shall soon see that the root of the index will move around over time). Therefore, from the time the file is created, and every time after that the root block moves, the file header must be updated immediately. If this is not done at the time, the system could crash and the file header will point to the "old root" but will have no idea how to locate the real top of the index.

Number of first data block.   Although the root of the index can move about over time, the block arbitrarily assigned to be the first data block at CREATE time will always be the first data block. This is because in an indexed file organization records are always added at the end of the file. If its location never changes, why is it necessary to record its value in the file's header block?

TABLE 13-2 FILE HEADER BLOCK: INDEXED FILES

Header information

Version ID
Date/time created
Date/time last modified
Link to next FHB block

File information

Volume name
Filename
File size
Allocation type
Next block to allocate   Number of the block that can be
                                           allocated next

Cluster size
File organization   Indexed
Block format
Maximum block size

Record information

Record format
Maximum record size

Access-method-specific information

Logical end-of-file

Keyed access methods only

Number of keys defined for file   Tells number of entries that follow

Key descriptions: one per key defined in file

Index number   Number of the index to which these
                                           data apply
Key location   Offset in bytes to beginning of the
                                           key field in the data record
Key size   Length of key in bytes
Key data type   Alphanumeric or other
Null key value   Byte defined as character identifying
                                           this key as being null.
Key attributes   Keys must be *unique*
                                         Keys may be *duplicated*
                                         Keys *can change*
                                         Keys *cannot change*

TABLE 13-2   (Cont.)

Key descriptions: one per key defined in file (Cont.)

Level of root block	Dictates depth of the index
Root block number	Indexed type files only
First data block number	Indexed type files only

File-processing statistics

Number of read operations	These data can provide useful
Number of write operations	information as to when the user's
Number of update operations	file should be reorganized; they
Number of delete operations	also tell how the file is being
Number of errors successfully recovered	processed
Number of file extensions performed	
Number of block splits performed	

TABLE 13-3   FILE CONTROL BLOCK: INDEXED FILES

Header information

Version ID
Link to next FCB
Status

User information

Job ID
I/O mode

File information

Volume name	
File name	
File size	
Physical end-of-file (PEOF)	Location of last block allocated to this file
Allocation type	
Next block to allocate	The next free (i.e., unallocated) block in the file
Cluster size	
File organization	Indexed
Block format	
Maximum block size	
File status	

Record information

Record format
Maximum record size
Access mode

TABLE 13–3 (Cont.)   FILE CONTROL BLOCK: INDEXED FILES

Record information (Cont.)	
Address of key definition block	Location where file's keys are all defined.
Number of keys defined	How many keys are defined for this file
Access-method-specific information	
Logical end-of-file (LEOF)	Location of last data record written into this file
File system internal information	
Last successful operation	
Current record pointer	Block number
	Key value
Address of IOBCT	
Address of DCT	
File-processing statistics	
Number of read operations	
Number of write operations	
Number of update operations	
Number of delete operations	
Number of errors successfully recovered	
Number of file extensions performed	
Number of block splits performed	

This is done primarily for integrity purposes. In other words, by being able to read the file's header, a system program can always know which block is the first data block. How often are changes being made in programs without all affected modules being modified? Disaster! On the other hand, it is critical that the access method and file system do nothing that could possibly jeopardize the integrity of the user's data. One of the ways to do this is to require a positive indication of where the first data block resides. Although this is not exactly earth shattering, it does, very simply and with minimal overhead, guarantee that the correct block will always be selected.

13.7.2 Block Structure

The indexed file is the first file structure in which the sequence of blocks may *not* be in consecutive numerical sequence. For example, in a relative file, the blocks are numbered from 1 to *n*. Thus, to find the next block in a RELATIVE file it was a simple matter of incrementing the current block number.

In the indexed file, the blocks may be assigned to the index structure or to the data level. Furthermore, it is impossible to know precisely what the next block of any specific level in the file structure really is. To get around this problem, it is necessary to link together all the blocks on a particular level. To accomplish this, the following information must be maintained in the *header* of each block. *The block header is a fixed-size number of bytes in each block set aside for file structural information and not for user data records.* Although this may seem to be more overhead, it allows the file to be processed correctly. Thus the block header contains the following information (refer to Figure 13-8):

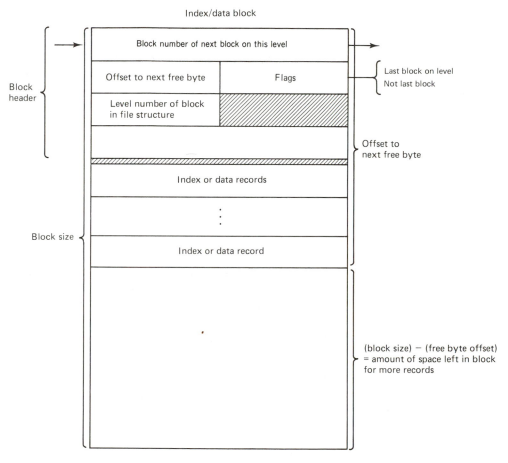

Figure 13-8 Block format.

- Block number of the next block on that level.
- A flag byte to mark the *last* block on that level. If set, the link above can be set to point to the first block on the level.
- Offset from the start of the block to the next available unused byte in the block. Thus the block size minus this offset allows the access method to determine whether a new record will fit in that block.

13.7.3 Index Records

All index records are formatted identically. However, there is a difference in the *content* of the index record depending on which *level of the index* the index record resides. The format of all index records is as follows:

- Key value of item pointed to by this record
- Block number containing the key value above

Note that all indexed records are *fixed length*. This is because the key is fixed in size and the block number can be allocated a fixed-size field. Thus it is a simple matter to calculate how many index records can fit within a block in the index.

Index records at level 2 or higher.   These index records point to the next-lower level in the index. Thus the key value represents the *highest key in the target index block*. The target block is identified by its block number.

Index records at level 1.   These index records reside in the lowest level of the index. Their function is to point to a specific user data record. Thus the key field is identical to the key field in the corresponding data record. The block number is the block in which the target data record resides.

13.8 SUMMARY

In this chapter we discussed the first file organization that allows both random and sequential access to user data records without any major penalties. In addition, we learned how to dynamically reorganize a file via block splitting techniques rather than to force all users into frequent file organizations. Finally, we learned that this file design provides the user with consistent random and sequential access performance. This was accomplished because there are no overflow areas to contend with.

KEY WORDS

Block header	Indexed file
Block splitting	Levels of an index
Dynamic file reorganization	Root index block

SUPPLEMENTAL REFERENCES

1. Comer, Douglas, "The Ubiquitous B-Tree." *Computing Surveys,* Vol. 11, No. 2, 1979, pp. 121–137. The purpose of this book was not to teach data structures. However, the indexed type file structure closely resembles variations on B-trees. Anyone wanting a

background on this kind of data structure should read this excellent article.

2. Hansen, Wilfred J., "A Cost Model for the Internal Organization of B+ Tree Nodes." *ACM Transactions on Programming Languages and Systems,* Vol. 3, No. 4, 1981, pp. 508–532. This is a very good article on the costs and trade-offs associated with B-tree file structures. Hansen includes several variations on the B-tree theme in his analysis so that the reader can understand the performance differences between several B-tree variations.

3. Held, Gerald, and Michael Stonebraker, "B-Trees Re-examined." *Communications of the ACM.* Vol. 21, No. 2, 1978, pp. 139–143. This short article discusses several problems associated with B-tree type file structures. Specifically, the authors discuss performance relative to secondary or alternate indices, concurrency problems, and issues associated with the depth of the index.

4. Martin, James, *Computer Data-Base Organization,* 2nd ed. Englewood Cliffs, N.J.: Prentice-Hall, Inc., 1975, Chap. 19. Martin has many excellent diagrams and pictures which show the various record addressing techniques available for indexed files.

5. Sussenguth, Edward H., "Use of Tree Structures for Processing Files." *Communications of the ACM,* Vol. 26, No. 1, 1983, pp. 17–20. This article provides background information concerning the application of *trees* for file structures. This is essentially a tutorial paper for those readers who have not had much experience with these types of structures.

6. Wiederhold, Gio, *Database Design.* New York: McGraw-Hill Book Company, 1977, Sec. 3–4. This book has a good discussion on various indexing techniques. Of special interest is the discussion of how to construct an indexed file that has multiple-key access.

EXERCISES

1. Design a file structure for the indexed file type that would allow the use of *multiple keys* to access the user data records.

2. What are the design and processing implications of using high-key versus low-key values in index data records? In other words, what if the index records contained the *low-key* value in the target block instead of the high-key value?

3. What is the sequence of I/O operations that would both add a new record into an indexed file and provide minimal risk of loss of data in case of a system crash?

4. Why is it important for the user to be aware of what the current level of the root of the index is? When and how should the user react to changes in the level of the root?

5. How can the file system determine if the user has changed the key of a record during an UPDATE operation? Be specific.

6. How many I/O buffers are needed to achieve a reasonable trade-off between performance and main memory? State clearly how you would use each I/O buffer that you would allocate.

7. How can sequential (i.e., READ_NEXT) performance be made as fast as that of a sequential file? List two recommendations you would make to achieve this goal.

8. If you had a very large user data record that did not fit in a block with the records of lower- or higher key values, how would you split the block? Be specific as to what data records would be copied into which blocks as a result of the split.

9. On a random READ operation, does finding an index record in level 1 of the index with an identical key value guarantee that the data record exists within the file? Why or why not?

10. Is there anything to be gained (e.g., performance) by presorting the user data records *before* they are inserted into the file? Be specific.

11. The section on block splitting discussed an algorithm that tried to balance the same *number* of data records in all the split blocks. List three other split algorithms, and then discuss the merits and drawbacks of each of them.

PROGRAMMING EXERCISES

1. Design and implement the CREATE file function for a single-key indexed file.

2. Design and implement a block-splitting algorithm that could be used in an indexed access method.

14

VSAM Files

CHAPTER OBJECTIVES

When you complete this chapter, you will be able to:

- Discuss the advantages and disadvantages of the integrated access methods, such as VSAM
- Discuss what block splitting is, why it is necessary, and how it is done
- Understand the terminology related to VSAM
- Discuss why overflow areas are not required
- Understand the concept of "fill factors" and why they are important to performance
- Discuss how, unlike ISAM, the VSAM file structure is not tied to specific disk characteristics

14.1 OVERVIEW

Up to this point in time, we have discussed the so-called traditional access methods. Each of them has been around for many years, in spite of the drawbacks that each has. In our discussions, we have tried to keep the user interface to the various access methods common. This has the major benefit of being much simpler for the user to learn. However, in reality, there are not many I/O systems in existence which provide such a level of commonality. One of the earliest versions of a common interface to perform I/O was incorporated into an IBM product known as VSAM (see Figure 14-0).

Previous to that product, a user had to learn one interface to request ISAM access to records and another interface to perform standard sequential I/O, and so on. This situation obviously was harder to support and write programs for. Thus one of the major breakthroughs that was achieved by VSAM and similar products was to take a major stride in standardizing the user/programming interface to the access methods and the basic file system.

Another point of concern relates to the fact that each of the file organizations discussed earlier presented to the user needed functionality, yet together with each file type came some fairly significant penalties. For example, sequential files can be read very rapidly, perhaps the fastest of any file organization, yet there is no random access capability.

Relative files provide the user with extremely fast random access to data records, yet the keys must be unique integers. Also, fixed-length cells are used even if the file's

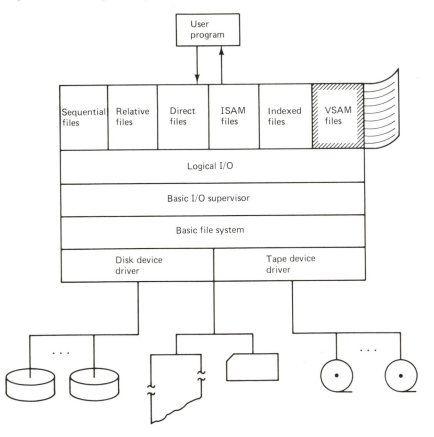

Figure 14-0   File system: VSAM access method.

records are declared to be of variable length. Alternatively, relative files provide both sequential and random access. However, performance of sequential access depends on whether the records in the file are dense or nondense.

Direct files gave the user "normal" key values (i.e., not restricted to integer values only). Direct also makes better use of the file's disk space than do relative files. However, in so doing, direct files take away from the user the capability to perform sequential access to the data records.

ISAM files provide the user with both random access to data records using "normal" key values and sequential access to the data. However, the user has to know a lot about the technical characteristics of the device being used, since the allocation of the file is directly related to the cylinder and track capacities of the specific drive. Also, by utilizing overflow areas, if the user guesses wrong on the design and allocation of the file, performance degrades dramatically.

Finally, INDEXED files get rid of overflow areas, and still provide sequential and random access to the user's data records. In addition, the user no longer has to be concerned with the technical details of the device on which the file happens to reside that day. However, sequential access has to take one level of indirection to get to the data (i.e., via the record pointer in the lowest level of the index, which is dense). Also, the user data records were not maintained in sequential order by ascending key values. Thus the sequential access performance of an INDEXED file was less than that of an ISAM file.

Therefore, although we have discussed many different methods to organize and structure data, we have yet to uncover a way in which we could have all the benefits mentioned above, yet have few of the drawbacks. VSAM and other current integrated access methods have taken major strides toward solving this dilemma once and for all. Since VSAM is one of the more widely used "access methods" in use today, in this chapter we delve into its design and structure. The terminology we use is based on IBM's definitions. There is similar, though not identical terminology in use by other products. We will, however, try and extend the file structures and control blocks discussed so far to incorporate VSAM-like capabilities. Thus what we discuss here is a VSAM modified to fit our overall design.

14.2 FILE DESIGN CONSIDERATIONS

The terminology used in discussing the VSAM file structure is somewhat different from the terminology used thus far in this book. If we examine Figure 14-1, what we see is the structure of a VSAM indexed file organization. Although it *appears* to be identical to that of an ISAM or indexed file structure, there are some important *structural differences* that will be discussed in the next section. For now, it is important for us to learn the terminology used by IBM in describing VSAM files.

All the levels of the index structure, with the exception of level 1, are known as the index set. This part of a VSAM file is identical to an ISAM or INDEXED

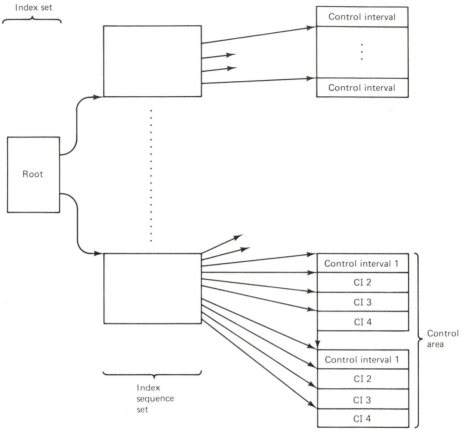

Figure 14-1 VSAM files.

file structure. Each index record in a block of the index set points to an index block at the next-lower level of the index. The index record itself consists of the following fields:

- Block number of index block at next-lower level in the index
- High-key value of the block being pointed to

    The lowest level of the index, level 1, is called the sequence set. The level 1 blocks in an INDEXED file contain one index record for every user data record in the file. Therefore, we say that level 1 is dense. In a VSAM file, the sequence set (i.e., level 1) is nondense. This means that there is one index record pointing to each *control interval* in the primary data level, not to each individual data record (see Figure 14-2a).
    The control interval is the amount of data that will actually get read, or written, whenever the file is accessed. Thus it is similar to the other file types that read and wrote *blocks*. The difference here is that a control interval could actually consist of one or more physical blocks on the disk track itself.

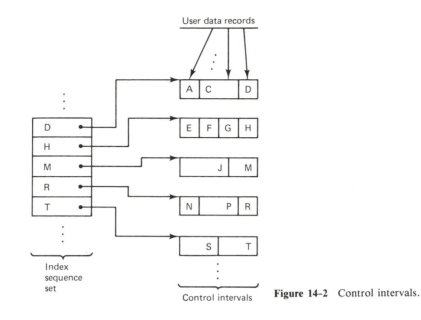

Index
sequence
set

Control intervals   **Figure 14-2**   Control intervals.

Finally, *one or more control intervals make up an allocated area of the file known as a control area.* The control intervals within a control area are contiguous. Thus the control area is a contiguous chunk of allocated space on the disk media. We can, for example, relate a control area to a cylinder on the disk. Thus the contiguous tracks (i.e., control intervals) within the cylinder (i.e., control area) make up the allocation unit within the file. A file can have many control areas, and each control area can have one or more control intervals. Thus in VSAM we have subdivided the primary data area of the indexed file into discrete components. We shall now see why this was done.

14.2.1 File Structure

The index records that reside within the blocks of the index set are maintained physically in ascending sequence by primary key value. The index records in the index set are nondense, meaning that there is only one index record per block at the next-lower level in the index.

The index records that make up the sequence set are also nondense. However, what distinguishes the sequence set index records from the other index records is the fact that now each index record points to a control interval (i.e., think block) within the user's data area known as the control area. This is not substantially different from what occurs in an ISAM file, except that in a VSAM file the user does not need to be aware of the technical details of the device. Here VSAM takes care of the problems of mapping the file onto the disk in an appropriate manner. This is an important point, since one of the major drawbacks to an ISAM file is that the file itself is intimately tied to the characteristics of the device. Thus, in the case of ISAM, the user has to calculate how many tracks and cylinders would be needed for the file and allocate them accordingly. If the calculations are wrong, or the underlying assumptions are not consistent with reality, the file structure has significant problems with overflow areas. In VSAM, the user allocates space in terms of control areas and control intervals, and VSAM handles all the concerns of how to map the control areas most optimally onto the selected target device.

The sequence set contains index records that point to every control interval allocated in the file. An index record in the sequence set contains the following:

- Control interval number
- Highest key value in that particular control interval

Within the control intervals that make up the control areas, the user data records are *physically stored in sequence by ascending primary key values.* Thus, as shown in Figure 14–3, the first control interval contains records with key values "A," "C," and "D." If a new record is added to the file with a key of "B," the records would have to be physically shuffled in order to get all four records to be in the correct key sequence on the disk.

One other point must be made concerning control intervals. It is possible to have *n* control intervals in a control area. However, it is also possible to only use *n-m* of those control intervals when populating the file with data records (see Figure 14–3). *The control intervals that are not used during the population of the file are effectively being set aside as distributed free space.* This is critical, since if we should ever add a record to the file and not have room in the target control interval, we could always push one or more records into this free-space area. Since all the control

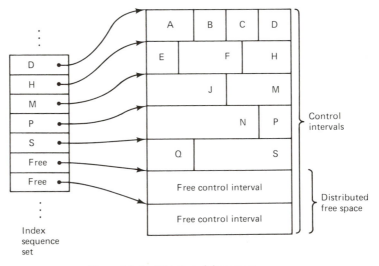

Figure 14–3   Distributed free space.

intervals are contiguous, a SEEK is not required, so that the operation is reasonably fast.

Within an ISAM file there is no concept of "free space," other than cylinder or file overflow areas. The distinction between the two is important. In ISAM the records that lie in the overflow area are not maintained in sequence by ascending primary key. Thus performance is adversely affected whenever the overflow area needs to be accessed. In VSAM, all user data records are maintained in key sequence, even in the control intervals allocated as distributed free space. Thus *a particular control interval can overflow into another control interval only if the new control interval is empty.* This, in turn, allows all records within a control interval to be in sequence by key, and therefore it can be accessed in the sequence set with one index record.

14.2.2 Record Addressing Algorithms

Within a VSAM file, user data records can be accessed either randomly by key, or sequentially.

Index tree walking.   To randomly access any record in the entire VSAM file, the user need only provide the VSAM access method with the key of the record desired. The walk down the index is identical to how it is performed both for ISAM and indexed access methods. When the tree transversal has reached the lowest-level index, the sequence set, the tree walk algorithm takes the pointer to the control interval in which the target record could reside.

Once the search has reached the control interval, there is only one last search that can be done, the search of the control interval. *The target user data record will either be found in that control interval, or it does not exist.* There is no overflow area in which to continue the search. This is one of the key benefits of the VSAM file organization. The time it takes to randomly access any record is the same no matter where in the file the record may be. This is because the depth of the index is always the same throughout the entire file. Also, since there is no overflow area, it means that the sequence set will always point to the only control interval in which the record might reside. Thus the search ends at the target control interval.

Sequential access.   To perform sequential access in a VSAM file, we must position to some key value within the index sequence set. Then we must take the control interval pointed to by that index record and retrieve the data records by ascending key values. This is easy, since the data records are kept physically in ascending key sequence within a control interval (see Figure 14–4). If there are no more records in the control interval, the next control interval in the control area is searched, and so on, until all the control areas have been searched in key sequence. The next control interval to search is identified within the index sequence set. Thus sequential access performance will approximate the READ_NEXT performance of a sequential file, and faster than that for indexed files.

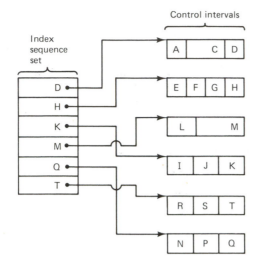

Figure 14-4 VSAM sequential processing.

Collisions.   We have collisions whenever a record is to be put into a file and the target location within the control interval is currently occupied. Then some alternative action must be taken. In the case of ISAM, we have to form overflow areas, while in indexed we simply keep extending the level 1 chain of records. In VSAM there can be collisions since the user data records are physically maintained in ascending key sequence. If there is no room in a control area for a new record, control interval splitting will take place. There are several possible alternatives that can occur, which are discussed in some detail in the following paragraphs:

- New record fits within the target control interval.
- New record does not fit in the target control interval, and therefore a control interval split is required.
- The control area is completely filled, so that a control area split will be required.

Space Available in Control Interval.   If the key value of the new record falls between the key values of two consecutive records in the control interval, the insertion algorithm says that the new record must be physically inserted between those two records (see Figure 14–5). If there is enough free space available at the end of the control interval to hold the new record, the following actions will take place.

1. All the records with a higher key value than the target record will be moved up in the control interval. This is done to create a chunk of free space between records with lower key values and records with higher key values. This movement of the records within the control interval takes place in the I/O buffer in main memory.
2. Once the hole has been created, the new record is moved into the opening within

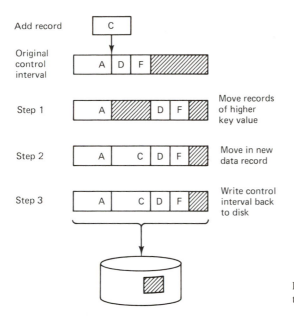

Figure 14-5 Record insertion into control interval.

the control interval. Upon completion of the move, all the records within the control interval will be physically in order by ascending key value.

3. Finally, this modified control interval is rewritten back to the file.

Empty Control Interval in the Control Area.   If the target record cannot fit in the proper control interval, a check must be made to see if an unused control interval exists within that control area. If there is a free control interval, the following actions take place (see Figure 14-6):

1. Determine where in the original control interval the target record should have been inserted had there been enough room within the control interval.
2. Locate the new empty control interval and copy all the records with *higher* key values from the original control interval into the new control interval.
3. If there is now enough space in the original control interval, copy the target record into the original control area.

    If there is still not enough room in the original control interval, check to see if there is enough room in the newly allocated control interval. If there is enough room, move all records with higher key values into the new control interval. This is done to create enough free space for the new user data record to be added.

    If there is still no room either in the original or new control interval, the access method must revert to taking some actions. Specifically, if there are no more control intervals available within this control area, an entirely new *con-*

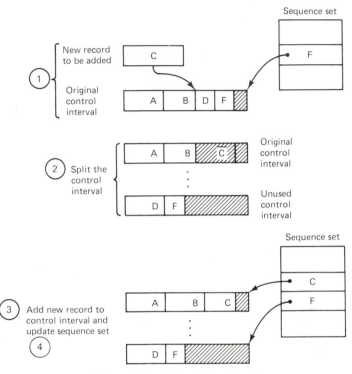

Figure 14-6 Control interval split.

trol area is allocated. This makes available all the control intervals within the new control area. Then the access method will copy the records with high-key values from the original control interval into their own control interval. The user data record is then copied into the control interval freed up by the move of the high-key values.

4. When all processing has been completed, the sequence set must be updated to correctly reflect the position of all the records that now reside in both the old and new control intervals.

No Room in the Control Area.   If there is simply no room in the control area, a new control area will be allocated and initialized. Then all records with key values *higher* than the target record's key value must be copied into the newly allocated control area. Next, the original target record that started all of this processing must be copied into either of the control areas, depending on whether the original control area has enough room for the record.

14.2.3 File Attributes

There are several file attributes that are important in VSAM files. The file attributes are saved in what we have called the file header. In the world of VSAM, the file header is merged into what is called the VSAM catalog. A catalog is simply a list of the files known to VSAM, together with an indication of file organization and other critical parameters.

File Organization.   A VSAM access method can support not only the VSAM indexed sequential file type, but also file organizations very similar to relative and indexed files. Thus the user must specify which of the possible file organizations is wanted.

File size.   Until now, we have always dealt with the file size as a key attribute of the file. For VSAM, the equivalent declaration relates to the user specifying the size and number of control intervals and control areas that will make up the file. Although VSAM can, and will, automatically extend the file on behalf of the user should there ever be a case in which there is no more room left in the file, it is always a better practice to preallocate as much of the file as is reasonable.

Control intervals and control areas.   Control interval size dictates the size of the unit of I/O data transfer. In other words, this is the number of bytes that will always be transferred whenever there is a read or write request to the file. It is important for performance reasons to make the control interval a multiple of the actual physical blocks on the disk itself (see Figure 14–7).

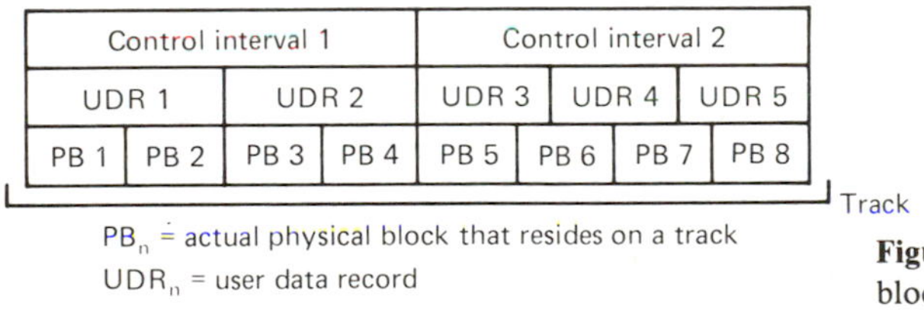

PB$_n$ = actual physical block that resides on a track
UDR$_n$ = user data record

Figure 14-7 Control intervals and disk blocks.

The size and number of the control areas should be large enough to hold the expected number of data records that will reside within the file. In addition, the control area size should take into consideration the amount of distributed free space that should be allocated within each control area throughout the file. This can have a very positive impact on the overall performance and responsiveness of write commands (e.g., WRITE, UPDATE).

Key position and key size.   Like the other indexed file types, records are inserted into the VSAM file based on the key which is physically part of the user's data record. For VSAM to know where to look for the key, the key position and size must be declared when the VSAM file is created.

Key attributes.   In most index files it is possible to allow more than one user data record to exist with the same primary key value. However, in VSAM files duplicate keys are *not* allowed. Thus VSAM files support *unique keys* only.

14.3 FILE OPERATIONS

The file operations that exist in VSAM are about the same functionally as we have discussed in previous file organizations. Thus only the differences that exist will be discussed here.

14.3 CREATE File

For many file types there is language support to create files from the high-level-language program itself. This is especially true of the simpler file types such as sequential files. However, as the file structure gets more complicated, the high-level language support tends to disappear rapidly. There are many reasons for this disappearing act, not the least of which is the fact that most languages simply do not support the syntax required to define the more complex file organizations. Also, since the various vendors have not standardized what is needed from the vantage point of high-level languages, it is almost impossible for any ANSI language committee to determine what capabilities must be supported within the language itself.

VSAM solves this problem by not having a CREATE file request. Instead, there is a utility program, called DEFINE, which users can run. DEFINE requests all the appropriate file attributes and file structure parameters and then goes off and physically creates the file. The parameters that users can set within DEFINE are defined as follows (this is a partial list showing only the key attributes):

- *File name:* This is the name by which the file will be cataloged within the VSAM master catalog. Its usage is identical to the way in which we have been using file names in previous chapters.
- *File organization:* Either a sequential, relative, or indexed organization can be selected. Here we are concerned only with the *key sequenced data set*, which is IBM's name for the indexed file structure.
- *Freespace:* The user has the capability of allocating distributed free space throughout the file. This space will not be used when the file is initially populated with user data records. However, it will be available for control interval splitting tasks.
- *Record size:* Here the VSAM user has somewhat greater flexibility. The user must specify not only the maximum record length but also the *average* record size. VSAM can use the average-size value to perform calculations as to how large, for example, a control interval must be.

When the DEFINE utility has completed its work, the VSAM file has been completely created and is ready to be populated with user data records.

14.3.2 OPEN File

The OPEN processing capability also exists within VSAM. Its purpose and function are the same as discussed in previous chapters. Specifically, in VSAM, the processing performed consists of the following tasks:

- The correct disk packs are mounted on the disks to ensure that the correct files are being processed.
- All internal table, control block, and I/O buffer space is allocated within main memory.
- File *password* information is checked to allow only authorized users into a particular data file.

When done, the VSAM file is ready to be used.

14.3.3 CLOSE File

The CLOSE function is also supported by VSAM. Specifically, the VSAM CLOSE operation performs the following tasks:

- All unwritten I/O buffers must be written back out into the file. This is performed to ensure that all data records that have been changed are written out onto the VSAM file.
- Control blocks, internal tables, and I/O buffer space is returned to the system's pool of available allocatable main memory space.

There are no surprises here, just reconfirmation that the CLOSE function is something that must be performed no matter what name it is known by.

14.4 RECORD OPERATIONS

VSAM has all of the usual capabilities that we have discussed in previous chapters. However, some of the names have been changed, and some interesting additional processing capabilities are offered. Thus we will now walk through the VSAM record operations, while relating the new concepts and terminology with the new terms.

Record access modes.   VSAM supports both sequential and random access of the user data records. Random access requires that the index structure be transversed, starting at the top of the index structure. The path followed down the index is based on comparing the user-supplied search key value against the key values in the index records. The path will be defined by taking those branches for which the user-supplied key value is less than or equal to the key value in the index record.

This is because the index record key value represents the highest possible key value in the control in the index block or control interval that is being pointed to.

Sequential access of the user data records is done by first positioning to one of the data records. This can be accomplished by either a random POSITION or random READ request. Once we are positioned at a specific data record in the file (i.e., the current record pointer is valid), we can perform fast sequential access. This is done simply by picking up the next valid data record that exists in the control interval. When the last record in the control interval has been read, the next control interval in the control area is accessed. The identification of the next control interval comes from the next index record in the sequence set.

Finally, when all of the control intervals within a control area have been accessed, a switch is made to the next control area allocated to the file. When there are no more control intervals or control areas, there are no more records in the file. Under these conditions, the next sequential READ_NEXT request will hit the logical end-of-file and will fail. The VSAM access method must then return to the calling program with the operation completion status of end-of-file condition detected. It is then up to the calling program to continue processing accordingly.

Record currency.   Since it is critical to the access method to maintain the current record pointer, it is necessary to describe its format in this file organization. Unlike indexed files, where the current record pointer referenced the lowest level of the index, effectively pointing to the pointer to the data record, we will again define the current record pointer to be the unique identifier of the data record. Thus the current record format will logically contain the following elements:

- Key of the data record
- Number of the control interval that contains the target user data record

14.4.1 POSITION to Record

The VSAM equivalent to the POSITION request is called *POINT*. In either format, the function is to allow the user to position to a specific data record in the file.

VSAM takes the key specified by the calling program and starting at the top of the index structure, walks down the tree until the data record position is located. The success, or failure, of the search depends on the search criteria defined by the user. For example, if an *exact* matching key value was requested, the record either exists or it does not exist. On the other hand, if the request was more generic (i.e., give me either a record with a matching key value or a data record with the next higher key value in the file). Then the request will always be successful unless there are literally no more records in the file.

The performance of the POSITION request is important, since other operations, (e.g., READ, WRITE) actually perform a POSITION operation as part of the overall request. The number of actual I/O operations that must be performed can be calculated as follows:

$$t_{\text{POSITION}} = \text{(number of levels in index)} + N$$

Since the entire tree must be transversed, the number of I/O operations must at least be equal to the number of levels in the index that must be searched. The parameter N has a value of from 1 to N, although usually N equals 2. The "1" is the I/O operation required to go from the level 1 sequence set to the control interval containing the target key range. If an exact match was requested, the record either exists in this specific control interval, or it does not. Thus N will always equal 1 in this case. On the other hand, if an *approximate* key search was specified, the target record found may or may not be found in this control interval. Therefore, other control intervals must be read and searched. Theoretically, it is *possible* that in some obscure case several control intervals would have to be searched before the next valid data record was found. For example, if most of the records had been deleted and new records tended to be added with new high-key values, this perverse case could occur. However, in most applications, the next valid record will be in either the current control interval or the next one. Thus N could range from values of 1 to 2.

14.4.2 READ Record

The READ request randomly retrieves a user-specified data record from the file and transfers it into a user-defined record buffer. The VSAM GET function call provides identical functionality.

By specifying the value of the key of the data record wanted, VSAM can then proceed to find the record and transfer it into the record buffer visible to the user's program. The READ operation performance can be defined as follows:

$$t_{\text{READ}} = t_{\text{POSITION}} + t_{\text{transfer to user buffer}}$$

The CPU time it takes to transfer the target record from the I/O buffer in main memory into the user-defined record buffer is neglible compared to the I/O times involved. We can therefore conclude that the READ operation will approximate the POSITION operation in overall time. This is reasonable since, by definition, the functionality of the POSITION and READ operations is identical except that READ goes one step further and actually copies the record from the I/O buffer to the user buffer.

14.4.3 READ_NEXT Record

The function of the READ_NEXT operation is to retrieve the next logical data record in the file for the user. To do this there must be a valid current record pointer to define the position in the file to begin the search for the next record.

READ_NEXT can search from control interval to control interval looking for the next valid record. In so doing it is really keeping one foot in the sequence set and the other in the control interval. Therefore, when the last data record has been retrieved from the control interval, the next control interval can be determined from the next sequential entry within the sequence set. Therefore, READ_NEXT performance can be quite fast.

Note the difference between ISAM, indexed, and VSAM sequential processing. With ISAM, the next sequential record is always the next record on the track. The only exception is when the records fall off into the overflow areas. Then the access method has to search for the next record, and depending on how long the overflow chain is performance could degrade very rapidly.

With indexed, there is no overflow areas. However, to locate the next sequential record we have to reaccess the lowest level of the index for every record in the file. This level of indirection could slow down sequential processing unless the lowest-level index blocks are kept in main memory at all times.

In the case of VSAM, we have a variant of indexed processing. Here we need to touch the lowest level of the index (i.e., the sequence set) only when the next control interval is needed. Again, if part of the sequence set could be kept in an I/O buffer in main memory, the sequential processing can be quite rapid.

14.4.4 WRITE Record

The WRITE operation adds new data records to the file. The VSAM equivalent operation is the *PUT* function. It happens quite frequently that the terms GET and PUT are used in place of READ and WRITE. However, this is typically just semantics, and the processing that is actually performed is the same.

As happened with the other indexed file organizations, *all records are added to a VSAM file by the value of the key found within the body of the data record itself*. To insert a new record into the file, the processing is as follows:

$$t_{WRITE} = t_{POSITION} + t_{insert\ record}$$

Again, the time it takes to position to the location in the file where the record should be placed is one of the key factors in determining how long the WRITE operation will take. The time to insert the record into the target control interval can also vary widely and in some cases can actually take much longer to perform than the time to POSITION to the control interval (i.e., when the control interval, control area, or index set splits).

How is a record inserted into a VSAM file? And what are the possible exception conditions that can be detected during the processing that affects how adding the record to the file takes place?

The processing steps that take place during a WRITE operation are as follows:

1. POSITION to Target Control Interval.   Data records are always inserted by the key value contained in the user data record itself. With that key, VSAM performs a POSITION or POINT to get to the control interval into which the new record *belongs*.

2. Free Space Exists in the Control Interval.   If, when the target control interval has been read into an I/O buffer in main memory, VSAM determines that there is enough available space in it, the data record can be copied into the I/O buffer and the insert is complete (see Figure 14–5 and the section on collisions). More specifically, if there is enough space, the space must be made available in the correct key sequence position. Therefore, the current records in the control interval may need to be shuffled about to open up enough free space *at the correct record position*. Then, and only then, can the data record be copied from the user's record buffer into the space in the control interval in the I/O buffer. When complete, the control interval can be rewritten back into the VSAM file, and thus the record will have been added to the file.

3. Space Is Available in Another Control Interval or Control Area.   When this occurs, the collision processing described in an earlier section takes place (see Figure 14–6). What is important to emphasize here is that collisions cause the VSAM file to dynamically reorganize themselves. Thus the data records in the control intervals, as well as the index records in the index set and sequence set, are always kept in sequence by ascending key value. This causes the WRITE times to vary widely, but it results in a reasonably optimal file for random access operations. This is important to understand, because the amount of splitting that occurs in a file is directly proportional to the amount of processing time that a WRITE operation will require.

14.4.5 UPDATE Record

The UPDATE operation does not really have a clean corresponding function call in VSAM. Instead, it is really a combination of calls. Specifically, to UPDATE a data record, the user must read the record with the intent to update (i.e., GET-for-Update) and then actually update the record by writing back the updated record (i.e., PUT-for-Update). Thus VSAM uses the GET and PUT operations for multiple logical processing functions. What determines the actual action taken (i.e., add a new record into the file or modify a currently existing record) is determined by the parameters supplied as part of the GET and PUT calls.

In VSAM files, the primary key value is not allowed to change once the data record has been inserted into the file. If the records are of variable length, it could be possible that the length of the record could be *shortened* enough so that part, or all, of the primary key is removed from the record. This situation must be detected by the access method, as a record is valid only if the record itself is long enough to hold the entire key field.

14.4.6 DELETE Record

The DELETE request logically removes a user data record from a file. To delete a record, the record must have been previously read successfully into memory. In other words, the current record pointer for the record to be deleted is valid. To accomplish the same functionality in VSAM, the target record must have been read with the GET call, with the "for update" option specified. Then the record can be deleted via the VSAM *ERASE* function.

By following our conventions, or VSAMs, the record to be deleted is the one identified by the previous read operation. Therefore, no key is required. The performance of the DELETE operation is quite fast since the data record can just be marked as being deleted or compressed out of the control interval so that it is physically removed from the file. In either case, the index structure in general, and the sequence set in particular, is not updated to reflect that the deletion took place. This is true even if the record deleted represented the high key in the control interval and thus had a matching record in the sequence set.

The key value in the index records of the sequence set initially reflect an actual data record that exists within the file. However, technically speaking, the key represents only the highest possible key within the associated control interval, whether or not the data record actually exists at any particular point in time.

14.5 PERFORMANCE CONSIDERATIONS

There are several factors affecting the performance of VSAM files:

- Depth of the index
- Number of I/O buffers
- Number of additions to the file
- Size of control intervals and control areas
- Fill percentage

Let us examine each of these in some degree of detail.

Depth of the index structure.   For random access to the data records, the depth of the index will dictate how many I/O operations are required to perform a READ operation. The root level of the index can grow higher and higher because of record insertions into the file, poorly chosen control interval sizes, and so on, which can cause an increase in splitting to occur.

Allocation of I/O main memory buffers.   This is done in the hopes that part of the index, usually the root, can be kept in main memory. If this happens, every tree walk will have one or more I/O operations that it will not need to perform. Since the usual number of I/O operations to access a record is fairly small, even the savings of one I/O operation can be quite significant.

For example, if we had a VSAM file that had a root level of, say, 4, then saving just one I/O operation can improve the responsiveness of the user requests from four I/O operations to three, an improvement of 25%, just by buffering in main memory those data that are critical to the overall operation.

Frequent additions into the VSAM file.   If many records are added into the VSAM file, the control areas will grow and split. Then the index may require splitting, which then causes the index to grow and slows down the job. The issue here is that additions take a relatively long time to accomplish. Also, if the additions to the file do not occur within the same blocks as those that have deleted record space, the data and index structure will change and the file will grow larger and larger.

Note that it is not the fact that the file grows larger that is the problem. Instead, it is the situation that deleted record space is not being reused, thus making for a net gain in the file. A larger file usually, though not always, makes for a larger index structure. This in turn makes for more I/O that needs to be performed, and thus lower performance of the file system and access method.

Size of control intervals and control areas.   Not only must enough space be allocated for the entire file, but the choice of how the space is divided up is also important. Control intervals should be a multiple of the disk's physical block size. In addition, there should be an integral number of control intervals per track without any wasted space. This last point is critical so that space on the disk will not be wasted. Finally, control intervals should be large enough to hold a number of user data records. With fixed-length records we could calculate closely how large to make a control interval. With variable-length records it is important to estimate the average size of a data record rather accurately.

Large enough control areas need to be allocated to hold a number of data records and still have room for distributed free space for expansion purposes. In addition, control areas should, whenever possible, be allocated completely within a cylinder or multiple cylinders. This will cut down on unnecessary SEEK times.

In summary, a critical part of performance is determined *before* the first data record is inserted into the file. How well we do at defining the parameters of the file at create time will determine how well the file performs for all its users.

Fill percentages.   Whenever a user expects to be adding or changing many records in a VSAM file, it is important to have space to insert the additions. What we really need to avoid is an unnecessary level of splitting. The fill percentage simply sets aside a certain number of control intervals within each control area for future growth and expansion. These can then be used without causing the entire control area to split.

14.5.1 File Population Techniques

As was the case for INDEXED files, there is nothing mandatory that must be done to populate the file. However, to improve performance, it is necessary to minimize the number of block or control interval splits.

One of the major ways in which to improve performance is to *sort* all the known data records by their key field. By so doing, the records will be presented to the access method in order by ascending key values. Furthermore, by telling the access method that the incoming records are in key sequence, it can optimize the process of how it moves records and when it rewrites control intervals. Therefore, there will be no need to perform any splits. The only processing to be performed is to add the new records to new blocks. This optimization process, known as *mass insert,* can improve file loading performance by an order of magnitude or more.

We can see how mass insert can work by referring to Figure 14–8. In Figure 14–8a, records "A" through "I" are added to the file. Note that there are no splits involved. VSAM simply adds the new records immediately following the last record. In the case of a split, VSAM would try and balance the number of data records left in each control interval. In mass-insert mode, this is not performed.

In Figure 14–8b, we are inserting a series of records into the file with keys that lie between the keys of two records that already exist within the file. Again, by knowing that mass insert is taking place, VSAM can perform the first split, and from then on there are no more splits.

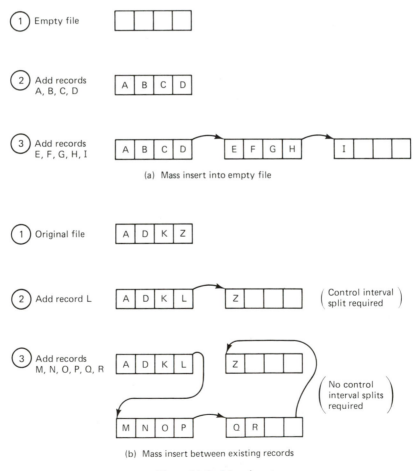

(a) Mass insert into empty file

(b) Mass insert between existing records

Figure 14–8   Mass insert.

14.5.2 File Reorganization

A VSAM file performs dynamic reorganizations by doing block or control interval/control area splitting. In this manner, the index is always kept in a reasonably optimal state. This means that whenever a random access operation is requested, the number of actual I/O operations is the same no matter where in the file the record exists. Again, this is because VSAM is constructed in a B-tree organization that dynamically adjusts as the file grows larger.

There are however, several conditions under which a VSAM file should be reorganized. First, if so many records have been added to the file that the number of levels in the index grows to the point of unacceptable performance, it is time to rebuild the file. Second, if there are many deletions occurring in the file, the amount of "wasted space" can grow considerably. Again, it is time to reorganize.

Level number of ROOT becomes too high.   As the file grows, control interval and control area splits will occur. Each time one of these occurs, the associated index must be updated to reflect the new control interval high-key values. Thus one or more records will be added to the index whenever a split at the data level arises. When the index block fills up with records, it can split into two blocks, thus causing the next higher level in the index to be modified. In this manner, both the data area and the index area can grow dynamically.

As the index grows, the top or root level of the index grows to a higher-and-higher number. This is important because the level number of the root is the same number of I/O operations that must be performed for every random access of a data record. Recall that the transversal of the index begins at the root block and works its way down to the sequence set. Therefore, as the root block splits, the random access time grows. When it becomes unacceptable, the file should be reorganized.

A VSAM file reorganization will reconstruct the file from scratch and then repopulate the file with the original data records. With all deleted record space removed, and perhaps the file allocation quantities changed to reflect the current and projected size of the file, the index structure can be rebuilt with the end result of a clean file and a lower level of the root.

Many DELETED records in the file.   It may be possible to reuse space within a block taken up by deleted records. However, it is possible that the application is such that most, or even possibly all, of the deleted record space will never be reused. For example, if we have a credit card file, all new records will usually tend to be added with new high-key values. Thus any accounts that are deleted will have lower key values, and therefore the space will never be reused. Thus the tree structure will just continue to grow larger and larger, even though the total number of current valid records may not be changing very much.

The way to reclaim the delected record space is to reorganize the VSAM file. The end result will be a VSAM file that has no wasted space and that has all indexes and data areas optimally loaded.

14.6 DESIGN TRADE-OFFS

The VSAM file organization solves many of the problems that the file types discussed earlier had. However, in choosing a file organization, the user must have intimate knowledge of the application being developed as well as the capabilities of the various access methods. Only then can an educated selection be made. Also, VSAM does have its own problems and drawbacks as well as highlights. Let us now examine the costs and benefits of VSAM keyed sequential files versus the other file organizations that we have already discussed.

14.6.1 File Size Calculations

Since the *overhead* of the VSAM file is rather high, it is beneficial to be able to determine in advance the space requirements for the file. To make these calculations, it is necessary to proceed step by step calculating the size of each of the components of the file.

Size of the primary data area.   First, it is necessary to know the approximate number of data records that will reside within the file. Next, it is necessary to estimate the average size of each data record. From these two values we can calculate the number of control intervals that will be needed to hold all the data records.

In addition, we must consider the size of a control area and determine how many of the control intervals in a control area are to be left as distributed free space. From this we can tell how many control intervals per control area can be used for data records when the file is first populated. Furthermore, based on our estimate of the number of records to exist in the file, we can then calculate how many control areas will be needed to initially hold all the user's data records.

Size of the index structure.   Once we have determined the total number of control intervals that will be needed in the file, we can calculate the size of the index structure. Since there is one index record that points to each control interval in the file, we know how many index records will be needed for the sequence set in the index.

Next, we need to calculate how many index records can fit within an index block. From this calculation we can determine how many blocks will be needed at level 1. We can then repeat this same procedure for level 2, level 3, and so on, until we arrive at the level that contains only one index block. That is the root index block and is the top of the index structure.

Finally, sum all of the preceding subtotals, and the result is the target file size. It is important, however, not to forget that within each structure (e.g., control interval . . .) VSAM adds certain control fields for its own use. These must be part of the calculation, but have been ignored here for simplicity purposes.

14.6.2 Costs and Benefits of the VSAM File Organization

As was the case for all of the preceding file organizations, VSAM files have both advantages and disadvantages. It is necessary to understand what these are in order to be able to successfully choose which file type is correct for any given application. Also refer to Table 14–1 on p. 390 to see how VSAM compares against the other file organizations previously discussed.

Costs
- VSAM files have variable WRITE performance since a split could occur at any point during the insertion of the new record.
- The size of the file is larger than similar file organizations, since VSAM can take advantage of distributed free space within the file.
- VSAM does not allow files to have duplicate key values.

Benefits
- VSAM files have no overflow areas.
- When the index structure is walked to locate a specific user data record, the exact control interval that contains the data record is always located.
- VSAM has consistent and predictable random access performance.
- VSAM sequential performance is very good and compares favorably with the performance gotten out of sequentially reading a sequential file.

14.6.4 Mainframe versus Microcomputers

As we proceed to more complicated and detailed file types, the end result is increased memory and disk space requirements. Also, performance is decreased because of the additional processing involved. Therefore, VSAM file organizations will have difficulty being implemented on many micros *unless* the functionality is reduced.

On larger machines, an integrated access method system has many benefits, such as a standardized interface and ease of use. Also, larger machines have the increased horsepower to process the additional functionality.

14.7 IMPLEMENTATION REQUIREMENTS

The file structure requirements are almost identical to the INDEXED file organization. However, we now have gone a step further by forcing the data records to be maintained in order by ascending key value. Therefore, the potential for block splitting has now rippled down to the level 0 primary data area.

If we conceptually take the structures defined for INDEXED files and link the data blocks together, we would have a VSAM-like structure. There are, of course, implementation differences, but the concepts are roughly the same. Thus, for the

TABLE 14–1: COMPARISON OF VSAM FILE CAPABILITIES

	Sequential Files	Relative Files	Direct Files	ISAM Files	Indexed Files	VSAM Files
Functionality						
READ – Sequential	Y	Y	N	Y	Y	Y
– Random	N	Y	Y	Y	Y	Y
WRITE – Sequential	Y	Y	N	N	N	Y
– Random	N	Y	Y	Y	Y	Y
UPDATE – In place	N	Y	Y	Y	Y	Y
– with length change	N	Y	Y	Y	Y	Y
DELETE – logical	Y	Y	Y	Y	Y	Y
– physical	N	N	Y	Y	—	Y
READ_NEXT	Y	Y	N	Y	Y	Y
Single-key Retrieval	—	Y	Y	Y	Y	Y
Unique key Required	—	Y	Y	Y	Y	Y
Performance						
READ_NEXT–one record	H	L-H	—	M-H	M-H	H
–entire file	H	L-H	—	M-H	M-H	H
READ one record	—	H	L-H	L-M	L-M	L-M
WRITE one record	H	H	L-H	L-M	L-M	L-M
#I/O's to READ record	0-1	0-1	0-N	0-N	0-N	0-N
#I/O's to WRITE record	0-2	0-2	0-N	0-N	0-N	0-N
Dependent upon order records get written into file?	N	N	N	Y	N	N
Costs						
File Space Utilization	H	L-H	H	M	M	L-M
Devices Supported: Disk	Y	Y	Y	Y	Y	Y
Tape	Y	N	N	N	N	N
Other	Y	N	N	N	N	N
Risk of Data Loss	L	L	L-M	L-M	L-M	L-M
File Needs frequent Re-Organization	N	N	Y	Y	N	N
Overflow Areas Required	N	N	Y	Y	N	N
#Index records at level 1	—	—	—	1/track	1/UDR	1/control interval

purposes of this book, we will leave them as being similar, but not identical. The important point here is to understand how to build a flexible index structure, such as VSAM's, not to know it at the bit and byte level.

14.7.1 File Header

The VSAM catalog is roughly equivalent to what we have generically called the file header. Simply put, the VSAM catalog contains the file attributes and other information required to allow VSAM to successfully process the file in the future. The catalog/file header contains the following kinds of information:

- All key definition information
- Size and locations of the control areas
- Statistics, such as the number of record insertions and number of splits

It is important to understand that no matter what name is used or who implements a particular product, the information we have discussed must be maintained somewhere. It could be in a VSAM catalog, a file header, or even an expanded entry in the user's directory. However, it does not matter where it is or what it is called. What is important is that the information be kept somewhere and that it always be kept in a standard location on the disk. Then it can always be found and the attributes read.

The file control block, key descriptor block, and the file header block discussed in Chapter 12 reflect the data needed to support a VSAM-like file capability. Indeed, if we take those definitions and add the following fields, we could support this new access method:

- File organization = VSAM
- Fill percentage

The latter field allows the user to specify how much of a block or control interval is to be filled when the file is populated with data records. Effectively, it allows the user to distribute free space throughout the file that can be used at a later time. This, in turn, can cut down on the number of splits that are needed, thus improving overall performance.

14.8 SUMMARY

We have just completed a discussion of one of the more powerful file organizations short of a full-blown data base management system. We learned how VSAM managed to design a structure that solved the overflow problems of ISAM and the sequential processing performance issues of indexed files. In addition, we learned about how an access method can artificially subdivide a file structure, with control intervals, control areas, and index sets, to help it manage both the space utilization problem and the performance problem.

In summary, VSAM and similar file organizations are a blend of a variety of old file structures that are pieced together in new ways to solve some of the ever-present problems with performance and time.

KEY WORDS

Catalog   Index set
Control area   Key sequenced data set
Control interval   Mass-insert mode
Control interval splitting   Sequence set
Distributed free space

SUPPLEMENTAL REFERENCES

1. Keehn, D. G., and J. O. Lacy, "VSAM Data Set Design Parameters." *IBM Systems Journal,* Vol. 13, No. 3, 1974, pp. 186–212. This is an excellent article on the design and performance issues of VSAM. It contains pictures, graphs, and formulas to back up its design.

2. Martin, James, *Computer Data-Base Organization,* 2nd ed. Englewood Cliffs, N.J.: Prentice-Hall, Inc., 1975, pp. 361–374. There is a brief discussion of VSAM here. The major advantage of this description of VSAM is Martin's excellent use of ISAM and VSAM pictures to convey how the record processing differs between them.

3. Schwenk, Ulrich, *VSAM Primer and Reference.* Santa Teresa, Calif.: IBM World Trade Systems Centers, 1979, No. G320-5774-01. This is a very good blend of reference book material and a beginning primer to VSAM. It contains a wide range of information, figures, and control structures of VSAM. Overall, it is a very readable manual.

4. Wagner, P. P., "Indexing Design Considerations." *IBM Systems Journal,* Vol. 12, No. 4, 1973, pp. 351–367. This is an excellent article on the design and performance issues of index structures. In particular, the VSAM indexed file is discussed in some detail. Also included in this article is a discussion on key compression techniques.

EXERCISES

1. An I/O error occurs that completely destroys the file header of a VSAM payroll file the night before the paychecks are to be distributed. Is it possible to write a program to retrieve all the valid data records and write them to a identically defined new file, or will the employees have a payless payday? Explain why or why not.

2. What is the difference between a *sequence set,* a *control interval,* and a *control area?*

3. In ISAM, when more space is needed for a user data record, it is added into the file's overflow area. Describe two ways in which VSAM processes user data records that do not fit in the block in the file where they belong.

4. Under what conditions should a user allocate distributed free space of 50% filled? When should the file be filled 100% (i.e., no distributed free space)?

5. Describe, in detail, the steps of the algorithm to walk down the index set and then to randomly read a specific user data record. Be sure to count the number of actual I/O operations required to do all this processing.

6. What information would you need about a VSAM-like file structure for you to determine that a file reorganization should now be done? Explain your decision.
7. Why is "mass insert" faster than normal WRITE inserts?
8. Design the mass-insert algorithm.
9. How many I/O buffers are needed to maximize performance and yet minimize space taken out of main memory?
10. What changes would you recommend be made to improve the VSAM-like access method discussed in this chapter? Justify your changes.

PROGRAMMING EXERCISES

1. Design and implement an algorithm to insert records into, as well as to split, index blocks and primary data area blocks. This will simulate a "VSAM-like" file structure and the subsequent control area split.
2. Design and implement the random READ operation to retrieve data records added into the file built by the program in Programming Exercise 1.

15

Multikey Indexed Files

CHAPTER OBJECTIVES

When you complete this chapter, you will be able to:

- Understand in detail the design and implementation of multiple keys
- Understand the costs and trade-offs in using multiple keys to access data records
- Understand how to select keys properly for optimal functionality and performance
- Describe the impact on performance when users change key values within data records

15.1 OVERVIEW

Up to this point in this book we have discussed a variety of access methods. Each had its benefits as well as a list of drawbacks. However, given any particular access method, we always implicitly assumed that the user's data records could be accessed by only *one* key. For example, an employee record could be accessed by the employee-number key. However, what if, in addition to the employee number, we wanted to access the same records in the same file by employee last name or years of service or skill set? When the records in a file need to be accessed by more than one key type, we must create a *multikey* file (see Figure 15–0).

In this chapter we discuss how this is done. The multikey functionality is not without considerable cost. However, if the need is there, the capability can become

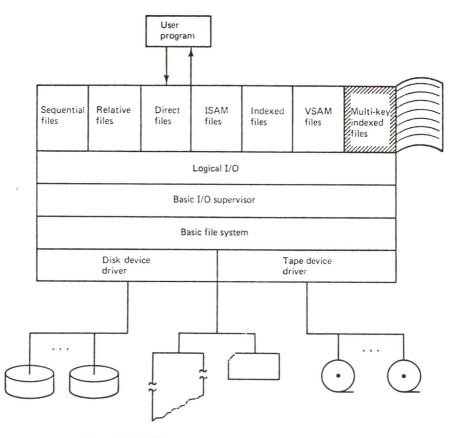

Figure 15-0   File system: multikey indexed access method.

a very powerful tool for the user. Let us now proceed to the design of a multikey INDEXED structure, while maintaining an outlook for ways in which to minimize the costs and maximize the benefits.

15.2 FILE DESIGN CONSIDERATIONS

First, let us standardize on the terminology that will be used. *The index whose index records are sorted in the same key sequence as the user's data records is called the primary index.* This is also the index in which the data records are inserted into the file. *The key represented by the primary index is called the primary key.*

All other indexes, except the primary index, are called alternate indexes or secondary indexes. In a similar manner, *the keys are known as the alternate keys or secondary keys.* Theoretically, there can be an unlimited number of alternate keys. Most products arbitrarily allow the definition of 255 or 256 alternate keys. This number usually comes from the use of a one-byte field to hold the number of the alternate key, not by some mysterious technical reason. In fact, since the performance of a system will degrade rapidly as the number of alternate keys being used grows, the limit of 255 or 256 is really a theoretical design limitation. The logical or reasonable limit is considerably smaller, on the order of a dozen or fewer keys.

If we have multiple keys, how many copies of the user's data records must we have in the file? Must there be one copy of the user's data for each key defined, or can we get away with less, or ideally even just maintain one copy of the data? These are some of the critical design issues that we will now investigate.

15.2.1 File Structure

In an indexed file, there are two critical elements in the structure. First there is the index, which provides the user with a vehicle to randomly access any user data record in the entire file. The second major element is the primary data area, which organizes the user's data in a very specific manner. The key point, then, is that *the index is separate from the data area*.

Why is a separate index so important? Because *if* the purpose of the index is to provide the capability of randomly accessing the data records in the file, *then* if there is one index, or many indexes, it does not matter. The user data records remain the same no matter how many indexes point into it. Thus we should be able to design a multikey index file by simply constructing one or more indexes that contain pointers into the primary data area.

How many copies of the user's data must we keep? It is absolutely critical that there be one and only one copy of the data records. Why? If there are multiple copies of the same data records, which copy is the correct one? What happens if the system crashes? How can we guarantee that all copies are absolutely identical? Each of these questions has a major impact on the performance of the access method and on maintaining the integrity of the user's data. The most straightforward method to answer these questions is to have only one copy of the user's data records. This not only solves the problems mentioned above, but it is also easy to implement. If indexes can be built that contain pointers to the data records, it does not matter whether there is one index with pointers, or many indexes pointing to the same data.

In summary, we must maintain one and only one copy of the user's data records. Also, we can construct one or more indexes that contain pointers to the specific data records. Thus, by referring to Figure 15-0, we can visualize a high-level view of what a multikey or multi-index file might look like.

How can we design these other indexes? To understand what some of the design criteria must be, let us examine the design of the primary index structure from a somewhat different point of view than was taken previously.

In each level of the index structure there exist at least two index records. These index records, other than at level 1, contain the highest possible key value of the block being pointed to by the index record. This key value is independent of the number of index records contained in that target block. Thus, at index levels 2 and above, there is one index record per index block at the next lower level.

At level 1 there is one index record per block in the primary data area of the file. This is again independent of the actual number of user data records that may currently exist in that target block. Thus we can observe that all levels of the index are *nondense*. In other words, there is one record pointing to a container of many records at the next lower level.

We can therefore conclude that it would be impossible to design an alternate index in an identical fashion. Why? Because, the primary data area records are in sequence by the primary key, not the alternate key. For example (see Figure 15–1), if the primary key was last-name, and the first alternate was social-security-number, the ordering of the records in the primary data area is not the same as is needed for the alternate index. Thus the alternate index cannot be constructed by using a single index record to point to a range of data records.

How, then, can we design the alternate indexes? What we need in a design is a structure in which there is *one index record in level 1 of the index, pointing to each individual user data record* instead of a range of data records (i.e., we have a dense index). We have already discussed a file structure in which there was one index record, at level 1 for every user data record in the primary data area. It is called the indexed file structure.

What we need to support multiple indexes, then, is a combination of structures which together provide the capability desired. Thus the overall design of a multikey Indexed file is shown in Figure 15–1. Next, we will proceed through the design and implementation of this file structure by walking through the various operations and structures of the file.

15.2.2 Record Addressing Algorithms

As was the case for VSAM, the user has been provided with the capability of performing either sequential or random access to the data records within the file. The complication with multikey Indexed files has to deal with *which key* or index is the one that should be used for a given operation. Therefore, with each record operation, there is an associated index number that tells the access method which index structure to use for the successful processing of the request. For example, assume that a user wants to randomly access records via social security numbers. Which key is the social security number? From the point of view of the access method, any index could be represented by social security number. Therefore, when the user makes a request, the identity of which index on which to perform the operation is also provided.

Index tree walking.   In ISAM, INDEXED, or single-key VSAM, the access method knew exactly where to look for a user data record because there was only one key and one index in the file. When we extend that to include files that can have multiple keys and thus multiple indexes, how can the access method know which index to walk down when the user says "here's a key, go find the record?"

In reality, only the user making the record request knows what kind of key is being passed to the access method. Therefore, it is up to the user to explicitly specify which index the access method should use in order to locate the target record.

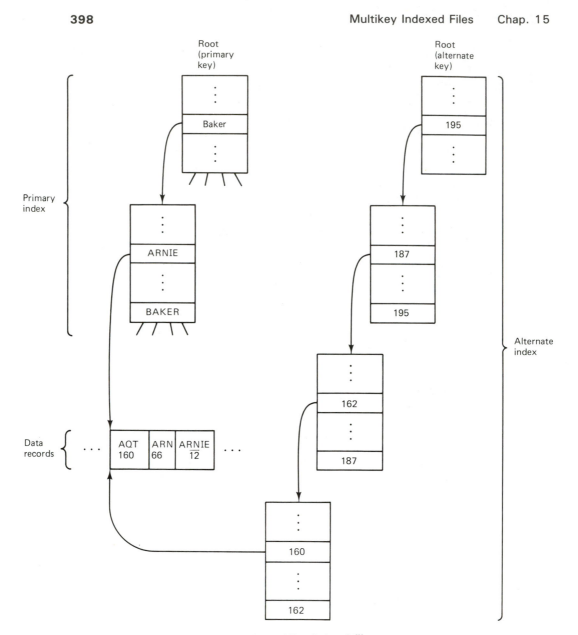

Figure 15-1 Multikey indexed file.

In any case, the technique of walking down the index structure will be the same no matter which index is finally chosen. Every time the access method walks down an index it must stop at the level 1 index block, which contains a pointer to where the target record resides in the file. Since there is only one index record per block, level 1 of the primary index must be *nondense*. Similarly, level 1 of each alternate index must be *dense*, since there is one index record for each and every data record in the primary data area of the file.

Sequential processing.   One of the key benefits of the "VSAM-like" file organizations is that sequential processing is relatively fast. This is really true only on the primary index, in which all the data records in the control intervals are physically in sequence by primary key values. On alternate indexes, sequential performance is possible, but not as fast.

Since the alternate indexes are similar to the INDEXED type file organization, we can conclude that sequential processing is possible because the level 1 index records are in sequence by that alternate key. Note that *the index records, not the data records, are in sequence in the alternate indexes.* What this means is that to sequentially process all the records in an alternate index, we must walk through the index records at level 1. Therefore, there will always be one additional I/O operation required than is required in the primary index. In other words, in the primary index, once we start going through the data records in level 0 of the structure, we do not need to refer to the index again. In an alternate index, the level 1 index must always be referenced in order to get the pointer to the next record (see Figure 15–2).

15.2.3 File Attributes

For a multikey file organization, file attributes, in particular key attribute definitions, are critical, because what and how many keys get defined will have a significant effect on the performance and usability of the overall system.

File organization.   The file must be declared as a "multikey indexed file," which is really a standard indexed file which has multiple-key definitions.

File size.   The amount of space to be allocated for the file should be calculated and declared when the file is being created. The reason for this is that the overall performance of the access method will be improved if we can minimize the number of times the file must be implicitly extended in order to successfully complete an operation.

The critical difference between single-key VSAM and multiple-key indexed files is that the file size that must be calculated must also include all the overhead for each of the declared index structures.

The trade-off here is between user-visible performance and optimal space utilization on the disk. If we were to make optimal use of disk space, we should allocate the bare minimum and let the file extend strictly on an as-needed basis. A variation of this might be reasonable for floppy-based microcomputer systems because disk space is at a much greater premium there. On the other hand, the result of doing this will be poor performance and responsiveness.

Alternatively, we can allocate the amount of space needed, and if it is too high just waste, or not use, the space. If this approach is taken, the estimation should

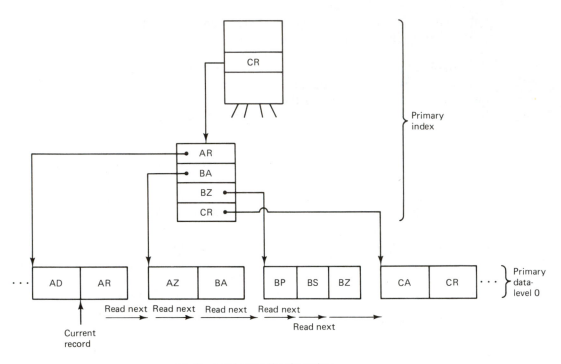

(a) Sequential access via primary key

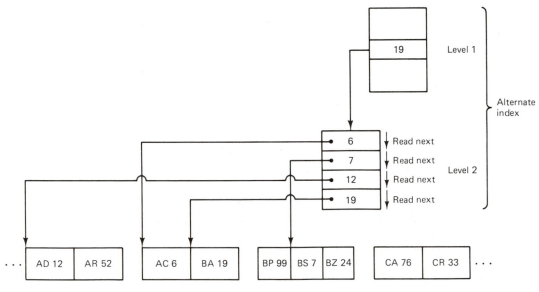

(b) Sequential access via alternate key

Figure 15-2 Sequential access in multikey file.

be on the high side (i.e., overestimate the projected number), so that if the original number turns out to be low, we can still minimize the number of implicit file extensions. In this manner we can provide the best possible performance at the potential cost of disk space.

Key position and key size.   This definition is no different from that required for the ISAM, indexed, or single-key VSAM file organizations. However, what is different is that we can now specify the definition of more than one key (see Figure 15–3). This is also a very critical choice that must be made. When we discuss the record operations, we shall see that the performance of some of them, WRITE and UPDATE in particular, can be reasonably responsive or absolutely unacceptably slow. One of the key determinants is the *number of keys* that must be manipulated to accomplish what appears to be a simple WRITE or UPDATE request from the user.

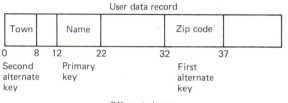

Key definitions:

Key/index	Location, in bytes, of key value
Primary	12–21
First alternate	32–36
Second alternate	0–7

Figure 15–3 Multiple keys in a user data record.

In the past, we selected a key size and location and perhaps a key data type. This is no longer enough information to allow the multikey indexed access method to successfully CREATE the desired file. The missing piece of information is the definition of which *index* the key size, location, and data type belong to. Previously, the index was implicitly defined as the primary index. Therefore, we never took the opportunity to define which index the parameters were being defined for. Now, however, it is mandatory that together with the key descriptions, the access method also be told for which index these declarations are being made.

Key attributes.   Keys themselves can have very specific attributes. In particular, keys can be allowed to be modified or even to duplicate within a file. On the other hand, both those attributes could be disallowed. Following is a discussion on each of these attributes and how they each affect the processing that needs to be performed.

Records with Duplicate Key Values.   In a multikey indexed file structure, the capability exists to allow more than one data record to be placed into the file with a key value that already exists. In this situation we say that the file organization allows *duplicate records* to be processed (see Figure 15-4). Most file types either totally disallow this feature, or at best make it an option selectable by the user.

   If we assume that the user chose the capability of having multiple records in the file with the same key value, how can the access method correctly process them? When a user requests a record with a particular key value, what if more than one record exists that corresponds to that search criterion? In what order should we insert a record when other records exist with the same key value. For example, should we add the new record at the end of the "list" or insert it first in the file?

   First, there may be a user-selectable option to dictate the correct insertion ordering algorithm. If not, COBOL requires that duplicates be inserted in a FIFO (i.e., first-in, first-out) manner. By convention, this could be the standard default.

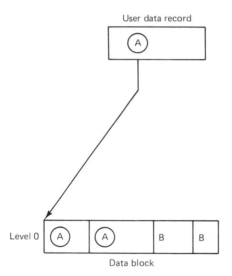

Figure 15-4 Records with duplicate keys allowed.

   Second, how can the records be read? Since a random READ operation specifies key value, which record will be retrieved? In every case, a random READ will return to the user the *first* record it finds with a matching key field no matter how many other matching records may exist in the file. Thus 10,000 random READs of a particular key value will *always* return the *first record* found that matches the key value. Thus how can we get access to the other duplicate records?

   Once we have read the first record in a chain of duplicate records, we have established a current record pointer. To read all the other duplicate records we need only perform READ_NEXT requests to sequentially go through all the records with duplicate keys. It is then the responsibility of the user's program to determine when the end of the duplicate chain has been reached.

   As can be gleaned from the discussion above, the processing of inserting records into a multikey indexed file can range from being very quick and dirty to quite long and requiring multiple I/O operations. This is the primary area in which a multikey index file pays the price, so to speak. READ performance is consistent and relatively fast in both access modes. However, the WRITE performance is variable, as possibly much restructuring of the file has to take place.

Keys Can/Cannot Be Changed.   Another characteristic of key fields is whether or not the field itself is to be allowed to change. In other words, can a user change the value of a key during an UPDATE operation? The answer is probably yes, especially in alternate indexes.

Both VSAM and COBOL require that the primary key be unique and cannot be changed. However, alternate keys are a completely different situation. For example, what if a person moved from Lexington to Concord. If "town" was as alternate key, it is reasonable that it be allowed to change to compensate for people moving into and out of various towns. Also, from this example it should be clear that keys should be allowed to duplicate, since there could be many people living in a town, and so on.

15.3 FILE OPERATIONS

The file operations for multikey indexed are the same as for VSAM. The difference is that now they either take significantly more time to process (e.g., CREATE) or must have an additional "index" parameter to tell on which index to perform the request (e.g., READ).

15.3.1 CREATE File

All of the functions that can be performed on a single-key indexed file must also be performed here. However, *during a CREATE operation for multikey indexed, all the indexes for the file must be built and initialized.* Thus it is similar to the VSAM CREATE for the primary key, plus the CREATE of the alternate indexes. Depending on the number of alternate indexes declared by the user, the time it takes to build a new multikey indexed file will vary considerably. However, in no case will it ever be as fast as the single-key VSAM CREATE case.

15.3.2 OPEN File

The purpose of the OPEN file request is the same regardless of file organization. during an OPEN, the file attributes are read from the disk into one of several control blocks used to correctly keep track of the processing against the file. In addition, the I/O buffers are allocated.

It is the responsibility of the OPEN processing programs to ensure that all of the required file attributes are correctly read and copied into one of the system control blocks. Not all information is required from the file's header block. However, enough data must be made resident so that the standard processing need not have to refer to the disk to do anything.

15.3.3 CLOSE File

There is no change in the CLOSE operation either. Here the primary function is to write out any dirty I/O buffers that have not yet been written out to disk. In addition, the I/O buffer space in main memory is deallocated, as are the internal control block used to process the file.

15.4 RECORD OPERATIONS

User data records in a multikey indexed file can be sequentially or randomly accessed via any index structure. The essential point for the record operations is that we must now specify which key is to be used to access the record.

Record access modes.   As was the case with ISAM and VSAM, user data records can be accessed in two modes, sequentially and randomly by key value. However, what multikey indexed files have is accessing capability on more than one index. In fact, a user could access data records sequentially or randomly on every index that is defined in the file.

Record currency.   Record currency is still vital to the successful processing of the data records within a multikey indexed file. However, we now have *two different record pointers* that need to be kept track of to process correctly.

First, within the primary index structure, the current record pointer references the user data record itself. Since the data records are maintained physically in sequence by ascending primary key value, it is a simple matter to locate the next record in the file.

Second, within the alternate indices, a pointer to the user's data record would serve no useful purpose. This is because the records in the alternate indexes are maintained in a different sequence than they are maintained within the primary index. Therefore, to process records out of the alternate indices correctly, it is necessary to have the current record pointer reference the level 1 index records. There is one index record per data record referenced by that index. Thus if the access method can remember, via the current record pointer, the last index record accessed in order to get to the current data record, it can easily pick up and find the next data record in that index structure.

15.4.1 POSITION to Record

The POSITION operation is the most complicated of the record operations. This is because it or its functionality must be executed in many different operations in order to reposition to the correct record in the file. Given the declaration of which index should be used for a specific operation, the POSITION operation will function as it did in the case of VSAM or indexed files.

Note that the operation is identical to the VSAM variant, but with the additional requirement of *which key* is to be used to perform this request. *In the alternate index(es), if a matching key value is not found in the level 1 index set, the data record does not exist in the file.* On the other hand, in the primary index, we only have a pointer to the control interval in which the record would exist if it was actually in the file. Thus the presence or absence of a record can usually be detected somewhat faster in an alternate index than in the primary index.

15.4.2 READ Record

The READ operation works on any of the indexes defined for the file. The READ operation will randomly access any data record in the file from the specified index.

Given the index on which the processing is to be done, the READ algorithm simply walks down that specific index tree until it gets to the index record that points to the location of the data record. Thus the performance can be seen as follows:

$$t_{READ} = t_{POSITION} + t_{transfer\ data\ to\ user\ buffer}$$

Again, the performance of the READ operation is completely dependent on the time it takes to POSITION to the requested data record. The performance is consistent across all keys because the file will get dynamically reorganized whenever it is necessary.

15.4.3 READ_NEXT Record

The READ_NEXT operation works identically to the single-key VSAM variant. However, since the READ_NEXT operation works off the current record pointer, which was set after the last input operation, the sequential access can be from within any index.

Note that there is no indication which index is to be used to access the next data record in the file. This information is retrieved from the current record pointer field maintained by the access method in order to successfully process the data records in the file. Thus, based on the last setting of the current record pointer, the index specification for the READ_NEXT has already been defined.

The performance of the READ_NEXT will vary depending on whether or not the access is via the primary index or an alternate index. In the latter case, we must always go back to the level 1 index set to get the pointer to the next record. We can improve on the overall performance here by allocating multiple I/O buffers in main memory. We can then save more of the level 1 index records in main memory so that we do not need to reaccess the disk as much. However, note that the user data records in an alternate index will not be in the same order as in the primary index, so that there will still be much disk I/O activity required to read in the control interval that contains the record.

15.4.4 WRITE Record

The most difficult and complex operation in any file organization is the WRITE operation, since the data record must be inserted into the file in such a way that it can be successfully retrieved. In multikey INDEXED, the WRITE takes this level of complexity to an extreme.

Note that there is no mention of which index to use in order to add this data record into the file. Why is this? The answer lies in the fact that *user data records are always inserted into the file by the primary key*. It does not matter how many keys exist in the data record. The data records always go into the file via the primary key value. If we think about that, we can realize that this is required because the primary key is defined to be the index in which the data are ordered in the same sequence as the index records. This can only be true in the index in which the data are actually inserted into the file, or in other words, the primary index.

The steps that must be taken to add a record into a multikey indexed file are as follows:

1. Insert the data record into the primary index, just as was done in the VSAM case.
2. For *each* alternate index, walk down that index tree and insert an index record in level 1 pointing to the data record.

What is perhaps not obvious from the foregoing sequence of steps is the amount of time it takes to perform those tasks. For example, to insert an index record in every alternate index, the access method must walk down each index tree, from its root block, to find the location in which to insert the index record pointer. Thus if there were 10 alternate indexes, each of the same index depth of five levels, there must be 50 (count them!) I/O operations just to position to the level 1 of each index. In addition, there must be five additional I/O operations to rewrite the new index record block back into the file. Thus there would be a minimum of 55 I/O operations just to insert the new data record pointers into the alternate indexes. This assumes that no block splitting is needed. If block splits occur, it is in addition to the 55 I/O operations. Add back the I/O to insert the data record into the primary control interval and you can end up with 60 plus I/O operations being performed simply to insert a new record into the file. This is significantly slower than any other WRITE operation discussed thus far in this book.

How long must a user data record be, assuming that the file has variable-length records? The data record is always inserted into the file based on the value of the primary key. Thus it is reasonable to assume that at a minimum, the data record must be at least long enough to hold the entire primary key field. Any length that does not include the entire primary key field results in an invalid key and thus the data record cannot be added into the file (see Figure 15–5a).

How long must a record be if the file has alternate keys? (See Figure 15–5b.) The critical key is the primary key field; since the record is added into the file by that field, the alternate key fields are not mandatory. If a record does not contain

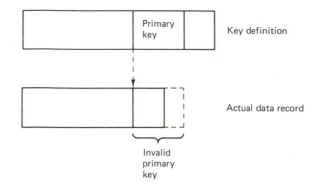

(a) Record not long enough to hold entire primary key

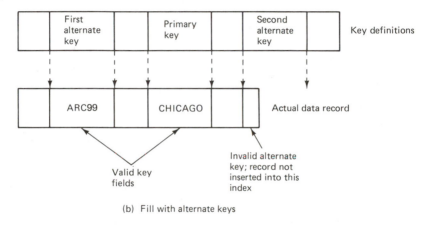

(b) Fill with alternate keys

Figure 15-5   Keys versus record lengths.

an entire key field, a record pointer is *not* inserted into that alternate index. For example, a person could take a job and be added to that company's payroll, yet a valid employee number might not yet exist. Thus that field could not be included in the data record.

There are two reasons for the slowness of the multi-index WRITE operation. First, data record must not only be inserted into the primary index, but index record pointers must also be inserted into every alternate index. Second, by performing this much I/O, it is likely that there will be considerable block or control interval splits occurring, which will slow it down even more.

The WRITE operation cost is high in terms of the amount of time it takes to insert new records into the file. However, once the data record has been added into the file, all other operations, with the possible exception of some special cases of UPDATE, will perform quickly and competitively with other file organizations.

There are several exception conditions that can occur when the file system attempts to write a new record into a multikey index file. First, what if one of the alternate key fields is filled with the null key character? The purpose of the null key value is to allow the user to state to the file system: "Don't add this key into the file." Thus for each key that is filled with the null key value, the file system simply skips over that key and does nothing.

A second condition that can arise is when a record is inserted into the file and a record with a duplicate key value already exists in the file. If *no duplicates are allowed,* the file attribute is set; then the file system has no choice but to reject this WRITE request. Sometimes this is easier said than done. What if 19 keys have already been successfully added into the various indexes for this data record, and on the twentieth and last key a duplicate record condition is discovered? Since this is invalid, *all alternate index records that were updated to point to this new record must be removed from each index.* In other words, everything done so far must be completely undone. This is extremely time consuming and leads to very poor response times.

15.4.5 UPDATE Record

The UPDATE operation performs in the same manner as was described for the VSAM. However, there are some important additional steps that must be considered due to the fact that multiple indexes exist within the file. Like the WRITE, there is no key or index specified by which to perform the operation. This is because the UPDATE operation always UPDATEs the data record identified by the current record pointer. Thus the processing will take place just as described in Chapter 14 as long as no alternate key values have been changed.

This last point is absolutely critical. If no keys were changed by the user, and we have prohibited the user from changing the primary key, the alternate index record pointers can remain the same. This is because the level 1 alternate index record consists of the key value and a block number containing the user data record with that specific key value. In other words, if the alternate key value in the data record has not been changed, the index records that already exist in the alternate indexes will remain valid.

In previous file organizations, we never considered the possibility that the key(s) might be changed by the UPDATE performed by the user. Now, however, there is a real probability that the alternate key values by which the record was originally inserted into the index will be modified by the user. For example, if one of the alternate indexes is defined to be zip codes, then whenever a person moves to another town, the zip code must be changed within the file.

The processing steps must be performed if the data record is moved, as might be the case for block splits or if an alternate key value is changed, are described below:

1. If the user data record increased in size after being modified by the user such that it no longer fits in the same block, a block split must occur. All data records that get moved because of the split must have their alternate index record pointers changed to reflect the new position of the data record in the file.

2. If the user modifies any alternate key value in the data record, then for each

key changed, the following must occur. First, the old index record must be deleted, since the key value is no longer valid (i.e., it has changed). Second, a new index record must reinserted into that alternate index by the new value of that key in the data record. Note that to accomplish this work, the alternate index must be transversed completely *twice* (i.e., once to delete the old index record and once to insert a new index record). Furthermore, this same kind of processing must occur for every alternate key value that is changed by the user.

It might be argued that the user should not make these kinds of changes. However, this is unreasonable, because the user should be able to do whatever is required to get the job done. What should occur, however, is that user's should be made aware of the cost of changing keys and defining large numbers of indexes. Define what is required by the application, not what might be needed only occasionally.

As was the case with the WRITE command, an UPDATE can run into a variety of problems, such as an invalid key change or a duplicate key encountered in an index. It is up to the file system to ensure that only those data records that are completely correct are added to the file.

15.4.6 DELETE Record

The DELETE operation is identical to that described for VSAM. The data record to be deleted is the one identified by the current record pointer. With multiple indexes, we have several choices as to how to delete a record. Should we simply mark the data record as being deleted and not change any index pointers? Or should we walk down each index and delete those index records also?

The fastest method is to mark the data record as being deleted and not touch the alternate indexes at all. There are two potential penalties with this method. First, if access is by an alternate index, we will find the associated index record and then try and get the data record. Only after reading the control interval will we discover that the record has been deleted. Thus an additional I/O operation must be performed that might have been avoided.

Second, by only flagging the data record as being deleted, we are wasting space. If another data record is to be added to that control interval and there is not enough space because the deleted record is still there, we could end up splitting the control interval unnecessarily. On the other hand, by not physically removing all remnants of the data record's existence, we can return to the calling program significantly sooner than would otherwise be possible.

If, however, we took the time to clean up the file, we would need not only to rewrite the original control interval with the deleted record now gone, but also rewalk all alternate indexes and remove all index records referencing that specific data record. The amount of time it would take to accomplish this completely would be considerable. Is it worth it? It really depends on the user's application and whether it is time sensitive or space constrained.

Alternatively, we can remove the alternate index records only as we access them in the future. When we find that the data record referenced was actually deleted, we could then remove that specific alternate index entry. Thus, over time, the alternate indexes would gradually be cleaned up.

15.5 PERFORMANCE CONSIDERATIONS

Since most of the processing time in a multikey indexed file is spent transversing one of the indexes, any real gains in performance must improve the tree-walking overhead. One of the ways in which this can be accomplished is to have the various indexes allocated to a fixed-head disk while leaving the data on the slower moving-head disks. What this does is to cut the SEEK time down to almost zero as the tree structure is transversed. Therefore, this should have an immediate impact on performance.

Alternatively, performance can be improved specifically by the user, by only defining those alternate indexes that are required to get the job done. If the user is not sensitized to the performance impact of defining multiple indexes, indexes might be defined only because "someday" it might be needed. Users must only allocate and define those alternate indexes that are needed, really needed, not just wanted. For example, by defining five alternate keys instead of 10, the user can double the performance and responsiveness of the system without changing a single line of code.

The other major impact on performance is the depth of each index structure. This is simply the level of the root block plus one. If the number of levels is high, it will take a relatively long time to read each index block on that path in order to reach the target user data record. Thus the level of the root is an indication of the number of I/O operations that must be performed to read a record in the file. If the level is high, the number of blocks to be read is high and performance is low.

15.5.1 File Population Techniques

To add data records into a multikey indexed file, it is necessary to effectively add the data record to each of the applicable indexes. Since the data records are inserted in the same sequence as the primary index, presort the user's data records and use the mass-insert option to build a more optimized file structure. This is similar to the situation we dealt with in the case of VSAM files.

However, the real question is whether anything can be done to improve the performance within the alternate index structures. Special utility software can be written to improve performance somewhat, but typically it will always take a considerable amount of time, since each index must be transversed for every data record added into the file.

Alternatively, with mass insert, the file system could just create the primary index and write out the data records but not create an alternate index. However, as this was being done, the file system could create a series of temporary files, one per alternate index, which contained the following information per data record:

- Alternate key value

- Location of the data record in the file
- Alternate index number, to identify in which index this record was to be inserted

With these files the file system could create the entire file structure. Basically, after the primary index and the data records have been added to the file, the file system need only sort each of these temporary files by their key values. Then it could simply build each alternate index from the records in these temporary files. Overall performance should improve greatly, since each index is built optimally and only making a single transversal of each index structure.

15.5.2 File Reorganization

Since the multikey indexed files perform dynamic file restructuring, file reorganizations will not be needed nearly as often as, say, an ISAM file needs them. However, file reorganizations will be required for the following reasons:

- To recover DELETEd data record space in the control intervals
- To recover space taken up by alternate index records which reference deleted data records
- To rebuild the file in a more optimal manner by redefining one of the key file attributes which dictate how the file will be built when it is initially created
- To reduce the number of keys defined for the file, or to try to reduce the depth of the index

In any of these cases, what is being done is that a "more optimal" file is being built. It is not a case, like ISAM's, in which the performance degrades to the point of unacceptability and the file must therefore be reorganized. A multikey indexed file is always optimally built within the constraints of the file's attributes.

15.6 DESIGN TRADE-OFFS

There are several major areas in the design and implementation of a VSAM-like file organization that can have a major impact on performance. First, how many alternate indexes will the access method allow the user to define? The user should very carefully select the number of alternate indexes that will *really* be needed. For performance reasons, the logical limit that the user can sustain is probably on the order of 10 to 15 alternate keys, or less.

Second, should the access method allow data records to increase in length during an UPDATE operation? If this is allowed, further block splitting might occur. On the other hand, the user should not be restricted to fixed-length records.

Third, what policy is to be implemented for DELETE operations? Should the file be completely cleaned up at the time of the DELETE, or can the file be cleaned up over time on an as-needed basis? The choice may be left to the user on larger systems with large disk capacities. However, in the area of microcomputers, disk space is usually at a higher premium. Thus the complete cleanup might be better in that situation.

15.6.1 File Size Calculations

How, then, do we calculate the total file size, including all the various indexes? We can perform this calculation by doing exactly what we did in the VSAM and IN-DEXED file organization chapters. Why? Because what we have designed is a combination of the single-key VSAM structure and the indexed file structure—without the user's data records. Therefore, this calculation is performed in the following steps:

1. Estimate the number of user data records that will be in the file during the lifetime of the file (i.e., until the next file reorganization, if there is one).
2. Calculate the size of the primary index and data areas by following the step-by-step VSAM calculations described in Section 14.6.1. This is done since the primary index and data area are identical to the structure of the single-key VSAM file.
3. Calculate the size of *each alternate index* by using the indexed file algorithm described in Section 13.6.1. *These calculations should be done only for index levels 1 and above, not for the level 0 user data record area.* The reason for this distinction is that there is only one copy of the user's data records and it was accounted for in step 2.
4. Sum up the estimates from steps 2 and 3. Note: Make sure to include the estimates for every alternate index that will exist in the file.
5. This total calculated above will serve as the base estimate for the file size parameter.

When the foregoing steps have been taken, it is necessary to make one last judgment on the file size. When the total calculated file size approximates n full tracks or cylinders, it might be best to round up the allocation to whole tracks or entire cylinders. Again, this is a judgment based on how close the estimate on number of user data records is thought to be, and on how tight disk space is at the user's installation. The logic here is that if we err on the high side, we will merely further minimize the risk of time-consuming implicit file extensions. There are no magic numbers that can be provided here to dictate what should be done and when. It depends entirely on the user's application requirements and the user's computer configuration.

15.6.2 Costs versus Benefits

The costs and benefits of a multikey indexed file organization are listed below and in Table 15-1:

Costs
- Insert (i.e., WRITE) performance is relatively slow due to the incremental file reorganizations that take place via splitting.
- UPDATE and/or DELETE processing can be slow if key values change or complete cleanup is required.
- The overhead of a multiindex file structure becomes much greater, since there must be an entire index structure built for every key defined by the user.

Benefits
- The file provides the user with fast sequential processing and consistent, reasonably fast, random processing.
- The user can sequentially process data records via any index.
- No overflow areas are required.
- The file is dynamically reorganized on an as-needed basis. The need for file reorganizations is greatly diminished.

Thus we can see that there are some significant advantages and benefits to multikey indexed files. However, to achieve the highest level of performance, the user must be aware of the cost of alternate indexes and thus choose them wisely. Table 15–1 summarizes all the file organizations discussed in this book.

15.6.3 Mainframe versus Microcomputers

Multikey indexed files have tended in the past to be located primarily on minicomputers and mainframes, but usually not on micros. The reason for this is that these kinds of file structures tend to consume ever-increasing amounts of disk space. Usually, the amount of disk space available on a micro is quite limited. Thus large file structures tend to be avoided, at least for now, on microcomputers.

15.7 IMPLEMENTATION REQUIREMENTS

All of the attributes discussed in Chapter 14 are applicable here also. However, the major difference is in the Key descriptor block. Now, instead of just a single block describing one key, we have the possibility of many KDBs linked together defining all the keys in the file. The file control block and the file header block remain essentially the same, except that the FHB now has more key descriptions in it.

15.7.1 Key Descriptor Block

Since we can now support more than one key definition, the file system must link all the KDBs together from the FCB to keep track of how the file was defined. In addition, each KDB has within it the following information:

TABLE 15-1 COMPARISON OF MULTIKEY INDEXED FILE CAPABILITIES

	Sequential files	Relative files	Direct files	ISAM files	Indexed file	VSAM	Multikey indexed
			Functionality				
READ							
Sequential	Y	Y	N	Y	Y	Y	Y
Random	N	Y	Y	Y	Y	Y	Y
WRITE							
Sequential	Y	Y	N	N	N	Y	Y
Random	N	Y	Y	Y	Y	Y	Y
UPDATE							
Inplace	N	Y	Y	Y	Y	Y	Y
With length change	N	Y	Y	Y	Y	Y	Y
DELETE							
Logical	Y	Y	Y	Y	Y	Y	Y
Physical	N	N	Y	Y	—	Y	Y
READ_NEXT	Y	Y	N	Y	Y	Y	Y
Single-key retrieval	—	Y	Y	Y	Y	Y	Y
Multiple-key retrieval	—	N	N	N	N	N	Y
Unique key required	—	Y	Y	Y	Y	Y	N

414

Performance

READ_NEXT							
One record	H	L-H	—	M-H	M-H	H	H
Entire file	H	L-H	—	M-H	M-H	H	H
READ_NEXT: multiple keys	—	—	—	—	—	—	M-H
READ one record	—	H	L-H	L-M	L-M	L-M	L-H
WRITE one record	H	H	L-H	L-M	L-M	L-M	L-H
Number of I/Os to READ record	0-1	0-1	0-N	0-N	0-N	0-N	0-N
Number of I/Os to WRITE record	0-2	0-2	0-N	0-N	0-N	0-N	0-N
Depend on what order records were written into file	N	N	N	Y	N	N	N

Costs

File space utilization	H	L-H	H	M	M	L-M	L-M
Device support							
Disk	Y	Y	Y	Y	Y	Y	Y
Tape	Y	N	N	N	N	N	N
Other	Y	N	N	N	N	N	N
Risk of data loss	L	L	L-M	L-M	L-M	L-M	L-H
Files need frequent reorganization	N	N	Y	Y	Y	N	Y/N
Overflow areas required	N	N	Y	Y	Y	N	N
Number of index records at level 1							
Primary index	—	—	—	1/track	1/data record	1/control interval	1/track
Alternate index	—	—	—	—	—	—	1/user data record

Note: Y, yes; N, no; L, low; M, medium; H, high.

- The *index number* for which this key definition is to apply. This is needed so that when the user tries to READ a record in "index 5" the file system can identify which index and key definition is being requested.
- The user can specify a *null key value*. When a record is long enough to completely contain an alternate key field and the user does *not* have a value for that field, it can be filled with this null key character and the file system will skip over processing this index. For example, if a new employee has just moved into town, he may not yet have a telephone number. Thus, if telephone number was one of the keys in the file, it could be filled with the null key so that the file system would not enter anything into that index for that data record. At a later date, when the employee gets a telephone number, the data record can be updated to show the true telephone number.

Note that the *primary key* can never be *null*. This is because the data records are inserted into the file by their primary key value, and if it was null, it would not be added. The KDB definition for multikey files is shown in Table 15–2

TABLE 15–2   KEY DESCRIPTOR BLOCK: MULTIKEY FILES

Header information

Version ID
Link to next KDB

Key information

Index number	Number of the index to which these data apply (0, primary key; 1, first alternate key; . . . ;*n* last alternate key)
Key location	Offset in bytes to beginning of the key field in the data record
Key size	Length of key in bytes
Key data type	Alphanumeric or other
Null key value	Byte defined as character identifying this key as being null
Key attributes	Keys must be *unique* Keys may be *duplicated* Keys *can change* Keys *cannot change*

Level of root block
Root block number
First data block number

15.8 SUMMARY

Multikey index files are really built from the components of previous file structures that were discussed. The primary index is just like the VSAM index, which contains one index record at level 1 for each *block* in the file. Also, the index records are sorted in the same sequence as are the data records.

On the other hand, the alternate indexes are identical to the indexed file structure. Here each alternate index is in a different sequence from the way the data records are sorted in the file. However, to make up for this apparent discrepency, there is one index record, at level 1 of each alternate index, for every user data record that exists in the file.

The primary index is nondense, and the alternate index is dense. Also, no matter how many keys exist in the file, there is only one copy of the user's data records. A change was made to the record operations—they now had to explicitly (e.g., POSITION, READ) or implicitly (e.g., READ_NEXT, UPDATE, DELETE) identify which index the record operation applied to. Thus the user could then be allowed to access data records through any of the indexes defined for the file.

KEY WORDS

Alternate index   Primary key
Alternate key   Secondary index
Null key   Secondary key
Primary index

SUPPLEMENTAL REFERENCES

1. Schwenk, Ulrich, *VSAM Primer and Reference.* Santa Teresa, Calif.: IBM World Trade Systems Centers, 1979, No. G320-5774-01. This is an excellent reference and user's guide to understanding VSAM and its structures. In addition, it covers not only the single-key case, but also the multikey VSAM file structure.

EXERCISES

1. If a random READ operation is requested, without specifying which index to use (i.e., the index number was "0"), what should the file system do? Explain your answer.

2. Must an alternate index have one level 1 index record for each and every user data record in the file, or can there be fewer index records than there are data records? Explain how this could happen, if true, or alternatively, why it cannot occur.

3. When a data record is deleted, is it better to physically remove all index records pointing to the data record from all of the indexes, or is it better to mark the data record as having been deleted? Explain why the approach you select is better than the other approach.

4. Why is the user not allowed to specify, on a WRITE operation, which index is to be used for the processing?

5. What happens if the user issues the following commands?

    - POSITION to "RWEGY" in index 12
    - WRITE record (any key value)
    - READ_NEXT

    Which data record is retrieved by the READ_NEXT, and where was the record inserted in the file as a result of the WRITE?

6. Is it possible for the user to be reading sequentially through more than one index at a time (i.e., just issuing READ_NEXT commands)? Explain why or why not.

7. Explain the processing that must occur when a user issues an UPDATE that changes the value of 3 of the alternate key fields and makes a fourth alternate key field all "null key characters." How many I/O operations are required to do this?

8. Write a formula that allows a user to calculate how many I/O operations will be performed whenever an UPDATE operation is requested. Assume multiple keys and that some or all can be changed.

9. For a given block size and format, record size and format, and a variable number of keys of different sizes, produce a formula that would allow a user to predict how much space a multikey file will take up on a disk.

10. Why is the *level of the root* block of an index a critical determinant to the performance the user will experience when referencing that index?

PROGRAMMING EXERCISES

1. Design and implement the code to CREATE a two-key index file.
2. Design and implement the code to WRITE records into the file created above.

Part IV

Miscellaneous Topics

In this book we have spent a great deal of time delving into the complexities of the overall file system. In so doing, we have avoided some of the major issues surrounding data management today. It is the purpose of this section to address some of these issues, not from the vantage point of presenting a solution, but to sensitize the reader to these critical issues.

16

File System Issues

CHAPTER OBJECTIVES

When you complete this chapter, you will be able to:

- Describe the impact of multiple users *sharing* the same files simultaneously
- Understand some of the issues concerned with *distributed data processing* and files
- Understand the concept of *high availability* and how it relates to file systems
- Understand the issues surrounding *data security* and personal computers
- Understand the *incompatibilities* between programming languages and their relationship to the file system

16.1 OVERVIEW

Throughout this book we have discussed many ways of organizing and accessing data. We have also discussed the costs and benefits of each of the file organizations. However, there are a variety of major issues and topics that are really beyond the scope of this book, yet which are critical to data management in the future. The purpose of this chapter is simply to raise these topics and some associated questions in order to make them more visible. For the most part, these issues remain to be solved with "ideal" solutions, although there are rough implementations for most of them.

16.2 FILE SHARING

In all of our discussions of access methods, we have implicitly assumed that we were the only person accessing the data at any given point in time. However, with the exception of single-user microcomputers, this is a very rare occurrence at best. What are some of the issues in a multiuser environment?

16.2.1 Which User Determines the Accessibility of the Data?

In many systems, the *first* person to actually OPEN a file has the right to declare which, if any, other users can access the data in parallel with the first user. Thus we can have situations in which there are no other users allowed to access the file. In this case the first user has *exclusive access rights*. Thus all other potential users must *wait* until the first user with exclusive access has completed its processing and has relinquished control.

If the first user allows only those other users who will *read-only* but not write or update the file, we have a condition of *one writer and many readers*. Alternatively, the first user could allow other users to write, in which case we would have a file that had *multiple readers and multiple writers*. With today's large files, this is usually the condition of choice.

The access rights declared by the first user program to access the file last until all the users have deaccessed and closed the file. Then the next person to open the file can again specify the access rights of the file.

A perhaps more acceptable solution is to have the person who creates the file specify which users have what rights of access. Then it no longer becomes a case of who gets to the file first gains access, but that anyone who needs access can get to the file whenever necessary. There are obviously special situations in which all access must be denied, but these situations are the exception and not the rule.

Although this may seem straightforward and somewhat trivial, let us probe for a while what it really means to have multiple users writing to the file at the same time.

- How can the access method prevent two or more users from changing the same record at the same time? For example, if two user programs each access the same record with the intent of updating it, which version of the record will actually be updated?

- If the access method choses to solve its problems by having multiple locks to prevent simultaneous updates, what gets locked? At what level of granularity should locks be applied within a file? Should the entire file be locked? Is locking a single control interval or block enough or too much? What is the minimum that can be locked and still enable the access methods to know that the data integrity of the file is intact? Can we lock only individual records? If so, how can this be done?

- How can we prevent deadlock situations from occurring? For example, if process 1 has record A and wants record B, and process 2 has record B and wants record A, we have a deadlock condition. What can the access methods do to minimize the potential for deadlock? For one thing, the file system could time-out all users who have been waiting more than a preset amount of time. Although this will hurt those users, it does serve to break the log jam and potentially free up resources needed by other users.

- If there was a procedure to lock and unlock data records within the file system, how could the average high-level-language program gain access to these new features? This is an issue because not all languages have the capability of supporting nonstandard features cleanly.

If we take a heavy-handed approach, we could lock the entire file. However, this would be intolerable from a system response mode. On the other hand, by marking only user data records as being locked, we open ourselves up to some complicated solutions if we go the entire route.

16.3 DISTRIBUTED DATA PROCESSING

Given the information above, what could be done if the users accessing the file were *not* located on the same machine? In this case, what does it really mean to update a record or to add a new record? For example, it should be possible for the access methods to tell whether or not the request was from a local or remote site. Then the following questions can be asked:

- Is it possible to access data from a remote terminal? If yes, how do all the various processes in memory know who has what information?

- If multiple users are accessing the same file, which user has the most current copy of the database?

- If we expanded the file's pathname to include the following data, would it make any difference?
  —"Node" name on which the user has his or her accounts
  —"Disk name," such as drive A for the IBM PC
  —"File name" of the file
  —"Record format"

- What if two users on different computers want the same record at the same time? Who gets the record? How can the file system guarantee that UPDATE operations will not cross each other?

Given the questions above, it should be clear that this issue is very complicated and very severe. It is made even worse through the advances being made in world wide communications that allow this type of processing to occur on a regular basis.

16.4 HIGH AVAILABILTY

With more and more business people running their companies via computers, it is becoming more and more obvious that what is really needed are systems that never fail! It is possible to get this done, but the cost is somewhat nebulous.

For example, the airline industry could lose millions of dollars of revenues if the systems on which they run ever failed. Thus, given the overall importance of computers to an industry, the next major task that is waiting to be defined is how to build systems that never fail.

There are many techniques that are being used today to achieve *high availability*. Some of these approaches are listed below.

16.4.1 Log Files

The intent here is to record all changes made to a file in a log or transaction file. Then should the disk fail, we need only to back to the last version of the file and restore it. Then we need to run all the changes in the log file through a utility function to bring the state of the file back to where it was when the disk crashed.

One of the difficulties with this approach is that the process is very time consuming. If we had an airline reservation system, it is unlikely that we would tolerate the system being down as long as it could possibly take to restore all files.

16.4.2 File Redundancy

One of the more standard approaches is to duplicate the critical elements of the systems. In this case, if the data files are the critical item of interest, the file system should duplicate the critical files. If one disk should fail, the disk containing the duplicate versions could be used immediately to allow processing to continue.

This procedure requires the file system to perform all I/O *twice*, once to the master file and once to the duplicate. If the devices themselves are connected to separate controllers and channels, the I/O can take place in parallel with each other. The writing of duplicate records and files is known as *shadow writing*.

The major gain here is the speed with which the application can continue after a critical file catastrophe. However, there is a significant additional cost in doubling all disks and their controllers. This additional cost is tolerable, however, for those applications that cannot afford to be down for long periods.

16.4.3 Error Detection and Correction

Much can be gained by simply recording all errors in a system log file. If this file is periodically scanned and analyzed, and the statistics maintained in a file, the appropriate maintenance can be performed *before* a component fails. Thus this step is more one of prevention than the other step, which deals with recovery after a failure.

16.5 DATA SECURITY

With so many different users accessing so many different files, how can we, the designers of the access methods, *guarantee* the security, privacy, and integrity of the data? How can we guarantee that only those users that have the correct access privileges get into the files? Or for that matter, why worry about security?

Business must be concerned about data security because critical competitive data, if visible to other companies, could have a major detrimental impact on future company revenues and profits. Also, we need to be concerned that personnel-related data are kept private. Finally, there are legal as well as ethical reasons why data must be protected. If these laws are violated, prosecution could result.

If it is not hard to understand why data must be protected, we must ask if *all* data must be protected to the same degree. To put this another way, all data are not created equal! To illustrate, let us examine the data that a typical business might maintain.

Data can be classified into several categories, such as the following:

- Historical data
- Current data
- Projected data
- Personnal Data

Historical data relate to what has already occurred, such as last year's sales or market share 10 years ago. Although many companies protect these data as well, they do not have as much significance in many industries. For example, in the computer industry, technologies are changing so rapidly that even last year's data might be worthless. Also, knowing historical data does not allow someone to accurately predict the future, since trends and technologies do change. In summary, historical data are useful to keep, but they do not seem to have the critical competitive importance that other data might have.

Current data reflect how business is doing today. This is of value in competitive situations and thus should be highly protected. To do so, privileged access codes might be placed on these files to limit who is authorized to see these data. However, current data only provide a small snapshot of what the company is really doing. Without historical and future data it is difficult to determine how well the company is really performing. Thus current data seem to be more important than historical data for many industries.

Future data are highly critical to an organization. What they tell us is where the company is planning on going (i.e., markets, competitors, products). Thus the future well-being of the firm rests in part on these data being protected and kept within the company itself. Of the three types of data discussed so far, these data are probably the most critical to protect.

Personal data must be protected because of laws and ethics. Due to these laws, firms must go to great lengths to protect the data or face possible lawsuits. Some of the methods used are putting these data on a completely separate machine and giving access privileges only to selected persons. In any case, they are sensitive data and must be protected.

Finally, with all of the technological changes going on in the communications industry, how can the data be protected? Many firms use microwave techniques to transmit data between various buildings and company locations. Also, many data are bounced off communications satellites. Once out in the open air, it is possible to intercept the data and gain access to the information without anyone knowing that the data have been "seen" by others. What can be done? Data can be encrypted, for example, but is this *the* answer?

Another problem the file system has to deal with is what to do when a highly sensitive file is deleted. What this means is that someone else could then create a file that takes the same space as the high-security file. If the new user just reads in the blocks and prints them, all the data that had been protected throughout the lifetime of the file have suddenly been lost when the file is deleted. The file system could perhaps zero out all the blocks of a file when it gets deleted. However, this is time consuming and may well affect how performance and system responsiveness are seen by the users. An alternative could be to define a file attribute that says "zero blocks when this file is deleted."

The issues raised above are not meant to be comprehensive or even valid for all companies in all circumstances. The goal here is to sensitize everyone to the fact that not all data should, or must, be treated and protected the same. Part of the solution belongs in the file system and the features it provides to allow for the appropriate level of security.

16.6 IMPACT OF PERSONAL COMPUTERS

With the increased use of personal computers and workstations, the user community will demand access to many different data bases and files of all kinds. Since the disk storage capacities of these machines are limited compared to minicomputers or mainframes, the data access certainly will be located remote from the micro.

There are, however, many serious issues related to microcomputers and intelligent workstations. In the preceding section we discussed the importance of classifying and protecting data. This job is difficult enough in a highly centralized environment. However, how can data be protected in an environment of distributed microcomputers?

In this situation, someone with all the correct access privileges (i.e., someone with both the right and need to know the data) can copy these data onto a disk in a microcomputer. Once copied, these highly sensitive data can be taken anywhere. Thus all of the security systems installed have just been bypassed. There is obviously no problem for all the people who do their job. However, with technologies changing rapidly, and with competitive positions changing daily, the protection of these data becomes an ever-increasing problem.

16.7 PROGRAMMING LANGUAGE INCOMPATIBILITIES

In this book we have discusssed a variety of file organizations and capabilities. We have thus established a basis of understanding on which to base future decisions as to which type of file organization is best for a particular application. However, nothing is ever as straightforward as it seems.

Today, there are many, many different languages available to users to implement systems and applications. The most popular currently are COBOL, FORTRAN, BASIC, and assembler language. Even if we restrict ourselves to these languages, we have many file-system-related issues. In fact, once we go beyond a single language we begin to have problems.

For example, no two languages agree precisely on the level of data management to be supported within the language itself. To illustrate, pick any two languages and then answer the following questions:

- What file organizations are supported within the language itself? In other words, what types of files do the language syntax provide support for?
- Even if it is possible to access the data records within a file, is it possible to CREATE any of the more complex file types other than sequential files?
- If the file is to be used by applications written in more than one language, what data types must be used in order that each program can process the *fields* correctly? Not all languages support all data types, and not every data type that appears to be the same is supported identically.

In addition to the issues above, it is frequently possible to implement new features within the file system and access methods. These new features may improve performance, security, or just add new functionality that seems to be worthwhile. How will the users take advantage of these new features? Do the languages being used support these new features? If not, how will all the languages being used be changed to provide the needed support?

An additional concern are the language *standards*. If the new features are not part of the standard language definition, what should be done? If we force the languages being used to adopt the new features, we force our languages to be nonstandard. This, in turn, means that our systems and applications become significantly harder to port to other, or newer, machines. Is it worth the effort? Do the benefits of the new features outweigh these drawbacks? Do the newer languages provide the needed support, or will we have similar problems there also?

The intent of this section is to make us aware of the seriousness of selecting, or adding, new file system features. It is much more than just the implementation effort within the file system. In fact, there will be a ripple effect across all the applications and languages that will be forced to use the new feature.

In summary, file system and access methods, in particular, need to choose their functionality wisely, since the ramifications can be quite major. The alternative, or course, is that the new features, no matter how useful or elegant, will simply not be used because the cost in time, effort, and program stability is not worth the risk.

16.8 INTERNATIONALIZATION

How can users in other countries use the file system product and capabilities when they probably cannot read the error and other messages very well? How can there be file system utility programs to create the more sophisticated file structures when all of the processing is interactive with the user, whose primary language may not be the language of the file system?

These issues are becoming more and more serious as machines are being sold not only all over the world, but also to less and less technically sophisticated users. Therefore, what can be done in the file system to help alleviate this problem?

First, all messages seen by users should be placed into a message-only file. This file can then be translated into the native language of the user's country and thus produce a much more acceptable and easier-to-use system. Thus the file system software could print "message 59" and it does not matter what language the message happens to be translated into.

This is a rather oversimplification of how to internationalize a product, but it is a significant enough problem that it should be discussed before the file system is coded.

16.9 SUMMARY

This chapter raised a number of serious issues related to how file systems do their job. As technology continues to change the parameters of the industry, it is getting more and more important to address each of these issues when the file system components are designed. In summary, issues of data security and integrity are critical to file systems because users assume that they are provided in the file system product itself.

KEY WORDS

Data security   Redundancy
Exclusive access   Shadow writing
High availability   Shared file
Internationalization

EXERCISES

1. At what level of granularity should the file system lock to allow multiple writers into the file at the same time—the entire file, the block containing the data record, or the data record itself?

2. Why is it acceptable to most user applications to be the only writer into the file, but also to allow other readers in the file at the same time? Is this equivalent to exclusive access? Explain why or why not.

3. Is there any way to protect data when the file can be accessed by users with personal computers? Explain why or why not.

4. Can you write a FORTRAN program that calls COBOL to perform all the I/O calls? Explain.

5. If you were a top security analyst for the government, how would you go about analyzing a series of competitive products as to how they address the issues of security, privacy, and integrity of the data?

6. What impact does *shadow writing* have on the overall performance of the system? Is there any way the performance can be improved? Explain.

7. Besides error messages, what are three other issues related to the internationalization of a file system?

8. How can the file system validate whether or not a user has the correct access authorization to be able to read and change a file? Take into consideration such factors as that log-on passwords tend to be passed around to many people.

9. How would you justify to a bank customer the amount of time it takes to validate the customer's bank account and the customer's need not to spend much time in the line?

10. What do you believe is the most serious issue facing file system designers today, and why?

PROGRAMMING EXERCISES

1. Design and implement an algorithm that allows multiple users to read, write, update, and delete data records at the same time (although not necessarily the same identical data record).

2. Design and implement a basic file system module that provides support for shadow writing of all data onto another disk.

Appendix A

Internal Data Structures

This appendix contains a detailed description of all the internal data structures discussed in this book. They are shown here in their complete form. In addition, Figure A–0 shows in a concise manner how the structures interrelate.

The structures summarized here are as follows:

Main Memory Control Structures
User interface control block (UICB)

File control block (FCB)

Key description block (KDB)

I/O request queue (IORQ)

Device control table (DCT)

I/O buffer control table (IOBCT)

USER INTERFACE CONTROL BLOCK

File structure	User information control block (UICB)
Function	Used to pass critical record processing information between the user's program and the file system; as such, it contains all the information that the user programs can pass on to the file system
Source of information	Setup by the compiler or run-time language support on behalf of the user program; if the user writes in assembler language, the user has total responsibility for this interface

430

USER INTERFACE CONTROL BLOCK (Cont.)

Linkage to file system	When a file is CREATEd or OPENed, the file system returns in the UICB the address of the associated FCB
How many	One per file currently open

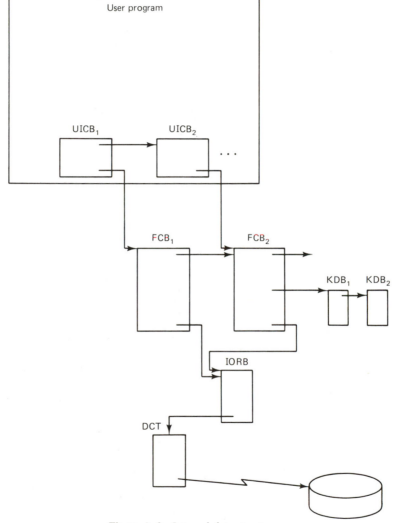

Figure A–0   Internal data structures.

USER INTERFACE CONTROL BLOCK (Cont.)

Header information

Version ID   Identifies which format this UICB conforms with;
                                      also allows for future expansion

Address of next UICB   Link all UICBs for user

User status   I/O successful
                                    HW unrecoverable error
                                    End-of-file
                                    Record not found
                                    Invalid key
                                    Space not available
                                    Invalid filename

File information

Job ID   Unique ID of job accessing this file

Filename   Name of the target file

File organization   Sequential file
                                    Relative file
                                    Direct file
                                    Indexed file
                                    ISAM file
                                    VSAM file
                                    Multikey indexed file

Address of FCB   Set when file is OPEN

Record information

Record format   Fixed-length records (FLR)
                                    Variable-length records (VLR)

Record structure   Spanned records
                                    Unspanned records

Record access mode   Input operations only
                                    Output operations only
                                    Input and output operations

Operation being requested   CREATE, OPEN, CLOSE, READ, READ_NEXT,
                                      POSITION, WRITE, UPDATE, DELETE

Index number   Number of the index from which the record should
                                      be read

Access mode   Sequential, by ascending key
                                    Sequential, by chronological order
                                    Random by key value
                                    Dynamic (i.e., both sequential and random access to
                                      be done)
                                    Mass-insert mode

Address of user record buffer   Location in memory where to get or put data for the
                                      user

Size of user record buffer   Number of bytes long

Target record size   Actual amount of record copied into URB by file
                                      system

USER INTERFACE CONTROL BLOCK (Cont.)

Address of search key buffer	For keyed access methods only
Size of key	Length of key in key buffer
Key definition	Full key in key buffer
	Partial key in key buffer
Key search rules	Exact match only
	Search key $\geq$ record's key
	Search key $>$ record's key
Block fill percentage	Amount of file's data blocks to be filled with records (default = 100%)

FILE CONTROL BLOCK

File structure	File control block (FCB)
Function	To hold most of the critical information needed by the file system to process user data record requests
Source of information	Filled in from information when file is created; at OPEN time, information comes from the file's header block
Linkage to file system	Links to UICB as well as internal file system control blocks which are built at OPEN time
How many	One per file currently OPEN

Header information

Version ID	Identifies which format this FCB conforms with; also allows for future expansion
Link to next FCB	All FCBs are kept in a linked list
Status	Area where processing status can be saved

User information

Job ID	Identification of job that is accessing this file (copied from UICB)
I/O mode	Input only (i.e., read)
	Output only (i.e., write)
	Input and output (i.e., all operations)

File information

Volume name	Name of disk or tape on which this file resides
Volume sequence number	ID of the volume of the file that is currently mounted (tape only)
Filename	User's name for this file
File size	Number of blocks, sectors, and so on
Physical end-of-file (PEOF)	Location of last block allocated to this file
Allocation type	Contiguous
	Noncontiguous
	Contiguous, if possible

FILE CONTROL BLOCK (Cont.)

Next block to allocate	The next free (i.e., unallocated) block in the file
Cluster size	Amount of space the file is to be extended whenever needed (in blocks, sectors, or tracks)
File organization	Sequential file Relative file Direct file ISAM file Indexed file VSAM file Multikey indexed file
Block format	Fixed-length blocks Variable-length blocks
Maximum block size	Size of largest block in the file, also size of each of the I/O buffers (in bytes)
File status	File NOT open (i.e., closed) File currently open
Block count	Number of blocks written to or read from the file (tape only)
Fill percentage	Percent of each block that should be used when populating a file

Record information

Record format	Fixed-length records Variable-length records Undefined record format
Maximum record size	If FLR, this is size of every record in the file If VLR, this is size of the largest possible record in the file
Maximum record number	Relative files only; if set, this is the highest record to be allowed in the file
Access mode	Sequential, by ascending key Sequential, by chronological order Random Dynamic Mass-insert mode
Address of key definition block	Location where file's keys are all defined
Number of keys defined	How many keys are defined for this file

Access-method-specific information

Logical end-of-file (LEOF)	Location of last data record written into this file
Cell size	Relative files only
Location of overflow area	Direct and ISAM only
Size of overflow area	How large the overflow area is in blocks, sectors, tracks, or cylinders

FILE CONTROL BLOCK (Cont.)

Next, overflow block to allocate	Direct and ISAM only

File system internal information

Last successful operation	READ, READ_NEXT, WRITE, UPDATE, DELETE, POSITION
	Index number
Current record pointer	Block number
	Current record size
	Offset in block to record (sequential only)
	Index number
	Key value
	Unique record identifier
Address of IOBCT	Pointer to linked list of IOBCTs; set when file is first opened
Address of DCT	Link to DCT for the device on which this file resides

File-processing statistics

Number of read operations
Number of write operations
Number of update operations
Number of delete operations
Number of errors successfully recovered
Number of file extensions performed
Number of block splits performed

KEY DESCRIPTION BLOCK

File structure	Key description block (KDB)
Function	To hold the precise definition of each of the keys defined for the file that is currently OPEN
Source of information	All information is defined at CREATE time; when file is subsequently OPENed, this information is read in from the file's header block
Linkage to file system	Constructed when file is OPENed, and linked to the associated FCB at that time
How many	One per each key defined for the file when the file was CREATEd

Header information

Version ID	Identifies which format this KDB conforms with; also allows for future expansion
Link to next KDB	All KDBs are kept in a linked list

KEY DESCRIPTION BLOCK (Cont.)

Key information

Index number	Number of the index to which data apply (0, primary key; 1, first alternate key; . . . ; n, last alternate key)
Key location	Offset in bytes to beginning of the key field in the data record
Key size	Length of key in bytes
Key data type	Alphanumeric or other
Null key value	Byte defined as character identifying this key as being null
Key attributes	Keys must be *unique*
	Keys may be *duplicated*
	Keys *can change*
	Keys *cannot change*
Level of root block	Indicates depth of the index
Root block number	Indexed type files only
First data block number	Indexed type files only
ID of hashing algorithm	Allows user to select which algorithm is to be used in a DIRECT file

I/O REQUEST QUEUE

File structure	I/O request queue (IORQ)
Function	Hold the queue of I/O requests that are targeted for this specific device
Source of information	Dynamically supplied by the file system when an I/O request is made
Linkage to file system	When a file is OPENed, the associated FCB is linked to the device (i.e., DCT) on which the file resides; in addition, the DCT itself is linked to the IORQ
How many	One per device

Header information

Version ID	Identifies which format this IORQ conforms with; also allows for future expansion
Link to next IORQ	All IORQs reside in a linked list
Status	No I/O request in progress
	I/O request in progress
	Waiting
Current position	Disk: track/cylinder/block number of current location
Queueing algorithm ID	Number of the queueing algorithm to be used on this IORQ
	1, FIFO
	2, job priority
	3, shortest SEEK first
Pointer to first queue entry	

I/O REQUEST QUEUE (Cont.)

Pointer to last queue entry	
Pointer to active entry	I/O request that is curently executing
Flags	Currently moving inward (disk)
	Currently moving out (disk)

IORQ request entries

Link to next entry	All I/O requests for a device are linked together
Address of FCB	Initiator of this specific I/O request
Job priority	Input to device I/O scheduling algorithm
Address of I/O request	Operation (e.g., read/write)
	Address of buffer
	Amount of data to be transferred
Queueing information	Data needed by the selected queueing algorithm, e.g.:
	Time in queue
	Number of times passed over

DEVICE CONTROL TABLE

File structure	Device control table (DCT)
Function	To maintain all device-specific information that is needed to succesfully drive the device
Source of information	Built when the operating system/file system is originally generated; the user usually has little or no control over these data
Linkage to file system	All DCTs are linked to each other; in addition, when a file is OPENed, the FCB is linked to the DCT for the device on which the user's file is located
How many	One per device in the system

Header information

Version ID	Identifies which format this DCT conforms with; also allows for future expansion
Link to next DCT	All DCTs reside in a linked list
Address of IORQ	IORQ associated with this specific device

General device information

Device status	Status information sent back from the device itself
	I/O successful
	I/O successful after error recovery
	Device not ready
	Illegal command
	Write protected media
	Unrecoverable error
	Invalid HW address

DEVICE CONTROL TABLE (Cont.)

	Device busy
	I/O in progress
	Invalid block/sector number
HW address of device	How to access the device
Volume name	Name of the volume currently mounted on this device
Device type	$5\frac{1}{4}$ -inch floppy disk
	$3\frac{1}{2}$ -inch floppy disk
	300-MB disk
	600-MB disk
	Cartridge tape
	Streamer tape
	Standard tape, etc.
Address of device driver	SW module that drives this device

Exception-processing information

Address of system error log	Central file into which all errors are written
Maximum number of retries: Device positioning commands	Limit on number of retries
Maximum number of retries: READs	
Maximum number of retries: WRITEs	
Number of current retry counter	For current error processing
Number of recoverable errors	Total number of errors detected and successfully recovered

Device-specific information: disk

Number of tracks per cylinder

Number of cylinders per disk pack

Number of sectors per track

Device-specific information: tape

Tape density	800 bpi
	1600 bpi
	6250 bpi, etc.
Volume sequence number	Multivolume tapes only
Label version standard	Labels can change format
Character set	ANSI 8-bit
	ANSI 7-bit
	EBCDIC etc.

I/O BUFFER CONTROL TABLE

File structure	I/O buffer control table (IOBCT)
Function	To hold the I/O block buffer information needed by the file system to correctly and efficiently manage the system's I/O buffers
Source of information	Dynamically supplied whenever an I/O request is made for a new block in a file
Linkage to file system	These buffers are allocated and linked to the file's FCB at OPEN time
How many	1-to-*n* I/O buffers, as requested by the user or defaulted by the system; the buffers may be owned by either the file system and shared with many users, or be specifically dedicated to individual open files

Header information

Version ID	Identifies which format this IOBCT conforms with; also allows for future expansion
Link to next IOBCT	All IOBCTs are kept in a linked list

Unique block identification

Device ID	Name of the device on which the block resides
Physical block number (PBN)	Actual physical location on the device of the block in the I/O buffer
Logical block number (LBN)	Number of block currently in the I/O buffer

Buffer information

Flags	Buffer is currently empty Block in buffer has been modified
Address of I/O buffer	Location in main memory of the I/O buffer into which the block will be read or written
Buffer size	Length, in bytes, of the I/O buffer

Appendix B

Common File Structures

This appendix contains a detailed description of all the common external file structures discussed in this book. They are shown here in their complete form, as well as to show in a concise manner how the structures interrelate.

The structures summarized here are as follows:

Common File Structures
Data record formats
Index record formats
Block format

RECORD FORMATS

File structure	User data record formats (Figure B-0)
Function	To specify the single format that all data records in the file will conform to

Source of information	Specified by user when the file is being CREATEd
	    Fixed length, unspanned
	    Variable length, unspanned
	    Fixed length, spanned
	    Variable length, spanned

Linkage to file system	The actual format specified for the file at CREATE time is written into the file's header block; at each subsequent OPEN, the file system reads the header block into memory and copies the declared record format, among other items, into the associated FCB
How many	One per file

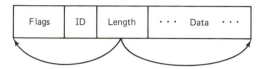

(a) Fixed-length record (unspanned)

(b) Variable-length record (unspanned)

(c) Fixed and variable-length records (spanned)

Figure B-0   User data record formats.

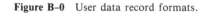

DATA RECORD FORMATS: UNSPANNED USER DATA RECORDS

Fixed-length record format (FLR)

Flags	No record currently present
	Valid record exists
	Record has been deleted
ID	Optional, unique number within a block, needed to support duplicates
Data	All records are same size

Variable-length record format (VLR)

Flags	No record currently present
	Valid record exists
	Record has been deleted
ID	Optional, unique number within a block, needed to support duplicates
Length of data record	Length, in bytes, of data plus all overhead
Data	(Data length-overhead) is amount of user data

DATA RECORD FORMATS: SPANNED USER DATA RECORDS

Fixed- and variable-length record formats

Segment control	Used to manage all the segments of a record
	0, record begins and ends in this segment
	1, record begins but does not end in this segment

DATA RECORD FORMATS: SPANNED USER DATA RECORDS (Cont.)

	2, record neither begins nor ends in this segment
	3, record ends but does not begin in this segment
Segment length	Length of this specific segment
Flags	No record currently present
	Valid record exists
	Record has been deleted
ID	Optional, unique number within a block, needed to support dups
Data	The actual data record is comprised of all the individudal data segments

INDEX RECORD FORMATS

File structure	Index record formats (Figure B-1)
Function	To define the standard format of all the index records built by the file system in support of index file organizations
Source of information	Defined when file system is designed and implemented
Linkage to file system	Not applicable
How many	One definition per file organization
Flags	Valid record
	Deleted record
Key value	Entire key that identifies this index record; size of key is in KDB
Block number	Block at next lower level in index which contains this key value
ID	Needed to support duplicate keys
Counter	"Rough" count of the number of duplicate records having this key value (only first record)

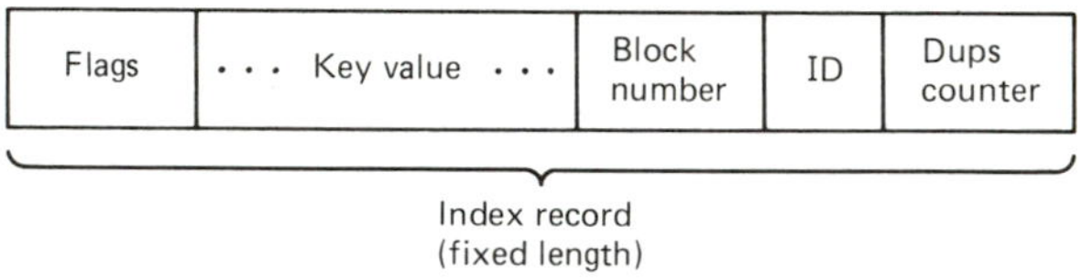

Index record
(fixed length)

Figure B-1 Index record format.

BLOCK FORMATS

File structure	Blocks within a file (Figure B-2)
Function	To define a standard format and structure of all blocks within a given file
Source of information	Defined when the file system is designed and implemented
Linkage to file system	Not applicable
How many	One format defined for a file
Current block number	Used as self-identification
Link to next block	Block number of next block on this level
Level number	Identifies where in the file structure this block belongs
Flags	Last block in linked list root index block
Offset to next free byte	Where the next record can be placed in the block, if there is enough room
Index or user data records	

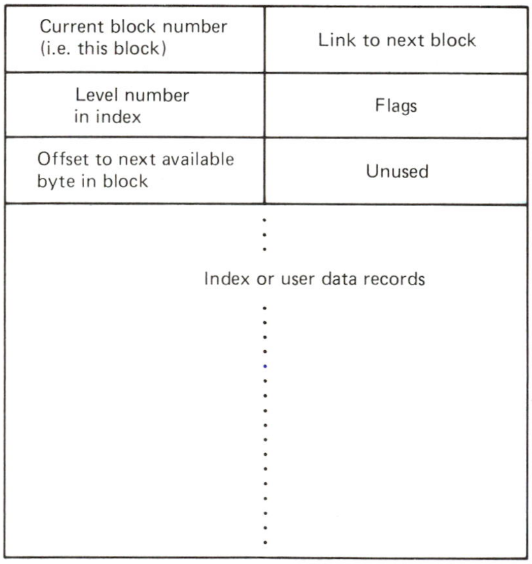

Figure B-2 Block format.

Appendix C

Disk File Structures

This appendix contains a detailed description of all the external file structures discussed in this book. They are shown here in their complete form as well as to show in a concise manner how the structures interrelate (see Figure C–0).

The structures summarized here are as follows:

External File Structures
Disk labels
Disk directory block format
Disk allocation table (DAT)
File allocation table (FAT)
File header block (FHB)
System error log

DISK LABELS

File structure	Disk volume label
Function	To give a disk volume a specific name
Source of information	Declared by the user when the disk is either being formatted and initialized, or later when only the volume name is being changed
Linkage to file system	It is up to the file system to ensure that the correct volumes are always being accessed; one way to accomplish this is to validate the name of the volume against a name supplied by the user

DISK LABELS (Cont.)

How many	One per disk pack, or volume
Volume name	Name of the disk pack
Version ID	Definition to which this label conforms; also allows for future expansion
Owner name	Person or organization that owns this disk
Creation date	Date this pack was originally initialized
Expiration date	Date this disk volume can be reinitialized
Security information	Information needed to restrict access, if necessary

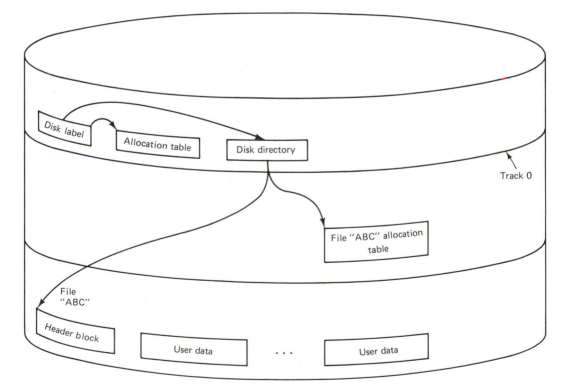

Figure C-0 On-disk file structures.

DISK DIRECTORY RECORD FORMAT

File structure	Disk directory record
Function	Allows the file system to keep track of all the files owned by a given user
Source of information	Supplied dynamically whenever a file is being CREATEd
Linkage to file system	At OPEN time, the file system reads the directory entry to verify that the file being OPENed exists, as well as to get the location of the first data block
How many	One directory record per file

Header information

Version ID	Used to identify the definition standard used for this directory structure; also allows for future expansion
Alternate directory	Optional; location where a mirror image of this directory exists; used primarily for backup purposes in case the regular directory gets destroyed

Directory record entry

Flags	Unused, or available, entry
	Valid file entry
	Deleted file
	Directory entry
Filename	Name of this specific file or directory
Block number	First block in the file
Address of file allocation table	Describes space allocated to this specific file
Security, access information	Full access
	Read-only access
	Update access
	No access
Password	For sensitive files, such as payroll
File size	Number of blocks allocated to this file

DISK ALLOCATION TABLE FORMATS

File structure	Disk allocation table (DAT)
	File allocation table (FAT)
Function	To define the space unallocated on the disk, or allocated to a particular file
Source of information	Disk is initialized when it is formatted; file allocation tables are set up when a file is CREATEd
Linkage to file system	Whenever space for a file is needed, it is taken from the DAT and added into the FAT, and vice versa
How many	One DAT per disk
	One FAT per file

DISK ALLOCATION TABLE FORMATS (Cont.)

Bit map	One bit per cluster on the disk
DAT	0 = cluster not allocated to any user
	1 = cluster allocated to a user
FAT	0 = cluster not allocated to this file
	1 = cluster allocated to this file

FILE HEADER BLOCK

File structure	File header block (FHB)
Function	To serve as a predefined block in every file into which all of a file's critical attributes have been recorded
Source of information	Most of the data are specified at CREATE time; the remainder are accumulated during the ongoing processing of the file itself
Linkage to file system	FHB is written out when the file is CREATEd; it is read into memory at OPEN time so that the file system can recapture all the attributes of this particular file
How many	One or more blocks unique to the file

Header information

Version ID	Identifies which format this header conforms with; also allows for future expansion
Date/time created	When was file created?
Date/time last modified	When was file last changed?
Link to next FHB block	All blocks making up the FHB are chained together

File information

Volume name	Name of disk or tape on which this file resides
Volume sequence number	ID of which volume of the file is currently mounted (tape only)
Filename	Name of the file, same as in the directory entry; can be used for recovery
File size	Number of blocks, sectors, and so on
Allocation type	Contiguous
	Noncontiguous
	Contiguous, if possible
Next block to allocate	Number of the block that can be allocated next
Cluster size	Amount of space the file is to be extended whenever needed (in blocks, sectors, or tracks)

FILE HEADER BLOCK (Cont.)

File organization	Sequential file
	Relative file
	Direct file
	ISAM file
	Indexed file
	VSAM file
	Multikey indexed file
Block format	Fixed-length blocks
	Variable-length blocks
Maximum block size	Size of largest block in the file, also size of each of the I/O buffers (in bytes)
Block count	Number of blocks written to or read from the file (tape only)
Fill percentage	Percentage of each block that should be used when populating a file

Record information

Record format	Fixed-length records
	Variable-length records
	Undefined record format
Maximum record size	If FLR, this is size of every record in the file
	If VLR, this is size of the largest possible record in the file
Maximum record number	Relative files only; if set, this is the highest record to be allowed in the file

Access-method-specific information

Logical end-of-file	LEOF
Address of file overflow area	Direct and ISAM only
Size of file overflow area	Direct and ISAM only
Next overflow block to be allocated	Next block to be assigned in the overflow area

Keyed access method only

Number of keys defined for file	Tells number of entries that follow

Key descriptions: one per key defined in file

Index number	Number of the index to which these data apply
Key location	Offset in bytes to beginning of the key field in the data record
Key size	Length of key, in bytes

FILE HEADER BLOCK (Cont.)

Key data type	Alphanumeric or other
Null key value	Byte defined as character identifying this key as being null
Key attributes	Keys must be *unique*
	Keys may be *duplicated*
	Keys *can change*
	Keys *cannot change*
Level of root block	Dictates depth of the index
Root block number	Indexed type files only
First data block number	Indexed type files only
Hashing algorithm number	Direct files only

File-processing statistics

Number of read operations	These data can provide useful infor-
Number of write operations	mation as to when the user's file
Number of update operations	should be reorganized; they also
Number of delete operations	tell how the file is being processed
Number of errors successfully recovered	
Number of file extensions performed	
Number of block splits performed	

SYSTEM ERROR LOG FILE

File structure	System error log file
Function	To record all the errors that the file system determines are important for future reference
Source of information	The file system, or operating system, decides when a particular error that was detected should be recorded
Linkage to file system	The DCT for a given device points to the associated system log file
How many	There is usually one per system, although there could be more

Header information

Version ID	Identifies which definition this file conforms with; also allows for future expansion

Device information

Device type	Identifies which device has failed
Device address	Identifies specific device in the configuration of the overall system
Volume	Name of volume or medium that was on the device when the error occurred

SYSTEM ERROR LOG FILE (Cont.)

Error information

Channel program or I/O command that failed	Copy of the I/O operation that failed
Status	All I/O status returned by this exception condition
Type of retries performed	Reread, rewrite, and so on
Number of retries performed	How many times the recovery procedures had to be run
Status of retries	Was error successfully and fully recovered?

Appendix D

Tape File Structures

This appendix contains a description of all the tape external file structures discussed in this book. They show in a concise manner how the structures interrelate.* All of these definitions have been extracted from this standard (see Figure D-0).

The structures summarized here are as follows:

Tape File Structures
Volume label
File header labels
End-of-Volume labels
End-of-File labels

VOLUME LABEL

File structure	Tape volume label
Function	To give a tape volume a specific name
Source of information	Declared by the user when the tape is created
Linkage to file system	It is up to the file system to ensure that the correct volumes are always being accessed; one way to accomplish is to validate the name of the volume against a name supplied by the user
How many	One per tape

---

*This material is reproduced with permission from American National Standard Magnetic Tape Labels and File Structure for Information Interchange, copyright 1978 by The American National Standards Institute. Copies of this standard may be purchased from the American National Standards Institute at 1430 Broadway, New York, N.Y. 10018.

451

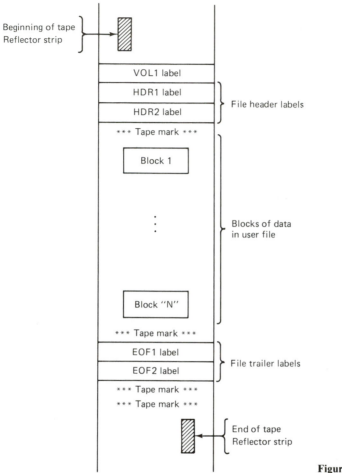

Figure D-0   Tape file structures.

VOLUME LABEL (Cont.)

Byte offset	Field	Description
1	Label identifier	"VOL" explicitly identifies this as a *VOL*ume label
4	Label number	"1"
5–10	Volume identifier	Name of this volume; usually the same as the label on the outside of the tape
11–37	Reserved	Reserved for future use
38–51	Owner identifier	Name of the owner of this tape
80	Label-standard version	Number of the standard to which these labels conform

FILE HEADER LABELS

File structure	File header labels
Function	To uniquely identify the name of a file on this tape; they also contain the critical file attributes that are needed to correctly process the file in the future
Source of information	Declared by the user when the file is first written (i.e., created)
Linkage to file system	It is up to the file system to ensure that the correct files are always being accessed; one way to accomplish is to validate the name of the file against a name supplied by the user; also, when the file is OPENed, the file system will read the header blocks and copy the file attributes into memory
How many	Two labels per file

Byte offset	Field	Description
	First header label	
1–4	Label identifier	"HDR1" identifies label
5–21	File identifier	*Name* of this file
22–41	Reserved	
42–47	Creation date	Date this file was created
48–53	Expiration date	Date this file can be deleted
54	Reserved	
55–60	Block count	Always set to 0
61–80	Reserved	
	Second header label	
1–4	Label identifier	"HDR2"
5	Record format	F = fixed length D = variable length S = spanned
6–10	Block length	Maximum number of bytes per block
11–15	Record length	Maximum number of bytes per data record
16–80	Reserved	

END-OF-VOLUME LABELS

File structure	End-of-volume labels
Function	To signal that the end of this tape volume has been detected, yet the file has more data to be written or read on another tape volume
Source of information	Declared by the user when the file is created

END-OF-VOLUME LABELS (Cont.)

Linkage to file system	It is up to the file system to ensure that the entire file is processed even if the file is contained on several tape volumes; the volume labels provide this linkage between a file's volume sequence
How many	Two per volume

Byte offset	Field	Description
	First end-of-volume label	
1–4	Label identifier	"EOV1" identifies label
5–54	Same as HDR1	
55–60	Block count	Set to *actual* number of blocks written into file
	Second end-of-volume label	
1–4	Label identifier	"EOV2" identifies label
5–80	Same as HDR2	

END-OF-FILE LABELS

File structure	End-of-file labels
Function	To identify that the end of a particular file has been reached
Source of information	When the user closes the file after writing the records into the file, the end-of-file labels are written
Linkage to file system	The information in the header labels is rewritten into the EOF labels, as well as the actual number of blocks that were written into the file
How many	Two per file

Byte offset	Field	Description
	First end-of-file label	
1–4	Label identifier	"EOF1" identifies label
5–54	Same as HDR1	

END-OF-FILE LABELS (Cont.)

Byte offset	Field	Description
55–60	Block count	Set to *actual* number of blocks written into file
61–80	Reserved	

END-OF-FILE LABELS

Byte offset	Field	Description
	Second end-of-file label	
1–4	Label identifier	"EOF2"
5–80	Same as HDR2	

Abbreviations

AM	Access method
ANSI	American National Standards Institute
AVR	Automatic volume recognition
BFS	Basic file system
BPI	Bits, or bytes, per inch
CA	Control area
CI	Control interval
CRP	Current record pointer
DAT	Disk allocation table
DCT	Device control table
FAT	File allocation table
FCB	File control block
FHB	File header block
FHD	Fixed-head disk
FLR	Fixed-length record
IOBCT	I/O buffer control table
IORQ	I/O request queue
IRG	Interrecord gap
ISAM	Indexed sequential access method
KDB	Key description block
LBN	Logical block number
LEOF	Logical end-of-file
LIO	Logical I/O
MBS	Maximum block size
MHD	Moving-head disk
MRN	Maximum record number
MRS	Maximum record size
PBN	Physical block number

PIO	Physical I/O
RFM	Record format
TM	Tape mark
UICB	User interface control block
URBS	User record buffer size
VLR	Variable-length record
VSAM	Virtual sequential access method

Glossary

Access Method. That part of the file system which processes user data records. There can be more than one access method since there are many ways in which the data records can be organized and retrieved. *Same as* Logical I/O.

Access Mode. When the file system is requested to read or write a record, the file system must know where and how to find that record. There are usually two access modes defined, sequential access mode and random access mode.

Alternate Index. *Same as* Secondary index.

Alternate Key. *Same as* Secondary key.

Alternate Track. A spare track that is used only when one of the primary tracks on a disk cannot be accessed because of an unrecoverable error. Most disks have a set of alternate tracks from which to allocate whenever a bad track is encountered.

Anticipatory Buffering. The ability of the file system to anticipate what the next block the user will request will be and to prefetch it into main memory. Thus by the time the user is ready to access records in a new block, the chances are high that the file system will already have read that block into memory. Therefore, performance will be improved.

Approximate Key Search. A type of searching for a user data record in which the user can specify the search criterion, such as exact match, any record with a higher key value, or any data record containing a key value that is equal to or greater than the key value supplied in the call. This search finds the first data record that fits the selected criterion.

Asynchronous I/O. This is the case when a user program can issue an I/O request and immediately resume execution. When, and only when, the program needs the data from the I/O request, it will wait for the completion of the I/O operation. Thus the execution of the user's program *and* the I/O request continue in parallel.

Attention Interrupt. *See* Unsolicited I/O interrupt.

Automatic Volume Recognition (AVR). The process in which the file system verifies that the correct tape or disk has been mounted in a device.

Bad Track File. A file into which every bad track on the disk is allocated. Since all tracks are allocated to some "file," it is convenient to allocate all bad tracks encountered during processing to this file so that they cannot be allocated to a valid user file.

Basic File System (BFS). That part of the file system software that interfaces directly with the external peripheral devices.

Bit Map. A method of managing the space available on a disk pack by having a single bit represent a single block or cluster of blocks on the disk.

Bits per Inch (bpi). The amount of data that can be recorded onto the track of a tape or disk. For tapes, bpi also defines *bytes* per inch, since the bits of a character are recorded on multiple parallel tracks.

Block. The actual unit of data that gets transferred between the main memory and the device, and vice versa.

Block Header. The overhead bytes of data at the front of a block which the file system uses to help maintain the data within the block.

Blocking Factor. The average number of complete records that occupy each of the blocks of a file.

Block Multiplexer Channel. A channel that can interleave blocks of data being transferred to multiple high-speed devices.

Block Operations. Those functions that allow the file system to read and write blocks onto the medium. See READ_BLOCK and WRITE_BLOCK.

Block Splitting. The process in which the contents of one block are split between two or more blocks. This occurs whenever a record is supposed to go into a specific block in a file and there is no room there for it. Then the block splits and the target record is copied into one of the split blocks.

Boot Block. A block or series of blocks on a disk pack which always reside at a specific location on the disk. The block(s) contain a software program that gets read into memory when the machine is turned on. This program is then given control to load into memory the operating system and thus to make the machine ready for use.

BPI. *See* Bits per inch *or* Bytes per inch.

Buffer. Space allocated in the main memory of the computer which is dedicated to holding or receiving data that are to be written or read from a device.

Bus. The physical wire that allows the various components of a computer system to be connected (e.g., main memory, devices, etc.).

Byte Multiplexer Channel. A channel that can interleave data transfers to multiple devices. Typically, it supports low-speed devices.

Bytes per Inch (bpi). The amount of data that can be written on 1 inch of a track on the medium. *See also* Bits per inch.

Cell. A fixed-size piece of a block which is large enough to hold the largest possible record that can exist in the file. There can be one or more fixed-length cells in a block. However, cells cannot span block boundaries.

Catalog. See Directory.

Channel. The physical wire or connection between the CPU and the peripheral controller.

Channel Program.   A command sequence sent as a unit to the device controller which is to be executed entirely before the CPU is to be notified of its completion. Essentially, it is a program that the device understands.

CLOSE File.   The access method function that stops a user from accessing a file which was previously opened. Effectively, it cuts the link between the user program and the internal file system tables needed to process the file correctly.

CLOSE_FILE.   The Basic file system function to deaccess a file that is currently open and in use.

Cluster.   The minimum number of disk blocks or sectors that can be allocated at any time. Thus if bit maps were used, each bit would represent a different cluster of contiguous blocks.

Cluster Size.   The number of disk blocks to be allocated whenever disk allocation is performed. Essentially, cluster size is the minimum number of disk blocks that the system will allocate, even if less space is requested.

Collision.   The condition where a user data record cannot be placed into a file because the space allocated for it has been taken by other records. Thus a collision occurs and the records must search further for available space. *See also* Overflow areas.

Compatibility.   The ability to take any file, or program, and have it run without any change on another system or device. Usually, as long as a user stays with the same type of machine and the same vendor, there are no problems. However, when you switch vendors or machine types, there are almost always problems. Full compatibility is when a user can take any program or any file and have it run successfully on another unit without having to make any modifications.

Contiguous Allocation.   Space allocation in which all the space is physically contiguous, without any gaps: for example, blocks 52 to 327.

Control Area.   One or more control intervals make up an allocated area of a VSAM file known as a control area. This is similar to a cylinder in an ISAM file, which contains the primary data area tracks.

Control Area Splitting.   The process, similar to block splitting, that occurs in a VSAM file when a particular control area is full.

Control Interval.   The unit of I/O data transfer in a VSAM file. It can consist of one or more physical blocks on the disk.

Control Interval Splitting.   Similar to the block splitting process, except that VSAM control intervals are being subdivided and split.

Controller.   The hardware box that connects the channel with a device. Specifically, it translates channel commands into commands the devices connected to it can understand.

CREATE File.   The access method function that allows a user to create or initialize a new file according to certain input parameters.

CREATE_FILE.   The basic file system function that creates new files (i.e., ones that do not currently exist).

Current Record.   The user data record that was the last data record successfully read.

Current Record Pointer.   The internal file system identifier of the last record successfully read by the user program. It usually consists of the block number in which the record resides, and the key, if any, of the data record.

Cylinder.   All tracks on a disk pack that can be accessed *without* moving the read/write heads.

Cylinder Index. That part of the index structure in an ISAM file which divides the file into key ranges within a given cylinder. Specifically, the cylinder index records define the highest key value to be found on a particular cylinder.

Cylinder Overflow Area. That part of an ISAM file into which the file system can add records if and when the primary data area has no room for the new record. This overflow area consists of one or more tracks on the same cylinder as the associated primary data area. It can accept overflows only from that cylinder.

Data Security. The situation in which the file system must protect the data from all unauthorized access.

Data Transfer Commands. Commands that the device drivers send to the devices to cause specific data blocks to be transferred to or from the device.

Defaults. A predefined value that the file system uses to replace a needed parameter that has not been supplied by the user.

Deferred Writing. The process in which an actual I/O operation is delayed until it is required to be performed, such as if that specific I/O buffer is needed for another block.

DEFINE. The name of the VSAM utility that is used to create all VSAM file structures.

DELETE_FILE. The basic file system function to erase a file from the directory and to return its space to the available space list.

DELETE Record. The access method that allows a user to delete a record that already exists in a file.

Dense File. A file in which almost every record position in the file contains a user data record. *See also* Nondense file.

Density. The number of data bits that can be written onto a device in a specific amount of space. For example, with tapes it is bits or bytes per inch. For disks, it is either bits per inch along the track or bits per square inch.

Device. A unit that can store and transmit data to and from the main memory of the computer.

Device Control Command. Commands that the device drivers send to the devices to reposition the read/write head on the medium (e.g., rewind a tape).

Device Control Table (DCT). A table in main memory that allows the file system to control and operate a specific device. There is one DCT for each device connected to the computer.

Device Driver. The lowest-level software routines that communicate directly with the external peripheral devices, such as tapes and disks. These modules are part of the basic file system.

Device Resource Manager. That part of the file system which is responsible for allocating and deallocating all devices owned by the system to the various user jobs.

Direct File. The file organization in which the user can do random reads and writes via a user-definable key value. Thus it differs from relative files in that a relative file creates integer keys for each record.

Directory. A special file maintained by the file system to keep track of all the files and other directories in a particular account. Also known as a catalog, VTOC.

Dirty Buffer. An I/O buffer which has been modified (i.e. it no longer is an identical match with the corresponding block on the medium).

Dirty Buffer Flag. The flag that is set whenever the contents of an I/O buffer have been changed or modified. This is used by the file system to detect when a block of data in memory has not been written back into the disk file.

Disk Allocation Table (DAT).   A file structure kept on a disk to allow the file system to manage the space on the disk pack.

Distributed Free Space.   Space that is allocated within a file but which is not used when the entire file is being populated. Instead, it is left available for when the user writes new records into the file. Thus available space is scattered throughout the file. This is similar to the cylinder overflow areas that each cylinder has in an ISAM file. Distributed free space, however, is not a overflow area, but simple space left unused in the file.

Double Buffering.   The situation in which two I/O block buffers are used to process all I/O for a particular file.

Duplicate Keys.   The situation in which there is more than one user data record within an indexed type file with the same identical key value.

Dynamic File Reorganization.   This occurs whenever a block within a file is forced to split. Then, the data records are copied into the most appropriate new block in the file. In effect, the file has been reorganized as the records were added to the file.

80/20 Rule.   *See* Pareto's rule.

End-of-File Label.   *See* Trailer labels.

End-of-Volume Label.   Same as a trailer label on tape, except that it indicates that the data in the file are continued on another tape volume. This occurs only when a file is spread over more than one tape (i.e., a multivolume file). The portion of a file that resides on a particular tape volume is known as a file section. All tapes but the last have end-of-volume labels. The last tape has a normal end-of-file label.

Error Recovery.   When a recoverable error is detected by the file system, it will attempt to retry the failing request. This process is known as error recovery.

Exclusive Access.   The condition under which only a single user can access a file.

EXTEND File.   The access method function that allows a user to request that a specific file be increase, or extended, in size.

EXTEND_FILE.   The basic file system function to implicitly or explicitly increase the size of a file.

Extent.   Disk allocation in units of tracks or full cylinders. Each of these contiguous units of tracks or cylinders is known as an extent.

Field.   An elementary data item, such as a name, phone number, or social security number.

Field Offset.   The number of bytes from the start of the record to the beginning of the target record.

FIFO I/O Request Queue.   A queue in which an incoming I/O request for a device is added at the end of the list. Alternatively, the first request into the queue is the first request out of the queue.

File.   A collection of related records.

File Activity Ratio.   This ratio indicates the percentage of records in the file that will be accessed. Specifically, it is the ratio defined as follows:

$$\text{file activity ratio} = \frac{\text{number of records accessed}}{\text{number of records in file}}$$

File Allocation Table (FAT).   The table that keeps track of the space allocated to a specific file. While the disk allocation table keeps track of all space available on the disk, every file has a FAT to keep track of the space that file has allocated to it.

463

File Attribute.   The characteristics that precisely define the structure of a file and how the records are to be processed: for example, file name and file organization.

File Control Block (FCB).   A control table that the file system uses to contain or point to all the information needed to successfully and effectively perform I/O against a file. There is one FCB per file the user currently has open.

File Header Block (FHB).   The first disk block(s) in a file, onto which are written all the file's attributes. In addition, any information that is critical to the correct processing of the data is also recorded here (e.g., next block to be allocated).

File Header Labels.   These are labels written onto a tape at the beginning of each file. These labels uniquely define the attributes of that file. For example, they include the name of the file, creation and expiration dates for the file, and size of each block in the file.

File Identifier.   A unique identification that directly connects a user file to a device. It allows a user to have more than one file open simultaneously.

Filename.   The actual name of the file. The filename differs from the pathname in that pathname really concatenates the filename with the device identifier, as well as directory names.

File Operations.   Those functions available either to the user or the file system, to operate on the file only, not the records in the file (e.g., create the file, extend the file, etc.).

File Overflow area.   When there is no room in an ISAM file in either the primary data area or the cylinder overflow area for that data area, the file system can add the record to the file's overflow area.

File Population.   The procedure of inserting all the data records into a file.

File Reorganization.   The procedure of reconstructing a file from scratch and then copying the data records from the original file to the new file. In this manner the user achieves better space utilization and potentially higher performance, as well as getting rid of previously deleted records.

File Size.   The actual number of blocks currently allocated to the file.

File Structure.   The information or overhead which is written into a file in addition to the data written by the user. The purpose of this overhead is to allow the various access methods to be able to read and write the user's data records correctly and efficiently.

File System.   The I/O software interface that lies between the user program and the external peripheral devices.

File Volatility Ratio.   A measure of how fast the records in the file are changing. Specifically, it is the following ratio:

$$\text{file volatility ratio} = \frac{\text{Number of additions } + \text{ Number of deletions}}{\text{Number of records in original file}}$$

Fixed-Head Disk (FHD).   A disk in which there is an individual read/write head for every track on the disk pack. This eliminates the SEEK time delay and results in rotational delay.

Fixed-Length Records (FLR).   A file in which all the records are identical in length.

Floppy Disk.   A disk manufactured from a very thin and flexible material.

Generic Key.   This is just a partial key value (i.e., the entire key need not be specified).

GET.   The VSAM function that is equivalent to the READ command.

Hard Disk.   A disk made of hard rigid material. These disks tend to be of significantly higher capacities than floppy disks.

Higher Availability.   The condition in which any component of a computer system can fail, yet the user's processing can continue. See Redundancy.

Hit Ratio.   *See* File activity ratio.

Indexed File.   A file organization that has an indexed structure that can be used to access data records randomly. Unlike ISAM, the data records are not kept in any kind of key sequence. Instead, the lowest level of the index tree contains one index for every user data record in the file and is maintained in sequence by ascending key value.

Index Set.   All the levels in the index of a VSAM file structure *except* level 1.

Interblock Gap (IBG).   *Same as* Interrecord gap.

Internationalization.   The capability to customize a product, such as a file system, to specific foreign markets (i.e. all messages are convertible to the native language).

Interrecord Gap (IRG).   This is the space that exists *between* the blocks that are written onto a tape or disk media.

I/O Buffer.   The space allocated in main memory into which, or from which, the block of data is to be transferred from, or to, the device.

I/O Buffer Size.   The size of the largest block that the file system expects to transfer to, or from, a file. It is really main memory dedicated for the transfer of blocks of data to, and from, the file.

I/O Buffer Control Table (IOBCT).   The internal table used by the file system to manage the contents of the I/O block buffer that it controls. There is one IOBCT per I/O block buffer allocated in the system.

I/O Commands.   Commands that the device drivers send to the devices to command them to perform specific functions, such as to read or write data.

I/O Exception Handling.   The processing that the file system performs whenever an unexpected event occurs, such as an I/O request that fails.

I/O Initiation.   Processing that includes the dequeueing of the next I/O request from the I/O request queue, and the actual starting of the device commands to fulfill this request.

I/O Interrupt.   The signal sent by the device, or its associated device controller, to signal that the I/O currently executing has just completed processing on the device. The signal returned includes an identification of the device that just completed the I/O operation, as well as status information regarding the success or failure of the request.

I/O Reduction Factor.   Also known as the *blocking factor*. It is the number of records that fit in a block. Thus a user can read all those records with just a single I/O to read the block. Therefore, the number of I/O operations is reduced by a factor of 1/(blocking factor).

I/O Request Queue (IORQ).   The queue in which all I/O requests for a particular device are placed until the current I/O operation has been completed.

I/O Supervisor.   That part of the basic file system software that is responsible for all I/O initiation and termination processing.

I/O Termination.   The processing involved with the handling of the I/O completion interrupt and the processing of the device status. If the I/O completed successfully, the I/O initiation module is called to start the next I/O request on that specific device.

ISAM   Indexed sequential access method. This is a file in which all the user data records are maintained in sequence by ascending key value. In addition, the records can be randomly accessed by walking down an index tree to the location in the file where the data record resides.

Job Scheduler. The part of an operating system that is responsible for the scheduling of all user jobs, as well as selecting which job will be next in line to get the CPU resource.

Key Attributes. The attributes that define whether a key is allowed to be changed during an UPDATE operation, or whether the file can have multiple records with the identical key values.

Key Data Type. The file attribute that defines the data format of the key field (e.g., ASCII, alphabetic, alphanumeric)

Key Description Block (KDB). The internal control structure into which the file system keeps all the key definitions and attributes.

Key Hashing. Used in direct files to convert a user's key into a disk address where the desired record is to be found.

Key Position. The file attribute that defines the starting location of the key field within the data record.

Key Sequenced Data Set. Another name for the indexed file component of VSAM.

Key Size. The file attribute that defines the length of a particular key field.

Label. A block of information that the file system writes onto a file which contains data needed to manage the file correctly. For example, the label could contain the name of the file, the block and record sizes, record format, and so on.

Length Field. A field that is appended to either a variable-length record or a variable-length block. The field contains the actual size of the variable-length record or block.

Levels of an Index. Each layer in an index tree is known as a level. The user data records reside at the lowest level in the index structure, known as level 0. All index layers have level numbers greater than 0.

Linear Search. In a direct file, when there is no space available for a data record in the primary data file, the file system must look for available room. With this method, the file system scans the following blocks in the file, scanning each one for available space.

Locate Mode. The method of processing data records in which the user is given a *pointer* to the data record that is still in the I/O buffer. The alternative is *move mode,* where the file system moves a copy of the data record into the user's record buffer.

Logical Block Number (LBN). The number of a block *relative to the first block of a file.* Unlike physical block numbers, which are relative to the first block on a disk, LBNs are directly associated with the blocks in a particular file.

Logical Compatibility. This relates to the compatibility of the file structure on the medium itself, between the old and new systems. For example, if the format of tape labels had not been standardized, then even though you could put your tape onto another machine, it might not be able to read the tape because its file system is expecting labels of a different format.

Logical Data Record. A user data record that is known and understood by the user program. As such, it is not tied to the physical characteristics of the device. Thus logical record 5 is the fifth user data record in the file, independent of the physical block where the record resides.

Logical Delete. The technique of simply marking a record having been deleted, but the record itself still resides within the block in the file.

Logical End-of-File (LEOF). The place in the file beyond which there are no user data records.

Logical I/O (LIO). That part of the file system which understands user data records and converts user record requests into basic file system block I/O requests. It is also known as the access methods.

Mass-Insert Mode. The technique of optimizing the file population process by sorting all records by their primary key values. The indexed file organizations can take advantage of this knowledge when they construct and write out the various index blocks.

Master Directory. The highest-level directory from which all other files and directories are referenced. Essentially, all user directories are subdirectories of the master directory.

Master File. The original version of a file, as opposed to a copy of the file.

Master Index. The highest-level index in an ISAM file. It can also be called the *root* of the index.

Maximum Block Size (MBS). The size of the largest possible block in a file of variable-length blocks.

Maximum Record Number (MRN). The value of the highest possible record key that can be written into a relative file.

Maximum Record Size (MRS). The maximum allowable size of data in a file that has variable-length records.

Move Mode. The buffering technique where the file system copies the target data record from the I/O buffer into the user's record buffer. *See also* Locate mode.

Moving-Head Disk (MHD). A disk in which the read/write access arm is required to move from one cylinder to another to access the proper data block.

Multiple-Key File. A file structure that allows a user to access the user data records via two or more keys. For example, a user could retrieve the data either by the employee's number or by his or her last name.

Noise Blocks. These are blocks of data on a tape that are too short for the tape hardware to distinguish between a valid block and dirt in a gap. Typically, these noise blocks are less than 13 or so bytes long. Thus the file system will always prohibit a user from trying to write any block to tape which is shorter than this critical length.

Noncontiguous Allocation. The situation in which space is allocated to a file in pieces that are not physically contiguous: for example, blocks 4, 17, 25, and 37 are allocated to a file.

Nondense File. A file in which most of the potential record positions have not yet been filled with valid user data records.

Nonshared Devices. Devices that can be allocated or owned by only one user at a time: for example, a tape drive or a card reader.

Non shared File. A file which can be accessed by only one user.

Null Key. A key value within a user data record for which all bytes of the key match with the defined null key character. This provides the user with a mechanism of telling the access method not to add an index entry for this record into the file.

Null Key Value. This is the user-defined value of a single byte of data, such that when the access method sees an alternate key with all bytes matching this value, the access method is to skip over this index for this index. In other words, no index entry will be made for a record key with a null value.

OPEN File. The access method function that allows a user to access, or *open*, a file that currently exists.

OPEN_FILE. The basic file system function that is used to establish a link between the user program and an already created file.

Overflow Areas.   Space that is allocated to take care of the condition that arises when a record cannot be inserted into a file because no space is available. Here the file system could look into the overflow areas and see if enough space is available.

Overflow Chain.   The linked list of blocks in an overflow area.

Overflow Search.   In a direct file, when a record is not located in the primary blocks of the file, the overflow blocks must be searched. This occurs on both READs and WRITEs.

Pareto's Rule.   Eighty percent of the results come from 20% of the tasks.

Pathname.   The entire unique name of a file, including device, directories, file name, and any suffixes.

Performance.   The user's perception of the system's responsiveness.

Physical Block Number (PBN).   The actual disk address of a particular block or sector. PBNs, or sectors, are numbered from 1 to N where N is the number of blocks on the entire disk.

Physical Compatibility.   The compatibility of the physical characteristics of the medium. For example, a tape cannot be inserted into a disk drive, and a $5\frac{1}{4}$-inch floppy disk cannot be inserted into a disk drive capable of processing 3-inch disks.

Physical Delete.   The technique of completely removing a record from within a file. When finished, the record no longer exists in any form in the file.

Physical End-of-File (PEOF).   The last block currently allocated to a file.

Physical I/O (PIO).   That part of the file system which handles the I/O interrupts as well as all I/O initiation and I/O termination.

POINT.   THE VSAM command that is equivalent to the POSITION command.

POSITION Record.   The access method function of accessing a particular data record but without actually transferring the data into a user record buffer. This is typically used to determine if a record exists within a file.

Preallocation of Files.   The situation when all of the space that a file is ever expected to need is preallocated when the file is created. Thus space is not allocated on an as-needed basis, but all at once at file create time.

Primary Data Area.   The tracks within an ISAM file which collectively hold all the user data records.

Primary Index.   The single index tree in an indexed file (e.g., ISAM, INDEXED, VSAM) in which the index records are maintained in the same sequence as that of the user data records.

Primary Key.   The name of the key that corresponds to the primary index within the user's data record.

PUT.   The VSAM equivalent of the WRITE or UPDATE commands.

Ram Disk.   A "disk" which is simulated in the main memory of the machine. It is primarily used to improve performance.

Random Access Mode.   This is how the file system is told to locate the data records in a file. In this mode, the user, or a system routine on behalf of the user program, will always supply a record identifier from which the file system can determine the location of that record in the file. For example, this might be a key such as a social security number.

READ_BLOCK.   A request to transfer a block of data *from* the device itself into the main memory of the machine.

READ_NEXT Record.   The access method function that allows a user simply to request the *next record* that exists in a file.

READ Record.   The access method function that allows a user to read data records in a file.

Record.   A collection of related fields.

Record Blocking.   The process of putting multiple data records into a single buffer. *See also Blocking factor.*

Record Buffer.   The portion of main memory that contains the data record which is to be written onto the target device. Alternatively, it is the area of main memory into which a record is to be copied.

Record Format (RFM).   The structure chosen for all the records within a file. For example, fixed- or variable-length record formats.

Record Unblocking.   The process of extracting a specific data record from a block containing multiple records.

Recoverable Errors.   Error conditions that occur during the processing of an I/O request on which the file system can attempt some form of error recovery procedures. Typically, errors that fall into this category are transient-type errors, such as a speck of dirt on a tape that goes away after several recovery attempts.

Redundancy.   The situation in which hardware components in a system are duplicated, so that if one fails, another is there to carry on. See High Availability.

Reflector Strip.   A small piece of aluminum foil tape which is placed onto the beginning and end of a tape. These pieces tell the tape drive hardware where it can start writing at the beginning of the tape and where it must stop writing at the end of the tape. If the reflector strip is on the inside of the tape, it signifies the start of the tape. A reflector strip on the outside edge of the tape signals the end of the recording area on the tape.

Relative File.   The file structure that allows users to randomly read and write any record in the entire file. The record key is an integer which dictates where in the file this particular record should be placed.

Resource Management.   A piece of software in the operating system or the file system which is responsible for allocating and managing a particular resource. For example, there are device resource managers and memory managers.

Root Index Block.   The highest level of an index structure; in other words, it is the top of the index tree.

Rotational Delay.   The amount of time it takes a disk to rotate around until the read/write heads reach the desired block on that track. While relatively time consuming, it is typically much less than the disk's SEEK time.

Secondary Index.   All the indexes within an indexed type file (e.g., ISAM, INDEXED, VSAM) other than the primary index.

Secondary Key.   Any key other than the primary key is an indexed type file structure.

Sector.   A fixed-length block on a disk.

SEEK Time.   The amount of time it takes a disk to move the read/write heads from one cylinder to another cylinder. This time is usually the major contraint on I/O performance since it is relatively long.

Selector Channel.   A channel that supports high-speed data transfer between main memory and a single peripheral device, and vice versa.

Sequence Set.   The lowest level in a VSAM index structure (i.e., level 1) is known as the sequence set. It contains index records that point to every control interval allocated in the file.

Sequential Access Mode.   The method by which the file system will retrieve the user's data records. In this case, the file system will always take the next data record from the current block or from the next physical block allocated in the file.

Sequential File.   The file organization in which each record has a predecessor and successor record (with the exception of the first and last records in the file). Examples are tapes, card decks, printers, backup files, and files created by most editors. All records in a sequential file are written at the logical end-of-file.

Serial Sequential File.   *Same as* Sequential file.

Shared Device.   A device that can be used by multiple users at the same time. For example, a disk can be used (i.e., shared) by many users at any one time.

Shared File.   A file that can be accessed by more than one user at the same time.

Shadow Writing.   The processing where each WRITE actually goes to 2 different devices, so that if one fails the other can continue. See High Availability.

Solicited I/O Interrupt.   Whenever an I/O request has been initiated, the file system expects to be notified when the I/O completes. Thus the interrupt notification is implicitly being solicited.

Spanned Records.   A record that is not completely contained within a single block and thus spans two or more blocks.

Sparsely Populated File.   A file in which most blocks are either partially filled, or empty.

Status.   In order for any routine to know if a requested function was completed successfully, it must somehow by explicitly notified. Status is defined to be that information which is returned to the calling program to notify it of the success or failure of that program's requested function.

Subdirectory.   A directory that exists within another directory: for example, the tax subdirectory that might exist in a payroll directory.

Synchronous I/O.   When a program issues an I/O request and then stops its own program execution until the I/O request has completed. In actuality, the execution of the user's program is synchronized with the completion of the I/O requests.

System Error Log.   A file into which the file system writes all errors that it encounters. Later, this file can be analyzed to determine what action needs to be taken.

Tape Mark.   A unique pattern of bits that tape drives can read and write to enable the file system to manage the data files on the tape.

Track Index.   That part of an ISAM tree structure which defines the key range available on a particular track in the primary data area of the file. Thus a track index record contains the highest key value to be located on a specific track.

Tracks.   That part of the surface of a tape or disk onto which the data are actually recorded. For tapes, the tracks run parallel to the edges of the tape. In the case of disks, the tracks are concentric circles that pass under the read/write head(s) as the disk rotates.

Trailer Labels.   Labels recorded at the end of every file on a tape. They are identical to the file's header labels, except that they contain a block count of the actual number of blocks written into this file on this particular tape volume.

Undelete a File.   A function, which could exist in any file system, that would allow a user to undo a DELETE_FILE operation that was accidentally requested. Thus the file could again be made available for processing, as if it had never been deleted.

Unrecoverable Errors.   Errors that may occur during the reading or writing of a data record which prohibit the request from completing successfully. These are usually fatal errors, such as a disk crash or a bad tape media.

Unsolicited I/O Interrupt.   This is the case in which an interrupt is sent to the file system, yet there is no I/O operation that can be associated with it. This is sometimes called an *attention interrupt*. For example, if a device had just been repaired and turned back on, an unsolicited attention interrupt would be sent to the file system stating that the device is now fixed and is ready and available to be used.

Unspanned Records.   A record that does not span blocks. Thus each record must fit entirely within a single block.

UPDATE Record.   The access method function that allows a user to modify a record that already exists within a file.

User Interface Control Block (UICB).   The control structure that serves as the interface between the user program and the file system.

User Record Buffer (URB).   The buffer set aside within the user's program to hold the data records that are passed to or received from the file system. It is as large as the largest record in the file.

User Record Buffer Size.   The size of the user's record buffer. This is given to the file system in order that the file system can know how much data there is to be written or received.

Variable-Length Records (VLR).   A file in which each record can be any length up to the declared maximum record size.

Volume Label.   The label that the file system writes onto a new disk or tape to identify the specific media volume. It contains, among other things, the name of the volume, name of the owner, creation data and so on.

Volume Table of Contents (VTOC).   See Directory.

VSAM.   The virtual sequential access method which runs on IBM mainframe machines. It combines both sequential and random access through multiple indexes to the user's data records.

WRITE_BLOCK.   A request to transfer a block of data from main memory to the peripheral device.

Write-Protect.   The condition in which the device is prohibited from doing any writing onto the medium: for example, a tape that does not have a write-ring.

WRITE Record.   The access method function that allows a user to write or add new records into a file.

Write-Ring.   A plastic ring that can be inserted into the back of a reel of tape. When present, data are allowed to be written onto the tape. When the write-ring is not present, data cannot be written onto the tape. This is a protection mechanism designed to minimize the risk of destroying valuable data on a tape.

Bibliography

ACM Curriculum Committee on Computer Science, *CURRICULUM '78* "Recommendation for the Undergraduate Program in Computer Science." *Communications of the ACM,* Vol. 22, No. 3, 1979, pp. 147–166.

Ahl, David H., "Floppy Disk Handling and Storage." *Creative Computing,* December 1983, p. 205.

ANSI, *American National Standard Magnetic Tape Labels and File Structures for Information Interchange.* New York: American National Standards Institute, Inc., 1977, ANSI-X3.27-1978.

ANSI, *American National Standard Programming Language COBOL.* New York: American National Standards Institute, Inc., 1974, ANSI-X3.23-1974.

Brown, D. T., R. L. Eibsen, and C. A. Thorn, "Channel and Direct Access Device Architecture." *IBM Systems Journal,* Vol. 11, No. 3, 1975, pp. 186–199.

Bulkeley, William M., "Microcomputers Gaining Primacy, Forcing Changes in the Industry." *The Wall Street Journal,* January 13, 1982.

Card, Chuck, "A Proposed Floppy-Disk Format Standard." *BYTE,* February 1983, pp. 182–190.

Claybrook, Billy G., *File Management Techniques.* New York: John Wiley & Sons, Inc., 1983, Chap. 10.

"Clean Machine," *Forbes Magazine,* December 5, 1983, p. 242.

Comer, Douglas, *Operating System Design, the XINU Approach.* Englewood Cliffs, N.J.: Prentice-Hall, Inc., 1984, Chaps. 9, 11, 12.

Comer, Douglas, "The Ubiquitous B-Tree." *Computing Surveys,* Vol. 11, No. 2, 1979, pp. 121–137.

Deitel, Harvey M., *An Introduction to Operating Systems.* Reading, Mass.: Addison-Wesley Publishing Company, Inc., 1984.

Freeman, Donald E., and Olney R. Perry, *I/O DESIGN: Data Management in Operating Systems.* Rochelle Park, N.J.: Hayden Book Company, Inc., 1977.

Hansen, Wilfred J., "A Cost Model for the Internal Organization of B+ Tree Nodes." *ACM Transactions on Programming Languages and Systems,* Vol. 3, No. 4, 1981, pp. 508–532.

Hanson, Owen, *Design of Computer Data Files.* Rockville, Md.: Computer Science Press, Inc., 1982.

Held, Gerald, and Michael Stonebraker, "B-Trees Re-examined." *Communications of the ACM,* Vol. 21, No. 2, 1978, pp. 139–143.

Johnson, Leroy F., and Rodney H. Cooper, *File Techniques for Data Base Organization in COBOL.* Englewood Cliffs, N.J.: Prentice-Hall, Inc., 1981, Chap. 3.

Keehn, D. G., and J. O. Lacy, "VSAM Data Set Design Parameters." *IBM Systems Journal,* Vol. 13, No. 3, 1974, pp. 186–212.

Krastins, Uldis, "Cache Memory Quickens Access to Disk Data." *Electronic Design,* May 13, 1982, pp. 77–80.

Leibson, Steve, "The Input/Output Primer, Part 2: Interrupts and Direct Memory Access." *BYTE,* March 1982, pp. 126–140.

Lister, A. M., *Fundamentals of Operating Systems,* 2nd ed. New York: Springer-Verlag, 1979.

Martin, James, *Computer Data-Base Organization,* 2nd ed. Englewood Cliffs, N.J.: Prentice-Hall, Inc., 1975.

Martin, James, *Principles of Data-Base Management.* Englewood Cliffs, N.J.: Prentice-Hall, Inc., 1976.

Microsoft, *Disk Operating System.* Boca Raton, Fla: International Business Machines Corporation, 1983, Version 2.0.

Miller, Stanley H. and Robert Freese, "Recording Densities Push the Limits." *Mini-Micro Systems,* October 1983, pp. 287–292.

Nicholls, John E., *The Structure and Design of Programming Languages.* Reading, Mass.: Addison-Wesley Publishing Company, Inc., 1975.

Norton, Peter, *Inside the IBM PC.* Bowie, Md: Robert J. Brady Company, 1983.

Prasad, N. S., *Architecture and Implementation of Large Scale IBM Computer Systems.* Wellesley, Mass.: QED Information Sciences, Inc., 1981.

Reece, Peter, "A Disk Operating System for FORTH." *BYTE,* April 1982, p. 322.

Schwenk, Ulrich, *VSAM Primer and Reference.* Santa Teresa, Calif.: IBM World Trade Systems Centers, 1979, No. G320-5774-01.

Sussenguth, Edward H., "Use of Tree Structures for Processing Files." *Communications of the ACM,* Vol. 26, No. 1, 1983, pp. 17–20.

Toby, J. Teorey, and James P. Fry, *Design of Database Structures.* Englewood Cliffs, N.J.: Prentice-Hall, Inc., 1982.

Wagner, P. P., "Indexing Design Considerations." *IBM Systems Journal,* Vol. 12, No. 4, 1973, pp. 351–367.

Wiederhold, Gio, *Database Design.* New York: McGraw-Hill Book Company, 1977.

Index

Access Methods (definition), 188 (Fig.
    8-0), 188
  CLOSE file, 196–198
  cost/benefits, 215
  CREATE file, 190–194
  DELETE record, 211
  direct file, 270
  EXTEND file, 198–199
  file attributes, 189
  file operations, 190
  file size calculations, 216
  indexed (definition), 338
  ISAM, 303
  multikey indexed, 394
  OPEN file, 194–196
  overview, 171
  POSITION to record, 201–203
  READ record, 203–205
  READ_NEXT record, 205–207
  record operations, 199–213
  relative files, 247
  sequential files, 225
  UICB, (table 8-2) 217
  UPDATE record, 210–211
  vs. basic file system, 188, 222
  VSAM, 367
  WRITE record, 207–209
Access modes (*see* Record access modes)
Access rights:
  exclusive, 422
  multiple readers and multiple writers,
    422
  one writer and multiple readers, 422
  read-only, 422
Activity ratio, file, 19

Algorithms:
  block splitting, indexed files, 341
  CLOSE file, 197–198
  CLOSE_FILE, 128
  collision processing, VSAM, 374
  CREATE file, 191–194
  CREATE_FILE, 122–123
  DELETE record, 212–213
  DELETE_FILE, 129–130
  disk space allocation, 89–90
  duplicate key processing, multikey
    indexed files, 402
  EXTEND file, 198–199
  EXTEND_FILE, 127
  file reorganization, 181
  I/O initiation, 151
  I/O termination, 153–154
  index tree walking, 309
  key hashing, 274
  OPEN file, 194–196
  OPEN_FILE, 125
  overflow area processing, direct files,
    278
  POSITION to record, 202
  READ record, 204
  READ_BLOCK, 133
    error recovery steps, 63–64
  READ_NEXT, relative files, 256
  UPDATE record, 210–211
  WRITE_BLOCK, 131
    error recovery steps, 64–65
  WRITE record, 208–209
Allocation type, FCB, 136
Alternate index, 305, 395
Alternate key, 395

Anticipatory buffering, 176
Approximate key search (definition), 312
Asynchronous I/O (definition), 32, 172
Attention interrupts (definition), 157
Attributes, file 13
Automatic volume recognition (disk), 85
Availability (*see* High availability)

Backspace command, tape (definition), 57
Basic file system (definition), 116
  commands, vs. access method
    commands, 222
  block operations, 130–134
  CLOSE_FILE, 128
  CREATE_FILE, 121
  DELETE_FILE, 129
  EXTEND_FILE, 127
  file control block (table 5-1), 136–137
  file operations, 117–130
  functions (Fig. 5-2), 119
  I/O buffer control table (Table 5-2),
    139
  OPEN_FILE, 124
  performance, 135
  READ_BLOCK, 133–134
  WRITE_BLOCK, 131–132
Basic I/O supervisor (*see* I/O supervisor)
Beginning-of-file detected, 60
Beginning-of-tape detected (definition),
  44, 60
Benefits:
  direct files, 293
  disk, 102
  indexed files, 358
  ISAM files, 329

Benefits *(Cont.)*
  multikey indexed, 413
  relative files, 262
  sequential files, 240
  tape, 69
  VSAM, 390
BFS *(see* Basic file system)
Bit maps (definition), 85 (Fig. 4–3), 86
  versus extents, 88
Bits per inch, 44
Block counts, 51
  end-of-file label, 455
  end-of-volume label, 454
  FCB, 137, 434
  file header label, 453
  FHB, 448
  tape error recovery, 66
Block I/O (definition), 130
  READ_BLOCK, 133
  WRITE_BLOCK, 131
Block multiplexer channel, 29
Blocks (Fig. 1–4), 10 (definition), 12
  addressing:
    disks, 82–83
    tape, 59–60
  direct files, 280
  fixed-length, 12
  format,
    FCB field, 137, 434
    FHB field, 448
    full definition, 442
    header, indexed files, 363
    indexed files (Fig. 13–8), 363
  function, 442
  indexed, 343
  ISAM, 312
  length field, 12
    tape, 51
  maximum size, 12
    FCB, 434
  operations, 130
  overflow chains, direct files, 279
  relative files, 250
  size, 169
  splitting, indexed (Fig. 13–2), 341–342
  tape, 58
  tape performance (Fig. 3–1), 71
  variable-length, 12
Blocking factor, 13 (Figure 1–7), 14, 176
  performance, 178
Blocking, record, 176 (Fig. 7–5), 178
BOF detection *(see* Beginning-of-file)
Boot block, disk, 84, 102
BOT detected *(see* Beginning-of-tape)
Buffer address, IOBCT, 439
Buffer flags, IOBCT, 439
Buffer size, IOBCT, 139, 439
Buffer-modified flag, 131
Buffers:
  block, 33
  I/O, 33
  record, 33
Bus, 27, 28
Byte multiplexer channel, 28
Bytes per inch, 44

Capabilities:
  direct files (Table 11–1), 293
  indexed files (Table 13–1), 358
  ISAM files (Table 12–1), 329–330
  multikey indexed (Table 15–1), 414–415
  relative files (Table 10–1), 263
  sequential files (Table 9–2), 239
  VSAM (Table 14–1), 389
Catalog, VSAM (definition), 390
Cell control flags, 251
  record deleted, 254
  record not present, 254
  valid record, 254
Cells, 247
  direct files, 272
  format, 265
  cell number, formula, 250
  relative files, 247, 250
  size, 248
    in FCB, 435
    formula, 265, 267
Channel program (definition), 31 (Fig.
    2–3), 32
  disk I/O, 36
  tape I/O, 35
Channels (Fig. 2–1), 27
  block multiplexer (definition), 29
  byte multiplexer (definition), 28
  selector (definition), 28
CLOSE file (definition), 196–198
  direct files, 282
  errors, 197
  explicit call, 198
  I/O buffer processing, 197
    ISAM, 316
  implicit processing, 198
  indexed files, 345
  ISAM, 316
  multikey indexed, 404
  physical end-of-file, 197
  relative file, 253
  sequential file, 232
  VSAM, 379
CLOSE_FILE (definition), 128
Cluster, 86
Cluster size:
  FCB field, 136, 434
  FHB field, 448
Collisions:
  alternatives in a direct file, 276
  direct files, 273, 275
  indexed files, 340
  linear search (Fig. 11–5), 277
  overflow areas, 277
  rehash (Fig. 11–4), 276
  WRITE record, 208
  VSAM, 374
Compatibility:
  logical,
    disk, 102
    tape, 68
  physical,
    disk, 101
    tape, 68
Constraints, resources, 18

Contiguous space allocation, 90
Control areas, VSAM, 371, 377
Control intervals (Fig. 14–2), 371
  overflow, 373
  READ_NEXT processing, 381
  VSAM, 370, 377
    splitting (Fig. 14–6), 376
Controller (definition), 28
  I/O interface, 29
Costs:
  direct files, 292
  disk, 103
  indexed files, 357
  ISAM files, 329
  multikey indexed, 413
  relative files, 262
  sequential files, 239
  tape, 69
  VSAM, 390
Count field, data transfer commands, 59
CR *(see* Current record)
CREATE file (definition), 190–194
  direct files, 281–282
  errors, 193
  file identifier, 193
  indexed processing, 343
  ISAM, 313
  location of file attributes (Fig. 8–1),
    192
  multikey indexed, 403
  relative files, 252
  sequential files, 231
  VSAM, 378
CREATE_FILE (definition), 121–123
  errors, 123
  processing algorithm, 122
  use of by CREATE, 191
Creation date, tape, 453
CRP, current record pointer, 200
Current position, IORQ, 159
Current record, 199 (Table 8–1), 200
  alternate index, 404
  direct files, 283–284
  FCB, 435
  indexed files, 346
  ISAM, 317
  multikeyed indexed, 404
  pointer (definition), 200
    sequential files, 242
  primary index, 404
  relative files, 267
  sequential files, 233
  state (Table 8–1), 200
    DELETE record, 213
      sequential files, 236
      VSAM, 383
    POSITION, 202
    UPDATE record, 210–211
      VSAM, 383
    WRITE record, 209
    VSAM, 380
Cylinder (Figure 4–1), 79, 80
  overflow area, 308
Cylinder index, 305 (definition), 306
  build processing, 314

record format, ISAM, 333

DAT, disk allocation table, 85, 108
Data:
   access to, 34
   changing on a device, 170
   loss of, 18
   transfer, 35
Data areas, direct files, 272
Data flow, 134, 169–170
Data records, sequence, ISAM, 307
Data security, 425
Data structures, 430–439
   link field, 37
   status field, 37
   version ID, 37
Data transfer commands (Fig. 2–4), 33
   count field (definition), 58
   disk, 96
   information needed for, 58
   tape, 58–59
DCT (see Device Control Table)
Deadlock, 423
Default values (definition), 117
Deferred writing, 177
   WRITE record, 209
Delete flag, direct files, 289
DELETE record (definition), 211–212
   direct files, 284, 289
   effect on current record, 213
   indexed files, 353
   ISAM (definition), 323
   logical delete, 130, 212
   multikey indexed, 409
   outputs, 213
   physical (definition), 129
   random deletions, 213
   relative files, 259
   sequential files, 236
   state of current record, 212
   VSAM, 383
DELETE_FILE (definition), 129
   processing algorithm, 129
Dense files:
   alternate index, 399
   performance, 260
   relative files, 250
Density:
   bits per inch, 44
   bytes per inch, 44
   DCT field, 438
   tape, 44
Design trade-offs:
   direct files, 291
   indexed files, 357
   ISAM files, 328
   logical I/O, 182–183
   multikey indexed, 411
   relative files, 261
   sequential, 228, 238
   VSAM, 388
Device:
   address of,
      DCT, 438
      error log field, 450

disk, 81
   status, DCT, 438
   tape, 41
   types, 29
      DCT, 438
      error log field, 450
Device allocation, 147
   nonshared devices, 148
   shared devices, 148
Device control commands, 32 (Fig. 2–4),
    33
   disk, 95–97
   I/O supervisor (Table 6–2), 161
   tape, 57–58
Device Control Table (definition), 37,
    (Table 2–1), 38
   address of in FCB, 435
   disk, 107 (Table 4–2), 108
   full definition, 437–439
   tape (Table 3–2), 72
Device drivers (definition), 26, 149
   address of, DCT, 149, 438
Device I/O (definition), 26, 29–30 (Fig.
    2–2), 31
   I/O commands, 30
   READ_BLOCK, 33
   record buffer, 30
   WRITE_BLOCK, 33
Device ID, IOBCT, 139, 184, 439
Device specific information (see also
    DCT)
Devices supported, sequential files, 236
Device type, DCT field, 438
Direct files (definition), 270
   benefits, 293
   capabilities, 293
   CLOSE, 282
   collisions, 273, 275–276
   control structures (Fig. 11–10), 299
   costs, 292
   CREATE, 281
   DELETE, 289
   design tradeoffs, 291
   duplicate key processing, 286
   file attributes, 280
   file control block (Table 11–2), 295–296
   file design considerations, 271
   file header block (Table 11–3), 296–297
   file operations, 281–283
   file population techniques, 290
   file reorganization, 291
   file size calculation, 292
   file structure, 272
   hashing algorithm criteria, 274
   key attributes, 281
   key change processing, 289
   key descriptor block, 294 (Table 11–4),
    297
   OPEN, 282
   organization (Fig. 11–1), 272
   overflow areas, 272
   performance considerations, 290
   POSITION, 284
   primary data area, 272
   READ, 285

READ_NEXT, 285
record access modes, 283
record addressing algorithm, 273
record currency, 283
record operations, 283–290
   UICB (Table 11–5), 298
   UPDATE, 287
   WRITE, 286
Directory:
   address of file, 94
   DELETE_FILE actions, 129
   disk, 90, 109
   file attributes, 94, 192
   file security, 94
   filename, 92
   pathname, 95
   subdirectory, 91
Dirty buffer flag, 174
Disk allocation table, DAT, 85, 108,
   full definition, 446–447
Disks:
   allocation, type of,
      FCB field, 434
      FHB field, 447
   automatic volume recognition, 85
   bad track handling, 100
   bit map, 85
   boot block (definition), 84
   cache, 107
   capacities (Table 4–1), 79
   cluster (definition), 86
      FCB field, 434
      FHB field, 448
   compatibility issues, 101
   contiguous space allocation, 90
   cylinder (Figure 4–1), 79 (definition),
    80, 82
   data transfer commands, 96
   device control commands, 95
   device control table, 108
   device types, 81
   directory (definition), 90
      entry (Table 4–3), 110
      record definition, 445–446
   error recovery, 98
      data transfer commands, 100
   extents (definition), 88
   FHB definition, 447
   file allocation bit map, 86
   file allocation table, 109
   file structures, 83
      full definition, 444–450
   fixed-head disk (definition), 82
   floppy disks, 78
   hard disks, 78
   hardware (Fig. 4–1), 79
   hardware characteristics, 78
   I/O, 36, 95–97
      exception handling, 97
      number per second (formula),
        104
   labels (definition), 444
   moving-head (definition), 82
   next block to allocate, 447
   noncontiguous space allocation, 90

Disks *(Cont.)*
 performance:
  bit maps vs. extents, 88
  characteristics, 103
  objectives, 105
  SEEKs, 105
  use of clusters, 87
  use of extents, 88
 physical block number, 82
 preallocated space, 90
 queueing, 106
 random access devices, 247
 READ_BLOCK command, 97
  error recovery, 101
 record number, 82
 rotational delay (definition), 80
 SEARCH command, 96
 sectors (definition), 82
 SEEK command, 80, 96
 space allocation algorithm, 89
 track (definition), 80
  number, 82
 volume label, 85, 109–110
 volume table of contents, 90
 WRITE_BLOCK command, 96
  error recovery, 101
Distributed data processing, 423
Distributed free space, VSAM (Fig. 14–3),
  372
Double buffering, 176
Duplicate keys, 401
 direct files, 286
 multikey indexed, 402
 relative files, 258

80/20 rule, 18
End-of-file, 199
 detection, tape, 60
 tape labels, 51, 75 (definition), 454
End-of-tape detection (definition), 45, 60
End-of-volume:
 detection, tape, 60
 label, 54
  tape (Table 3–5), 75
   (definition), 453–454
 READ processing, 61
 WRITE processing, 61
EOF detection (*see* End-of-file)
EOT detection (*see* End-of-Tape)
EOV detection (*see* End-of-Volume)
Erase-Block command, tape (definition),
  57
Error correction, 424
Error detection, 424
Error log, 160 (Table 6–3), 163
 address, DCT, 161, 438
 contents, 155
 full definition, 449–450
Error recovery, 156
 block counts, 66
 disk, 98
 disk bad tracks, 100
 disk data transfer, 100
 disk READ_BLOCK command, 101
 disk write protected, 100

disk WRITE_BLOCK command, 101
 number retries (DCT), 161, 438
 READ_BLOCK on tapes, 63
 SEARCHs, 99
 SEEKs, 99
 tape, 62–67
 write-protected tape, 65
 WRITE_BLOCK on tapes, 64
Errors:
 CLOSE file, 197
 CLOSE_FILE, 128
 CREATE file, 193
 CREATE_FILE, 123
 EXTEND_FILE, 127
 hardware unrecoverable, 156
 invalid record number, 255
 OPEN file, 196
 OPEN_FILE, 126
 POSITION to record, 203
  relative files, 255
 READ record, 204
 READ_BLOCK, 133
 record not found, 255
 SEARCH, 99–100
 SEEK, 99
 UPDATE record, 210
 WRITE record, 209
 WRITE_BLOCK, 132
Exception handling:
 disk, 97–101
 goals of, 98
 normal errors, 155
 tape I/O, 60–67
  normal errors, 60
  recoverable errors, 62
  unrecoverable errors, 62
 unexpected errors, 155
Expiration date, tape, 453
EXTEND (definition), 198
 processing algorithm, 198
 required parameters, 198
EXTEND_FILE (definition), 127
 errors, 127
 explicit, 127, 131
 implicit, 127, 131
 processing algorithm, 127
 required parameters, 127
Extents, versus bit maps, 88

FAT (*see* File allocation table)
FCB (*see* File control block)
FHB (*see* File header block)
Field (definition), 7 (Fig. 1–4), 10
 offset (Figure 1–2), 8
FIFO queueing, 150
 disk, 106
File (definition), 9 (Fig. 1–4), 10
 activity ratio (definition), 19
 allocation table, disk, 109, 446–447
 characteristics, 9
 filename, 9
 nonshared files, 11
 record format, 8
 shared files, 11
 volatility ratio (definition), 19

File allocation table, 109
 full definition, 446–447
File attributes (definition), 14
 access methods, 189
 direct files, 280–281
 disk directory, 94
 how change, 169
 in directory entry, 192
 in file header block, 220
 indexed files, 341–343
 ISAM, 312
 logical I/O, 168–169
 multikey indexed, 399–403
 OPEN file access, 194
 relative files, 250–251
 sequential files, 230
 VSAM, 376–377
 written by CREATE, 191
File control block (definition), 123 (Table
  5–1), 136
 address of in UICB, 432
 direct files (Table 11–2), 295–296
 full definition, 433–435
 indexed files (Table 13–3), 361
 ISAM (Table 12–3), 332–333
 relative files (Table 10–3), 266–267
 sequential files (Table 9–3), 240–241
 VSAM, 391
File design:
 alternate index, 397
 considerations, direct files, 271
 design ratios, 19
 key issues, 15
File header block (definition), 218 (Table
  8–3), 220–221
 direct files (Table 11–3), 296–297
 full definition, 447–449
 indexed files (Table 13–2), 360–361
 ISAM (Table 12–2), 331–332
 relative files, 248, 264 (Table 10–2), 265
 sequential files (Table 9–4), 243
File header labels, tape definition, 453
File header, VSAM, 390
File identifier (definition), 193
File in use, OPEN_FILE, 126
File labels, 48, 50
File location, file attribute, 13
File locks, 422
File name, 136
 disk directory entry, 446
 FCB field, 433
 FHB field, 447
 UICB field, 92, 432
File not found, OPEN_FILE, 126
File operations:
 access methods, 190
 direct files, 281–283
 indexed, 343–345
 ISAM, 313–316
 multikey indexed, 403–404
 relative files, 252
 sequential files, 230–232
 VSAM, 378–379
File organization, 169
 design considerations, 189

direct files, 280
FCB, 137, 434
FHB field, 448
indexed, 343
ISAM, 312
multikey indexed, 399
relative files, 250
sequential file FCB, 242
standard set, 168
UICB, 432
VSAM, 377
File overflow area (Fig. 12-4), 308
File population techniques:
  direct files, 290
  indexed files, 356
  ISAM, 325
  multikey indexed, 410
  relative files, 260
  sequential files, 237
  VSAM, 385
File redundancy, 424
File reorganization (definition), 180, 214
  direct files, 291
  indexed files, 356
  ISAM, 327
  multikey indexed, 411
  processing algorithm, 181, 214
  relative files, 260
  sequential files, 237
  VSAM, 387
File section, tape, 54
File sharing, 422
File size attribute, 169
  direct files, 280
  FCB, 136, 434
  FHB field, 447
  file attribute, 13
  indexed, 343
  ISAM, 312
  multikey indexed, 399
  relative files, 251
  sequential files, 230
  VSAM, 377
File size calculation:
  direct files, 291
  indexed files, 357
  ISAM, 328
  multikey indexed, 412
  relative files, 262
  sequential files, 238
  tape, 71
  VSAM, 388
File status, FCB, 137, 434
File structure (definition), 47
  compatibility, disk, 102
  direct files, 272–273
  disk, 83–84
  indexed (Fig. 13-1), 338–340
  ISAM, 304–311
  multikey indexed, 396–397
  sequential files, 228 (Fig. 9-1), 229
  tape, 47–55
  VSAM, 371–373
File system (definition), 2
  basic, 116

functionality, 16
goal, 12
inputs (Fig. 5-1), 118
issues, 421
objectives, 6
performance, 16
resources, 16 (Fig. 1-9), 17
standard I/O interface, 30
tradeoffs, 16
Filename (definition), 9, 13, 169
  default, 122
  FCB, 433
  file attribute, 13
  location of file, 10
  UICB, 432
Fill percentage:
  FCB, 434
  FHB, 448
  UICB, 433
  VSAM, 385
Fixed-head disk, 82
Fixed-length records (definition), 8
  length field, 9
Flags, IOBCT, 139
Floppy disk, 78
FLR, fixed-length record, 8
Format:
  blocks, 442
  cylinder index record, ISAM, 333
  index records, 442
    indexed files, 364
    ISAM, 333
    VSAM, 372
  record cells, 267
  user data records, 441
  VSAM current record, 380
Formulas:
  cell size, 265
  disk I/Os per second, 104
  file size,
    relative files, 262
    sequential files, 238
  I/O reduction factor, 178
  number of ISAM POSITION I/Os, 318
  relative file hashing formula, 250
  tape file size, 71
Forwardspace block command, tape
    (definition), 57
Fragmentation, I/O buffers, 173
Full key exact search (definition), 311

Generic key search (definition), 311

Hard disks, 78
Hashing algorithm:
  direct files, 274–280
  relative files, 248–250
Header labels, 50
  tape (Table 3-4), 74
High availability, 424

I/O, 1 (see also Input/output)
  actual, 16
  asynchronous, 32, 172
  block, 130

data movement (Fig. 2-5), 34
performance constraints, 5
synchronous, 32, 172
user's perspective, 5
why study?, 3
I/O asynchronous, 172
I/O buffer, 33, 439 (see also Buffers)
  address, IOBCT, 139, 184
  allocation, 123
  buffer-modified flag, 131
  CLOSE file, 197
    ISAM, 316
  CLOSE_FILE processing, 128
  dirty flag, 174
  double buffer processing, 176
  flags, IOBCT, 184
    dirty, 174
    modified, 174
  importance of, 173
  memory resident, 147
  multiple buffer processing, 176
  performance impact, 173
  processing techniques, 173
  sharing, 173
  single buffer processing, 174
  size, 173 (IOBCT), 184
  space allocation (OPEN_FILE), 125
  space fragmentation, 173
  status, WRITE record, 209
  tape, 58
I/O buffer control table (Table 5-2),
    138–139, 176 (Table 7-2), 184
  address of in FCB, 435
  full definition, 439
I/O commands:
  data transfer, 30
  device control, 30
I/O data flow,
    134
I/O exception handling (see Exception
    handling)
I/O initiation, 118, 151
  performance, 158
  processing (Fig. 6-4), 152
I/O mode in FCB, 433
I/O programming, 35
I/O reduction factor (formula), 178
I/O request queues, 137, 149 (Table 6-1),
    159
  FIFO, 150
  format (definition), 437
  priority based, 150
I/O statistics, FCB, 435
I/O supervisor (definition), 143
I/O termination, 118
  performance, 158
  processing, 151
Incompatibilities, programming languages,
    427
Index record format:
  definition, 442
  indexed files, 364
  ISAM, 333
  VSAM sequence set, 372
Index set (definition), 369

Indexes:
  alternate, 305 (definition), 395
  cylinder, 305
  cylinder index records, 307
  ISAM, 303
  levels in, 338
  master, 305
  nondense, 397
  number of,
    KDB, 436
    multikey indexed, 416
    UICB field, 432
  primary, 305 (definition), 395
  root, 305
  secondary (definition), 395
  track, 307
  tree walking:
    ISAM, 309
    multikey indexed files, 397–399
    VSAM, 373
Indexed files:
  access method, 338
  benefits, 358
  block splitting, 341
  block structure, 362
  CLOSE, 345
  costs, 357
  CREATE, 343–344
  DELETE, 353
  design trade-offs, 339–357
  file control block (Table 13-3), 361–362
  file design trade-offs, 339
  file header block (Table 13-2), 360–361
  file operations, 343–345
  file population techniques, 356
  file reorganization, 356
  file size calculations, 357
  file structure, 338
  OPEN, 344
  POSITION processing, 347
  READ, 348
  READ_NEXT, 348
  record access modes, 345
  record addressing algorithms, 340
  record operations, 345–353
  UPDATE, 350
  WRITE, 348
Input operations, 170
Input/output, 1, 16
Interblock gap (Fig. 3-4), 47
Internal data structures, 430–439
Internationalization, 428
Interrecord gap, 47
Interrupt handler, 153–154
Interrupts, 153
  solicited, 154
  unsolicited, 154
Invalid record number, 255
IOBCT table definition (*see also* I/O
    buffer control table)
  address of in FCB, 435
IORQ (*see also* I/O request queues)
  address in DCT, 437
ISAM files:
  access method (definition), 303
  benefits, 329

CLOSE, 316
costs, 329
CREATE, 313
  tasks, 315
current record format, 317
cylinder index, 306–307, 314
cylinder overflow area, 308
DELETE processing, 323
design trade-offs, 328
file attributes, 312
file control block, 332–333
file header block, 331–332
file operations, 313–316
file overflow area, 308
file population techniques, 325
  nonsorted data records (Fig. 12-9),
    326
    sorted data records (Fig. 12-8),
    325
file reorganization, 327
file size calculations, 328
file structure, 304 (Fig. 12-3), 306
index record format, 333
index tree walking (Fig. 12-5), 310
master index, 305–306, 314
OPEN, 316
performance considerations, 324
POSITION, 317
primary data area, 307
random access mode, 317
READ (definition), 319
READ_NEXT (definition), 319
READ_NEXT performance, 319
record addressing algorithms, 311
record operations, 316–324
search algorithm, 308
search criteria, 310
sequential access mode, 317
track index, 307, 315
UPDATE processing, 322
WRITE (definition), 321

Job control language, 117
Job ID:
  FCB, 136, 433
  UICB, 432
Job priority:
  I/O request queueing, 150
  IORQ, 160
Job scheduler (definition), 145 (Fig. 6-1),
  146

KDB (*see* Key descriptor block)
Key attributes:
  direct files, 281
  FHB, 449
  KDB, 436
  multikey indexed, 401
  VSAM, 377
Key buffer address, UICB, 433
Key change processing:
  direct file, 289
  indexed files, 351
  ISAM, 322
Key data type:
  direct files, 280

FHB, 449
indexed, 343
ISAM, 313
KDB, 436
Key descriptor block (*see also* KDB):
  address of in FCB, 434
  direct files, 294 (Table 11-4), 297
  full definition, 435–436
  multikey indexed, 413 (Table 15-2), 416
  VSAM, 391
Key field, WRITE record processing, 207
Key position:
  direct files, 280
  indexed, 343
  ISAM, 313
  KDB, 436
  multikey indexed, 401
  VSAM, 377
Key search rules:
  approximate (definition), 312
    indexed files, 346
    VSAM, 381
  exact, 311
    VSAM, 381
    indexed files, 346
  full key, 311
  generic key, 311
  greater than or equal to, ISAM, 318
  partial key, 311
  partial, indexed files, 346
  UICB field, 433
Key size:
  direct files, 280
  FHB, 449
  indexed, 343
  ISAM, 313
  KDB, 436
  multikey indexed, 401
  UICB field, 433
  VSAM, 377
Key to disk address conversion, 208
Keys, 201
  alternate (definition), 395
  change attribute, 403
  direct file, 271
  duplicates:
    relative files, 258
    multikey indexed, 401
  hashing (definition), 274
  integer, 248
  matching, ISAM, 318
  null, 416
  number of, 448
  part of data record, direct files, 273
  primary (definition), 395
  secondary (definition), 395
  unique, ISAM, 317

LBN (*see* Logical block number)
LEOF (*see* Logical end-of-file)
Levels, indexed files, 338
Link field (definition), 37
LIO (*see* Logical I/O)
Locate mode, 171
Lock:
  files, 422

records, 423
Log files, 424
Logical block number (definition), 83
    IOBCT, 138, 139, 184, 439
    READ_BLOCK, 133
    WRITE_BLOCK, 131
Logical delete, 130
    DELETE record, 211–212
    ISAM, 323
    multikey indexed, 409
    sequential files, 236
Logical end-of-file, 137 (definition), 201
    FCB, 137, 435
    FHB, 448
    ISAM processing, 333
    READ_NEXT processing, 206
    sequential files, 228, 241
Logical I/O (definition), 166–167
    design trade-offs, 182
    performance characteristics, 181
    status processing, 183
Logical records, 167

Magnetic tape device, 41
Main memory allocation, 147
Mass insert, VSAM (Fig. 14-8), 386
Master index:
    build processing, 314
    ISAM, 305–306
    OPEN processing, ISAM, 316
    record format, ISAM, 333
Maximum block size, 12, 13
    FCB field, 434
    FHB field, 448
Maximum record number (definition), 249
    FCB field, 434
    FHB field, 448
    processing, 251
    relative files, 264
Maximum record size:
    FCB field, 137, 434
    FHB field, 448
    file attribute, 13
Mechanical I/O, bottleneck, 33
Move mode, 171
Moving-head disk, 82
MRN (see Maximum record number)
Multikey indexed:
    access method, 394
    alternate index, 395
    capabilities (Table 15-1), 414–415
    CLOSE, 404
    costs/benefits, 413
    CREATE, 403
    DELETE, 409
    design trade-offs, 411
    file attributes, 399–403
    file operations, 403–404
    file population techniques, 410
    file reorganization, 411
    file size calculations, 412
    file structure, 396–397
    index number, 416, 448
    index tree walking, 397–399
    key descriptor block, 413 (Table 15-2),
        416

OPEN, 403
    performance considerations, 410
    POSITION, 404
    primary index, 395
    primary key, 395
    READ, 405
    record access modes, 404
    record operations, 404–410
    secondary index, 395
    secondary key, 395
    sequential processing, 399
    UPDATE, 408
Multiple I/O buffers, 176 (Fig. 7-4), 177

Next block to allocate:
    FCB field, 136
    FHB field, 447
    sequential file FCB, 242
Node, 423
Noise blocks, tape, 62
Noncontiguous, space allocation, 90
Nondense files:
    index files, 397
    relative files, 250
Nonshared files, 11
Null key (definition), 416
    FHB field, 449
    KDB field, 436

Offset to field, 8
OPEN file (definition), 194–196
    access modes, 194
    direct files, 282
    errors, 196
    indexed files, 344
    ISAM, 316
    multikey indexed, 403
    relative files, 253
    sequential file, 232
    VSAM, 379
OPEN_FILE (definition), 124
    errors, 126
    processing algorithm, 125
    required parameters, 125
Output operations, 170
Overflow areas:
    address of in FCB, 435
    address of in FHB, 448
    block chains, 279
    control intervals, 373
    cylinder (ISAM files), 308
    direct files, 272, 278
    file (ISAM files), 308
    processing algorithm, 278
Overhead, sequential files, 238

Pareto's rule (see 80/20 rule)
Parity bit, 44
Partial key search (definition),
    311
Pathname (see also File name)
    (definition), 9 (Fig. 1-5), 11
PBN (see Physical block number)
PEOF (see Physical end-of-file)
Performance:
    #I/O operations, indexed WRITE, 353

access method file reorganizations, 214
basic file system, 135
bit maps vs. extents, 88
blocking factor, 178
characteristics,
    disk, 103
    direct files, 290
    indexed files, 353
    ISAM, 324
    multikey indexed, 410
    VSAM, 384
data transfer, 35
deferred writing, 177
disk cache, 107
disk objectives, 105
disk SEEKs, 105
file population techniques, 214
file reorganization, 180
I/O buffers, 173
I/O initiation, 158
I/O operations per multikey indexed
    WRITE, 406
I/O request queueing, 159
I/O termination, 158
ISAM POSITION to record, 318
ISAM record operations, 317
limiting factors in, 5, 103–107
logical I/O, 181
mechanical I/O bottleneck, 33
preallocation of disk space, 90
READ_NEXT:
    ISAM, 319
relative files, 260
tape, 70
    effect of block size, 71
use of disk clusters, 87
use of extents, 88
user perception of, 11
VSAM:
    control area size, 385
    POSITION, 380
    control interval size, 385
    depth of index, 384
    fill percentages, 385
    frequent additions, 385
    I/O buffers, 384
    level of root, 387
    number of deleted records, 387
    WRITE, relative files, 258
Personal computers, impact, 426
Physical block number, 82
    IOBCT, 138, 139, 184, 439
    READ_BLOCK, 133
    WRITE_BLOCK, 131
Physical delete, 129
    DELETE record (Fig. 8-8), 212
    sequential files, 236
Physical end-of-file, 136, 201, 197
    FCB field, 434
Physical I/O (definition), 167
PIO (see Physical I/O)
POSITION to record (definition),
    201–203
    direct files, 284
    errors, 203
    indexed files, 346

Position to Record *(Cont.)*
  ISAM, 317
  multikey indexed, 404
  outputs, 203
  relative files, 254
  sequential files, 232
  VSAM, 380
Primary data area, 307
  direct files, 272
Primary index, 305, 395
Primary key, 395
Protection, write-ring, 44

Queueing:
  algorithm ID, IORQ, 159
  device specific, 151
    IORQ field, 437
  FIFO (disk), 106, 150
  ordered SEEKs (disk), 106
  performance, 159
  priority based, 150

Ram disk, 107
Random access:
  devices, disks, 247
  to records, 246
READ record (definition),
    203–204
  at end-of-volume, 61
  direct files, 285
  errors, 204
  indexed files, 348
  ISAM, 319
  multikey indexed, 405
  relative files (definition), 255
  sequential files, 233
  VSAM, 381
READ_BLOCK (definition), 33, 133
  command, 36
    disk, 97
    tape, 58
  data flow, 134
  disk error recovery, 101
  errors, 133
  tape error recovery, 63 (Fig. 3–13), 64
Ready, tape condition, 66
READ_NEXT record (definition & Figure
    8–4), 205–207
  direct files, 285
  error conditions, 206
  index files, 348 (Fig. 12–6), 320
  ISAM, 319
  multikey indexed, 405
  relative files (definition), 255–256 (Fig.
    10–5), 257
  sequential files, 233
  vs. READ record, 206
  VSAM, 381
Record access modes:
  access methods, 199
  direct files, 283
  FCB field, 434
  indexed files, 345
  ISAM, 317
  multikey indexed, 404
  random access, 199

relative files, 254
sequential access, 199
sequential files, 232
UICB field, 432
VSAM, 373, 379
Record addressing:
  direct files, 273
  indexed, 340
  ISAM, 311–312
  multikey indexed, 397
  relative files, 248–250
  sequential files, 229–230
Record blocking, 176
Record buffer, 33, 170
  device I/O, 30
Record control flags:
  deleted, 242
  valid, 242
Record currency, *(see* Current record)
Record Format, 8, 169
  FCB, 137, 434
  FHB field, 448
  file attribute, 13
  fixed-length records, 8
  full definition 440–443
  function, 440
  tape, 51
  UICB, 432
  user data, 441
  variable-length records, 9
Record hashing algorithm, relative files,
    248
Record insertion, VSAM (Fig. 14–5), 375
Record not found, relative files, 255
Record number, maximum, FCB, 434
Record operations:
  access methods, 199
  direct, 283–290
  indexed files, 345–353
  ISAM, 316–324
  multikey indexed, 404–410
  relative files, 254
  sequential files, 232–236
  VSAM, 379–384
Record order, chronological, 228
Record size, 51, 169
  file header label, tape, 453
  maximum, FCB, 434
  relative files, 250
Record structure field, UICB, 432
Record unblocking, 176
Records (definition), 8 (Fig. 1–4), 10
  characteristics, 8
  logical, 167
  spanned, 12
  unspanned, 12
Recoverable errors, 156
Reflector strips *(see* Tape)
Relative files:
  access method, 247
  benefits, 262
  capabilities (table 10–1), 263
  cell format, 247–248
  CLOSE file, 253
  costs, 262
  CREATE processing, 252

DELETE record, 259
design tradeoffs, 261
duplicate record numbers, 258
file attributes, 250–252
file control block (Table 10–3), 266–267
file header block (Table 10–2), 264–265
file operations, 252–253
file population, 260
file reorganization, 260
file size, 251
hashing algorithm (Fig. 10–2), 249
integer keys, 248
MRN, 249
OPEN file (Fig. 10–4), 253
performance, 260
POSITION to record, 254
READ record, 255
READ_NEXT record (Figure 10–5),
    255
record access modes, 254
record operations, 253–259
UPDATE record, 258
WRITE record, 256
Reorganization of files, *(see* File
    reorganization)
Resource management:
  devices, 147
  main memory, 146
Resource, constraints, 18
Retries *(see* Error recovery), 63
REWIND command, 35
Rewind command, tape (definition), 57
Root block:
  block number,
    FHB field, 449
    KDB field, 436
  in an index, 305
  indexed files, 338
  level of,
    FHB field, 449
    KDB field, 436
  OPEN processing, ISAM, 316
Rotational delay, 80

Search algorithm, ISAM, 308
SEARCH command, 36, 96
Search criteria, ISAM keys,
    310
Secondary index, 305, 395
Secondary key, 395
Sectors, disk, 82
Security, data, 425
SEEK command, 36 (definition), 96
  disk, 80
SEEK queueing, disk, 106
Selector channel, 28
Sequence set (definition), 372
  VSAM, 370
Sequential access:
  alternate key (Fig. 15–2b), 400
  multikey indexed, 399
  primary key (Fig. 15–2a), 400
  tape, 59
  VSAM, 373 (Fig. 14–4), 374
Sequential file (definition), 227
  benefits, 240

capabilities (Table 9-2), 239
CLOSE file, 232
costs, 239
CREATE files, 231
current record pointer, 242
DELETE record, 236
devices supported, 236
file attributes (Table 9-1), 230
file control block (Table 9-3), 240-241
file header block (Table 9-4), 243
file operations, 230-232
file population techniques, 237
file reorganization, 237
file structure, 228
I/O buffering techniques, 237
logical end-of-file, 241
OPEN file, 232
performance considerations, 237
POSITION to record, 232
random reads, 233
read all records, 234
READ record, 233
READ_NEXT, 233
record access modes, 232
record addressing, 230
record flag byte, 242
record operations, 232-236
vs. serial sequential file, 228
UPDATE processing algorithm,
    234-235
WRITE processing (Fig. 9-5), 234
Serial sequential file, 228
Shared files, 11
Single buffer I/O, 174
Size, cell, FCB, 435
Solicited interrupts, 154
Space allocation:
    bit maps, 85
    clusters (Fig. 4-4), 87
    contiguous, 90
    CREATE_FILE, 123
    deleted record processing, direct files,
        289
    direct files, 272
    disks, 85
        algorithm, 89
        allocation table, 85
        clusters, 86
        extents, 88
    EXTEND_FILE, 127
    file allocation bit map, 86
    I/O buffers, 123, 125
    noncontiguous, 90
    overflow areas, direct files, 282
    preallocation of space, 90
    tradeoffs in a direct file, 279
    type, FCB, 434
Space deallocation:
    CLOSE_FILE, 128
    DELETE_FILE, 129
Spanned records (definition), 12 (Fig.
    1-6), 13
Splitting:
    blocks, indexed files, 341
    control intervals, VSAM files, 376
Start I/O, 149

Statistics, I/O:
    FCB field, 435
    FHB field, 449
Status:
    device, DCT, 438
    FCB, 136, 433
    field (definition), 37
    IORQ, 159, 436
    logical I/O processing, 183
Subdirectory, 91-92
Synchronous I/O, 32, 172
System error log (see Error log)

Tape:
    beginning-of-file detection, 60
    beginning-of-tape detection, 44, 60
    block addressing, 59
    block counts, 51, 66
    block length, 51, 58
    BOT detection (Fig. 3-4), 45
    characteristics, 42
    compatibility, 68
    cost/benefits, 69
    creation date, 50, 453
    data transfer commands, 43, 58
    density (definition), 44
    device control commands, 43, 57-58
    device control table (Table 3-2), 72
    device driver (Fig. 3-0), 42
    end-of-file detection, 60
    end-of-file labels, 51 (Fig. 3-8), 52
        (Table 3-6), 75
        (definition), 454
    end-of-tape detection, 45 (Fig. 3-4), 46,
        60
    end-of-volume detection, 60
    end-of-volume label (definition), 54
        (Table 3-5) 75
        (definition), 453
    error recovery, 62
    expiration date, 50
    file header labels definition, 453
    file identifier, 50
    file labels (definition), 50
    file section, 54
    file size calculation, 71
    frame (Figure 3-1), 43
    header label, 50 (Fig. 3-7), 51 (Table
        3-4), 74
    I/O buffer, 58
    interrecord gaps, 47
    label identifier, 50
    label, version of, 50
    labels (definition), 48-52
    multifile tape (Fig. 3-11), 56
    multivolume tape (Fig. 3-10), 55
    noise blocks (definition), 62
    normal I/O exceptions, 60 (Fig. 3-12),
        61
    not ready errors, 66
    owner identifier field, 50
    parity bit, 44
    performance characteristics, 70
    record format, 51
    record length, 51
    recoverable I/O errors, 62

reflector strips, 44-45
sequential access, 59
skipping blocks in error recovery, 66
tape mark, 47
tracks, 43
trailer label (Fig. 3-8), 52
trends (Figure 3-2), 45
unrecoverable errors, 62
version, 49
volume identifier, 50
volume label (Fig. 3-6), 49 (Table 3-3),
    74, (definition), 451-452
write protection errors, 65
write-ring (definition), 44
Tape device, 41
Tape I/O, 55-60
Tape mark (definition), 47 (Fig. 3-5), 48
    multifile tapes, 54
    write-tape-mark command, 58
Tape structure:
    full definition, 451-455
    multifile tapes, 54
    multivolume files, 54
    single file, 52-53
Track, 80
Track index (definition), 307
    record format, ISAM, 333
    build processing, 315
Tracks, tape (definition), 43
Trade-offs, logical I/O, 182
Trailer labels, 51

UICB (see also User interface control
    block)
    address of in FCB, 432
Unblocking, records, 176, 178
UNDELETE, relative files, 259
Unlock, records, 423
Unrecoverable hardware errors, 156
Unsolicited interrupts (see Attention
    interrupts), 154, 157
Unspanned records (definition), 12
    (Fig. 1-6), 13
UPDATE record (definition), 210-211
    access modes, 210
    direct files, 287
    errors, 210
    indexed files, 350
    ISAM (definition), 322
    key changes, indexed files, 351
    multikey indexed, 408
    no key change, indexed files, 350
    relative files, 258
    sequential files, 234
    state of current record, 210, 211
    VSAM, 383
URB, user record buffer, 170
User data record format, 441
User interface control block, access
    methods, 217
    full definition, 430-433
User record buffer, 33, 170 (see also
    Record buffer)
    address, UICB, 432
    size, UICB, 432
    READ record command, 203

User status, UICB, 432
User, requirements, 15

Variable-length records (definition), 9
Version ID, 37
Virtual sequential access method (*see*
    VSAM)
VLR, variable-length record, 9
Volatility ratio, file, 19
Volume label:
   DCT field, 438
   disk, 85, 109
   tape, 49 (Table 3–3), 74
     definition, 451–452
Volume name:
   error log field, 450
   FCB field, 136, 433
   FHB field, 447
Volume sequence number:
   DCT field, 439
   FCB field, 136, 433
   FHB field, 447
Volume table of contents, disk, 90
VSAM files:
   access method, 367
   benefits, 390
   capabilities (Table 14–1),
     389
   catalog (definition), 390
   CLOSE, 379
   collisions, 374
   control areas, 371
   control interval, 370
   costs, 390

CREATE, 378
current record, 380
DELETE, 383
design trade-offs, 369–371, 388
distributed free space, 372
file attributes, 376–377
file control block, 391
file header, 390
file operations, 378–379
file population techniques, 385
file reorganization, 387
file size calculations, 388
file structure, 371–373
index set, 369
index tree walking, 373
key descriptor block, 391
key position and size, 377
mass insert, 386
OPEN, 379
performance considerations, 384
POSITION, 380
READ, 381
READ_NEXT, 381
record access modes, 373, 379
record operations, 379–384
sequence set (definition), 370
sequential access mode, 373
UPDATE, 383
WRITE, 382
VTOC (*see* Volume table of contents)
Wait state, interrupt processing, 154
WRITE record (definition), 207–208
   at end-of-volume, 61
   collision processing, 208

deferred writing, 209
direct files, 286
errors, 209
explicit file extension, 207
I/O buffer status, 209
implicit extension, 207
indexed files, 348
ISAM, 321
integer key, relative files, 257
key field, 207
multikey indexed, 406
   no duplicates allowed, 408
outputs, 209
performance in relative files, 258
relative files, 256–257
sequential files, 234
state of current record, 209
VSAM, 382
Write-ring, 44 (Figure 3–3), 46
   usage with WRITE_BLOCK
     commands, 58
Write-tape-mark command, tape
     (definition), 58
WRITE_BLOCK (definition), 33, 36, 131
     (Fig. 5–6), 132
   data flow, 134
   deferred writing, 177
   disk, 96–97
   disk error recovery, 101
   errors, 132
   explicit extend file, 131
   implicit extend file, 131
   tape, 58
   tape error recovery, 64 (Fig. 3–14), 65